GRS

Geriatrics Review Syllabus

Sixth Edition

Questions and Critiques/Book 3

A Core Curriculum in Geriatric Medicine

The Chief Editors were Peter Pompei, MD, and John B. Murphy, MD; Syllabus Editors were Colleen Christmas, MD, Steven R. Counsell, MD, G. Paul Eleazer, MD, Anne R. Fabiny, MD, and Susan Schultz, MD; Question Editors were William J. Burke, MD, Alison A. Moore, MD, MPH, and Gail M. Sullivan, MD, MPH; Consulting Editor on Ethnogeriatrics was Carmel Dyer, MD; Consulting Editor on Pharmacotherapy was Todd P. Semla, PharmD, MS; Special Advisors were James T. Pacala, MD, MS, and Stephanie Studenski, MD, MPH; Consulting Question Reviewers were Itamar B. Abrass, MD, and Jane F. Potter, MD; Medical Writers were Barbara B. Reitt, PhD, ELS(D), and Dalia Ritter; Indexer was L. Pilar Wyman; and Managing Editor was Andrea N. Sherman, MS.

Many thanks to Fry Communications for assistance in organizing the *Geriatrics Review Syllabus* material onto an editorial content management Web site and all production work including typesetting, graphic design, CD-ROM development, and printing. With more than 60 years in the information industry, Fry offers printing and ancillary services to publishers and other content providers.

Citation: Pompei P, Murphy JB, eds. *Geriatrics Review Syllabus: A Core Curriculum in Geriatric Medicine*. 6th ed. New York: American Geriatrics Society; 2006.

Geriatrics Review Syllabus: A Core Curriculum in Geriatric Medicine, 6th Edition. Cataloging in publication data is available from the Library of Congress.

Library of Congress Control Number: 2005938012

ISBN Number Book 3: 978-1-886775-15-2

Printed in the United States of America

10 9 8 7 6 5 4 3 2 1

INTRODUCTION

The core mission of the American Geriatrics Society (AGS) is to promote the optimal health, function, and well-being of older persons. Through the *Syllabus*, we advance this goal by providing health care providers with a current fund of knowledge that is evidence based and incorporates the most recent advances in health care. In 1989 the AGS published its first *Geriatrics Review Syllabus (GRS)*. This publication was enormously successful and has become the standard resource in the field of medicine to assist clinicians in staying current and providing the best possible care to their older patients. We update the *GRS* to keep pace with advances in medical knowledge. It is with a great sense of accomplishment that the AGS publishes this sixth edition (*GRS6*) authored largely by AGS members who are leaders in the field of geriatric medicine.

The *GRS6* is available as a 3-volume set of books or in CD-ROM format. Book 1 contains the *Syllabus* of 59 chapters, annotated references that allow the interested reader to pursue topics in greater depth, and an appendix with assessment instruments and practical resources. Book 2 contains 263 case-oriented, multiple-choice questions and is accompanied by an answer sheet for those participating in the continuing education program. Book 3 repeats the questions and contains answers, supporting critiques, and references, providing an effective self-assessment tool. The CD-ROM format comprises the entire program.

The *Syllabus* is divided into five sections—Current Issues in Aging, Approach to the Patient, Syndromes, Psychiatry, and Diseases and Disorders—that encompass 59 chapters. Each chapter provides a synopsis of the current thinking about a particular topic or field. The goal of the *GRS* editorial board is to provide a comprehensive resource that covers the scope of geriatric medicine. Accordingly, discussions of certain subjects that are well-covered in other resources are kept brief, and participants are referred to more in-depth discussions in an annotated bibliography. In compiling the bibliography, the Editorial Board has made every attempt to restrict the references to journals listed in Index Medicus. By intention, *GRS6* focuses on recent developments since the publication of the fifth edition rather than on basic principles of caring for older persons. Finally, little attention is devoted to topics that are core components of medicine and are not unique to the care of older persons; this information can be found in standard medical texts.

The Question Editors, using questions drafted by a team of question writers, have developed an entirely new set of 263 case-oriented, multiple-choice self-study questions. These questions are designed to complement material in the *Syllabus* chapters, and they draw on the entire knowledge base of geriatric medicine, rather than limiting themselves to the text of the *GRS Syllabus*. We recommend that participants prepare for answering these questions by first carefully reading through the *Syllabus* chapters. Any material addressed in the questions that is not discussed in the chapters is amply discussed in the critiques. The questions have been developed independently of any specialty board and will not be a part of any secure board certification examination.

GRS6 is the result of a major collaborative effort by AGS members and staff. The Editorial Board selected over 100 authors to develop the 59 chapters and 263 questions with answers, explanations, and references.

All *GRS* authors were encouraged to include information on health disparities among racial and ethnic minorities in those areas where accurate data exist. Although there has been an increase in the understanding of the health outcomes and diseases among older minorities, these populations remain insufficiently studied. Clinicians must recognize the differences between various ethnic groups and are encouraged to be sensitive to cultural issues in the care of older persons. *Doorway Thoughts: Cross-Cultural Health Care for Older Adults* (a series of volumes also published by the AGS) is a useful companion to the *GRS* for readers who are interested in exploring cultural issues in more depth.

Topics for inclusion were carefully selected by the editorial team. Authors were chosen on the basis of their in-depth knowledge of a particular area and their ability to condense large amounts of information into clinically applicable, succinct essays. Editors and authors are experienced in caring for geriatric patients and emphasize the geriatrics perspective in the preparation of manuscripts, bibliographies, and questions.

With each new edition, the *Syllabus* has included increasing amounts of information about drugs commonly used in treating older adults, though no effort is made to provide comprehensive coverage of available drugs for each disease or disorder. (See the AGS *Geriatrics At Your Fingertips*, published annually, for details about individual agents.) When *Syllabus* authors have chosen to discuss specific drugs, we have made certain that the information provided was up to date at the time of publication and that any mentions of uses not specifically approved by the U.S. Food and Drug Administration (so called "off-label" uses) are so tagged.

Another product supplementing the *GRS* is the AGS *GRS Teaching Slides*, available as a subscription through the AGS Web site. The slide presentations in

Microsoft® Power Point® are based on *GRS* chapters and suitable for faculty, fellows, residents, and students. Each presentation is designed for approximately a 1-hour seminar and may be used as a stand-alone lecture or to complement the lecturer's personal teaching materials.

Chapters new to *GRS6* include those on perioperative care, cultural aspects of care, persistent pain, and diabetes mellitus. Also new to the *GRS* are key points provided at the beginning of each chapter. The Appendix offers material that clinicians find useful in clinical practice.

The *GRS* self-assessment program provides participants with the option of applying for 75 Continuing Medical Education (CME) credits through the American Medical Association, American Academy of Family Physicians, and American Osteopathic Association. For information on self-scoring or submitting answer sheets for CME credit, please see the Program Guidelines (p 000). In addition to the CME credit offered by successfully completing the *GRS6*, the American Board of Internal Medicine (ABIM) has approved the CD-ROM version of the *GRS6* self-assessment program for 100 lifelong learning points for ABIM diplomates who are enrolled in the Maintenance of Certification program.

We hope the *GRS* will meet our goal of improving participants' knowledge base in geriatrics and thus enhancing the practice patterns of clinicians who care for older persons by providing a self-study tool that is current, concise, scholarly, and clinically relevant. We encourage your comments and suggestions, as the AGS continually strives to better serve its members, other health professionals, and the older persons they treat.

Learning Objectives

At the conclusion of this program, participants will be better able to:

• Describe the general principles of aging and the biomedical and psychosocial issues of aging;

• Discuss legal and ethical issues related to geriatric medicine;

• Evaluate the financing of health care for older persons;

• Identify the basic principles of geriatric medicine, including assessment, pharmacology, prevention, exercise, palliative care, rehabilitation, and sensory deficits;

• Diagnosis and manage geriatric syndromes, including dementia, delirium, urinary incontinence, malnutrition, osteoporosis, falls, pressure ulcers, sleep disorders, pain, dysphagia, and dizziness;

• Use state-of-the-art approaches to geriatric care while providing care in hospital, office-practice, nursing-home, and home-care settings;

• Apply relevant information from the fields of internal medicine, neurology, psychiatry, dermatology, and gynecology to the care of older patients;

• Adjust patient care in the light of evidence-based data regarding the particular risks and needs of ethnic, racial, and sexual patient groups; and

• Employ evidence-based data to increase the effectiveness of teaching geriatrics to all health professionals.

PROGRAM GUIDELINES

CONTINUING EDUCATION CREDITS

Accreditation

The American Geriatrics Society (AGS) is accredited by the Accreditation Council for Continuing Medical Education (ACCME) to provide continuing medical education (CME) for physicians.

CME Credit Hours

The AGS designates this educational activity for a maximum of **75 Category I credits toward the American Medical Association (AMA) Physician's Recognition Award (PRA)**, provided that the answers are submitted for computer scoring and at least 70% of the questions are answered correctly. Each physician should claim only those credits that he/she actually spent in the activity. Diplomates of the American Board of Internal Medicine who are recertifying may also obtain Maintenance of Certification credits from the GRS6. This is in addition to Category 1 credit and is more fully described below.

The GRS6 is accredited for physicians wishing to earn AMA PRA CME credits through December 2008. The AGS will review the program in November 2008, and a determination regarding extension of CME credits through December 31, 2009, will be announced in January 2009.

The GRS6 has been reviewed and is acceptable for up to **75 Prescribed credits from the American Academy of Family Physicians**, provided that the answers are submitted for computer scoring and at least 70% of the questions are answered correctly. The initial approval of the GRS6 for 75 Prescribed credits is for the period January 1, 2006, to December 31, 2007. The AGS will apply for renewal of Prescribed credits for the period January 1, 2008, to December 31, 2009, following the review of the GRS6 for currency of content in mid-2007.

The **American Osteopathic Association (AOA)** has determined that the GRS6 is eligible for up to **75 hours in Category 2-B of AOA CME**, through December 31, 2009, provided that the answers are submitted for computer scoring and at least 70% of the questions are answered correctly.

Instructions for Submitting Answer Sheets for CME Credit

CME credit hours are awarded to participants on a one-time basis after participants submit the answer sheet enclosed with the GRS6 and if the program is successfully completed by answering 70% of the questions correctly. The type of CME credit requested must be indicated on the answer sheet. Upon program completion, the answer sheet must be submitted in the envelope addressed to Program Management Services, Inc. (PMSI).

Notification of CME Examination Performance

PMSI will evaluate answers and mail an individualized performance report to each participant. For those who successfully complete the program, a CME certificate will be enclosed with the report. For those who do not successfully complete the program, another answer sheet will be enclosed with an offer of the opportunity to take the examination again. Both types of notices will be sent within 3–4 weeks of submission. All score results are considered confidential.

Questions about CME certificates should be directed to PMSI at 1-800-232-4422.

User Eligibility for CME Credits

Each copy of the GRS6 program is valid for CME credits only for one participant.

Maintenance of Certification Credits

For those applying for ABIM Maintenance of Certification (MOC) credits, please see the GRS6 CD-ROM program guidelines. MOC credits are *only* available through the GRS6 CD-ROM program and by using its electronic submission form. MOC credits are not offered by completing the enclosed paper exam answer sheet.

QUESTION ANALYSIS

AGS will post an analysis of participant performance on the Syllabus Questions to the AGS Web site (http://www.americangeriatrics.org) once 250 answer sheets have been scored.

USER EVALUATION

The AGS would appreciate participants' comments about the GRS6 program through the user evaluation enclosed with the program. Comments and suggestions will be taken into consideration by those planning the next edition.

CONGRUITY OF CONTENT BETWEEN SYLLABUS AND QUESTIONS

Since the *Syllabus* chapters and the questions with critiques are written by different authors, questions may not always correlate directly with the *Syllabus*. In the event that a question's content is not addressed in the correlating chapter, its answer is fully supported in the question critique.

UPDATES AND ERRATA

Important updates, such as medication alerts, will be posted as necessary on the AGS Web site: http://www.americangeriatrics.org.

Please report any errata to: info.amger@americangeriatrics.org, Attention: *GRS* Managing Editor. Identified errata will be posted on the AGS Web site: http://www.americangeriatrics.org.

AGS GERIATRICS RECOGNITION AWARD

The Geriatrics Recognition Award (GRA) was developed by the AGS to encourage health care professionals to acquire special knowledge and keep abreast of the latest developments in geriatrics through continuing education programs. The GRA demonstrates a health care professional's commitment to providing quality care to patients by participating in continuing education programs in geriatrics. It provides professional recognition of a health care professional's special knowledge in geriatrics sought by many employers.

CME credits earned from successfully completing the *GRS6* may be applied toward the GRA. To receive more information and an application, please provide your mailing address to the American Geriatrics Society CME Department, Empire State Building, Suite 801, 350 Fifth Avenue, New York, NY 10118, telephone (212) 308-1414, fax (212) 832-8646.

GRS6 ONLINE (Web version)

The *GRS6* will soon be available online via the Web through institutional subscriptions. Subscribers can purchase yearly access to the full *GRS6* Syllabus along with the questions and critiques for all of their students and faculty to use through their institution intranets. For more information on this great teaching resource, please call Elvy Ickowicz at 212–308–1414 or e-mail her at eickowicz@americangeriatrics.org.

NORMAL LABORATORY VALUES*

FOR BLOOD, PLASMA, AND SERUM CHEMISTRIES, HEMATOLOGY, AND URINE
Referenced in the Questions and Critiques (Books II and III)

BLOOD, PLASMA, SERUM CHEMISTRIES

Aminotransferase, alanine (ALT, SGPT)   0–35 U/L

Aminotransferase, aspartate (AST, SGOT)   0–35 U/L

Bicarbonate (CO_2)   21–30 mEq/L

Blood gas studies:

   PO_2 83–108 mm Hg

   PCO_2 Female: 32–45 mm Hg; Male: 35–48 mm Hg

   pH   7.35–7.45

   Oxygen saturation   95%–98%

Calcium   8.8–10.3 mg/dL

Calcium, ionized   4.5–5.6 mEq/L

Carcinoembryonic antigen   < 2.5 ng/mL

Chloride   98–106 mEq/L

Cholesterol:

   Total   Recommended: < 200 mg/dL; Moderate risk: 200–239 mg/dL; High risk: ≥ 240 mg/dL

   High-density lipoprotein (HDL)   Female: < 35 mg/dL; Male: < 29 mg/dL

   Low-density lipoprotein (LDL)   Recommended: < 130 mg/dL; Moderate risk: 130–159 mg/dL; High risk: ≥ 160 mg/dL

Creatinine   0.7–1.5 mg/dL

Creatine kinase   Female: 26–140 U/L; Male: 38–174 U/L

Digoxin (therapeutic level)   0.8–2.0 ng/mL

Folate   2.2–17.3 ng/mL

Glucose   Fasting: 70–105 mg/dL; 2-h postprandial: < 140 mg/dL

Iron   50–150 µg/dL

Iron-binding capacity, total   250–450 µg/dL

Lactate dehydrogenase   60–100 U/L

Magnesium   1.8–3.0 mg/dL

Parathyroid hormone   10–65 pg/mL

Phosphatase, acid   0.5–5.5 U/L

Phosphatase, alkaline   20–135 U/L

Phosphorus (age 60 and over)   Female: 2.8–4.1 mg/dL; Male: 2.3–3.7 mg/dL

Potassium   3.5–5 mEq/L

Prostate-specific antigen   < 4 ng/mL, normal; > 10 ng/mL, abnormal; 4–10 ng/mL, equivocal

Protein, total   6.4–8.3 g/dL

   Albumin   3.5–5.5 g/dL

   Globulin   2.0–3.5 g/dL

Rheumatoid factor, latest test   > 1:80 is abnormal

Sodium   136–145 mEq/L

Testosterone:

   Women   < 3.5 nmol/L

   Men   10–35 nmol/L

Thyrotropin (TSH)   0.5–5.0 µU/mL

Thyroxine (T_4)   Total, 5–12 µg/dL; free, 0.9–2.4 ng/dL

Triglycerides   Recommended: < 250 mg/dL

Urea nitrogen (BUN)   8–20 mg/dL

Uric acid   2.5–8.0 mg/dL

Vitamin B_{12} 190–900 pg/mL

HEMATOLOGY

Erythrocyte count   Female: 4.2–5.4×10^6/µL; Male: 4.7–6.1×10^6/µL

Erythrocyte sedimentation rate (Westergren)   0–35 mm/h

Ferritin   Female: 10–120 ng/mL; Male: 20–150 ng/mL

Hematocrit   Female: 33%–43%; Male: 39%–49%

Hemoglobin   Female: 11.5–15.5 g/dL; Male: 14.0–18.0 g/dL

Hemoglobin A_{1c} 5.3%–7.5%

Leukocyte count and differential   4800–10,800/µL; 54%–62% segmented neutrophils, 3%–5% band forms, 23%–33% lymphocytes, 3%–7% monocytes, 1%–3% eosinophils, < 1% basophils

Mean corpuscular hemoglobin   28–32 pg

Mean corpuscular volume   86–98 fL (86–98 mm^3)

Platelet count   150,000–450,000/µL

URINE

Creatinine clearance   90–140 mL/min

Creatinine, urine   Female: 11–20 mg/kg per 24 h; Male: 14–26 mg/kg per 24 h

Urine, postvoid residual volume   < 50 mL, normal; > 200 mL, abnormal; 50–200 mL, equivocal

---

* Note: As normal ranges vary among laboratories, data in this table may not conform with all laboratories' data.

QUESTIONS, ANSWERS, CRITIQUES, AND REFERENCES

Directions: Each of the questions or incomplete statements below is followed by four or five suggested answers or completions. Select the ONE answer or completion that is BEST in each case and darken in the circle or place an "X" through the letter you have selected for each answer on the answer sheet. The table of Normal Laboratory Values on the facing page may be consulted for any of the questions in this book.

1. A 75-year-old woman had a left hemisphere stroke with right hemiparesis and mild expressive aphasia 2 weeks ago. She was transferred to a skilled nursing facility on hospital day 4 because she was unable to participate in rehabilitation secondary to delirium attributed to a urinary tract infection. Her prestroke cognitive status was normal, and she had been living independently in an apartment by herself. At present she is dependent in transfers and toileting, and she requires assistance in dressing. Her cognitive status has returned to baseline. The physical therapist in the nursing home reports that she is actively engaged in therapy and follows three-step commands, but tires easily. Occupational therapy and speech therapy have not been provided.

Which of the following is the most appropriate next therapeutic step?

(A) Initiate occupational therapy, speech, and language pathology consultations.
(B) Refer the patient to an in-patient stroke rehabilitation service.
(C) Ask the physical therapist to continue therapy more slowly.
(D) Discharge the patient with a referral for home-based rehabilitation.

ANSWER: B

Stroke rehabilitation is probably best provided in specialized stroke settings. This patient is likely to respond well to rehabilitation. First, her cognitive status is good; this is probably the most important factor influencing outcomes. Her prestroke independence also bodes well for a good outcome. She is not at an advanced age, and advanced age may be a risk factor for poor outcomes. Delirium is a negative risk factor in rehabilitation, but it appears to have been transient in this case. Rehabilitation efforts may begin after the patient has been medically stabi-

lized, which may take some time in an older patient. This patient's ability to follow three-step commands indicates that she has good receptive speech capabilities and memory. Generally, expressive speech deficits do not provide added risk for a poor outcome in stroke rehabilitation. Though she appears to have some deconditioning (that is, she tires easily in physical therapy), the addition of occupational and speech therapy would allow her to receive up to 3 hours of therapy per day and meet Medicare reimbursement guidelines for inpatient rehabilitation. The correct answer is B.

Asking the nursing home to request occupational therapy and speech and language pathology consultations would be the next best option. Studies have shown that stroke rehabilitation provided in a skilled nursing facility is beneficial, and nursing homes capable of rehabilitation are increasingly common. It probably should be reserved for those patients requiring a slower pace or unable to tolerate 3 hours of combined therapy per day. It is also probably not appropriate to use rehabilitation based in a nursing home for stroke simply for financial reasons, though some managed care companies may request this.

Asking the physical therapist to continue therapy more slowly would probably lead to a worsening of the deconditioning and would not address the patient's occupational therapy needs related to activities of daily living or speech therapy needs related to aphasia.

Discharging the patient with a referral for home-based rehabilitation is a reasonable choice for patients with a good support system and caregivers willing to participate in the rehabilitation plan. It is also helpful for patients requiring a slower pace of rehabilitation. This patient lives alone, and home rehabilitation would probably be less effective than rehabilitation in a dedicated stroke unit. Further, because she needs assistance with transfers, toileting, and dressing, discharge to her own home without 24-hour help would not be safe.

References

1. Gresham GE, Duncan PW, Stason WB, et al. *Post-Stroke Rehabilitation: Assessment, Referral, and Patient Management.* Quick Reference Guide for Clinicians, No. 16. Rockville, MD: U.S. Department of Health and Human Services, Public Health Service, Agency for Health Care Policy and Research. AHCPR Pub. No. 95-0663. May 1995.
2. Landi F, Bernabei R, Russo A, et al. Predictors of rehabilitation outcomes in frail patients treated in a geriatric hospital. *J Am Geriatr Soc.* 2002;50(4):679–684.
3. Murray PK, Singer ME, Fortinsky R, et al. Rapid growth of rehabilitation services in traditional community-based nursing homes. *Arch Phys Med Rehabil.* 1999;80(4):372–378.

2. A 72-year-old obese man who is not depressed comes to the office because he has insomnia and fatigue. His wife hears him snoring loudly in a separate bedroom and notes that he sleeps a lot during the day. History includes hypertension and mild heart failure. His body mass index is 40.

Which of the following is most likely to be helpful for this patient?

(A) Bright-light therapy administered between 7 PM and 9 PM
(B) Continuous positive airway pressure administered nasally
(C) Implementation of sleep hygiene routines
(D) Lorazepam 1 mg administered at bedtime
(E) Zolpidem 10 mg administered at bedtime

ANSWER: B

Symptoms of sleep apnea include loud snoring and excessive daytime sleepiness, both of which increase at least up to age 70. Increased body weight is a risk factor because it enhances upper airway collapsibility and is associated with decreased muscle strength and endurance. Sleep apnea is also more likely with anatomic changes that occur with age, including lengthening of the soft palate, an increase in the size of pharyngeal fat pads, and changes in the shape of bony structures of the pharyngeal airway. In persons with sleep apnea and heart failure, mean survival is less than 2.7 years. The treatment of choice is continuous positive airway pressure, a device that applies positive pressure through a nosepiece to keep the airway open at night. This device is useful in older adults, including those with mild dementia, and may have an added benefit of improving depressive symptoms in dementia patients and their caregivers.

Sedating agents such as zolpidem and lorazepam may worsen the condition. Bright-light therapy may be useful in treatment of advanced sleep phase in older adults, but it has not been shown to be useful in sleep apnea. Focusing on sleep hygiene alone may be useful but does not produce a therapeutic effect or address the basic biologic disturbances that lead to sleep apnea.

References

1. Ancoli-Israel S, DuHamel ER, Stepnowsky C, et al. The relationship between congestive heart failure and mortality in older men. *Chest.* 2003;124(4):1400–1405.
2. Bliwise DL. Sleep apnea, APOE4 and Alzheimer's disease 20 years and counting. *J Psychosom Res.* 2002;53(1):539–646.
3. Malhotra A, Crowley S, Pillar G, et al. Aging-related changes in the pharyngeal structure and function in normal subjects. *Sleep.* 2000;23:A42–A48.

3. A 76-year-old woman comes to the office for follow-up evaluation of hypertension. Her blood pressure was 148/82 mm Hg at a recent examination. She returned for repeat measurements on two occasions; the average of all these readings is 146/83 mm Hg. She is in good general health and has no history or evidence of coronary artery disease or diabetes mellitus. Her current medications are a daily multivitamin and a calcium supplement. She lives alone, eats out frequently, and does not participate in a regular exercise program. She does not smoke or consume alcohol.

Evaluation to date has not identified a secondary cause for hypertension. She is obese (BMI [kg/m^2] = 31), and her waist circumference is 92 cm.

Laboratory studies:

Fasting glucose	115 mg/dL
Total cholesterol	220 mg/dL
High-density lipoprotein	42 mg/dL
Triglycerides	200 mg/dL

Which of the following is most appropriate regarding management of her hypertension?

(A) Recommend life-style interventions for 6 months.
(B) Begin a β-blocker.
(C) Begin a thiazide-type diuretic.
(D) Begin an angiotensin-converting enzyme inhibitor.
(E) Begin a calcium channel blocker.

ANSWER: A

The initial assessment and evaluation of this patient confirmed that she met criteria for stage 1 essential hypertension. In addition, the constellation of this patient's findings (central obesity, hypertension, hypertriglyceridemia, low level of high-density lipoprotein, and impaired fasting glucose level) satisfies criteria for the metabolic syndrome. The most appropriate management of this patient's hypertension is a 6-month trial of life-style interventions. Most older persons with hypertension are sedentary, overweight, insulin resistant, and salt sensitive, so the blood-pressure reduction that follows effective life-style changes may be even greater among older patients. The Trial of Nonpharmacologic Interventions in the Elderly (TONE) demonstrated that relatively modest reductions in dietary sodium (average decrease of 40 mmol/day) and body weight (average reduction of 4.7 kg) lowered blood pressure to a degree comparable to that achieved with a single antihypertensive drug (average reduction of 5 mm Hg systolic and 3 mm Hg diastolic). The Dietary Approaches to Stop Hypertension (DASH) study demonstrated similar findings. Exercise training is an effective intervention to lower blood pressure in hypertensive patients; it confers additional benefits with respect to improving insulin sensitivity and the lipid profile.

None of the medications listed in the other options is indicated for initial treatment for stage 1 hypertension. If life-style interventions do not result in systolic blood pressure below 140 mm Hg after 6 months, then adding the use of a medication should be considered. A thiazide-type diuretic would be the best option to select at that time.

Patients with stage 1 hypertension and features of the metabolic syndrome are at greater risk for cardiovascular events. The role of more aggressive treatment of the lipid abnormalities (with statins or other drugs) or insulin resistance (with insulin-sensitizing drugs) is not yet clear. The life-style interventions for blood pressure will confer similar benefits on manifestations of the metabolic syndrome.

References
1. Grundy SM, Hansen B, Smith SC Jr, et al. Clinical management of metabolic syndrome: report of the American Heart Association/ National Heart, Lung, and Blood Institute/ American Diabetes Association conference on scientific issues related to management. *Circulation.* 2004;109(4):551–556.
2. Hagberg JM, Park JJ, Brown MD. The role of exercise training in the treatment of hypertension: an update. *Sports Med.* 2000;30(3):193–206.
3. Moore TJ, Vollmer WM, Appel LJ, et al.; DASH Collaborative Research Group. Effect of dietary patterns on ambulatory blood pressure: results from the dietary approaches to stop hypertension (DASH) Trial. *Hypertension.* 1999;34(3):472–477.
4. Whelton PK, Appel LJ, Espeland MA, et al. Sodium reduction and weight loss in the treatment of hypertension in older persons: a randomized controlled trial of nonpharmacologic interventions in the elderly (TONE). TONE Collaborative Research Group. *JAMA.* 1998;279(24):839–846.

4. A 70-year-old new patient comes to the office because she has had fever, chills, nausea, vomiting, and headache for 3 days. Over the past 2 days, progressive and prominent weakness of her right leg and some urinary incontinence has developed. On examination, the patient is mildly lethargic, but she does not have significant meningeal signs. Her right leg is flaccid and she is unable to move it. Mild weakness is evident in the left leg and right arm, but the left arm is normal. Reflexes are absent in the right leg and reduced in the left leg and right arm, but sensation is intact throughout. A mild tremor involving the chin and both arms is also evident. The patient does not know if the tremor was present before this illness.

Which of the following is the most likely diagnosis?

(A) Amyotrophic lateral sclerosis
(B) Guillain-Barré syndrome
(C) Hypokalemic periodic paralysis
(D) Poliomyelitis
(E) West Nile virus infection

ANSWER: E

Acute flaccid paralysis secondary to West Nile virus infection is the most probable diagnosis in this patient. West Nile virus infections have been reported throughout much of the United States in recent years. This flavivirus is transmitted from birds to humans via mosquito bites. Most cases occur in summer, but some states have reported cases occurring as late as December. Transmission by blood transfusion, organ transplantation, and breastfeeding has also been reported. Usually, the infection produces only a mild febrile illness, but in some patients acute neurologic involvement becomes evident.

The most common neurologic presentation is that of encephalitis or meningitis, but acute flaccid paralysis, reminiscent of poliomyelitis, has also been documented. Acute flaccid paralysis due to West Nile virus infection is characterized by acute onset of asymmetric, painless limb weakness with prominent progression over 48 hours. The weakness is accompanied by hyporeflexia or areflexia, but no sensory changes are seen. Lumbar puncture demonstrates a cerebrospinal fluid pleocytosis, typically of 150 to 200 cells, predominantly but not exclusively lymphocytes, and modest protein elevation (50 to 200 mg/dL). Rest and action tremors, myoclonus, and parkinsonism have been reported in affected patients, including those with acute flaccid paralysis.

Clinical and electrophysiologic examinations of patients with acute flaccid paralysis due to West Nile virus infection suggest involvement of anterior horn cells in the spinal cord, and this has been documented both in experimentally infected monkeys and in naturally infected horses and birds. Anterior horn cell involvement in a human who died following West Nile virus infection has been confirmed.

Amyotrophic lateral sclerosis selectively affects motor neurons and produces a clinical picture of both upper and lower motor neuron involvement without sensory impairment. However, amyotrophic lateral sclerosis develops over months to years and is not accompanied by a febrile illness. Guillain-Barré syndrome (acute inflammatory demyelinating polyradiculoneuropathy) often develops several weeks after an infection, but not typically during its acute phase. The weakness in Guillain-Barré syndrome is usually symmetric. It is often accompanied by painful distal dysesthesias and sometimes by sensory impairment. Bowel and bladder dysfunction are rare in Guillain-Barré syndrome and encephalopathy does not occur. Lumbar puncture is characterized by elevated protein with a normal cell count. Hypokalemic periodic paralysis is characterized by episodic muscle weakness accompanied by hypokalemia. Episodes may be triggered by eating a high-carbohydrate meal or consuming alcohol and typically first appear during adolescence. The disorder often follows an autosomal-dominant inheritance pattern. Poliomyelitis, due to poliovirus infection, produces a clinical syndrome virtually identical to that seen with West Nile virus infection, but it has been eradicated from the United States.

References
1. Sampathkumar P. West Nile virus: epidemiology, clinical presentation, diagnosis, and prevention. *Mayo Clin Proc.* 2003;78(9):1137–1143.
2. Sejvar JJ, Haddad MB, Tierney BC, et al. Neurologic manifestations and outcome of West Nile virus infection. *JAMA.* 2003;290(4):511–515.
3. Sejvar JJ, Leis AA, Stokic DS, et al. Acute flaccid paralysis and West Nile virus infection. *Emerg Infect Dis.* 2003;9(7):788–793.

5. A 79-year-old woman has longstanding hypertension, diabetes mellitus, osteoporosis, osteoarthritis, and peptic ulcer disease. She is enrolled in traditional Medicare Parts A and B programs and has no other health insurance. She is contemplating a switch to a Medicare Advantage plan.

What likely benefit would a switch to a Medicare Advantage plan have over traditional Medicare coverage for her health needs?

(A) Expanded coverage of benefits

(B) Coverage of long-term nursing-home care

(C) Option of retaining her own primary care physician

(D) Coverage of outpatient laboratory tests to monitor diabetes mellitus and hypertension

(E) Option of going to an endocrinologist of her choice for diabetes care

ANSWER: A

A Medicare Advantage plan (Medicare Managed Care, formerly Medicare Plus Choice, or Medicare HMO) is a health plan that receives a capitation payment for its Medicare enrollees from the Center for Medicare and Medicaid Services (CMS). Under its contract with CMS, the Medicare Advantage plan must provide all the services that are covered under traditional Medicare Parts A and B. Through cost-saving measures, such as managing enrollees' use of services within a smaller network of providers with whom the plan has negotiated contracts, a Medicare Advantage plan often can offer expanded benefits over the traditional Medicare package and commonly includes partial or full coverage for eyeglasses, durable medical equipment, and preventive services not covered by traditional Medicare. Coverage for long-term care is very limited for both traditional Medicare and Medicare Advantage. The patient is less likely to be able to retain her own primary care physician in a Medicare Advantage plan because such plans often have a smaller network of providers to achieve cost savings. Both traditional Medicare Part B and Medicare Advantage plans cover outpatient laboratory tests.

Medicare Advantage plans generally maintain a closed panel of consulting subspecialists and manage access to the subspecialists. Thus, it is very possible that the patient may not have the option of seeing her choice of endocrinologist.

Reference

1. Medicare Plan Choices page. Available at http://www.medicare.gov/Choices/Overview.asp (accessed September 2005).

6. A 72-year-old healthy woman is in a nursing facility for rehabilitation after hemiarthroplasty. Her nurse reports that she seems needy, frequently asking for help with tasks that she can handle. The patient's husband died 9 months ago. According to her daughter, the patient relied on her husband to make decisions, has had difficulty adjusting to his death, and has few interests of her own. She now calls her daughter often for help with routine decisions. On examination, she shows no evidence of depression or memory impairment and relates that she enjoys community activities. She is anxious about her discharge home and fears that no one will take care of her.

Which of the following is the most likely diagnosis?

(A) Avoidant personality disorder

(B) Schizoid personality disorder

(C) Dependent personality disorder

(D) Borderline personality disorder

ANSWER: C

Although increased dependence is common in medically ill persons, particularly in those with realistic functional decline, this woman is otherwise healthy and has few limitations. She manifests a longstanding pattern of relying on those around her, particularly her husband, for everyday decisions. She has had relatively few interests of her own and seems to fear that no one will take care of her. All of these features suggest a dependent personality disorder. Patients with this condition commonly have increased anxiety when they lose the person who was the primary object of their dependence.

Patients with avoidant personality disorder may restrict activities and social contacts because they fear rejection or criticism. There is no suggestion that this woman fears criticism. She seems to invite interaction with others and attends community activities in the nursing facility.

Patients with schizoid personality disorder may exhibit anxiety in an institutional care setting, as it brings them in close contact with others. These patients prefer solitary activities and show no interest in relationships; they would avoid community activities. They would also tend to show relief with impending discharge back to a home situation where they can resume their solitary life style.

In the patient with borderline personality disorder, the idea of discharge from an institutional setting may prompt anxiety related to fears of abandonment. These patients, however, would be expected to display anger, outbursts of strong emotion, and disruptive behavior. They may also try to manipulate discharge plans. The patient in this case does not exhibit any of these features.

The differential diagnosis for this patient may also include depression and bereavement. Many depressed or bereaved older patients have difficulty making decisions and become more dependent on family members. In this case, however, no depressive symptoms are described. Although she may be bereaved, her dependent behaviors began before her husband's death. This suggests that the normal bereavement process may be more complicated in this patient.

References
1. Agronin ME, Maletta G. Personality disorders in late life: understanding and overcoming the gap in research. *Am J Geriatric Psychiatry.* 2000;8(1):4–18.
2. Coolidge FL, Segal DI, Hook JN, et al. Personality disorders and coping among anxious older adults. *J Anxiety Disorders.* 2000;14(2):157–172.

7. An 82-year-old nursing-home resident is evaluated because she has developed full-thickness pressure ulcers on both heels. She has a history of multiple sclerosis, dementia, and urinary incontinence.

Which of the following is the most appropriate mattress for this patient?

(A) Air mattress
(B) Foam mattress
(C) Water mattress
(D) Low-air-loss mattress
(E) Air-fluidized mattress

ANSWER: D

The support system for redistributing pressure is important in pressure-ulcer care. Medicare and Medicaid reimburse for static devices that do not require electricity, devices powered by electricity or pump, and air-fluidized electric beds.

Static devices that do not require electricity include air, foam, gel, and water overlay mattresses. They are ideal for a patient at low risk for developing a pressure ulcer, but if reactive hyperemia develops on bony prominences, a dynamic surface should be considered. Devices powered by electricity or pump, such as pressure alternating and low-air-loss mattresses, are considered dynamic and are ideal for patients with moderate to high risk for pressure ulcers or for patients who have full-thickness pressure ulcers, as in this case.

Air-fluidized electric beds contain silicone-coated beads and are also considered dynamic. They are used for patients with nonhealing, full-thickness pressure ulcers or numerous truncal full-thickness pressure ulcers. They are not needed in this case where the ulcers are not truncal and have not had a trial of usual therapy.

References
1. Cullum N, McInnes E, Bell-Syer SE, et al. Support surfaces for pressure ulcer prevention. *Cochrane Database Syst Rev.* 2004;(3):CD001735.
2. Lyder CH. Pressure ulcer prevention and management. *JAMA.* 2003;289(2):223–226.
3. Theaker C. Pressure sore prevention in the critically ill: what you don't know, what should know and why it's important. *Intensive Crit Care Nurs.* 2003;19(3):163–168.

8. A 78-year-old thin woman comes to the office because she has acute lower back pain that began when she tried to open a stuck window. The pain is so severe that she has difficulty standing or sitting. The pain lessens when she lies down, and increases when she rolls to the side. The pain does not radiate to her legs.

On physical examination, there is marked tenderness in the mid-lumbar spine area and moderate paravertebral muscle spasm in the lumbar region. Bilateral straight leg raise tests are normal. She has full motor strength of the proximal and distal muscles of both lower legs.

Radiography of the lumbar spine shows diffuse disk space narrowing and vertebral osteophytosis throughout the lumbar region.

What is the most likely diagnosis?

(A) Herniated lumbar disk at L-4, L-5
(B) Instability of the lumbar spine
(C) Lumbar spinal stenosis
(D) Vertebral compression fracture
(E) Ruptured abdominal aortic aneurysm

ANSWER: D

This patient's clinical presentation is typical for vertebral compression fracture. The acute onset of lower back pain in an elderly woman after trying to open a window is a classic scenario. Spasm of the paravertebral muscles and tenderness of the lumbar spine are also typical. Vertebral compression fractures rarely cause neurologic signs, and the absence of leg weakness also favors this diagnosis. Compression fractures of the vertebrae may not be apparent on plain radiographs of the spine for up to 4 weeks after the injury. Technetium bone scans and magnetic resonance imaging identify compression fractures earlier than plain radiographs.

Herniation of the lumbar disk is rare in persons older than 55 years, as the nucleus pulposus of the disk loses water content with age, becomes less gel-like, and does not herniate outside the lumbar disk space. In addition, disk herniation is likely to cause mild weakness of the L-4, L-5 innervated muscles of the legs with a positive straight leg raise test.

Instability of the lumbar spine can cause acute lower back pain but does not usually cause pain when the patient rolls to the side. Severe pain from sitting or standing is rare. Radiography of the lumbar spine will often demonstrate one disk space that is narrowed and sclerotic out of proportion to other disk spaces.

The pain of lumbar spinal stenosis develops after prolonged standing and walking and is relieved when the patient sits. Lumbar spinal stenosis does not cause acute lower back pain or pain from rolling side to side.

Although a visceral source should always be considered in patients with acute onset of back pain, this patient's presentation is not consistent with a ruptured aneurysm. Ruptured aneurysm is associated with persistent and severe pain that is not relieved by lying down. Tenderness and muscle spasm in the lumbar spine are uncommon in a patient with a ruptured aneurysm.

References

1. Kim DH, Silber JS, Albert TJ. Osteoporotic vertebral compresson fractures. *Instr Course Lect.* 2003;52:541–550.
2. Lyles KW. Management of patients with vertebral compression fractures. *Pharmacotherapy.* 1999;19(1 Pt 2):21S–24S.
3. Wu SS, Lachmann E, Nagler W. Current medical, rehabilitation, and surgical management of vertebral compression fractures. *J Womens Health.* 2003;12(1):17–26.

9. A 70-year-old man comes to the office for advice regarding treatment of prostate cancer. The patient recently had transurethral resection of the prostate for increasingly bothersome lower urinary tract symptoms. His symptoms markedly improved, and he has had no side effects. Tissue analysis shows evidence of prostate cancer (Gleason grade 5). His prostate-specific antigen level is 3.8 ng/mL. He is otherwise healthy and takes no medication other than a multiple vitamin.

His urologist explained to him that radical prostatectomy would reduce his risk of dying from prostate cancer. They also discussed radiation therapy, hormone therapy, and watchful waiting. The patient states that he is uneasy about "having a cancer" and prefers active treatment in hope of a quick, definitive solution. However, he is concerned about maintaining sexual function and is troubled by the prospect of incontinence. He is unsure of how to proceed.

What is the most appropriate therapy to recommend?

(A) Radical prostatectomy
(B) External beam radiation
(C) Brachytherapy
(D) Chronic hormone therapy
(E) Watchful waiting

ANSWER: C

This patient desires treatment, is otherwise healthy, and has a reasonably long life expectancy. Gleason grade 5 indicates a moderately differentiated, moderately aggressive form of cancer. The relatively low prostate-specific antigen (PSA) level indicates a low likelihood of distant or local spread at this time. Most experts would recommend treatment.

Gleason grade 5 cancer responds well to brachytherapy alone. Given the patient's concerns about sexual side effects, brachytherapy is the treatment of choice because it is associated with a lower risk of sexual dysfunction and incontinence than radical prostatectomy or external beam radiation. Radical prostatectomy is more effective than hormonal therapy and in early prostate cancer may reduce death from prostate cancer more effectively than watchful waiting, but there is no evidence that surgery is superior to brachytherapy or external beam radiation.

References

1. DeMarzo AM, Nelson WG, Isaacs WB, et al. Pathological and molecular aspects of prostate cancer. *Lancet.* 2003;361(9361):955–964.
2. Holmberg L, Bill-Axelson A, Helgesen F, et al. Scandinavian Prostatic Cancer Group Study Number 4. A randomized trial comparing radical prostatectomy with watchful waiting in early prostate cancer. *N Engl J Med.* 2002;347(11):781–789.
3. Jani AB, Hellman S. Early prostate cancer: clinical decision-making. *Lancet.* 2003;361(9362):1045–1053.
4. Klein EA, Kupelian PA. Localized prostate cancer: radiation or surgery? *Urol Clin North Am.* 2003;30(2):315–330.

10. A 78-year-old woman with longstanding chronic obstructive pulmonary disease, metastatic lung cancer, and recurrent left-sided malignant pleural effusion is admitted to home hospice. She was recently hospitalized for worsening dyspnea. Therapeutic thoracentesis resulted in immediate improvement in her symptoms, and she underwent pleurodesis several days later. The dyspnea returned after she was discharged home 1 week ago, and she refuses to go back to the hospital for further tests or treatment because she is frustrated by how quickly her symptoms reappeared. She states that she can barely catch her breath. She has had no recent fever or chills and no change in her chronic cough. Her only medications are ipratropium and albuterol inhalers, both of which she is now using every 4 hours with no improvement. She increased her supplemental oxygen level from 2 L per minute to 4 L per minute by nasal cannula, with minimal improvement. Since her discharge from the hospital, she is unable to perform activities of daily living except for feeding, she requires the assistance of a 24-hour caregiver, and she spends most of her time in bed. Her appetite has diminished in the past 3 weeks and she has lost about 3.6 kg (8 lb).

On examination, she is lying in a hospital bed in her living room and appears anxious and uncomfortable. She is afebrile. Blood pressure is 103/54 mm Hg, pulse is regular at 88 per minute, and respiratory rate is 22 per minute. She is clearly using her accessory respiratory muscles. The lower half of the left lung field is dull to percussion, and there are no wheezes or crackles. Oxygen saturation is 96% on oxygen via nasal cannula at 4 L per minute.

Which of the following is the most appropriate next step in management?

(A) Start acetaminophen with codeine 300 mg/30 mg every 6 hours.
(B) Start oral morphine 5 mg every 4 hours.
(C) Start oral lorazepam 1 mg every 8 hours.
(D) Start nebulized ipratropium bromide every 4 hours.
(E) Change oxygen supplementation to a face mask.

ANSWER: B

Dyspnea, the subjective experience of breathing discomfort, is one of the most distressing symptoms for patients with cancer. The symptom is common in patients with advanced lung disease and present in 70% of patients with terminal cancer. Self-report is the gold standard for diagnosis of dyspnea. Measurements of respiratory rate, oxygen saturation, and arterial blood gases often do not correlate with severity of symptoms and do not measure dyspnea. Dyspnea results from interactions among multiple physiologic, psychologic, social, and environmental factors. A thorough history and examination are necessary to evaluate the source of dyspnea.

The optimal therapy is treatment of the underlying cause. However, for many patients, especially those with advanced cancer, the cause cannot be reversed and treatment must focus on symptom management. Opioids are first-line therapy in the symptomatic treatment of dyspnea. They reduce minute ventilation and decrease the sensation of breathlessness. Use of these agents may be limited by carbon dioxide retention and related somnolence, as well as by a decreased respiratory response to hypoxia. Opioid receptors are found throughout the peripheral and central nervous system and in the tracheobronchial tree. Typically less potent opioids (codeine, hydrocodone) are used for patients with mild dyspnea; more potent opioids (morphine, oxycodone, hydromorphone) are used for more severe cases. Randomized controlled trials have not shown a consistent benefit from nebulized morphine for dyspnea. This patient with moderate to severe dyspnea should receive scheduled low-dose morphine. Acetaminophen with codeine is recommended for patients with milder symptoms.

Benzodiazepines such as lorazepam may help manage anxiety associated with terminal cancer or dyspnea, but they do not improve breathlessness.

Inhaled β_2-agonists such as albuterol and the anticholinergic ipratropium bromide are used to manage dyspnea in patients with chronic obstructive pulmonary disease (COPD). They reduce the work of breathing by reducing airway resistance and the associated hyperinflation that compromises diaphragmatic function. Although this patient has COPD, she is not likely to benefit much from a nebulized

formulation, since her symptoms appear to be primarily related to mass effect of tumor and pleural effusion, and she has not had relief with metered-dose inhalers.

Supplemental oxygen may improve symptoms in patients with advanced lung disease, and the Medicare hospice benefit covers home oxygen therapy for dyspnea associated with terminal illness. This patient has already increased her oxygen level without significant improvement in symptoms. A higher level may not improve her symptoms and increases the risk of carbon dioxide retention, given her history of COPD. A face mask is unlikely to provide a greater benefit than nasal prongs, given her current oxygen saturation. Face masks are typically avoided in terminally ill patients, as they may interfere with speaking and eating, can create a sense of suffocation, and may be isolating, frightening, and uncomfortable for patients.

References

1. Abernethy AP, Currow DC, Frith P, et al. Randomised, double blind, placebo controlled crossover trial of sustained release morphine for the management of refractory dyspnea. *BMJ.* 2003;327(7414):523–528.
2. Luce JM, Luce JA. Perspectives on care at the close of life: management of dyspnea in patients with far-advanced lung disease: "once I lose it, it's kind of hard to catch it . . .". *JAMA.* 2001;285(10):1331–1337.
3. Thomas JR, von Gunten CF. Clinical management of dyspnoea. *Lancet Oncol.* 2002;3(4):223–228.
4. Webb M, Moody LE, Mason LA. Dyspnea assessment and management in hospice patients with pulmonary disorders. *Am J Hosp Palliat Care.* 2000;17(4):259–264.

11. A 74-year-old man is evaluated for a pressure ulcer that has developed on his left heel over the past few days. He was recently admitted to the nursing home and has a history of mild dementia, non–insulin-dependent diabetes mellitus, hypertension, and coronary artery disease. He has left hemiparesis from a stroke.

On examination, the ulcer is 5 cm × 3 cm. There is necrosis of the subcutaneous tissue, partial exposure of the underlying fascia, a moderate amount of slough, and a large amount of exudate. Erythema surrounds the ulcer, but there is no induration.

Which of the following is the most appropriate treatment for the ulcer?

(A) Calcium alginate dressing
(B) Collagen granules covered with dry gauze
(C) Sequential use of calcium alginate and hydrocolloid dressings
(D) Wet-to-dry dressing

ANSWER: C

This patient has a stage III pressure ulcer with a large amount of exudate and necrotic tissue. Maintenance of a moist wound environment is the primary goal of a dressing. Exudates must be controlled, but the wound should not be desiccated. Hydrocolloid dressings are good for stage II or III pressure ulcers with low to moderate drainage. In a recent randomized multicenter trial of stage III or IV pressure ulcers, sequential treatment first with calcium alginate and then with hydrocolloid dressing was found to promote faster healing than treatment with hydrocolloid alone.

Small trials have shown favorable results with topical collagen. A recent study, however, did not show appreciable benefit of collagen over hydrocolloid dressing. As collagen is more costly, hydrocolloid remains the first choice for appropriate ulcers.

Calcium alginate dressings alone will dry the exudate but not promote a moist environment for healing. Wet-to-dry dressing will also dry the wound environment.

References

1. Belmin J, Meaume S, Rabus MT, et al. Sequential treatment with calcium alginate dressings and hydrocolloid dressings accelerates pressure ulcer healing in older subjects: a multicenter randomized trial of sequential versus nonsequential treatment with hydrocolloid dressings alone. *J Am Geriatr Soc.* 2002; 50(2):269–274.
2. Dimant J. Implementing pressure ulcer prevention and treatment programs: using AMDA clinical practice guidelines. *JAMDA.* 2001; 3(3):315–325.
3. Graumlich J, Blough L, McLaughlin R, et al. Healing pressure ulcers with collagen or hydrocolloid: a randomized, controlled trial. *J Am Geriatr Soc.* 2003;51:147–154.
4. Lyder CH. Pressure ulcer prevention and management. *JAMA.* 2003;289(2):223–226.

12. A 72-year-old woman is brought to the office by her daughter, with whom she lives. The patient has asthma. The daughter has just been diagnosed with influenza, by a nasal swab antigen test. The mother has consistently refused to get the influenza vaccine because she says she "always got the flu from the shot," but she agrees to be immunized now.

In addition to immunization, prophylaxis using which of the following would best prevent influenza in this patient?

(A) Amantadine
(B) Rimantadine
(C) Oseltamivir
(D) Zanamivir

ANSWER: C

Both neuraminidase inhibitors, oseltamivir and zanamivir, are available for treatment of influenza. Only oseltamivir is approved for prophylaxis of influenza. Unlike amantadine and rimantadine, which cover only influenza A, neuraminidase inhibitors protect against both influenza A and B. Oseltamivir is preferred because it is administered orally, whereas zanamivir requires an inhalation device, which is often difficult for older adults to use, and zanamivir can trigger bronchospasm in patients with reactive airway disease.

Oseltamivir and zanamivir should be considered in older adults even if the documented strain is influenza A, as amantadine causes marked adverse effects and requires dose adjustment to prevent kidney failure. Rimantadine has fewer adverse effects and does not need adjustment for reduced kidney function, but it is more expensive than amantadine.

The effect of neuraminidase inhibitors on such secondary end points as hospitalization and death has been examined only in a few small studies. Thus, in patients without a strict contraindication, drug prophylaxis does not replace the vaccine, which has proven efficacy for preventing hospitalization and death. Furthermore, the vaccine's protective efficacy lasts several months, whereas chemoprophylaxis is useful only for as long as it is taken (usually 2 weeks).

References

1. Harper SA, Fakuda K, Uyeki TM, et al. Prevention and control of influenza: recommendations of the Advisory Committee on Immunization Practices (ACIP). *MMWR Recomm Rep.* 2004;53(RR-6):1–40.
2. Treanor JJ, Hayden FG, Vrooman PS, et al. Efficacy and safety of the oral neuraminidase inhibitor oseltamivir in treating acute influenza: a randomized controlled trial. US Oral Neuraminidase Study Group. *JAMA.* 2000;283(8):1016–1024.
3. Welliver R, Monto AS, Carewicz O, et al. Effectiveness of oseltamivir in preventing influenza in household contacts: a randomized controlled trial. *JAMA.* 2001;285(6):748–754.

13. An 84-year-old man with a history of advanced dementia is admitted to the hospital for aspiration pneumonia. This is his third hospitalization for aspiration pneumonia in 6 months. His health has been steadily declining over the past year; he has lost 9.5 kg (20 lb) over the past 10 months and has a sacral pressure ulcer. He is nonverbal, unable to ambulate, and dependent for all of his activities of daily living. The patient never wanted to go to a nursing home; with the assistance of home-health aides, his wife has cared for him at home.

After the pneumonia resolves, the patient continues to receive wound care for his pressure ulcer. A bedside swallow study is obtained, and results indicate that all food consistencies are unsafe for the patient. The hospitalist suggests initiation of tube feeding.

The patient's advance care plan states that his wife is his agent and that he does not want any extraordinary measures taken to extend his life—specifically, no cardiopulmonary resuscitation, mechanical ventilation, or artificial nutrition. The wife asks the patient's primary physician for advice.

What is the most appropriate recommendation for this patient?

(A) Long-term placement of a feeding tube and discharge to a skilled nursing facility
(B) Short-term placement of a feeding tube and discharge to a skilled nursing facility until the pressure ulcer has healed
(C) Discharge to a skilled nursing facility for wound care until the pressure ulcer has healed
(D) Discharge home with home-health services
(E) Discharge home with home hospice

ANSWER: E

This patient has end-stage dementia. His physical condition has progressively deteriorated and he is now nonverbal and bedbound, with severe dysphagia and recurrent infections. He stated in his living will that he does not want artificial nutrition. His wife holds his durable power of attorney, and her decisions should reflect his wishes. A feeding tube would be contrary to his expressed preferences and therefore should not be placed. His request to not go to a nursing home should be honored if possible. Although a home-health agency would provide the patient with wound care, the best option for this patient is referral to home hospice.

To receive the Medicare hospice benefit, patients must have a terminal condition with a prognosis of 6 months or less. The National Hospice Organization developed hospice eligibility guidelines for noncancer diagnoses, including end-stage dementia, and Medicare has made recommendations that are based on these criteria. The criteria include having a score on the Reisburg Functional Assessment Staging (FAST) of 7 or greater (this score is given to patients with limited ability to speak, loss of ambulation, and urinary and fecal incontinence), a history of comorbid conditions in the past 6 months (such as aspiration pneumonia, septicemia, decubitus ulcers, pyelonephritis), dysphagia, and an inability to maintain fluid and caloric intake to sustain life. Advanced age, impaired nutritional status, and severe functional impairment have been shown to be better predictors of decreased survival than the FAST score. These additional factors should be taken into consideration along with the guidelines.

The hospice multidisciplinary team typically includes a physician, a nurse, a social worker, and a chaplain as well as home-health aides and various therapists (such as music therapists, physical therapists). The primary goal of care is comfort and relief of suffering. The patient and family are the unit of care, and bereavement services are offered to the family for 13 months after the patient dies.

References

1. Luchins DJ, Hanrahan P, Murphy K. Criteria for enrolling dementia patients in hospice. *J Am Geriatr Soc.* 1997; 45(9):1054–1059.
2. Schonwetter RS, Han B, Small BJ, et al. Predictors of six-month survival among patients with dementia: an evaluation of hospice Medicare guidelines. *Am J Hosp Palliat Care.* 2003;20(2):105–113.
3. Shuster JL. Palliative care for advanced dementia. *Clin Geriatr Med.* 2000; 16(2):373–386.
4. Volicer L. Management of severe Alzheimer's disease and end-of-life issues. *Clin Geriatr Med.* 2001; 7(2):377–391.

14. An 80-year-old man has hypertension, heart failure, osteoarthritis, and visual and hearing impairments. He is enrolled in the traditional Medicare Parts A and B programs and is considering taking out a supplemental insurance policy.

Which of the following services are not covered under traditional Medicare Parts A and B and should be considered by a patient when selecting supplemental insurance?

(A) Cataract surgery
(B) Cochlear implant
(C) Hearing aid
(D) Diagnostic audiogram
(E) Evaluation by an ophthalmologist

ANSWER: C

Medicare Part A primarily covers acute care related to hospitalization; Part B provides coverage for outpatient and clinician services comprising diagnosis and treatment (including surgery) of medical illness. Medicare provides coverage for cataract surgery and diagnostic evaluations of hearing and visual deficits. Medicare covers cochlear implants for patients with bilateral severe or profound sensorineural hearing impairment who have limited benefit from hearing or vibrotactile aids. Parts A and B do not cover many types of medical equipment, including hearing aids and eyeglasses, or many

preventive services. Diagnostic services, including diagnostic tests and consultation with specialists, are partially or completely covered by Part B.

References

1. Health Care Financing Administration. *Medicare Coverage Issues Manual*, transmittal 134, HCFA Publication 6. Available at http://www.cms.hhs.gov/manuals/pm_trans/R134CIM.pdf (accessed September 2005).
2. Centers for Medicare and Medicaid Services. Medicare Coverage Database page. Available at http://www.cms.hhs.gov/mcd/search.asp? (accessed September 2005).

15. A 72-year-old previously healthy man was hospitalized 8 days ago with an acute ruptured appendix. His weight at presentation was 71.8 kg (158 lb; body mass index 26 [kg/m^2]), which was unchanged from the prior year, and serum albumin was 3.9 g/dL. Sepsis developed postoperatively, but he was much improved after 4 days of antibiotic therapy. At that time, albumin was 2.2 g/dL; leukocyte count, electrolytes, and renal function were normal. Ileus also developed, but the patient was able to resume a regular diet 3 days ago. Nurses' notes indicate that his appetite has been "fair."

Yesterday evening the patient's temperature spiked to 39°C (102.2°F) after 4 days with no fever. Fever work-up suggested probable urinary tract infection, and the antibiotic regimen was changed. This morning the patient feels much better; he is sitting in a chair and starting to eat breakfast. Temperature is 37°C (98.6°F) and weight is 71 kg (157 lb). Physical examination is remarkable for a noninflamed surgical wound, which is being allowed to heal by secondary intent. He has 1+ pretibial and presacral edema.

Which of the following is best for assessing the patient's nutritional risk?

(A) Obtain repeat serum albumin level.
(B) Obtain serum prealbumin level.
(C) Order detailed calorie counts for 3 days.
(D) Measure biceps and triceps skinfold thickness and arm muscle circumference.

ANSWER: C

At this point, it is important to know how well the patient is eating. The combination of bed rest and acute disease-induced inflammation and anorexia can result in rapid loss of lean tissue mass and fat stores in older patients. This patient most likely has had a significant deterioration in nutritional status during the 8 days of hospitalization. As is often the case, the amount of body mass loss is masked by the presence of edema.

Since nursing staff often overestimate how well older patients are eating, formal calorie counts should be obtained for high-risk patients. Although the calorie count should be followed for 3 days, the data should be assessed as it is collected. A very low nutrient intake would be apparent from data collected within the first 24 hours. Three-day counts are helpful to assess patients who have fluctuating or borderline nutrient intake.

The serum secretory proteins, albumin and prealbumin, are of limited value in assessing the patient's nutritional risk at this point. Since the serum concentration of both drops in response to acute inflammation, they will likely be low in this patient. After the acute inflammatory disorders resolve, the prealbumin level may prove useful—a persistently low value suggests inadequate nutrient intake. Albumin is not a good indicator of the adequacy of an older patient's nutrient intake in any situation.

Skinfold and arm muscle circumference measurements provide an indirect assessment of the patient's nutritional reserves. However, the most important information needed at this time is an accurate assessment of his nutrient intake.

References

1. Laporte M, Villalon L, Thibodeau J, et al. Validity and reliability of simple nutrition screening tools adapted to the elderly population in healthcare facilities. *J Nutr Health Aging.* 2001;5(4):292–294.
2. Mowe M, Bohmer T. Reduced appetite: a predictor for undernutrition in aged people. *J Nutr Health Aging.* 2002;6(1):81–83.
3. Omran ML, Morley JE. Assessment of protein energy malnutrition in older persons, part I: history, examination, body composition, and screening tools. *Nutrition.* 2000;16(1):50–63.
4. Sullivan DH. What do the serum proteins tell us about our elderly patients? *J Gerontol A Biol Sci Med Sci.* 2001;56A(2) M71–M74.

16. An 80-year-old man has been homebound for a decade since a stroke left him with hemiplegia. He called his physician with symptoms of dysuria and fever to 38.3°C (101°F). The patient has a history of depression that is currently being treated. He pays someone to help him dress in the morning and assist him back to bed at 5 P.M. He is wheelchair bound during the day and has meals-on-wheels delivered. He has been very demanding with home-health aides, and no agency will provide him with further assistance. He has consistently stated that he never wants to go to a nursing home; after his most recent hospitalization for urosepsis 2 months ago, he insisted that he never wants to be hospitalized again or to be stuck with needles. At that time, Adult Protective Services and psychiatry consultation stated that he was capable of making his own decisions. In response to his call, a home-care nurse is sent to evaluate him and to obtain a urine specimen. Culture of the urine grows bacteria that are resistant to broad-spectrum antibiotics. The physician ascertains that the patient, while lethargic, is still able to make decisions, and the patient insists on staying in his home.

Which of the following should the physician do next?

(A) Call an ambulance to take him to the hospital.
(B) Admit him to a nursing home.
(C) Begin intravenous antibiotics at home under the skilled home care Medicare benefit.
(D) Ask the patient if he agrees to a hospice consultation.
(E) Adjust the antidepressant medication.

ANSWER: D

The physician's goal should be to support the decisions the patient has made even if the physician may not agree with them.

If the patient agrees to a hospice referral, this may be the best option. Though hospice may not accept him because of the ambiguity of his illness and his marginally supported living situation, many hospice programs are flexible enough to take on a patient such as this.

If the patient refuses all intervention, the medical team may not feel comfortable in supporting this unsafe situation and can withdraw services as well. Team discussions should be encouraged, and team members involved in the case should be supported in these difficult cases.

Calling an ambulance and taking him to the hospital or admitting him to a nursing home or starting intravenous antibiotics at home are not appropriate actions in this case. The patient has consistently expressed his wish not to be hospitalized, admitted to a nursing home, or stuck with needles, and the medical team should respect this, even if he cannot physically resist such an intervention. The patient may need adjustment of his antidepressants, but it is still appropriate to respect his previously stated preferences.

References

1. Blank K, Robison J, Doherty E, et al. Life-sustaining treatment and assisted death choices in depressed older patients. *J Am Geriatr Soc.* 2001;49(2):153–161.
2. Cobbs EL. Improving quality in end-of-life care: dying at home. *J Am Geriatr Soc.* 2001;49(6):831–832.
3. Fried TR, Pollack DM, Drickamer MA, et al. Who dies at home? determinants of site of death for community-based long-term care patients. *J Am Geriatr Soc.* 1999;47(1):25–29.
4. Rosenfeld K, Wenger NS. Measuring quality in end-of-life care. *Clin Geriatr Med.* 2000;16(2):387–400.
5. Singer PA, Martin DK, Kelner M. Quality end-of-life care: patient's perspectives. *JAMA.* 1999;281(2):163–168.

17. A 68-year-old woman comes to the office because she has pain and stiffness in several joints. Her sleep has been poor, and she is fatigued, irritable, and weak. She attributes her symptoms to the antibiotic she has been taking for a nonproductive cough.

On physical examination, temperature is 38°C (100.4°F) and blood pressure is 170/95 mm Hg. She has tenderness to palpation of the small joints of her hands and feet, epitrochlear and cervical adenopathy, and an erythematous rash over her chest and back that she had not noticed. Her strength is normal.

Laboratory studies:

Leukocyte count	3.0/μL
Platelet count	492,000/μL
Hematocrit	26%
Antinuclear antibody	1:160
Anti-double-stranded DNA antibody	Positive
Urinalysis (clean catch)	2+ protein, no cells

Which of the following is most consistent with this patient's features?

(A) Dermatomyositis
(B) Drug-induced lupus
(C) Late-onset lupus
(D) Rheumatoid arthritis
(E) Fibromyalgia

ANSWER: C

Late-onset systemic lupus erythematosus (SLE) is characterized by polyarthritis, serositis, rash, and cytopenia, and occasionally also by fever in older adult. The symptom complex is clinically similar to drug-induced lupus erythematosus but is distinguished by its proteinuria and antibody response to double-stranded DNA. Although late-onset disease is thought to have a better prognosis than SLE in young adults, occasionally kidney involvement can progress to failure; therefore, treatment should be pursued aggressively.

This patient does not have the proximal muscle weakness prominent in dermatomyositis. Rheumatoid arthritis can cause polyarthritis of the small and intermediate-sized joints in patients with a positive antinuclear antibody titer, but it is not associated with an antibody response to double-stranded DNA. Fibromyalgia can accompany any rheumatic condition but would not in itself explain this symptom complex.

References

1. Beyan E, Uzuner A, Beyan C. An uncommon cause of fever in the elderly: late-onset systemic lupus erythematosus. *Clin Rheumatol.* 2003;22(6):481–483.
2. Favalli EG, Sinigaglia L, Varenna M, et al. Drug-induced lupus following treatment with infliximab in rheumatoid arthritis. *Lupus.* 2002;11(11):753–755.
3. Pu SJ, Luo SF, Wu YJ, et al. The clinical features and prognosis of lupus with disease onset at age 65 and older. *Lupus.* 2000;9(2):96–100.

18. A 74-year-old man comes to the office because he has pain in his right arm. He had a stroke with right hemiparesis 4 months ago and underwent 2 weeks of in-patient rehabilitation. On examination of his right upper extremity, he has trace muscle strength at the shoulder. Muscle tone is slightly spastic. Passive range of motion of the shoulder and elbow is full but elicits pain. There is swelling over the hand and slight erythema of the hand and forearm. The skin is sensitive to touch. There are no lesions on the hand or arm. Vital signs are normal.

Which of the following is the next step in management of this patient?

(A) Physical therapy consultation
(B) Elevation of patient's arm on a pillow while sleeping
(C) Diagnostic ultrasonography of the arm
(D) Nighttime elastic wrapping of right hand and forearm
(E) Empiric antibiotic treatment

ANSWER: A

This patient has a number of features commonly seen in reflex sympathetic dystrophy, or shoulder-hand syndrome (also called *causalgia*). The most disturbing symptom is pain, usually described as burning or deep, that is aggravated by movement. It does not follow a dermatomal distribution. Pain may be worsened by non-noxious stimuli (allodynia). The pain is usually accompanied by local edema and vasomotor changes. Early on, the skin is commonly erythematous and warm, and later it may appear cyanotic and mottled, as with livedo reticularis. Finally, the skin may become shiny and thin, and nails become brittle. Reflex sympathetic dystrophy is common after a stroke and may be more common in the presence of subluxation of the shoulder or spasticity, affecting as many as 27% of hemiplegic patients. Bone scan may be abnormal and plain radiography may show patchy osteopenia, but the diagnosis is based on clinical findings.

Treatment comprises prevention (managing subluxation and spasticity and maintaining range of motion) and physical therapy. Rest is not recommended and may aggravate symptoms. The challenge in therapy is getting the patient to allow adequate movement to start the healing process. Adequate pain relief and perhaps corticosteroids are needed to allow physical therapy to proceed.

Upper extremity venous thrombosis is rare, even in hemiplegia, although the presence of reflex sympathetic dystrophy makes it more likely. However, there would be venous distension with thrombosis.

The application of an elastic bandage will not lead to improvement and, because of allodynia, is likely to be extremely uncomfortable. Cellulitis is unlikely since there is no history of infection or localized lesions on the arm, and vital signs are normal.

References

1. Braus DF, Krauss JK, Strobel J. The shoulder-hand syndrome after stroke: a prospective clinical trial. *Ann Neurol.* 1994;36(5): 728–733.
2. Gispen JC. Painful shoulder and the reflex sympathetic dystrophy syndrome. In: Koopman WJ, Moreland LW, eds. *Arthritis and Allied Conditions.* Palo Alto, CA: Skolar/Wolters Kluwer Health; 2001.
3. Wasner G, Schattschneider J, Binder A, et al. Complex regional pain syndrome: diagnostic, mechanisms, CNS involvement and therapy. *Spinal Cord.* 2003;41(2):61–75.

19. A 79-year-old patient comes to the office at the insistence of family members who believe that she has been behaving differently over the past 2 years. She is a college-educated former teacher who has been retired for 10 years and lives with her husband. She has a history of well-controlled hypertension, mild macular degeneration, and mild osteoarthritis. She used to play golf and bridge, but now she seems less interested in these activities and is less social with family and friends. Her family reports that she takes initiative less often than before and is more easily distracted once she starts an activity. She now occasionally says things, such as criticizing family members, which surprise and concern her family. The patient says that she is fine and has no complaints. When asked about the symptoms her family describes, she answers that sometimes she does not want to do things as often as before, but that she still enjoys playing golf and bridge. She denies any depressive symptoms. Physical examination, including a complete neurologic examination, is within normal limits. Her score on the Mini–Mental State Examination is 29 of 30.

Which of the following is the most appropriate next step?

(A) Reassure the patient and family that her function is appropriate for her age.
(B) Obtain neuroimaging.
(C) Order formal neuropsychologic testing.
(D) Have the patient return in 2 weeks for repeat testing.

ANSWER: C

Executive function refers to the area of cognition responsible for regulation of complex goal-directed behavior. Problems with executive functioning may manifest as lack of initiative, difficulty maintaining attention and focus, perseveration, lack of insight, poor judgment, disinhibition, and changes in personality. Loss of executive control is associated with functional decline. The Mini–Mental State Examination (MMSE) assesses a number of different cognitive functions, such as orientation, registration, recall, attention and calculation, language, and visual-spatial skills. Although a score of 29 is reassuring, the MMSE incompletely assesses executive functioning. Because the patient's symptoms may indicate a problem in this area, neuropsychologic testing of executive function would be more likely to determine if dysfunction exists. Simple office-based assessment of executive functioning is possible, although normal results may not obviate further testing by a neuropsychologist. The clock-drawing test assesses executive control and visual-spatial skills, both of which are incompletely assessed by the MMSE. The test involves asking the patient to draw a clock face, to put in all the numbers, and to set the hands at a particular time (commonly 1:45, 2:50, and 11:10). Word-list generation or the use of standardized questionnaires, such as the Executive Interview (EXIT) test of executive function, would also be appropriate.

Given the family's description, and level of concern, the possibility of cognitive problems is sufficiently strong that reassurance without further assessment would be inappropriate in spite of the near-normal MMSE. Neuroimaging with computed tomography or magnetic resonance imaging is not the most appropriate next step for this patient, since the nature of her cognitive problems has not yet been elucidated adequately. Testing results are unlikely to change over the next 2 weeks.

References

1. Craft S, Cholerton B, Reger M. Aging and cognition: what is normal? In: Hazzard WR, Blass JP, Halter JB, et al., eds. *Principles of Geriatric Medicine and Gerontology.* 5th ed. New York: McGraw Hill; 2003:1355–1372.
2. Juby A, Tench S, Baker V. The value of clock drawing in identifying executive cognitive dysfunction in people with a normal Mini-Mental State Examination score. *CMAJ.* 2002;167(8):859–864.
3. Royall DR, Mahurin RK, Gray KF. Bedside assessment of executive cognitive impairment: the executive interview. *J Am Geriatr Soc.* 1992;40(12):1221–1226.

20. An 80-year-old woman in an assisted-living center is evaluated because she has become withdrawn. She no longer attends activities and prefers to eat in her room. She has macular degeneration and arthritis. She moved to the center 2 months earlier because she was unable to prepare her own meals, needed to use a wheelchair outside of her house, and, because of vision loss, was unable to manage finances. At first she was happy with the move, made friends, and used her wheelchair to attend activities. She now no longer goes to the community library or picks up her paper. There are no other new findings on history or physical examination.

Which of the following is most likely to have caused increased disability resulting in behavior change?

(A) Cataracts
(B) Arthritis
(C) Macular degeneration
(D) Dementia

ANSWER: C

This patient most likely has a worsening of her macular degeneration, which causes central blindness. Patients become unable to recognize faces and feel embarrassed and isolated. For many persons, fear of blindness is greater than fear of cancer or heart disease. Loss of vision in the elderly population has a great impact on quality of life: Up to 39% of patients over age 65 with low vision meet criteria for major depression. In some studies, quality-of-life ratings in patients with severe vision loss are lower than or equal to those of patients with chronic obstructive pulmonary disease, acquired immunodeficiency syndrome, or bone marrow transplant. Low-vision specialists can improve functional status and enhance quality of life for patients with severe vision loss.

Although arthritis can produce significant dysfunction, this patient is using a wheelchair for mobility and appears to have adjusted well to this modality. The patient does not complain of the blurring or glare that are characteristic of cataracts, and disability from cataracts develops over more than 2 months. Similarly, dementia is unlikely to progress this rapidly.

References

1. Brodie SE. Aging and disorders of the eye. In: Tallis RC, Fillit HM, eds. *Brocklehurst's Textbook of Geriatric Medicine and Gerontology.* 6th ed. London: Churchill Livingston; 2003:735–747.
2. Brody BL, Gamst AC, Williams RA, et al. Depression, visual acuity, comorbidity, and disability associated with age-related macular degeneration. *Ophthalmology.* 2001;108(10):1893–1901.
3. Scott IU, Smiddy WE, Schiffman J, et al. Quality of life of low-vision patients and the impact of low-vision services. *Am J Ophthalmol.* 1999; 128(1):54–62.

21. An 88-year-old nursing-home resident is evaluated because she has vertebral compression fractures found on lateral chest radiographs obtained after a positive PPD test for tuberculosis. They have occurred since her admission to the nursing home 3 years ago. She has mild dementia and Barrett's esophagitis. Her medications include a proton-pump inhibitor, calcium, and vitamin D. Evaluation suggests primary osteoporosis; femoral neck T score is −3.0 and combined lumbar T score is −2.8.

Which of the following is the most appropriate additional treatment for her osteoporosis?

(A) Alendronate
(B) Calcitonin
(C) Conjugated equine estrogen
(D) Etidronate
(E) Parathyroid hormone (teriparatide) Forteo

ANSWER: E

Parathyroid hormone is available for the treatment of osteoporosis. It seems particularly effective for preventing spinal fractures; fracture reduction at other sites is less certain. Unlike bisphosphonates, which are antiresorptive, parathyroid hormone stimulates bone formation. Clinical trials have shown improved bone density and reduced number of fractures in persons taking parathyroid hormone in comparison with a placebo group. In a randomized controlled trial comparing parathyroid hormone with the bisphosphonate alendronate, the incidence of nonvertebral fracture was found to be significantly lower for the parathyroid hormone group. Adverse effects are nausea, headache, and transient hypercalcemia. Parathyroid hormone must be administered by daily injection; treatment courses are limited to less than 2 years until more is known about long-term effectiveness and adverse effects.

In this case, the patient has preexisting esophageal disease and a remote history of gastric ulcer. Calcitonin, like parathyroid hormone, requires parenteral administration and its efficacy is limited. Estrogen replacement therapy[OL] is associated with adverse reactions. It would have to be cycled or used in conjunction with a progestational agent, and patient acceptance is often low. Etidronate[OL] has been supplanted by other bisphosphonates that have been more widely used and studied.

References

1. Black DM, Greenspan SL, Ensrud KE, et al. The effects of parathyroid hormone and alendronate alone or in combination in postmenopausal osteoporosis. *N Engl J Med.* 2003;349(13):1207–1215.
2. Body JJ, Gaich GA, Scheele WH, et al. A randomized double-blind trial to compare the efficacy of teriparatide [recombinant human parathyroid hormone (1-34)] with alendronate in postmenopausal women with osteoporosis. *J Clin Endocrinol Metab.* 2002;87(10):4528–4535.

[OL] Not approved by the U.S. Food and Drug Administration for this use.

3. Crandall C. Parathyroid hormone for treatment of osteoporosis. *Arch Intern Med.* 2002; 162(20):2297–2309.
4. Neer RM, Arnaud CD, Zanchetta JR. Effect of parathyroid hormone (1-34) on fractures and bone mineral density in postmenopausal women with osteoporosis. *N Engl J Med.* 2001;344(19):1434–1441.

22. An 87-year-old woman is admitted to your service at a skilled nursing facility. She has an ischemic cardiomyopathy with a left ventricular ejection fraction of 15% and a progressive dementia. She does not understand her condition or the possible outcomes with treatments and therefore lacks decisional capacity. She has no advance directives. She has outlived most of her friends, was never married, and has no children, although she does have a niece. The niece, although caring, has never discussed illness or end-of-life decisions with her aunt. You do know that the patient was combative with hospital care, needing both chemical and physical restraints during the hospitalization prior to this admission. You are discussing care options with the niece. You have told her, considering her aunt's cardiac and functional level, that attempting resuscitation would be a relatively futile procedure, and on this basis she has agreed with a do-not-attempt-resuscitation–do-not-intubate order. You then turn the conversation to the available treatment options for an exacerbation of her aunt's heart failure. You give her the option of sending her aunt to the hospital or having her remain in the nursing home and receive the maximum monitoring, treatment, and palliation available in that setting.

In guiding the niece as to how she should make this decision, it is appropriate that you tell her which of the following?

(A) Look at the benefits and burdens of these treatments for all demented patients.
(B) Consult a lawyer before making this type of decision.
(C) Look at benefits and burdens of this intervention for her aunt.
(D) Use the substituted-judgment standard.

ANSWER: C

The cascade of decision making for incapacitated patients is (1) the patient's expressed wishes, (2) substituted judgment, and (3) beneficence. In this case, the patient has not given any specific directions before becoming incapacitated. In order to make the decision by substituted judgment, the decision maker must have a sense of the patient's values, preferences, and thoughts about issues of health care and end of life. The niece does not have this information, and there is no one else who could be of assistance in this.

Therefore, the appropriate standard for decision making is beneficence; that is, looking at the potential benefits and burdens of treatment is the standard for decision making. This decision must be made on the basis of the possible benefits and burdens for this particular patient in this particular circumstance. Hospitalization may be more or less traumatic for different demented patients; therefore, a general statement should not be made of the relative burden of hospitalization that would hold up for all patients with dementia. For this patient, the possible advantages of hospitalization include increased cardiac monitoring and intravenous positive inotropic agents. These could potentially be life prolonging. This must be weighed against her difficulties with coping with the strange and confusing environment of the hospital and the functional loss that would occur if chemical and physical restraints were used, all of which would affect her quality of life. Consulting a lawyer in this case would not be helpful, as the timeline for decision making would likely preclude a lawyer's involvement, and a lawyer would have no additional information about the patient's wishes.

References
1. The Hastings Center. *Guidelines for the Termination of Life-Sustaining Treatment and the Care of the Dying.* Briarcliff Manor, NY: Hastings Center; 1987.
2. President's Commission for the Study of Ethical Problems in Medicine and Biomedical and Behavioral Research. *Making Health Care Decisions. A Report on the Ethical and Legal Implications of Informed Consent in the Patient-Practitioner Relationship.* Washington, DC: US Government Printing Office; 1982:217–261.

23. A 78-year-old woman who lives alone comes for an office visit as a new patient. She has osteoarthritis, macular degeneration, hypertension, and mild hearing loss. She has no symptoms except knee pain when she walks. On examination, she is thin (body mass index [kg/m²] of 19.2), and crepitus is present in both knees. The rest of the examination is within normal limits. Hemoglobin and hematocrit are normal, as was a colonoscopy approximately 10 years ago.

What is the most appropriate next step in evaluating her nutritional status?

(A) Check serum cholesterol.
(B) Check serum albumin.
(C) Check lymphocyte count.
(D) Inquire about recent weight loss.
(E) Perform anergy skin testing.

ANSWER: D

Body mass index (BMI, kg/m²) below 20 suggests poor nutritional status. It is not clear, however, that her current BMI represents a change for her. The easiest and quickest way to assess whether there is an ongoing serious problem affecting her nutrition is to inquire about recent weight loss. In fact, asking a question about recent weight loss complements the BMI as a screening strategy and may uncover nutritional problems in people with normal BMIs. Unintentional weight loss of greater than 5% over the prior 6 months is associated with increased mortality and strongly suggests the need for further evaluation, including an assessment of such factors as concurrent medical illness, depression, inability to shop or cook, inability to feed oneself, or financial hardship. In this woman who lives alone, one or more of these factors may play a role. Validated tools such as the Mini-Nutritional Assessment—Short Form (MNA–SF) are also useful for screening for undernutrition.

Both low albumin and low cholesterol in frail older adults are risk markers for increased mortality and may be a reasonable part of the evaluation of undernutrition or stress. For example, studies have demonstrated a graded increase in mortality with albumin levels lower than 5.0 g/dL. However, in addition to the cost and time involved in obtaining these tests,

neither one alone is particularly sensitive or specific, and all laboratory tests are affected by non-nutritional factors. Total lymphocyte counts and anergy skin testing are not useful nutritional markers for older adults.

References

1. Hensrud DD. Nutrition screening and assessment. *Med Clin North Am.* 1999; 83(6):1525–1546.
2. Rubenstein LZ, Harker JO, Salva A, et al. Screening for undernutrition in geriatric practice: developing the short-form mini-nutritional assessment (MNA-SF). *J Gerontol A Biol Sci Med Sci.* 2001;56(6):M366–M372.
3. Sullivan DH, Johnson LE. Nutrition and aging. In: Hazzard WR, Blass JP, Halter JB, et al., eds. *Principles of Geriatric Medicine and Gerontology.* 5th ed. New York: McGraw Hill; 2003:1151–1169.

24. A 71-year-old woman comes to the office to establish care. Her husband died 8 months ago, and she recently moved to the city to be near her daughter. She has a 45-year history of generalized anxiety disorder, for which she has taken diazepam 10 mg daily for the past 30 years. She asks for a prescription to continue the diazepam.

Which of the following is most appropriate at this time?

(A) Continue diazepam.
(B) Withdraw diazepam.
(C) Substitute buspirone for diazepam.
(D) Substitute venlafaxine for diazepam.

ANSWER: A

Given that this is the woman's first contact with the physician, that she is adjusting to a move to a new city after her husband's death, and that there is no imminent risk from continuing the diazepam, it is prudent to maintain the diazepam for now. It is also appropriate to arrange a follow-up appointment with her to discuss the possibility of withdrawing diazepam in the future, at which point it would be important to establish whether she still has generalized anxiety disorder, whether she currently has symptoms of depression, and whether she has a recent history of falls or cognitive impairment. It would also be important to determine whether she previously tried withdrawing the diazepam and, if so, whether this was associated with exacerbation or recurrence of anxiety.

If she is relatively asymptomatic and has not recently tried discontinuing the diazepam, then a slow withdrawal of the drug, by 1 mg per week, would be appropriate. If the history or attempt at withdrawal suggests that she needs ongoing treatment, appropriate options are to continue diazepam at the lowest effective dose, cognizant of the potential risks as she grows older; to substitute buspirone for diazepam if she does not have significant depressive symptoms; or to substitute with an antidepressant that is effective in generalized anxiety disorder, especially if she has comorbid depressive symptoms. Citalopram, escitalopram, sertraline, or venlafaxine are suitable antidepressants. Buspirone and antidepressant medications have a delayed onset of action and do not suppress withdrawal symptoms of benzodiazepines. Thus, if one of these medications is substituted for the benzodiazepine, it needs to be given at a therapeutic dose for 4 weeks before the benzodiazepine is gradually withdrawn. Despite this approach, some patients are less satisfied with the anxiolytic effects of buspirone than with a benzodiazepine.

References

1. Davidson JR, DuPont RL, Hedges D, et al. Efficacy, safety, and tolerability of venlafaxine extended release and buspirone in outpatients with generalized anxiety disorder. *J Clin Psychiatry.* 1999;60(8):528–535.
2. DeMartinis N, Rynn M, Rickels K, et al. Prior benzodiazepine use and buspirone response in the treatment of generalized anxiety disorder. *J Clin Psychiatry.* 2000;61(2):91–94.
3. Katz IR, Reynolds CF, Alexopoulos GS, et al. Venlafaxine ER as a treatment for generalized anxiety disorder in older adults: pooled analysis of five randomized placebo-controlled clinical trials. *J Am Geriatr Soc.* 2002;50(1):18–25.
4. Rickels K, DeMartinis N, Garcia-Espana F, et al. Imipramine and buspirone in treatment of patients with generalized anxiety disorder who are discontinuing long-term benzodiazepine therapy. *Am J Psychiatry.* 2000;157(12):1973–1979.

25. A 72-year-old man comes to the office to establish care. He has no symptoms, and examination is normal except for hypertension.

Laboratory studies:
Hemoglobin	12.0 g/dL
Mean corpuscular volume	90.0 fL
Mean corpuscular hemoglobin	90.0 pg/cell
Serum protein	9.5 g/dL (elevated)
Serum immunoglobulins	
IgG	2500 mg/L (elevated)
IgA	230 mg/dL (normal)
IgM	150 mg/dL (normal)
Serum protein electrophoresis	monoclonal M spike

Bone marrow biopsy reveals 8% plasma cells. Skeletal survey is normal.

What is the most appropriate management now?

(A) Reassessment in 1 year
(B) Chemotherapy
(C) Radiation therapy
(D) Bone marrow transplantation

ANSWER: A

This patient has a monoclonal gammopathy of undetermined significance (MGUS). MGUS occurs in up to 2% of persons 50 years old, and in up to 4% of patients over age 70. In a 35-year follow-up series, MGUS was found to progress to multiple myeloma, IgM lymphoma, primary amyloidosis, macroglobulinemia, chronic lymphocytic leukemia, or plasmacytoma in 115 of 1384 patients. In 32 additional patients, the monoclonal protein concentration increased to more than 3 g/dL, or the percentage of plasma cells in the bone marrow increased to more than 10% (smoldering multiple myeloma) without progression to overt myeloma or related disorders. The cumulative probability of progression was 12% at 10 years, 25% at 20 years, and 30% at 25 years. The risk of progression of MGUS to multiple myeloma or related disorders is about 1% per year. Thus, treatment is not warranted at this time.

The 5-year survival rate for multiple myeloma is between 25% and 30%, and is usually lower in older patients. Clinical progression to multiple myeloma is associated with anemia in 66% of patients, chronic renal insufficiency in 25%, hypercalcemia in 20%, bone pain in 60%, and lytic lesions in 70%. Prognostic markers include elevated β_2-microglobulin, lactate dehydrogenase level, and chromosome 13 abnormalities. Most elderly patients cannot undergo bone marrow transplantation. Treatment usually includes melphalan and prednisone, high-dose dexamethasone, or dexamethasone plus thalidomide. Radiation therapy would be appropriate for painful bone lesions.

References

1. Kyle RA, Rajkumar SV. Monoclonal gammopathies of undetermined significance. *Hematol Oncol Clin North Am.* 1999;13(6):1181–1202.
2. Kyle RA, Rajkumar SV. Monoclonal gammopathies of undetermined significance: a review. *Immunol Rev.* 2003;194:112–139.
3. Kyle RA, Therneau TM, Rajkumar SV, et al. A long-term study of prognosis in monoclonal gammopathy of undetermined significance. *N Engl J Med.* 2002;346(8):564–569.

26. A 76-year-old woman returns to the clinic for follow-up after 1 month of treatment for stress incontinence. Initial therapy consisted of the insertion of an estradiol vaginal ring and pelvic muscle exercises taught during pelvic examination and reinforced with an instruction booklet. Her symptoms are unchanged, and she remains very bothered by the stress incontinence. Her only other medical problem is systolic hypertension, for which she is treated with hydrochlorothiazide.

Which of the following is the most appropriate next step in treatment?

(A) Remove the estradiol vaginal ring and begin oral estrogen therapy.
(B) Refer patient for biofeedback-assisted pelvic muscle training.
(C) Refer patient for periurethral collagen injections.
(D) Begin pseudoephedrine 30 mg three times daily.

ANSWER: B

The most appropriate next step in treating the patient is biofeedback-assisted pelvic muscle

training. Although some healthy, motivated older women can learn the proper execution of pelvic muscle exercises during a pelvic examination with reinforcement by educational materials, many benefit from biofeedback to assist in identifying the correct muscles and contracting them without simultaneously increasing abdominal pressure.

Oral estrogen replacement may not be as effective as local estrogen for lower urinary tract symptoms, so switching to oral therapy from the vaginal ring is unlikely to be of benefit. Referral to a surgeon for a procedure for stress incontinence, such as periurethral collagen injections, is an option, but it is probably better reserved for those older women who do not improve with optimal conservative management. Pseudoephedrine[OL] may help some older women with stress incontinence, but hypertension is a relative contraindication.

References

1. Burgio KL, Goode PS, Locher JL, et al. Behavioral training with and without biofeedback in the treatment of urge incontinence in older women: a randomized controlled trial. *JAMA.* 2002;288(18):2293–2299.
2. Burgio KL, Locher JL, Goode PS, et al. Behavioral vs drug treatment for urge urinary incontinence in older women: a randomized controlled trial. *JAMA.* 1998;280(23):1995–2000.
3. Hay-Smith EJ, Bo K, Berghmans LC, et al. Pelvic floor muscle training for urinary incontinence in women. *Cochrane Database Syst Rev.* 2001;1:CD001407.
4. Hendrix SL, Cochrane BB, Nygaard IE, et al. Effects of estrogen with and without progestin on urinary incontinence. *JAMA.* 2005;293(8):935–948.

27. A 75-year-old white woman who lives in a nursing home is evaluated because she has a rash on her face and scalp. The patient states that the rash has developed gradually over 6 months. The rash does not itch. She has a history of Parkinson's disease for several years. On examination, there are erythematous scaling lesions in the nasolabial folds, on the eyebrows, forehead, and scalp, and along the hairline. The scales are greasy and yellow.

Which of the following is the most likely diagnosis?

(A) Psoriasis
(B) Seborrheic dermatitis
(C) Discoid lupus erythematosus
(D) Pityriasis rosea
(E) Rosacea

ANSWER: B

Seborrheic dermatitis is a common chronic inflammatory disorder that affects more than 20% of older people. It is particularly common in patients with Parkinson's disease. It manifests with erythematous patches or plaques with loose, yellowish, greasy scales, and it affects areas where sebaceous glands are most prominent: scalp, eyebrows, nasolabial folds, ears, chest, and intertriginous areas. Scalp seborrhea can vary from mild dandruff to dense, diffuse adherent scales. The cause of seborrheic dermatitis is thought to be in part an inflammatory reaction to *Pityrosporum ovale,* as this yeast is found in increased numbers in the lesions.

Facial and trunk seborrhea is treated with a mild corticosteroid (such as hydrocortisone 1%) or ketoconazole^OL 2% cream. Scalp seborrhea is treated with shampoos containing selenium sulfide, pyrithione zinc, or ketoconazole. If the eyelids are involved (marginal blepharitis), they should be cleaned every night with a cotton swab dipped in a mild baby shampoo.

In psoriasis, the lesions are well-demarcated erythematous plaques with adherent silvery scales and usually involve the extensor surfaces of the elbows, knees, scalp, and trunk, but not eyebrows and nasolabial folds. Discoid lupus erythematosus is a chronic indolent disease with plaques in sun-exposed areas. The plaques are sharply demarcated, and red-violaceous with scaling and atrophy. Older lesions may have hypopigmentation surrounded by hyperpigmentation. Scalp lesions can cause scarring alopecia. Pityriasis rosea develops in patients 10 to 35 years old. It manifests as an erythematous maculopapular rash with fine scaling, mainly in the trunk and arms. It starts with a "herald" patch that precedes the others by 1 to 2 weeks. Pruritus may be present. It is most likely caused by a virus and resolves spontaneously. Rosacea is characterized by facial flushing with telangiectasias, inflammatory

papules, pustules, and nodules. It is also called "adult acne" and does not have scales.

References

1. Freeman A, Gordon M. Dermatologic diseases and problems. In: Cassel CK, Leipzig RM, Cohen HJ, et al., eds. *Geriatric Medicine: An Evidence-Based Approach.* 4th ed. New York: Springer-Verlag; 2003:869–881.
2. Johnson BA, Nunley JR. Treatment of seborrheic dermatitis. *Am Fam Physician.* 2000;61(9):2703–2710, 2713–2714.
3. Powell FC. Clinical practice: rosacea. *N Engl J Med.* 2005;352(8):793–803.

28. A 70-year-old left-handed woman comes to the office because she has a 1-month history of pain in her left shoulder. She recalls no trauma. She has a history of mild arthritis, for which she takes ibuprofen as needed, but this pain has not been relieved with ibuprofen. It is starting to affect her daily activities.

On examination, she has active abduction to 90 degrees, with limitation beyond 90 degrees because of weakness, external rotation to 45 degrees, and full passive range of motion. There is no warmth over the joint. There is some tenderness in the deltoid and supraspinatus muscle areas.

Which of the following is the best choice in management of this patient?

(A) Obtain anteroposterior and lateral radiographs of the shoulder.
(B) Refer for physical therapy.
(C) Inject the shoulder joint with a combination of lidocaine and corticosteroid.
(D) Obtain magnetic resonance imaging of the shoulder.
(E) Teach the patient shoulder range-of-motion exercises.

ANSWER: D

This patient most likely has a rotator cuff tear. These are common in older age and may happen spontaneously or with minimal trauma. The classic finding is limitation in abduction. According to recent clinical findings, the presence of supraspinatus weakness, external rotation weakness, and impingement confers a 98% likelihood of rotator cuff tear. If a patient has only two of these three findings and is over

---

^OL Not approved by the U.S. Food and Drug Administration for this use.

age 60, the chance of rotator cuff tear remains 98%. Magnetic resonance imaging is sensitive for detecting rotator cuff tears and can assist the orthopedic surgeon in making recommendations. Often, highly functioning older adults need a surgical solution.

Radiography of the shoulder is helpful in diagnosing adhesive capsulitis or osteoarthritis, but it does not reveal soft-tissue problems. In this case, radiography may produce a false-negative result.

Physical therapy is useful for all shoulder problems and is the primary treatment for conditions that last longer than 1 month with conservative therapy. It is especially useful for frozen shoulder, bursitis, or biceps tendonitis. This patient's clinical findings do not fit these diagnoses, however, and most physical therapists prefer that the diagnosis is clarified before beginning therapy.

Corticosteroid injections help limit pain and facilitate physical therapy. Opinion is divided as to whether patients with shoulder problems other than rotator cuff tears should begin therapy with physical therapy or with a shoulder injection. However, a corticosteroid injection to the shoulder would not facilitate the proper treatment in this case.

Codman, or shoulder range-of-motion, exercises are useful in the treatment of frozen shoulder. This patient has full passive range of motion and would receive no benefit from these exercises.

References

1. Murrell GA, Walton JR. Diagnosis of rotator cuff tears. *Lancet.* 2001; 357(9258): 769–770.
2. van der Windt DA, Koes BW, Deville W, et al. Effectiveness of corticosteroid injections versus physiotherapy for treatment of painful stiff shoulder in primary care: randomised trial. *BMJ.* 1998;317(7168):1292–1296.

29. A 94-year-old woman who lives in a nursing home is referred for evaluation of increasing lower extremity edema. The patient has a history of coronary artery disease, including two myocardial infarctions and coronary artery bypass at age 79, and she has type 2 diabetes mellitus, hypertension, moderate Alzheimer's disease, depression, and severe osteoarthritis of both hips. She has an indwelling Foley catheter for urinary incontinence. Over the past few weeks, the nursing-home staff has noted progressive swelling of both legs up to the level of the mid-thigh. The patient is wheelchair bound and requires assistance with most activities. Current medications include aspirin, lisinopril, furosemide, metformin, nortriptyline, donepezil, and haloperidol. Additional history is fragmentary, but the nursing-home staff reports no recent complaints of chest pain or shortness of breath. The patient's living will specifies no cardiopulmonary resuscitation and no artificial life support.

On physical examination, the patient is frail, alert, pleasant, and oriented only to name. She responds to questions but with inconsistent answers. Heart rate is 84 per minute and regular, blood pressure is 130/70 mm Hg, and respiratory rate is 18 per minute. There is no jugular venous distention. A few bibasilar crackles are heard. She has a regular, grade I-II/IV systolic murmur and an S_4, with no S_3. The abdomen is not tender and has no masses. There is moderate to marked edema to the level of the mid thigh bilaterally. She has no focal neurologic deficits.

Laboratory studies:

Hemoglobin	11.3 g/dL
Leukocyte count	5400/µL
Platelet count	217,000/µL
Creatinine	1.0 mg/dL
Blood urea nitrogen	24 mg/dL
Glucose	124 mg/dL
Serum electrolytes	normal
Albumin	3.4 g/dL
Liver enzymes	mildly elevated

Which of the following is the most appropriate approach to managing this patient's edema?

(A) Obtain a B-type natriuretic peptide level and an echocardiogram.

(B) Obtain a plasma D-dimer level and lower extremity venous Doppler ultrasonography

(C) Apply bilateral lower extremity pneumatic compression device.

(D) Apply support stockings and elevate her legs.

(E) Restrict dietary sodium moderately and increase diuretic dosage.

ANSWER: E

The cause of this patient's lower extremity edema is likely multifactorial. Potential contributing factors include worsening heart failure, venous thromboembolic disease, chronic venous insufficiency, excess dietary sodium, and medication side effects. Because of the patient's dementia and physical disabilities, conservative management, emphasizing comfort measures, is appropriate. To this end, a trial of moderate sodium restriction and increased diuretic dosage is the most appropriate course. The results of B-type natriuretic peptide level testing and echocardiography are unlikely to affect management significantly. D-dimer has low specificity in this setting, and the patient is a poor candidate for anticoagulation, even if venous Doppler ultrasonography indicates the presence of deep-vein thrombosis. Support stockings and elevation of the legs are noninvasive and nonpharmacologic, but may be difficult to implement in an elderly patient with dementia and severe osteoarthritis of the hips; in addition, they are unlikely to be effective as the sole treatment for edema. Pneumatic compression devices would also be difficult to implement and probably ineffective in this patient.

References

1. Hunt SA, Baker DW, Chin MH, et al. ACC/AHA guidelines for the evaluation and management of chronic heart failure in the adult: executive summary. *J Am Coll Cardiol.* 2001;38(7):2101–2113.

2. Page J, Henry D. Consumption of NSAIDs and the development of congestive heart failure in elderly patients: an under-recognized public health problem. *Arch Intern Med.* 2000;160(6):777–784.

3. Redfield MM, Rodeheffer RJ, Jacobsen SJ, et al. Plasma brain natriuretic peptide concentration: impact of age and gender. *J Am Coll Cardiol.* 2002;40(5):976–982.

30. A 73-year-old black man comes to the office with a painless lesion on his left heel. He states that the lesion has slowly been getting bigger, but he is not sure how long he has had it. He does not recall trauma and reports no drainage or bleeding. History includes chronic venous insufficiency with venous stasis ulcers and osteoarthritis of the knees. He ambulates with a four-point cane. When he watches television, he sits in a recliner to keep his legs elevated. On examination, his left plantar heel has a firm, black raised plaque with irregular margins. It measures 4.5 × 3.7 cm. The patient has 1+ pulses bilaterally and normal sensation.

Which of the following is the most appropriate next step?

(A) Radiography of the foot
(B) Shave biopsy of the lesion
(C) Incisional biopsy of the lesion
(D) Arterial Doppler ultrasonography
(E) Bone scan

ANSWER: C

As this patient's raised lesion has grown and has irregular margins, acral lentiginous melanoma (ALM) should be suspected, and the lesion should be biopsied. ALM can occur on the palm, sole, nail bed, and mucous membrane. It is a variant of melanoma (other variants are lentigo maligna melanoma, superficial spreading melanoma, and nodular melanoma). Black persons have a lower incidence of melanoma than white persons. In black persons, ALM most commonly appears on the acral surface of the foot. Blacks with cutaneous melanoma are more likely to present with advanced disease, with a median survival of 45 months. White persons with melanoma are 3.6 times more likely to present with early disease and have a median survival of 135 months. Diagnosis in black persons may be delayed for many reasons, such as infrequent inspection of the feet compared with other parts of the body, low suspicion for melanoma in black persons, and atypical presentation. In a retrospective case review, ALM was misdiagnosed as wart, callous, fungal disorder, foreign body, crusty lesion, sweat gland condition, blister, nonhealing wound, mole, and keratoacanthoma. Subungual ALM was misdiagnosed as subungual hematoma, onychomycosis, ingrown toenail, and defective or infected toenail.

When melanoma is suspected, the best approach is excisional biopsy, which permits measurement of thickness. Shave biopsy is contraindicated when melanoma is suspected. Incisional biopsy through most of the dark, raised area is appropriate when the lesion is large or in an area where excisional biopsy cannot be performed, such as the face, hands, or feet. Melanoma should be in the differential diagnosis of heel ulcers; it would be a mistake to manage this raised lesion as a pressure ulcer with dry dressing and avoidance of weight bearing. Radiography or a bone scan of the foot to look for fracture or chronic osteomyelitis is not appropriate, as the physical examination does not suggest fracture or an infected wound. Arterial Doppler ultrasonography would be done for an ischemic heel ulcer, but this patient has pulses (although diminished), and the lesion's irregular margins indicate possible melanoma.

References

1. Bellows CF, Belafsky P, Fortgang IS, et al. Melanoma in African-Americans: trends in biological behavior and clinical characteristics over two decades. *J Surg Oncol.* 2001;78(1):10–16.
2. Soon SL, Solomon AR Jr, Papadopoulos D, et al. Acral lentiginous melanoma mimicking benign disease: the Emory experience. *J Am Acad Dermatol.* 2003;48(2):183–188.

31. A 72-year-old woman comes to the office because she has had vulvar burning and itching for several weeks. The pruritus is so intense that it disrupts her sleep. On pelvic examination, she has no evidence of vulvar inflammation, but the labia minora is fused with the labia majora. Speculum examination is difficult because of stenosis of the introitus.

Which of the following is the mostly likely diagnosis?

(A) Cutaneous candidiasis
(B) Atrophic vaginitis
(C) Lichen sclerosus
(D) Squamous cell hyperplasia
(E) Vulvar intraepithelial neoplasia

ANSWER: C

Vulvar burning and itching in older women can be due to vulvar diseases or to generalized skin diseases that also affect the vulva. The most common vulvar disease to cause burning and itching is lichen sclerosus. The itching may be so severe that it interferes with sleep. Dyspareunia is often a late symptom associated with introital stenosis. Dysuria and difficulty voiding can occur especially when there is fusion of the labia minora over the urethra. On physical examination, thin, white, wrinkled skin extends over the labia minora or labia majora and possibly the perianal area. As the disease progresses, the distinction between the labia majora and minora is lost and the clitoris becomes buried under the fused prepuce. Shrinkage of the clitoris leads to dyspareunia. A vulvar biopsy with immunofluorescent stain is performed for diagnosis. Treatment is with topical high-potency corticosteroids, such as clobetasol 0.05 mg or halobetasol propionate 0.05 mg daily for 6 to 12 weeks and then one to three times per week for maintenance.

Vulvar candidiasis causes pruritus, burning, and occasionally dysuria and dyspareunia. It causes large patches of erythema of the labia majora, genitocrural folds, perianal areas, and inner thighs. White, cottage cheese–like discharge may be present. The diagnosis is made by visualization of candidal organisms via microscopy in vaginal discharge treated with 10% potassium hydroxide. Treatment consists of topical antifungals, such as clotrimazole or nystatin, or a single 150-mg oral dose of fluconazole.

Atrophic vaginitis is a consequence of estrogen deficiency and is common in postmenopausal women who are not on hormone replacement therapy. Symptoms include vulvar pruritus, dyspareunia, burning, and loss of vaginal secretions. On physical examination, the vaginal epithelium is pale and smooth with few or no vaginal folds. In severe cases, the vaginal epithelium can be erythematous and friable, and it may bleed easily. Introital stenosis and decreased vaginal depth may be seen. Treatment consists of estrogen delivered either topically (estradiol cream or conjugated equine estrogen cream) or in a hormone-releasing ring (Estring).

Squamous cell hyperplasia generally presents as a single vulvar plaque but may be present as multiple lesions involving the labia majora, outer aspects of the labia minora, and hood of the clitoris. Lesions appear thickened and hyperkeratotic, and there may be pruritus, burning, dyspareunia, or pain. Diagnosis is by vulvar biopsy. Treatment is with potent topical corticosteroids.

Vulvar intraepithelial neoplasia refers to neoplastic or dysplastic changes in the vulvar squamous epithelium. Lesions are white, red, or hyperpigmented; they are unifocal or multifocal, rough, and well circumscribed, and are not usually precancerous. Although most patients are asymptomatic, pruritus is the most common symptom. Diagnosis is by vulvar biopsy, and treatment involves wide local excision by a gynecologic oncologist.

References

1. American College of Obstetricians and Gynecologists. *Vulvar Non-neoplastic Epithelial Disorders.* ACOG Education Bulletin No. 241. Washington, DC: American College of Obstetricians and Gynecologists; 1997.
2. Bachmann GA, Nevadunsky NS. Diagnosis and treatment of atrophic vaginitis. *Am Fam Physician.* 2000;61(10):3090–3096.
3. Powell JJ, Wojnarowska F. Lichen sclerosus. *Lancet.* 1999;353(9166):1777–1783.

32. A healthy 68-year-old man comes to the office for a physical examination. Ten years ago he had four adenomatous polyps removed; follow-up colonoscopy 5 years ago was negative.

Which of the following is the most appropriate colon cancer screening recommendation for him?

(A) Immunohistochemical fecal occult blood testing
(B) No further screening
(C) Colonoscopy
(D) Flexible sigmoidoscopy plus occult blood testing
(E) Virtual colonoscopy

ANSWER: C

Colonoscopy is the most appropriate screening for a healthy older person with a risk factor for colon cancer, such as an adenomatous polyp, who has a life expectancy of 10 years or longer. Patients with a family history of colorectal cancer, with more than two adenomas, with adenomas 1 cm or larger, or with adenomas with high-grade dysplasia or villous architecture should be screened more intensively. As this patient has a life expectancy of more than 10 years, repeat endoscopy is the preferred screening test. A frequency of every 5 years in this patient with previous polyps is appropriate.

In patients without risk factors, appropriate screening for colon cancer can be annual fecal occult blood testing, flexible sigmoidoscopy every 5 years, annual fecal occult blood testing with flexible sigmoidoscopy every 5 years, double-contrast barium enema every 5 years, or colonoscopy every 10 years. There is insufficient evidence to recommend one of these approaches over another, and the choice must be individualized.

There is insufficient evidence to recommend colon cancer screening with computed tomography colonography (virtual colonoscopy), immunohistochemical fecal occult blood testing, stool test for detection of altered human DNA, or video endoscopy.

References

1. Miller K, Waye JD. Colorectal polyps in the elderly: what should be done? *Drugs Aging.* 2002;19(6):393–404.
2. Smith RA, Cokkinides V, Eyre HJ. American Cancer Society. American Cancer Society guidelines for the early detection of cancer, 2004. *CA Cancer J Clin.* 2004;54(1):41–52.

33. A 77-year-old man comes to the office because of a 12-month history of pain over the posterior aspect of his right calf after prolonged standing or walking. At first, the pain occurred only after he walked 10 to 12 blocks, but it now occurs after he walks less than a block. He also has pain when he stands for more than 10 minutes. The pain is relieved immediately with sitting.

On physical examination, pulses are full in both legs. The skin is normal, with full skin hair throughout both legs. Bilateral straight leg raise tests are normal. There is good mobility of both hips without pain. There is mild weakness of the right great toe extensor, right hip abductor, and right hip extensor.

Radiography of the lumbar spine shows diffuse degenerative changes of the lumbar disks and facet joints. There is evidence of mild to moderate osteoarthritis of the right hip.

What is the most likely cause of this patient's pain?

(A) Bone or joint disease of the hip
(B) Vascular insufficiency
(C) Lumbar spinal stenosis
(D) Ruptured popliteal cyst
(E) Metastatic cancer to the bone

ANSWER: C

This patient's pain occurs after prolonged standing and walking, and is relieved immediately with sitting. Such a presentation is typical of lumbar spinal stenosis, and the weakness of the muscles of the right leg innervated by L-4, L-5 and L-5, S-1 is consistent with this diagnosis. The most appropriate next step in the evaluation of this patient would be to perform a diagnostic imaging test to look for signs of lumbar spinal stenosis.

Hip disease can cause pain in the groin, buttock, thigh, and knee, but rarely in the lower leg. The distribution of pain and the normal hip examination make hip disease an unlikely cause of this patient's pain, despite the abnormal hip radiograph.

Calf pain while walking is a symptom of arterial insufficiency, but this patient has normal pulses and no skin findings, and pain on standing is rare in patients with arterial insufficiency.

Although a ruptured popliteal cyst can cause acute calf pain, the prolonged duration of this patient's pain, with progressive worsening over 12 months, suggests a different cause.

This patient does not have a typical history of metastatic cancer. The association with position is unusual for a cancer, and the history of pain after walking that is relieved with sitting is not consistent with a tumor.

References

1. Binder DK, Schmidt MH, Weinstein PR. Lumbar spinal stenosis. *Semin Neurol.* 2002;22(2):157–166.

2. Yukawa Y, Lenke LG, Tenhula J, et al. A comprehensive study of patients with surgically treated lumbar spinal stenosis with neurogenic claudication. *J Bone Joint Surg.* 2002;84-A(11):1954–1959.

34. A 77-year-old man with poor vision and severe osteoarthritis was admitted to a nursing home 6 weeks ago because he is unable to live independently. He has a history of diabetes mellitus, coronary artery disease, gastroesophageal reflux, and osteoarthritis. He reports poor appetite, poor sleep, and low energy.

Physical examination is consistent with the medical history. He has lost 9.5 kg (21 lb) since moving to the nursing home. His responses are delayed and he frequently says "I don't know" when asked about recent events, even though he is able to give a detailed personal history. He admits he is sad and attributes his depression to cancer. Complete laboratory work-up for weight loss does not identify an acute physical problem or evidence of cancer, but he remains unconvinced.

Which of the following treatments is most likely to restore this patient's appetite and to stop his weight loss?

(A) Megestrol
(B) Mirtazapine
(C) Olanzapine
(D) Individual psychotherapy
(E) Electroconvulsive therapy

ANSWER: E

Electroconvulsive therapy is the treatment of choice in a frail older patient with delusional depression in whom rapid response is needed to forestall further physical deterioration. It is well tolerated and associated with rapid and sustained response in many of these patients. Delusional depression (major depression with psychotic features) is more common than generally realized. In older patients, delusional depression typically has melancholic features (such as pervasive sadness, significant anorexia, early-morning awakening, psychomotor retardation or agitation) and cognitive impairment. Delusions are often somatic (as in this patient's fixed belief that he has cancer) or associated with themes of guilt, worthlessness, or hopelessness. Delusions occurring in the context of severe depression have been attributed to the marked dysregulation of the hypothalamic-pituitary-adrenal axis and elevated cortisol levels observed in these patients. If left untreated, delusional depression is associated with high morbidity and mortality. It is the most difficult form of depression to treat. The recommended pharmacotherapy for delusional depression is a combination of an antidepressant and an antipsychotic, both at high doses. However, even when they tolerate this combination, older patients tend to respond slowly and relatively poorly.

Depression should not be treated as a random collection of unrelated symptoms requiring targeted treatment. It is not effective to use medications to target specific depressive symptoms (such as megestrol for anorexia, methylphenidate or modafinil for low energy, a benzodiazepine for sleep problems) or to select a psychotropic medication by matching its most prominent side effect to a target symptom (such as mirtazapine or olanzapine to promote weight gain).

References

1. Fink M. Electroconvulsive therapy update: recognizing and treating psychotic depression. *J Clin Psychiatry.* 2003;64(3):232–234.
2. Meyers BS, Klimstra SA, Gabriele M, et al. Continuation treatment of delusional depression in older adults. *Am J Geriatr Psychiatry.* 2001;9(4):415–422.
3. Mulsant BH, Sweet RA, Rosen J, et al. A double-blind randomized comparison of nortriptyline plus perphenazine versus nortriptyline plus placebo in the treatment of psychotic depression in late life. *J Clin Psychiatry.* 2001;62(8):597–604.
4. Rothschild AJ. Challenges in the treatment of depression with psychotic features. *Biol Psychiatry.* 2003;53(8):680–690.

35. A 75-year-old man comes to the office because he has excessive daytime sleepiness and insomnia characterized by awakenings throughout the night. He also has disagreeable leg sensations during the day that are relieved only when he moves his legs. His partner confirms that the patient kicks frequently when he is asleep.

Which of the following treatments is most likely to help this patient?

(A) Pramipexole 0.125 mg at bedtime
(B) Celecoxib 200 mg at bedtime
(C) Mirtazapine 15 mg at bedtime
(D) Modafinil 100 mg twice daily
(E) Zolpidem 10 mg at bedtime

ANSWER: A

Periodic limb movements are a major cause of insomnia in older persons. The distinctive periodic motor output, in which the legs kick at 20- to 40-second intervals throughout the night, may be related to changes in arterial blood pressure or supraspinal factors that lead to brief arousals and fragmented sleep. The prevailing hypothesis is that a deficit in dopaminergic transmission contributes to this disorder, since affected patients have lower binding of the D2 receptor in the basal ganglia, and treatment with dopamine agonists is effective. Periodic limb movements can be treated with dopaminergic agents, such as pramipexole or levodopa-carbidopa[OL], which decrease both the number of kicks and arousals during the night.

The cyclooxygenase inhibitor celecoxib[OL] is not indicated for periodic limb movements. Antidepressants, such as mirtazapine[OL], and hypnotics, such as zolpidem[OL], have not been shown to benefit patients with periodic limb movements. Modafinil[OL] may improve daytime drowsiness but does not help the nighttime awakenings and limb movements.

References

1. Ancoli-Israel S. Sleep disorders in older adults. *Geriatrics.* 2004;59:37–40.
2. Milligan SA, Chesson AL. Restless legs syndrome in the older adult: diagnosis and management. *Drug Aging.* 2002;19(10):741–751.
3. Rothdach AJ, Trenkwalder C, Haberstock J, et al. Prevalence and risk factors of RLS in an elderly population: the MEMO study: Memory and Morbidity in Augsburg Elderly. *Neurology.* 2000;54(5):1064–1068.

OL Not approved by the U.S. Food and Drug Administration for this use.

36. A 71-year-old man comes to the office because his right foot has become warm and swollen over the past 6 weeks. He has no pain, fever, chills, nausea, or vomiting. He has noticed that the arch in the foot has gradually collapsed during this time and that the foot feels "unstable." He has a 15-year history of insulin-dependent diabetes mellitus and no history of trauma or recent change in activity.

On physical examination, temperature is 36.5°C (97.7°F), pulse is 80 per minute, respiration rate is 16 per minute, and blood pressure is 150/90 mm Hg. Examination of the right foot demonstrates a unilateral flatfoot deformity with marked swelling and warmth. No ulcerations or breaks in skin are seen. Palpation of the dorsalis pedis and posterior tibial artery demonstrates bounding pulses. There is markedly diminished sensation in the feet and ankles.

Laboratory studies:

Leukocyte count	8000/μL
Hematocrit	42.5%
Erythrocyte sedimentation rate	30 mm/h
Urea nitrogen	28 mg/dL
Glucose	139 mg/dL
Creatinine	1.4 mg/dL

Radiographs of the right foot show osseous fragmentation and subluxation along the tarsometatarsal joint with "rocker bottom" foot shape and absence of the normal arch changes. No gas is seen in the tissues. Technetium Tc 99m medronate bone scan shows increased activity and uptake to midfoot on all three phases of bone scan.

Which of the following is the most likely diagnosis?

(A) Ruptured plantar fascia
(B) Osteomyelitis
(C) Charcot's foot
(D) Gout

ANSWER: C

Charcot's foot (diabetic neuroarthropathy) is the progressive degeneration and malalignment of the foot induced by severe neuropathy. Once more commonly associated with tabes dorsalis, this foot deformity is now most often caused by longstanding diabetes. Charcot's foot will develop in 1% to 2% of the approximately 16 million diabetic persons in the United States. The deformity is induced by peripheral neuropathy and repetitive stress to the foot, which results in recurrent joint injury, breakdown, and malalignment. Patients generally present with a painless, erythematous, swollen foot, which is commonly misdiagnosed as osteomyelitis. The destructive radiographic changes and the positive bone scan both mimic osteomyelitis, but the normal leukocyte count, erythrocyte sedimentation rate, glucose level, and temperature, as well as the absence of ulceration, exclude osteomyelitis and gas gangrene. Differentiating Charcot's foot from osteomyelitis is more difficult when there is also an infected ulcer, which affects the laboratory values, as the radiographic findings are similar.

A plantar fascial rupture is unlikely, as it would not cause the destructive radiographic changes, nor would it demonstrate uptake in the third phase of the bone scan. Gout, although uncommon in the midfoot, can cause sudden warmth and swelling with an acute flare-up. However, it also would be unlikely to produce the dramatic findings seen on radiograph of Charcot's foot.

Reference

1. Jude EB, Boulton AJ. Update on Charcot neuroarthropathy. *Curr Diab Rep.* 2001;1(3):228–232.

37. An 82-year-old woman who lives alone is brought to the emergency department because she has been confused and weak for approximately 1 week. The patient has gone to the same primary care doctor for 10 years. History includes systolic hypertension, osteoporosis, and depression. Medications include hydrochlorothiazide, calcium with vitamin D, and low-dose aspirin. At her last office visit 4 weeks ago, the patient reported fatigue, weight loss, poor sleep, and an overall sense of hopelessness since her husband died 6 months earlier. Her mental status examination was otherwise normal. A selective serotonin-reuptake inhibitor was prescribed at that time.

In the hospital, the patient is confused and does not recognize her primary care doctor. Blood pressure is 154/88 mm Hg with no orthostatic changes. Pulse is 86 per minute, respirations are

15 per minute, and she has no fever. Rectal examination reveals no occult blood.

Laboratory studies:

Blood urea nitrogen	5 mg/dL
Serum creatinine	1.2 mg/dL
Serum electrolytes	
Sodium	110 mEq/L
Potassium	3.5 mEq/L
Chloride	75 mEq/L
Bicarbonate	28 mEq/L
Urinalysis	Specific gravity 1.018; glucose and protein negative; leukocytes 0–5/hpf

Which of the following is the most likely cause of this patient's hyponatremia?

(A) Adrenal insufficiency
(B) Dehydration secondary to decreased thirst and appetite
(C) Syndrome of inappropriate antidiuretic hormone (SIADH)
(D) Heart failure
(E) Age-related change in sodium concentration

ANSWER: C

This patient most likely has euvolemic hyponatremia, or syndrome of inappropriate antidiuretic hormone (SIADH). While often seen with neoplasm or head trauma, in older adults it is a common complication of drug therapy. This patient is taking two classes of drugs (thiazide diuretics and selective serotonin-reuptake inhibitors) that are associated with hyponatremia. In older adults, hyponatremia may be an incidental finding or may present acutely with an unpleasant sweet taste in the mouth, fatigue, vomiting, weakness, or confusion. Comparison of plasma and urine osmolarity and measurement of urine excretion of sodium would be appropriate at this time. With an abnormal mental status, this patient is beginning to exhibit neurologic findings, which may precede seizure and death. Too-rapid correction of hyponatremia has been associated with diffuse cerebral demyelination. It is generally accepted that raising the serum sodium concentration approximately 0.6 to 2.0 mEq/L hourly, or no more than 12 mEq/L in the first 24 hours, is safe. Discontinuation of hydrochlorothiazide and the selective serotonin-reuptake inhibitor is appropriate, as is restriction of fluid intake (approximately 1500 cc per 24 hours or less).

Adrenal insufficiency is unlikely, since the patient has no orthostatic changes and a low potassium level. There is no evidence of volume overload to support heart failure and hyponatremia with volume excess. Although creatinine clearance may decrease with age, serum sodium concentration should remain normal.

References

1. Andreoli TE. Water: normal balance, hyponatremia, and hypernatremia. *Ren Fail.* 2000;22(6):711–735.
2. Fabien TJ, Amico JA, Kroboth PD, et al. Paroxetine-induced hyponatremia in older adults: a 12-week prospective study. *Arch Intern Med.* 2004;164(3):327–332.
3. Kugler JP, Hustead T. Hyponatremia and hypernatremia in the elderly. *Am Fam Physician.* 2000;61(12):3623–3630.
4. Smith DM, McKenna K, Thompson CJ. Hyponatremia. *Clin Endocrinol.* 2000;52(6):667–678.

38. An 83-year-old man with mild dementia lives alone in a suburban area not served by public transportation. He continues to drive despite having had one moving violation and one minor accident in the past 12 months. His nearest family member lives more than 40 minutes away. He has a score of 27 on the Mini–Mental State Examination (MMSE). When a discussion is initiated about his driving, he says he is a good driver and that forcing him to stop would be like "cutting off my legs." He limits his driving to local stores and does not drive at night or on the highway any more. His family agrees that he is a safe driver. His corrected visual acuity is better than 20/40, he does not have any physical limitations, and he does not drink alcohol or use any medications that might affect his alertness.

Which of the following is the most appropriate next step in assessing this patient's safety as a driver?

(A) No further assessment is necessary.

(B) He should stop driving.

(C) He should have formal neuropsychologic testing.

(D) He should have a formal driving evaluation.

ANSWER: D

Any recommendation to stop driving should be made with careful consideration. For people who live in areas without public transportation or who do not have family or friends to drive for them, the inability to continue driving may make their current living situation untenable. Moreover, cessation of driving is associated with depression and reduced activity. Although there is a point in the course of dementia when safe driving is not possible, the presence of mild dementia alone may not be sufficient reason to cease driving. In patients with mild dementia, visual-spatial impairment, as suggested by the inability to copy intersecting pentagons, and loss of visual attention are particularly concerning, as is any evidence of recent moving violations or accident. Physical impairment, visual impairment, and the use of alcohol or psychoactive medications are other factors that increase risk related to driving.

Because of this patient's mild dementia and history of driving incidents, further assessment is warranted. The steps he has taken to limit his driving do not in themselves demonstrate that he is a safe driver. On the other hand, his dementia is not severe enough to warrant driving cessation without further assessment, particularly if he is unwilling to stop driving and has no alternate transportation. Formal neuropsychologic testing will help describe the extent and nature of his cognitive impairments, and it may shed light on the quality of his judgment; however, it will not assess his actual driving performance.

An on-road driving evaluation performed by an occupational therapist may clarify whether the patient can continue to drive a car safely and can also offer potential adaptive strategies or equipment. Motor vehicle departments can also perform on-road testing. Regardless of whether the testing is done through an occupational therapy program or through a state motor vehicle department, the physician must be aware of the state's reporting requirements.

At present, the ability of particular driving assessments to predict future accidents is not clear. Similarly, the effectiveness of interventions to improve driving skills in patients with dementia is unknown. A recent review sponsored by the American Medical Association and the National Highway Traffic Safety Administration summarizes current thinking regarding safety of older drivers.

References

1. American Medical Association. *Physician's Guide to Assessing and Counseling Older Drivers.* Available at http://www.ama-assn.org/ama/pub/category/10791.html (accessed September 2005).
2. Duchek JM, Hunt L, Ball K, et al. Attention and driving performance in Alzheimer's disease. *J Gerontol B Psychol Sci Soc Sci.* 1998;53(2):P130–P141.
3. Fox GK, Bowden SC, Smith DS. On-road assessment of driving competence after brain impairment: review of current practice and recommendations for a standardized examination. *Arch Phys Med Rehab.* 1998;79(10):1288–1296.
4. Marottoli RA, de Leon CFM, Glass TA, et al. Consequences of driving cessation: decreased out-of-home activity levels. *J Gerontol B Psychol Sci Soc Sci.* 2000;55(6):S334–S340.
5. Wang CC, Carr DB, for the Older Drivers Project. Older driver safety: a report from the Older Drivers Project. *J Am Geriatr Soc.* 2004;52(1):143–149.

39. A 73-year-old man comes for a routine office visit. He has hypertension, mildly abnormal cholesterol levels, and osteoarthritis. He takes hydrochlorothiazide 25 mg once daily, lisinopril 5 mg once daily, and ibuprofen 200 to 400 mg as needed for joint pain. He exercises and watches his diet carefully. For several years he has had three glasses of red wine with dinner most evenings. He remarks that he read that alcohol may lower the risk of coronary artery disease and stroke. His blood pressure is 146/87 mm Hg and has been somewhat difficult to control.

Which of the following is the most appropriate advice for this patient regarding his current drinking pattern?

(A) It is safe for him to continue.
(B) It may increase longevity.
(C) It may raise his low-density lipoprotein levels.
(D) It may exacerbate his hypertension.
(E) It places him at risk for alcoholism.

ANSWER: D

Regular use of alcohol is hazardous in a patient who has one or more health conditions that can be exacerbated or caused by alcohol, or who takes medications that interact adversely with alcohol. The risk associated with this patient's use of alcohol climbs substantially, because this amount of alcohol exacerbates or may even cause hypertension, and because his blood pressure is elevated even with hydrochlorothiazide and lisinopril. Moreover, alcohol can interact with nonsteroidal anti-inflammatory drugs to increase the potential for gastrointestinal bleeding.

The guidelines of the National Institute on Alcohol Abuse and Alcoholism (NIAAA) for safe use of alcohol recommend that both men and women aged 65 and older consume no more than one standard drink (12 oz beer, 5 oz wine, 1.5 oz of 80-proof liquor) per day, or seven standard drinks per week. However, focusing only on the amount and frequency does not address other specific factors that may increase the risk of drinking for individual patients.

Low or moderate use of alcohol can lead to heavier drinking and alcoholism in some people, but the information provided for this patient does not allow accurate prediction of risk for accelerated drinking or alcoholism. The fact that he has been drinking at about the same amount and frequency for several years argues against his risk's being higher than the risk for other older people who drink in ways consistent with the NIAAA's recommendations.

Moderate use of alcohol may offer vascular protection. This benefit has largely been attributed to elevation of high-density lipoprotein cholesterol and increased fibrinolysis and decreased platelet aggregation. However, the amount of benefit attributable to alcohol remains controversial. Moreover, guidelines continue to recommend caution about applying results of epidemiologic studies on the effects of alcohol to the care of individual patients.

Substances found in red wine, including resveratrol, have been associated with increased life span in certain organisms, but the relevance of this to humans is unclear.

References

1. Lieber CS. Alcohol and health: a drink a day won't keep the doctor away. *Clev Clin J Med*. 2003;70:945–946, 948, 951–953.
2. Moore AA, Beck JC, Babor TF, et al. Beyond alcoholism: identifying older, at-risk drinkers in primary care. *J Stud Alcohol*. 2002;63(3):316–324.
3. Mukamal KJ, Conigrave KM, Mittleman MA, et al. Roles of drinking pattern and type of alcohol consumed in coronary artery disease in men. *N Engl J Med*. 2003; 348:109–118.
4. U.S. Department of Agriculture/U.S. Department of Health and Human Services. Home and Garden Bulletin No. 232. *Nutrition and Your Health: Dietary Guidelines for Americans*. 5th ed. Washington, DC: Superintendent of Documents, U.S. Government Printing Office; 2000.

40. Which group of older women has the greatest risk of osteoporotic fracture?

(A) Black Americans
(B) White Americans
(C) Chinese Americans
(D) Japanese Americans

ANSWER: B

Over 1.3 million osteoporotic fractures occur each year in the United States. The risk of all fractures increases with age; among persons who survive until age 90, 33% of women and 17% of men will have a hip fracture. The number of postmenopausal women in the United States will double over the next 20 years, such that the number of osteoporotic fractures is expected to triple by the year 2040.

Bone mineral density, fracture rates, and bone turnover vary among women of different ethnicities. Most reports suggest that bone mineral density is highest in black Americans, lowest in Asian Americans, and intermediate in white Americans. However, when the data are adjusted for body size, there are no differences among black American, Chinese American, and Japanese American women, all of whom have higher bone mineral density than white American women.

The risk of hip fractures is considerably lower in black American women than in white

American women. Two factors contribute to the relative protection against fracture: peak bone mass is higher and the rate of bone loss after menopause is lower. Asian American women also have a lower risk of fractures than white American women.

References

1. American Geriatrics Society, Adler R, Kamel H. *Doorway Thoughts: Cross-Cultural Health Care for Older Adults.* Boston, MA: Jones and Bartlett; 2004.
2. Finkelstein JS, Lee ML, Sowers M, et al. Ethnic variation in bone density in premenopausal and early perimenopausal women: effects of anthropometric and lifestyle factors. *J Clin Endocrinol Metab.* 2002;87(7):3057–3067.
3. NIH Consensus Development Panel on Osteoporosis Prevention, Diagnosis and Therapy. Osteoporosis prevention, diagnosis and therapy. *JAMA.* 2001; 285(6):785–795.

41. An 85-year-old man is brought to the office by his family because he sees hallucinations of children and small animals when he is alone in a room. At times he has been disturbed and agitated by these hallucinations. His family also notes that he is having more difficulty walking and at times has hand tremors when he sits quietly. He has a 1-year history of short-term memory loss and word-finding difficulties. Examination is unremarkable except for cogwheel rigidity and resting tremors.

Which of the following is the most likely diagnosis?

(A) Parkinson's disease
(B) Alzheimer's disease
(C) Dementia with Lewy bodies
(D) Huntington's disease

ANSWER: C

The occurrence of a dementia within 1 year of onset of extrapyramidal symptoms (lead-pipe or cogwheel rigidity, bradykinesia, resting tremor) with prominent, distinct visual hallucinations indicates a diagnosis of dementia with Lewy bodies. Family members should be questioned about the presence of fluctuating cognition, another core feature of dementia with Lewy bodies. Other signs and symptoms that support the diagnosis are unexplained falls, depression, and delusions. Although Parkinson's disease presents with extrapyramidal symptoms, initially these occur without memory loss or psychosis. Hallucinations may develop in patients with Alzheimer's disease, but extrapyramidal symptoms usually occur later in the disease course. Huntington's disease is characterized by cognitive impairment and choreiform movement disorder.

References

1. Sink KM, Holden KF, Yaffe K. Pharmacological treatment of neuropsychiatric symptoms of dementia: a review of the evidence. *JAMA.* 2005;293(5):596–608.
2. Wilcock GK. Dementia with Lewy bodies. *Lancet.* 2003;362(9397):1689–1690.

42. A 72-year-old nursing-home resident with moderate cognitive impairment is evaluated because she has fatigue when walking. History includes hypertension, chronic renal insufficiency, and osteoarthritis. Her medications include hydrochlorothiazide and acetaminophen. Hemoglobin is 9% and mean corpuscular volume is 92 fL.

Which of the following is most likely to improve her anemia?

(A) Iron
(B) Vitamin B_{12}
(C) Folic acid
(D) Erythropoietin

ANSWER: D

Chronic renal insufficiency is the most likely cause of the anemia with a normal mean corpuscular volume. Recombinant human erythropoietin is effective treatment for anemia of chronic renal insufficiency. Its use has been associated with partial regression of left ventricular hypertrophy among dialysis and nondialysis patients with heart failure. Anemia of chronic renal insufficiency remains prevalent, under-recognized, and undertreated. Folate deficiency and B_{12} deficiency are more likely manifested by an elevated mean corpuscular volume, and iron-deficiency anemia is usually manifested by a reduced mean corpuscular volume.

References

1. Balducci L. Epidemiology of anemia in the elderly: information on diagnostic evaluation. *J Am Geriatr Soc.* 2003;51(3 Suppl):S2–S9.
2. Kausz AT. Anemia management in patients with chronic renal insufficiency. *Am J Kidney Dis.* 2000; 36(6 Suppl 3):S39–S51.
3. Kikuchi M, Inagaki T, Shinagawa N. Five-year survival of older people with anemia: variation with hemoglobin concentration. *J Am Geriatr Soc.* 2001;49(9):1226–1228.

43. A 74-year-old man with a history of coronary artery disease had three-vessel coronary artery bypass 3 days ago. He was extubated on postoperative day 1. He now requires evaluation because he remains agitated despite chemical and physical restraints. He pulls at the oxygen tubing despite wrist restraints. Because of his confusion, ambulation has been limited and the Foley catheter is continued. Vital signs are normal. Recommendations include removal of the Foley catheter and obtaining a urinalysis and urine culture.

Which of the following may significantly reduce his agitation and promote resolution of the delirium?

(A) Limit mobility to chair transfers until delirium clears.
(B) Remove the wrist restraints.
(C) Place him in a geri-chair near the nurse's station.
(D) Assist with feeding.

ANSWER: B

A multifaceted targeted intervention is most effective in preventing and treating delirium in hospitalized patients. All potential contributors to delirium should be identified and addressed if possible. Nonpharmacologic strategies are extremely important and often overlooked. Physical restraints may precipitate or contribute significantly to the agitation. If there are no major concerns for traumatic withdrawal of life-saving devices such as endotracheal tubes, removing the restraints and allowing the patient to move at will can greatly reduce anxiety. The patient may require close monitoring and perhaps supervision from the family. Family members may provide a calming effect if they are educated about delirium and its reversibility.

Limiting mobility in any respect is detrimental at this point. The patient needs ambulation at least three times daily. Programs that focus on early mobilization of postoperative hip fracture patients show better outcomes. Although nutritional intake is extremely important in the overall care of this patient, it is feasible that the patient would not require assistance if the restraints were removed and the patient were allowed to feed himself. Spoon-feeding an agitated patient may increase agitation. Placing the restrained patient near the nurse's station will not improve his delirium.

References

1. Inouye SK, Bogardus ST, Charpentier PA, et al. A multicomponent intervention to prevent delirium in hospitalized older patients. *N Engl J Med.* 1999;340(9):669–676.
2. Marcantonio ER, Flacker JM, Wright RJ, et al. Reducing delirium after hip fracture: a randomized trial. *J Am Geriatr Soc.* 2001;49(5):516–522.
3. Weintraub D, Spurlock M. Change in the rate of restraint use and falls on a psychogeriatric inpatient unit: impact of the Health Care Financing Administration's new restraint and seclusion standards for hospitals. *J Ger Psych Neur.* 2002;15(2):91–94.

44. A 79-year-old man comes to the office because of increasing agitation. His wife notes that for the past 1 to 2 years he has had memory difficulties, increasingly unsteady gait, and several falls. For the past 3 months, he has complained of seeing small black spiders all over the house; when his wife tells him he is imagining these and refuses to call an exterminator, he becomes agitated and threatening. History includes hypertension treated with hydrochlorothiazide.

On physical examination, he demonstrates mild cogwheel rigidity with no tremor. On cognitive assessment, he scores 22 of 30 on the Mini–Mental State Examination, losing 4 points for orientation, 3 points for delayed recall, and 1 point for design copying.

Which of the following is the most appropriate management for his hallucinations and agitation?

(A) Rivastigmine *Exelon*
(B) Risperidone
(C) Haloperidol
(D) Citalopram
(E) Divalproex sodium

ANSWER: A

This patient possibly has dementia with Lewy bodies, which is characterized by cognitive impairment, parkinsonism, and prominent visual hallucinations. Neuropathologically, dementia with Lewy bodies is notable for severe deficits of acetylcholine. At least one randomized controlled trial demonstrated significant benefits with rivastigmine[OL] for behavior and cognition, including decreased hallucinations and anxiety.

Patients with dementia with Lewy bodies may demonstrate significant sensitivity to typical antipsychotics like haloperidol, which may increase morbidity and mortality. Treatment with atypical antipsychotics like risperidone may be necessary, though these drugs may also dramatically worsen extrapyramidal symptoms even in low doses. Citalopram[OL] has been shown to decrease agitation and psychosis in patients with Alzheimer's disease, though similar studies have not been done in patients with dementia with Lewy bodies. Divalproex sodium[OL] has also been shown to decrease agitation and aggression in patients with Alzheimer's disease, but no specific effect on hallucinations has been noted in these studies.

References

1. McKeith I, Del Ser T, Spano P, et al. Efficacy of rivastigmine in dementia with Lewy bodies: a randomised, double-blind, placebo-controlled international study. *Lancet*. 2000; 356(9247):2031–2036.
2. McKeith IG. Dementia with Lewy bodies. *Br J Psychiatry*. 2002;180:144–147.
3. Pollock BG, Mulsant BH, Rosen J, et al. Comparison of citalopram, perphenazine, and placebo for the acute treatment of psychosis and behavioral disturbances in hospitalized, demented patients. *Am J Psychiatry*. 2002;159(3):460–465.
4. Porsteinsson AP, Tariot PN, Erb R, et al. Placebo-controlled study of divalproex sodium for agitation in dementia. *Am J Geriatr Psychiatry*. 2001;9(1):58–66.

[OL] Not approved by the U.S. Food and Drug Administration for this use.

45. A 75-year-old patient comes to the office for his annual check-up. He had complained of hearing loss for several years but until recently had declined to visit an audiologist because he did not think his hearing was bad enough. The audiology report indicates that he has a mild to moderate bilaterally symmetric sensorineural hearing loss with good word recognition scores. During today's interview, he does not seem to follow the discussion, even though he is wearing his new hearing aids. He states that he rarely uses the hearing aids because they do not seem to work in the situations that are most difficult for him. His wife agrees, but also mentions that he has not returned to the audiologist for his follow-up visit.

Which of the following is the most appropriate recommendation?

(A) Return to the audiologist for a hearing aid check, and counseling.
(B) Return these hearing aids to the audiologist to exchange for more effective aids.
(C) Substitute an assistive listening device for hearing aids in the situations that are most difficult for him.
(D) Schedule a cochlear implant evaluation.
(E) Screen for hearing handicap with the Hearing Handicap Inventory for the Elderly—Screening Version (HHIE–S)

ANSWER: A

Success with hearing aids depends in large part on whether audiologic rehabilitation is under-taken to help hearing-impaired persons recover lost physical, psychologic, or social skills. Patients should return to the audiologist within 3 weeks to ensure that the characteristics and fit of a new hearing aid are adequate and that the patient can operate the hearing aid appropri-ately. An individualized orientation is critical for identifying hearing aid components, teaching care and maintenance, setting realistic expecta-tions, and counseling to facilitate adjustment. The orientation may include training for auditory visual integration, which focuses on combining visual and auditory input to promote receptive communication.

It is premature to return the hearing aid before adjustments are attempted to optimize audibility and speech understanding. All hearing aid companies offer a free trial period (excluding some minimal expenditures) to ensure customer satisfaction.

Assistive listening devices are used to complement, not replace, hearing aids. They use remote microphone technology to overcome communication problems created by noise or distance. The microphone is placed 3 to 6 inches from the sound source, which overcomes the negative effects of distance on speech under-standing. Different assistive devices offer sound enhancement, television or media enhancement, telecommunications, and signal-alerting technology, and they can be purchased without a prescription. Audiologists can help patients identify the most appropriate assistive listening device.

Individuals with mild to moderate sensorineural hearing impairment are not candidates for cochlear implants, because they have a relatively large amount of residual hearing and can benefit from hearing aids.

The Hearing Handicap Inventory for the Elderly—Screening Version is used to identify individuals at risk for hearing impairment who may require follow-up. This patient has already had a complete audiologic evaluation, so functional screening is not appropriate. He should be referred back to the audiologist, and his wife should accompany him if possible.

References

1. Kricos P, Lesner S. *Hearing Care for the Older Adult.* Boston: Butterworth-Heineman; 1995.
2. Weinstein B. *Geriatric Audiology.* New York: Thieme Medical Publishers, Inc; 2000.

46. An 89-year-old woman comes to the office because she has "spins" that last about 30 seconds and occur only with position changes of her head, such as when she lays down, gets out of bed in the morning, or looks up to get something from a top bookshelf. Between spells, she feels completely normal.

Which of the following tests should be used to diagnose the likely cause of her vertigo?

(A) Pure-tone audiography with speech discrimination
(B) Magnetic resonance imaging of the internal auditory canal with gadolinium
(C) Positioning maneuver with head hanging back
(D) Electroencephalography
(E) Multiple sleep latencies test

ANSWER: C

Benign paroxysmal positional vertigo (BPPV) is one of the most common causes of vertigo for which older patients see a physician. It is caused by otolithic calcium carbonate crystals (a normal part of the human vestibular microanatomy) that become loose and cause excitation of the posterior semicircular canal. Typically, the patient has spells of vertigo, generally briefer than 1 minute, that occur when he or she looks up (top-shelf vertigo), bends forward, or rolls over in bed. The spells tend to be worse at night or in the morning because the otoconia accumulate and clot to form a plunger effect. During the Dix-Hallpike positioning maneuver (answer C), the clot moves and stimulates the semicircular canal crista to produce vertigo and nystagmus. Repeated positioning causes fatiga-bility because of dispersion of single particles from the clot, making the plunger less effective. Latency before onset of nystagmus is explained by the delay in setting the clot into motion. The condition is treated by the modified Epley maneuver, which is designed to relocate the otoliths from the posterior canal to the utriculus where they can be reabsorbed.

Answer A is incorrect, as these tests assess hearing, not causes of vertigo. Answer B is not correct, as this test is used to diagnose acoustic neuroma, not BPPV. Answer D is incorrect, as EEG is used to diagnose seizures. Answer E is incorrect, as this test is used to diagnose narcolepsy.

References

1. Hain TC. Benign paroxysmal positional vertigo. June 26, 2005. Available at http://www.dizziness-and-balance.com/disorders/bppv/bppv.html (accessed September 2005).
2. Hilton M, Pinder D. The Epley manoeuver for benign paroxysmal positional vertigo—a systematic review. *Clin Otolaryngol.* 2002;27(6):440–445.

3. Parnes LS, Agrawal SK, Atlas J. Diagnosis and management of benign paroxysmal positional vertigo (BPPV). *CMAJ.* 2003;169(7):681–693.

47. Which of the following is the most likely mechanism of the thrombocytopenia seen in chronic B-cell lymphoma when the bone marrow shows exuberant megakaryocytopoiesis?

    (A) Myelodysplasia
    (B) Autoimmune thrombocytopenia
    (C) Drug-induced thrombocytopenia
    (D) Primary disorder of platelet production in the bone marrow

ANSWER: B

In the geriatric population thrombocytopenia is usually secondary to an underlying systemic illness. It is therefore worthwhile to investigate the cause of thrombocytopenia by bone marrow aspiration or biopsy. The histologic finding of a clonal lymphoproliferative process in the marrow is good evidence for an immune-mediated process causing thrombocytopenia. Immune-mediated thrombocytopenia is a relatively common complication of indolent lymphoproliferative disorders, or it may occur with chronic viral infection. Autoimmune complications of chronic lymphocytic leukemia and low-grade B-cell non-Hodgkin's lymphoma include autoimmune thrombocytopenia, autoimmune hemolytic anemia, and pure-erythrocyte aplasia. These disorders presumably result from immune dysregulation rather than from clonal secretion of autoreactive antibodies by the neoplastic clone itself.

An aspirate that shows evidence of exuberant megakaryocytopoiesis indicates that the bone marrow is not the source of thrombocytopenia, but is active in response to a decrease in peripheral platelets. Thus, both myelodysplasia and primary disorder of platelet production are excluded by the histologic findings in the bone marrow. Peripheral consumption of platelets or shortened platelet survival can be mediated by splenic sequestration, microangiopathy, intravascular coagulation, or an immune-related phenomenon. Drug-induced thrombocytopenia is possible with almost any medication, but it is a diagnosis of exclusion, as there is no sensitive test, and the measurement of antiplatelet antibodies is nonspecific.

References
1. Diehl LF, Ketchum LH. Autoimmune disease and chronic lymphocytic leukemia: autoimmune hemolytic anemia, pure red cell aplasia, and autoimmune thrombocytopenia. *Semin Oncol.* 1998;25(1):80–97.
2. Khouri I, Tuan B, Grant K. Immune thrombocytopenic purpura. *N Engl J Med.* 2002;347(6):449–450.
3. Ward JH. Autoimmunity in chronic lymphocytic leukemia. *Curr Treat Options Oncol.* 2001;2(3):253–257.

48. An 89-year-old man comes to the office for follow-up of mild renal insufficiency (serum creatinine of 1.4) and osteoarthritis of the knees. Knee pain initially limited his ability to climb stairs and walk but now persists after rest and at night. Acetaminophen 1 g three times daily provides no relief, and he does not tolerate narcotic agents.

Physical examination reveals valgus deformity, warmth and effusions of both knees; range of motion is limited by pain. Radiography confirms the presence of osteoarthritis with marked medial joint-space narrowing, sclerosis, and osteophyte formation.

Which of the following should be tried next?

    (A) Celecoxib 100 mg orally twice daily
    (B) Ibuprofen 600 mg three times daily
    (C) Intra-articular triamcinolone
    (D) Intra-articular hyaluronic acid
    (E) Arthroscopy with lavage and debridement

ANSWER: C

Osteoarthritis of the knee is disabling and interferes with mobility. Management focuses on pain relief, quadriceps strengthening exercises, and weight reduction when appropriate. The best next step for this patient is a single intra-articular injection of triamcinolone.

Acetaminophen remains the first line of management in osteoarthritis, largely because of its favorable safety profile. Although cyclooxygenase-2 (COX-2) selective inhibitors have lower gastrointestinal bleeding risk than nonselective nonsteroidal anti-inflammatory agents (NSAIDs) such as ibuprofen, COX-2 inhibitors offer no advantage over NSAIDs with regard to renal events, such as exacerbation of hypertension, peripheral edema, and kidney failure. This 89-year-old patient's mild kidney impairment is a relatively strong contraindication for COX-2 inhibitors and NSAIDs. Although intra-articular injection of hyaluronic acid polymers can result in clinical benefit for up to 6 months, this should follow, not precede, a trial of intra-articular corticosteroids.

Total joint arthroplasty is the definitive intervention for this patient. Arthroscopy with lavage and debridement has recently been shown to achieve symptom and functional improvement comparable to sham intervention and therefore would not be indicated unless there are symptoms of locking or give-way weakness. High tibial osteotomy can be considered in patients with varus deformity. This procedure results in valgus deformity and therefore would not benefit this patient.

References

1. Curtis SP, Ng J, Yu Q, et al. Renal effects of etoricoxib and comparator nonsteroidal anti-inflammatory drugs in controlled clinical trials. *Clin Ther.* 2004;26(1):70–83.
2. Geba GP, Weaver AL, Polis AB, et al. Efficacy of rofecoxib, celecoxib and acetaminophen in osteoarthritis of the knee. *JAMA.* 2002;287: 64–71.
3. Jordan KM, Arden NK, Bannwarth B, et al. EULAR Recommendations 2003: an evidence based approach to the management of knee osteoarthritis: report of a task force of the standing committee for International Clinical Studies Including Therapeutic Trials (ESCISIT). *Ann Rheum Dis.* 2003;62:1145–1155.
4. Lo GH, LaValley M, McAlindon T, et al. Intra-articular hyaluronic acid in treatment of knee osteoarthritis. *JAMA.* 2003;290(23):3115–3121.

49. A 68-year-old man who has had obsessive-compulsive disorder for 45 years comes to the office to discuss changing treatment. He is currently taking clomipramine, 100 mg daily. A recent electrocardiogram revealed left bundle branch block, which was not present on an electrocardiogram performed 12 months earlier.

Which of the following medications could be substituted for the clomipramine to reduce risk of exacerbating the heart block?

(A) Bupropion
(B) Buspirone
(C) Lorazepam
(D) Sertraline

ANSWER: D

Clomipramine, a tricyclic antidepressant, is an effective treatment for obsessive-compulsive disorder (OCD). Tricyclic antidepressants can slow cardiac conduction and pose a risk in persons with left bundle branch block. Controlled studies have found that selective serotonin-reuptake inhibitors (SSRIs), such as sertraline, are an effective alternative to clomipramine for OCD. In this patient's case, it would be prudent to withdraw the clomipramine over at least 2 weeks and then start sertraline at 50 mg daily, increasing to 100 mg daily after 7 days as tolerated. Ideally, the dosage of sertraline should be maintained at 100 mg daily for 4 to 6 weeks before its efficacy is evaluated. If the patient's symptoms are not adequately treated, the dosage can then be increased to 150 mg daily and, if necessary, to 200 mg daily 2 weeks later.

The efficacy of bupropion as a treatment for OCD has not been established in randomized controlled studies. According to a meta-analysis of drug treatments for OCD, antidepressants without selective serotonergic properties are not as effective as clomipramine or SSRIs. Since bupropion has no significant effect on serotonin, it likely is not as effective as established drug treatments for this disorder.

Buspirone, a nonbenzodiazepine anxiolytic, is by itself not an effective treatment for OCD. Further, in two controlled studies of OCD, buspirone was found to be no more effective than placebo as an adjuvant to SSRIs. Lorazepam has not been investigated in a controlled treatment trial of OCD. A recent study found that another benzodiazepine, clonazepam, is no more effective than placebo in this disorder.

References
1. Kaplan A, Hollander E. A review of pharmacologic treatments for obsessive-compulsive disorder. *Psychiatr Serv*. 2003;54(8):1111–1118.
2. Skoog G, Skoog I. A 40-year follow-up of patients with obsessive-compulsive disorder. *Arch Gen Psychiatry*. 1999;56(2):121–127.

50. A 79-year-old man with a history of prostate cancer comes to the office because he has had worsening back pain for 3 weeks. He recalls no recent accident or injury. The pain limits his ability to dress and bathe himself, and he has become increasingly dependent on his wife. He cannot get comfortable in his bed and has been sleeping in a reclining chair for the past few nights. He took acetaminophen with codeine last night with no relief.

Physical examination is normal except for tenderness on palpation over his lower spine. Bone scan demonstrates metastatic disease in the lumbar spine and pelvis.

Which of the following is the most appropriate initial management strategy for this patient's pain?

(A) Immediate-release oxycodone
(B) Sustained-release oxycodone
(C) Propoxyphene
(D) Transdermal fentanyl
(E) Acetaminophen with codeine

ANSWER: A

This patient has moderate to severe pain that is adversely affecting his functional status and quality of life. He requires scheduled dosing of an opioid. His pain would be best managed with initiation of a potent fast-acting opioid such as immediate-release oxycodone. This medication should be given around the clock and the dose increased as needed to achieve adequate pain control. Once the patient's pain is under control, the amount of immediate-release oxycodone required in 24 hours should be calculated. The regimen can then be converted to an equianalgesic dose of a long-acting opioid, such as sustained-release oxycodone or transdermal fentanyl patch. These agents should not be initiated until the amount of opioid required for pain control has been determined. Even then, fentanyl has incomplete cross-tolerance with other opioids and should

usually be started at the lowest dose. Propoxyphene has efficacy similar to that of aspirin or acetaminophen alone, with a significantly higher risk of side effects, including dizziness and ataxia. It is unlikely that propoxyphene would provide adequate pain relief for this patient. Because using the acetaminophen with codeine offered no relief, using it in this patient is unlikely to provide him sufficient pain control.

References
1. AGS Panel on Persistent Pain in Older Persons. The management of persistent pain in older persons. *J Am Geriatr Soc*. 2002; 50(6):S205–S224.
2. Bruera E, Kim HN. Cancer pain. *JAMA*. 2003;229(18):2476–2479.
3. Doyle D, Hanks G, Cherny N, et al., eds. *Oxford Textbook of Palliative Medicine*. 3rd ed. Oxford: Oxford University Press; 2003.

51. In which of the following settings is the prevalence of depressive symptoms and diagnosable major depression highest?

(A) Community
(B) Outpatient medical clinic
(C) General hospital
(D) Long-term-care facility

ANSWER: D

The cross-sectional prevalence of major depression among older persons is between 1% and 3% in the community, 10% and 12% in primary (ambulatory) care, 10% and 15% in acute (medical-surgical hospital) care, and 15% and 25% in chronic or long-term (nursing-home) care. In all these settings, the prevalence of significant depressive symptoms is two to three times higher than the prevalence of diagnosable major depression, ranging from 10% in the community to 40% in nursing homes. The higher prevalence of depression in treatment settings has been attributed to the association of depression with physical illness and disability. The prevalence of major depression is 13% in patients with diabetes mellitus, 16% in those with coronary artery disease, 17% in those with arthritis, and 22% in those with acute stroke. Depression is also associated with Alzheimer's and Parkinson's diseases, other neurodegenerative disorders, cancer, thyroid disease, end-organ failure, hip fracture, vitamin B_{12} deficiency, fibromyalgia, chronic fatigue syndrome, irritable bowel syndrome, and chronic pain. In controlled studies, depressed patients with medical illness have been found to respond to antidepressant treatment or psychotherapy similarly to depressed patients without comorbid medical illness.

References

1. Blazer DG. Depression in late life: review and commentary. *J Gerontol A Biol Sci Med Sci.* 2003;58(3):249–265.
2. Charney DS, Reynolds CF 3rd, Lewis L, et al.; Depression and Bipolar Support Alliance. Depression and Bipolar Support Alliance consensus statement on the unmet needs in diagnosis and treatment of mood disorders in late life. *Arch Gen Psychiatry.* 2003; 60(7):664–672.
3. Lenze EJ, Rogers JC, Martire LM, et al. The association of late-life depression and anxiety with physical disability: a review of the literature and prospectus for future research. *Am J Geriatr Psychiatry.* 2001;9(2):113–135.
4. Mulsant BH, Ganguli M. Epidemiology and diagnosis of depression in late life. *J Clin Psych.* 1999;60(Suppl 20):9–15.

52. A 66-year-old man with a 10-year history of Parkinson's disease comes to the office because of increasingly prominent and aggravating peak-dose dyskinesia over the past year. Although his carbidopa-levodopa dosage has been adjusted by decreasing the individual dose and increasing the dosage frequency, the dyskinesia continues to be a problem.

Which of the following agents should be added next?

(A) Amantadine
(B) Benztropine
(C) Coenzyme Q_{10}
(D) Entacapone
(E) Selegiline

ANSWER: A

Amantadine, a glutamate antagonist, has been shown to reduce levodopa-induced dyskinesia. It also is modestly effective in treating the motor symptoms of Parkinson's disease itself. Therefore, it can be an effective management step for the patient who has progressive diffi-

culty with motor fluctuations in the form of peak-dose dyskinesia and end-of-dose wearing off.

Benztropine is an anticholinergic drug that can reduce tremor but has little effect on other features of Parkinson's disease and is of no benefit in treating dyskinesia. Coenzyme Q_{10} has shown promise as a neuroprotective agent in Parkinson's disease, but it does not provide symptomatic benefit or reduce dyskinesia. Both entacapone (a COMT inhibitor) and selegiline (a MAO-B inhibitor) prolong the benefit of a dose of levodopa by inhibiting levodopa metabolism, but they may actually increase dyskinesia.

References

1. Blanchet PJ, Verhagen Metman L, Chase TN. Renaissance of amantadine in the treatment of Parkinson's disease. *Adv Neurol.* 2003;91:251–257.
2. Shults CW. Treatments of Parkinson's disease circa 2003. *Arch Neurol.* 2003;60(12):1680–1684.
3. Van Laar T. Levodopa-induced response fluctuations in patients with Parkinson's disease: strategies for management. *CNS Drugs.* 2003;17(7):475–489.

53. Which of the following describes expected age-related changes in pulmonary function?

(A) Stable total lung capacity; decreased vital capacity, decreased forced vital capacity, decreased FEV_1, and increased residual volume
(B) Decreased total lung capacity, decreased forced vital capacity, decreased FEV_1, and decreased residual volume
(C) Increased total lung capacity, increased forced vital capacity, increased FEV_1, and increased residual volume
(D) Decreases in all volumes
(E) Decreased lung capacity, decreased residual volume, increased forced vital capacity, and increased FEV_1

ANSWER: A

With normal aging there is a loss of static elastic recoil of the lung that is balanced by an increased stiffness of the thoracic cage; this generally results in a maintenance of total lung capacity at volumes equal to those of younger adults. The loss of elastic recoil and an increase in closing volume result in a predictable increase in residual volume (the volume of air remaining in the lungs after the forced vital capacity maneuver). Consequently, there is a reduction in vital capacity, which is the difference between total lung capacity and residual volume. The FEV_1 reaches a maximal volume in young adulthood and then declines steadily over a person's life.

References

1. Enright P. Aging of the respiratory system. In: Hazzard WR, Blass JP, Halter JB, et al., eds. *Principles of Geriatric Medicine & Gerontology.* 5th ed. New York: McGraw Hill; 2003:511–515.
2. Enright PL, McClelland RL, Buist AS, et al.; Cardiovascular Health Study Research Group. Correlates of peak expiratory flow lability in elderly persons. *Chest.* 2001;120(6):1861–1868.
3. Zeleznik J. Normative aging of the respiratory system. *Clin Geriatr Med.* 2003;19(1):1–18.

54. A 66-year-old woman comes to the office because she is concerned that she has colon cancer. She has had no weight loss, pain, change in appetite, or change in color or consistency of her stools. Over the past 3 years she has had recurrent worries of having cancer. She was referred to a gastroenterologist 8 months ago; at that time the results of a complete blood cell count, liver function tests, and colonoscopy were normal. Current physical examination is unremarkable, and stool guaiac test is negative. She says that she understands her worries may be irrational, but she cannot dispel the idea that something may have been missed.

Which of the following is the most appropriate management for this patient?

(A) Prescribe low-dose antipsychotic medication.
(B) Reassure the patient and schedule a follow-up visit in the near future.
(C) Refer the patient back to the gastroenterologist.
(D) Repeat complete blood cell count and liver function tests.

ANSWER: B

This patient has hypochondriasis, which is a type of somatoform disorder. Other types include conversion disorder and somatization disorder. In somatization disorder, patients have multiple physical complaints with no adequate medical explanation; in hypochondriasis, the patient has the persistent fear of having an illness. These fears may or may not be accompanied by physical complaints. Patients with hypochondriasis try to dispel their fears by repeatedly seeking unnecessary and expensive medical tests and evaluations. The normal test results may reassure the patient, but often the reassurance is short-lived. Affected persons often respond to a schedule of regular contact with their primary care physician, where they can discuss their fears and develop trust in the physician's judgment. This works best if the physician listens empathically, provides reassurance, protects the patient from unnecessary testing, and listens for health concerns that may require legitimate evaluation. There is no need to repeat a specialist referral or order further testing. Ordering additional tests may in fact reinforce the patient's fears and be interpreted that the physician is concerned as well.

The differential diagnosis for this patient includes delusional disorder, somatic type. Patients with this condition believe that they have an illness but are not able to see that their beliefs are irrational. Since this patient recognizes the irrational nature of her beliefs, she does not have a psychotic disorder, and antipsychotic medication would not be helpful.

References

1. Sheehan B, Bass C, Briggs R, et al. Somatization among older primary care attenders. *Psychol Med.* 2003;33(5):867–877.
2. Wijeratne C, Hickie I. Somatic distress syndromes in later life: the need for paradigm change. *Psychol Med.* 2001;31(4):571–576.

55. A 75-year-old man is brought to the office by his wife because of his increasing agitation. He has been treated for Alzheimer's disease with donepezil 10 mg daily for 2 years. Over the past 3 months, he has become increasingly quiet and withdrawn, refusing to accompany his wife out of the house and, when pressed, shouting at her to leave him alone. He no longer watches television, a previously enjoyable pastime. He is eating poorly and has lost 4.5 kg (10 lb). His wife is extremely disturbed by his behavior and has considered long-term care. On examination, he appears sad and complains of frustration related to his inability to work and drive a car. He sees no reason to go on living but has no thoughts of harming himself.

What is the most effective initial management strategy for this patient?

(A) Enrollment in an adult day program
(B) Caregiver education and training in coping skills
(C) Nortriptyline
(D) Sertraline
(E) Electroconvulsive therapy

ANSWER: D

Depression associated with Alzheimer's disease is best managed with a selective serotonin-reuptake inhibitor. Sertraline or citalopram is less likely than fluoxetine or paroxetine to cause drug interactions. A recent double-blind randomized trial confirmed the effectiveness of sertraline therapy (dosage 25 to 150 mg/day) for treating depression in Alzheimer's disease, noting significant improvements in depression symptoms, activities of daily living, and caregiver distress.

Enrollment in an adult program would be a useful nonpharmacologic intervention, though given the severity of his depression and the associated weight loss, pharmacologic intervention should be considered initially.

Nortriptyline is a tricyclic antidepressant that has been well studied in older adults. Because of its anticholinergic effects, potential for orthostatic hypotension, and toxicity in overdose, selective serotonin-reuptake inhibitors are a safer first choice.

Electroconvulsive therapy can be used for the treatment of depression in patients with Alzheimer's disease. However, because it may increase cognitive impairment and induce delirium in patients with preexisting cognitive impairment, it should be reserved for severe or refractory cases.

References

1. Lyketsos CG, DelCampo L, Steinberg M, et al. Treating depression in Alzheimer disease: efficacy and safety of sertraline therapy, and the benefits of depression reduction: the DIADS. *Arch Gen Psychiatry.* 2003;60(7):737–746.
2. Lyketsos CG, Olin J. Depression in Alzheimer's disease: overview and treatment. *Biological Psychiatry.* 2002;52(3):243–252.
3. Marriott A, Donaldson C, Tarrier N, et al. Effectiveness of cognitive-behavioural family intervention in reducing the burden of care in carers of patients with Alzheimer's disease. *Br J Psychiatry.* 2000;176:557–562.

56. Of the following features that may be available from a patient history, which best distinguishes syncope from an unexplained fall?

(A) Tonic-clonic movements
(B) Urinary incontinence
(C) Postictal state
(D) Loss of consciousness
(E) Loss of postural tone

ANSWER: D

Distinguishing syncope from falls can be difficult. These syndromes often have separate causes, but they have considerable clinical overlap in elderly patients. The clinical feature that distinguishes the two presentations is loss of consciousness. Many elderly patients have retrograde amnesia regarding the event; in one study, 32% of older adults with normal cognition could not remember falling 3 months after the event. Often a witnessed account is unavailable. Falls not resulting from an obvious cause, such as impaired gait or balance, often have a cardiovascular cause (particularly bradycardia or neurally mediated blood-pressure disorders). Thus, in the elderly person, syncope and unexplained falls may be indistinguishable clinical manifestations of the same pathophysiologic process.

Seizures are a common cause of unexplained loss of consciousness but do not constitute true syncope. Patients with seizures often have a history of prior seizures or have other neurologic symptoms or findings that suggest the diagnosis. Many patients with syncope have myoclonic jerks that can be mistaken for seizure activity by witnesses. In a study of 94 consecutive patients who had transient loss of consciousness, the best discriminatory finding was orientation immediately after the event according to the eyewitness. Nausea and sweating before the event were useful to exclude a seizure but incontinence and trauma were not discriminatory. Another study found that lateral tongue biting is 24% sensitive and 99% specific for diagnosis of generalized tonic-clonic seizures. In a recent standardized evaluation of 671 patients with loss of consciousness, head turning and being unconsciousness were predictive of seizures, whereas dizziness or diaphoresis prior to the event or loss of consciousness after prolonged sitting or standing suggested syncope.

References

1. Benbadis SR, Wolgamuth BR, Goren H, et al. Value of tongue biting in the diagnosis of seizures. *Arch Intern Med*. 1995;155(21):2346–2349.
2. Shaw FE, Kenny RA. The overlap between syncope and falls in the elderly. *Postgrad Med J*. 1997;73(864):635–639.
3. Sheldon R, Rose S, Ritchie D, et al. Historical criteria that distinguish syncope from seizures. *J Am Coll Cardiol*. 2002;40(1):142–148.

57. A 71-year-old woman comes to the office because she has acute back pain. History includes moderate gastroesophageal reflux disease, hypertension, and depression. Medications include pantoprazole 40 mg daily, lisinopril 10 mg daily, hydrochlorothiazide 12.5 mg daily, citalopram 20 mg daily, calcium carbonate 500 mg tablets three times a day, and a daily multivitamin. She usually consumes three to four servings of dairy products daily. She walks 2 miles three times each week and does not smoke or drink alcohol.

Radiography of the spine confirms vertebral fractures and osteopenia. Dual-energy x-ray absorptiometry (DEXA) results show a bone mineral density T score of –2.7 at the femoral neck and –2.9 in the spine.

Which of the following is the most important initial change to make?

(A) Change calcium carbonate to calcium citrate.
(B) Add calcitonin 200 IU intranasally once daily.
(C) Add risedronate 35 mg once weekly.
(D) Use a hip protector.

ANSWER: C

This patient has osteoporosis, as indicated by her low bone mineral density at the femoral neck and spine (T score below −2.5). Bisphosphonates are first-line agents in patients with osteoporosis, as several studies have shown reduced fracture risk at both the spine and hip. Moderate gastroesophageal reflux disease is not a contraindication for bisphosphonates.

Since calcium carbonate requires an acidic environment for optimal absorption, it is best given with meals. Proton-pump inhibitors increase the gastric pH and theoretically may reduce the absorption of calcium carbonate products, although this has not been formally tested. Alternatively, calcium citrate does not require an acidic environment for absorption. This patient receives from 900 to 1200 mg of calcium daily from her diet (goal, 1200 to 1500 mg of elemental calcium) in addition to 600 mg of elemental calcium from supplements. She therefore is probably meeting her calcium needs with the current regimen. Since she seems to tolerate dairy products, she should be encouraged to routinely consume at least four servings of calcium-containing products daily.

Calcitonin is not a first-line agent since it is not as effective as bisphosphonates and has not been shown to reduce hip fractures. Although calcitonin may be beneficial for acute pain secondary to vertebral fractures, it should be used in combination with a bisphosphonate in established osteoporosis. A hip protector would not be effective in preventing further vertebral fractures.

References

1. Follin SL, Hansen LB. Current approaches to the prevention and treatment of postmenopausal osteoporosis. *Am J Health Syst Pharm*. 2003;60(9):883–901.
2. McClung MR, Geusens P, Miller PD, et al. Effect of risedronate on the risk of hip fracture in elderly women. Hip Intervention Program Study Group. *N Engl J Med*. 2001;344(5):333–340.

58. A 71-year-old woman who lives in a retirement community comes to the office for her annual examination. She had a diarrheal illness 1 week ago that resolved; others in her retirement community also had the illness. On examination, blood pressure is normal. Laboratory studies are normal except for a sodium level of 132 mEq/L.

Which of the following age-related physiologic changes most likely explains the low sodium level?

(A) Decreased thirst
(B) Decreased β-adrenergic response
(C) Increased α-adrenergic activity
(D) Diminished ability to conserve sodium

ANSWER: D

The ability of the kidney to conserve sodium decreases with age, as manifested in this patient by a low sodium level after a diarrheal illness. In older patients, clinical symptoms often resolve before correction of electrolytes has occurred. After an episode of viral gastroenteritis, electrolytes such as sodium remain abnormal days after the patient is symptom free.

Age-related reduction in thirst is associated with hypernatremia due to delay in oral repletion. Age-related increased α-adrenergic responses and decreased β-adrenergic responses protect against positional hypotension and are not related to sodium level.

References

1. Forman DE, Rich MW. Heart failure in the elderly. *Congest Heart Fail.* 2003;9(6):311–321.
2. Lamb EJ, O'Riordan SE, Delaney MP. Kidney function in older people: pathology, assessment and management. *Clin Chim Acta.* 2003;334(1–2):25–40.

59. A 70-year-old woman comes to the office because she is worried about her risk of stroke. Her mother died from a stroke earlier this year. The patient's history includes hypertension and type 2 diabetes mellitus. Medications include glipizide, aspirin, enalapril, and atorvastatin. She smokes one pack of cigarettes daily and does not exercise. On examination, blood pressure is 150/80 mm Hg. Laboratory studies include hemoglobin A_{1C} of 8% and low-density lipoprotein level of 110 mg/dL.

Which of the following is associated with the greatest risk reduction of stroke?

(A) Achieving optimum hemoglobin A_{1C} level
(B) Achieving optimum blood-pressure control
(C) Adding an antioxidant
(D) Quitting smoking
(E) Achieving optimum LDL cholesterol level

ANSWER: B

Systolic hypertension, which is common in older adults, is a more important risk factor for cerebrovascular disease than diastolic blood pressure and is more difficult to treat. Studies suggest that the target goal should be under 130/80 mm Hg to prevent organ disease in patients with diabetes. The incidence of stroke is reduced by up to 44% when blood pressure is controlled in patients with diabetes and hypertension.

Statins can be used for primary and secondary prevention of major vascular diseases in older adults. Statins are effective in decreasing stroke risk, although less so than controlling hypertension. Treatment with a statin reduces the incidence of stroke by 33% in persons with diabetes without known coronary disease.

Tighter blood glucose control prevents microvascular complications of diabetes and coronary disease rather than stroke. Vitamin E, an antioxidant, has not been shown to be effective in several large studies. Smoking is an independent risk factor for ischemic stroke, with a relative risk of 1.5. From 2 to 5 years after smoking cessation, the risk of stroke reverts to that of nonsmokers.

References

1. Chobanian AV, Bakris GL, Black HR, et al. Seventh report of the Joint Committee on Prevention, Detection, Evaluation and Treatment of High Blood Pressure. *Hypertension.* 2004;43(1):1–3.
2. Gorelick PB, Sacco RL, Smith DB, et al. Prevention of first stroke: a review of guidelines and a multidisciplinary consensus statement from the National Stroke Association. *JAMA.* 1999;281(12):1112–1120.
3. Straus SE, Majumdar SR, McAlister FA. New evidence for stroke prevention: scientific review. *JAMA.* 2002;288(11):1388–1395.

60. A 68-year-old man comes to the office because of lower urinary symptoms associated with benign prostatic hyperplasia. He awakens once or twice each night to urinate; the frequency of his nocturia has increased gradually over the past 4 years. He has no other urinary tract symptoms. He has coronary heart disease that is well managed with metoprolol 100 mg and aspirin 81 mg daily.

On physical examination, blood pressure is 140/70 mm Hg, and pulse is 55 per minute. On digital rectal examination, the prostate is not enlarged, has no nodules, induration, or asymmetry. Prostate-specific antigen (PSA) level is 6 ng/mL (increased from 2.5 ng/mL at age 65 and 3 ng/mL at age 67).

What is the most appropriate next step in the evaluation of this patient?

(A) Remeasure the PSA level.
(B) Refer to a urologist for a prostate biopsy.
(C) Order a transrectal ultrasound.
(D) Order a bone scan.

ANSWER: A

This patient has had a relatively orderly progression of his prostate-specific antigen (PSA) level, with a sudden rise. Serial PSA levels can vary for several reasons, including subclinical prostatitis and vigorous prostatic massage. Often the cause is unknown. Any single abnormal PSA level should be confirmed 4 to 6 weeks later before proceeding with work-up for prostate cancer.

Referral to a urologist is appropriate if the increase in PSA level is confirmed. Transrectal ultrasound is not a diagnostic test for prostate cancer and should be used as part of a transrectal prostate biopsy. A bone scan is used to stage known prostate cancer.

References

1. Clements R. The role of transrectal ultrasound in diagnosing prostate cancer. *Curr Urol Rep.* 2002;3(3):194–200.
2. Eastham JA, Riedel E, Scardino PT, et al. Polyp Prevention Trial Study Group. Variation of serum prostate-specific antigen levels: an evaluation of year-to-year fluctuations. *JAMA.* 2003;289(20):2695–2700.

61. A 79-year-old man comes to the office for a routine visit. He feels well. He has a history of hypertension, stable kidney insufficiency, and coronary artery disease, with myocardial infarction 2 years ago (ejection fraction, 35%). He takes aspirin 81 mg daily, furosemide 20 mg twice daily, metoprolol 25 mg twice daily, and pravastatin 40 mg daily.

On examination, blood pressure is 165/79 mm Hg, consistent with readings over the past few visits.

Laboratory studies:
Sodium	137 mEq/L
Potassium	4.3 mEq/L
Urea nitrogen	25 mg/dL
Creatinine	2.3 mg/dL (stable)

Which of the following is the most appropriate intervention?

(A) Add lisinopril.
(B) Increase metoprolol.
(C) Substitute hydrochlorothiazide for furosemide.
(D) Add amlodipine.

ANSWER: A

This patient has structural heart disease from myocardial infarction and longstanding hypertension, but has no symptoms of heart failure. Despite his kidney insufficiency (estimated creatinine clearance of 25 mL/min), the use of an angiotensin-converting enzyme (ACE) inhibitor is indicated. ACE inhibitors improve survival and reduce morbidity after myocardial infarction. Kidney function may deteriorate acutely when an ACE inhibitor is initiated, and patients with chronic kidney insufficiency are especially susceptible. A transient 10% to 20% increase in serum creatinine can be anticipated when ACE inhibitor therapy is started and is not a reason to discontinue therapy. Serum creatinine and electrolytes should be evaluated before and 1 to 2 weeks after starting therapy.

Given this patient's kidney function, hydrochlorothiazide will probably not be effective for reducing blood pressure. Increasing metoprolol or adding amlodipine may reduce his blood pressure but, given his history of myocardial infarction, lisinopril is the best choice.

References
1. Jessup M, Brozena S. Heart failure. *N Engl J Med*. 2003;348(20):2007–2018.
2. Schoolwerth AC, Sica DA, Ballermann BJ, et al. Renal considerations in angiotensin converting enzyme inhibitor therapy: a statement for healthcare professionals from the Council on the Kidney in Cardiovascular Disease and the Council for High Blood Pressure Research of the American Heart Association. *Circulation*. 2001;104(16):1985–1991.

References
1. McCurry SM, Gibbons LE, Logsdon R, et al. Training caregivers to change the sleep hygiene practices of patients with dementia: the NITE-AD Project. *J Am Geriatr Soc*. 2003;51(10);1455–1460.
2. McCurry SM, Reynolds CF, Ancoli-Israel S, et al. Treatment of sleep disturbance in Alzheimer's disease. *Sleep Med Rev*. 2000;4(6):603–608.
3. Teri L, Logsdon RG, McCurry SM. Nonpharmacological treatment of behavioral disturbance in dementia. *Med Clin North Am*. 2002;86(3):641–656.
4. Vitiello MV, Boorson S. Sleep disturbances in patients with Alzheimer's disease: epidemiology, pathophysiology and treatment. *CNS Drugs*. 2001;15(10):777–796.

62. An 89-year-old woman who lives with her daughter and son-in-law is evaluated because she recently has become more agitated and is often tearful. She repeats stories and packs her bags several times a day, stating that she is "going home." She is up frequently at night, wandering and crying loudly. History includes moderate dementia and hypertension. Her medications include galantamine and lisinopril. She requires assistance in all instrumental activities of daily living (IADLs), but in basic activities of daily living she is dependent only in bathing. The daughter reminds her to take her medications, which she often resists, and bathes her.

Which of the following burdens on caregiving is most likely to lead to nursing-home placement?

(A) Repetitive questioning
(B) Packing behavior
(C) Nighttime disruptive behaviors
(D) Needing assistance in IADLs
(E) Refusal to take medications

ANSWER: C

Behavior problems of frail older adults are the primary cause of nursing-home placement from the community. With support and counseling, families can learn techniques to address some behavioral difficulties. However, when an older adult is up at night and interrupts the caregivers' sleep, daytime functioning and overall coping skills of the caregivers diminish. Disruptive sleep behaviors can be addressed through increased daytime activities and, as a last resort, medications, such as low-dose trazodone at bedtime.

63. A 62-year-old woman comes to the office for evaluation of dementia. History includes personality change over 2 to 3 years (comprising apathy, excessive familiarity in social situations, disinhibition), followed by memory loss and prominent expressive aphasia. There are no other psychiatric symptoms or psychiatric history. The patient has a history of well-controlled coronary disease, heart failure, hypertension, and hypercholesterolemia. There is no history of cerebrovascular events.

Physical, neurologic, and general mental status examination is normal. Her Mini–Mental State Examination score is 21 of 30 (losing 3 points on orientation, 2 on serial sevens, 3 on recall, 1 on sentence repetition). Laboratory studies are normal.

Which of the following brain imaging studies would be most helpful in identifying the cause of her dementia?

(A) Positron emission tomography
(B) Noncontrast magnetic resonance imaging
(C) Noncontrast computed tomography
(D) Magnetic resonance imaging with gadolinium contrast

ANSWER: A

In the differential diagnosis of dementia, brain imaging is best used to answer a specific question. In this patient, the most likely differential is between frontotemporal degeneration and Alzheimer's disease. Frontotemporal dementia is suggested by the younger age of the patient, the onset of personality change before the memory loss, the history of prominent expressive aphasia, and the results of the Mini–Mental State Examination—especially the difficulty with repetition. In a 62-year-old, the probability that any case of dementia is due to Alzheimer's disease is higher than the probability that it is due to frontotemporal dementia. However, frontotemporal dementia is more common in this age group, has a different prognosis, and does not respond well to cholinesterase inhibitors. Therefore, differentiating between Alzheimer's and frontotemporal dementias may be important, although at this time there appears to be little correlation between a clinical diagnosis of frontotemporal dementia and specific neuropathologic findings. Structural imaging, especially magnetic resonance imaging, occasionally reveals differential atrophy in frontal and anterior temporal areas consistent with frontotemporal dementia. In cases where differentiation of frontotemporal dementia and Alzheimer's disease is not clear after clinical evaluation and structural imaging, Medicare has agreed to cover the cost of FDG PET (fluorodeoxyglucose positron emission tomography), which is more sensitive to neuronal loss in specific brain regions.

Most practice guidelines recommend the use of noncontrast computed tomography (CT) to exclude causes of dementia other than Alzheimer's disease. However, given its limited resolution, CT usually contributes little to the understanding of the clinical picture. In addition to detecting brain atrophy, CT is useful in detecting larger brain tumors, larger infarcts, and hydrocephalic ventricular enlargement. In this patient, the clinical picture does not suggest vascular dementia since the cognitive decline is gradual, there is no history of cerebrovascular accidents, and the neurologic examination is normal. Therefore, imaging findings of infarcts, whether on CT or magnetic resonance imaging, are unlikely, they would be in brain areas not directly involved in cognition, and they would not necessarily explain the dementia. Further, in the absence of gait disorder or urinary incontinence, normal-pressure hydrocephalus is highly unlikely, so any ventricular enlargement is most likely to be secondary to atrophy. Measurement of the hippocampus is being studied as a possible indicator of Alzheimer's disease. However, this is early work that has not been

shown to differentiate among types of dementia or to have other clinical utility.

References

1. Centers for Medicare and Medicaid Services. Decision Memo for Positron Emission Tomography (FDG) and Other Neuroimaging Devices for Suspected Dementia (CAG-00088R). Available at http://www.cms.hhs.gov/mcd/viewdecisionmemo.asp?id=104 (accessed September 2005).
2. Good C. Dementia and aging. *Brit Med Bull.* 2003; 65:159–168.
3. Knopman DS, DeKosky ST, Cummings JL, et al. Practice parameter: diagnosis of dementia (an evidence-based review). Report of the Quality Standards Subcommittee of the American Academy of Neurology. *Neurology.* 2001;56(9):1143–1153.
4. McKhann GM, Albert MS, Grossman M, et al; Work Group on Frontotemporal Dementia and Pick's Disease. Clinical and pathological diagnosis of frontotemporal dementia: report of the Work Group on Frontotemporal Dementia and Pick's Disease. *Arch Neurol.* 2001; 58(11):1803–1809.

64. A 69-year-old woman with mild mental retardation comes to the office with one of her residential caregivers, who describes gradually worsening anger, agitation, and isolation over the past 12 months. Approximately 6 months ago she began treatment with a selective serotonin-reuptake inhibitor, but her response has been negligible despite titration of the medication to the maximum recommended dose. She has no previous history of emotional or behavioral problems. She takes acetaminophen for mild pain due to degenerative arthritis, and she has bilateral cataracts but is reluctant to proceed with surgery.

She has enjoyed working in a noncompetitive setting for over 20 years, but this activity is now in jeopardy because her visual impairment interferes with the work. She has no supportive family and only a small network of peer friendships. She is her own guardian and has always been involved in decisions about her life and health.

Which of the following is the most appropriate next step in caring for this patient?

(A) Begin psychotherapy, focusing on helping her with health care decisions.

(B) Begin a medication to augment the antidepressant.

(C) Add an atypical antipsychotic agent to decrease her agitation.

(D) Arrange for neuropsychological testing.

(E) Discontinue the antidepressant and begin a medication for anxiety.

ANSWER: A

Older persons with mental retardation have limitations in insight, judgment, coping ability, and family support systems. It is likely that, as this patient's sensory impairment worsened, she was less able to cope with work and with the associated stress of needing to make health care decisions. A course of psychotherapy focusing on health care decisions and her fears and expectations is the best choice of the options listed. The ideal outcome would be for her to choose treatment for the visual impairment that has radically changed her environment.

Augmenting her current antidepressant treatment is less than ideal, given the limited clinical evidence that she is depressed or that it would best be treated with medication.

Adding a low-dose atypical antipsychotic to decrease agitation may be appropriate in some situations, but at this point it is more prudent to avoid a medication with potentially serious adverse effects. Typical and atypical antipsychotic medications may succeed in decreasing some target behaviors, but at the cost of dampening all behavior.

Although some psychologic testing might be beneficial, it is inappropriate to defer active treatment while trying to arrange for a battery of neuropsychological tests. The most pertinent testing would offer insight into her cognitive and adaptive skills and information regarding her mood and behavior. Much of this could be assessed by gathering information on the patient and spending time in therapy with her.

Given the clinical picture, the patient seems anxious. However, beginning a benzodiazepine anxiolytic medication at this point could worsen her mood and behavior and cause serious adverse effects.

References

1. Cooper SA. The relationship between psychiatric and physical health in elderly people with intellectual disability. *J Intellect Disabil Res.*1999;43(Pt 1):54–60.

2. Heller T, Janicki M, Hammel J, et al. *Promoting Healthy Aging, Family Support, and Age-Friendly Communities for Persons Aging With Developmental Disabilities: Report of the 2001 Invitational Research Symposium on Aging with Developmental Disabilities.* Chicago: The Rehabilitation Research and Training Center on Aging with Developmental Disabilities, Department of Disability and Human Development, University of Illinois at Chicago; 2002.

3. Janicki MP, Davidson PW, Henderson CM, et al. Health characteristics and health services utilization in older adults with intellectual disability living in community residences. *J Intellect Disabil Res.* 2002;46(Pt 4):287–298.

4. McCulloch DL, Sludden PA, McKeown K, et al. Vision care requirements among intellectually disabled adults: a residence-based pilot study. *J Intellect Disabil Res.* 1996;40(Pt 2):140–150.

65. An 82-year-old woman who lives in a long-term-care facility is evaluated for agitation that occurs during the day and when she awakens from sleep. She has mild Alzheimer's dementia. She spends most of the day sitting in front of the television in a lounge with low lights, occasionally dozing off. The patient is mobile and fully participates in all basic activities of daily living. Review of her medications and physical examination reveal no apparent cause for the agitation. Mental status examination reveals only mild cognitive impairment.

Which of the following nonpharmacologic interventions is most likely to benefit this patient?

(A) Ask staff to exercise the patient twice daily.

(B) Ask staff to discourage the patient from watching television and to introduce nighttime diapers.

(C) Ask staff to keep the patient in a bright environment during the day and a quiet, dark environment at night without interruptions.

(D) Ask staff to prevent daytime napping and implement enforced sleeping hours, with restriction of evening fluid intake.

(E) Provide the patient with a soft nightlight, familiar items and photographs at the bedside, and orienting objects, such as a clock.

ANSWER: C

Disrupted, brief sleep at night is common in the long-term-care setting, and patients are commonly asleep during the day. According to actigraphic data (from a device usually worn on the wrist that measures activity), nursing-home patients are rarely asleep or awake for a full hour throughout the night and day. Low lighting, noise, and interruptions by staff to wake and turn patients are partially responsible for poor sleep consolidation. Patients in nursing homes need to be in bright environments during the day and in a quiet, dark environment at night. Awakenings at night are often accompanied by agitation and may result in greater daytime agitation. Even severely demented nursing-home patients spontaneously change shoulder and hip position throughout the night, obviating the need to awaken them to prevent bedsores related to incontinence.

Exercise may be generally helpful, but it does not address the environmental concerns and nighttime awakening that are likely responsible for this patient's agitation. Similarly, removing the television does not address the daytime low light and napping. Fluid restriction, enforced sleep hours, and prevention of napping are not reasonable expectations of the staff and generally are difficult to enforce in a long-term-care facility. The provision of a nightlight, orienting objects, and a familiar nonthreatening environment is useful in dementia syndromes and delirium, especially for patients with "sundowning" or loss of orientation, which is not the case with this patient.

References

1. Ancoli-Israel S. Sleep disorders in older adults. *Geriatrics.* 2004;59:37–40.

2. Martin J, Marler M, Shochat T, et al. Circadian rhythms of agitation in institutionalized Alzheimer's disease patients. *Chronobiol Int.* 2000;17(3):405–418.

3. Schnelle JF, Alessi CA, Al-Samarrai NR, et al. The nursing home at night: effects of an intervention on noise, light, and sleep. *J Am Geriatr Soc.* 1999;47(4):430–438.

66. The primary care provider for a 79-year-old woman with advanced dementia is called by the police when the patient is found dead at home. She lived with her son, who had called paramedics when he discovered that she was not responsive. The paramedics found an elderly woman lying almost naked on her bed, and they were concerned about her appearance. They described a thin woman with feces on her buttocks and abdomen, elongated fingernails and toenails caked with dirt, two large pressure sores (stage IV on her buttock and stage III on her right shoulder), and matted, dirty hair.

It has been difficult to care for her. Her son always reported that she did not want him to bring her to the doctor, and she had refused a home-health aide when she was in an earlier stage of dementia. On her last visit to the office, 18 months ago, she was found to have lost a substantial amount of weight and was disheveled and somewhat dirty. Home-health care was initiated, but her son refused their services when they came to his house, saying that he was able to care for her and that she did not want anyone else to help.

For religious reasons, the son wants the death certificate signed as soon as possible so that she can be buried within 24 hours. The police request direction about what to do next. Which of the following is the most appropriate response?

(A) Request transport of the body to an emergency department for further evaluation.
(B) Sign the death certificate.
(C) Release the body to the mortuary and make a referral to Adult Protective Services.
(D) Request an evaluation by a coroner or medical examiner.

ANSWER: D

This may be a case of fatal neglect and should be reported to the coroner or medical examiner for expert postmortem evaluation and autopsy. Some signs of neglect may be difficult to distinguish from chronic illness. For example, dehydration, malnutrition, and pressure sores may be unavoidable as persons with multiple medical problems become more debilitated. In cases of medical neglect, however, the caregiver fails to seek appropriate medical care for the patient. It is important in these circumstances for the clinician to confer with the coroner or medical examiner's office about appropriateness of care. The medical examiner may perform an autopsy or toxicology screening and may look for evidence to support or refute the possibility of fatal neglect.

A death certificate should not be signed under these circumstances. First, it has been 18 months since the patient's last examination, suggesting that she has not been under active care. Also, there is reason to suspect neglect: the person is found in filthy conditions with severe pressure sores and possible malnutrition. Although extenuating circumstances may explain the situation (in this case, a person who refused care), it is not within the clinician's purview to make this determination.

Once a patient is pronounced dead, it is not necessary or appropriate to bring the body to an emergency department if abuse or neglect is suspected. Similarly, it is not appropriate to make a referral to Adult Protective Services once a person has died.

References

1. Collins KA, Bennett AT, Hanzlick R. Elder abuse and neglect. *Arch Intern Med.* 2000;160(11):1567–1568.
2. Ortmann C, Fechner G, Bajanowski T, et al. Fatal neglect of the elderly. *Int J Legal Med.* 2001;114(3):191–193.
3. Thomas DR. Are all pressure ulcers avoidable? *J Am Med Dir Assoc.* 2001; 2(6):297–301.

67. The family of an 82-year-old nursing-home resident reports that she seemed more confused when they visited her the previous evening. The staff reports that the confusion seems to vary through the day. There has been no decrease in her appetite. History includes Alzheimer's disease, atrial fibrillation, depression, and osteoarthritis. For the past 3 years she has taken digoxin and warfarin; fluoxetine was added 4 months ago and ibuprofen 1 month ago. On examination, blood pressure is 130/80 mm Hg, respiratory rate is 18 per minute, and pulse is 54 per minute.

Which of the following is the most likely cause for her worsening confusion?

(A) Advancing Alzheimer's disease
(B) Worsening depression
(C) Digoxin toxicity
(D) Dementia with Lewy bodies

ANSWER: C

This presentation is consistent with possible delirium. The patient's current medication regimen places her at increased risk for drug-related side effects and interactions, which is a common problem in the nursing home. Of the options presented, the most likely is digoxin toxicity caused by the recent introduction of ibuprofen, which may cause renal insufficiency and fluid retention. Renal insufficiency leads to a decrease in digoxin clearance and places her at increased risk for digoxin toxicity. Although Alzheimer's disease, worsening depression, and dementia with Lewy bodies may increase one's risk for delirium, they are unlikely to cause acute changes in mental status.

References

1. Giovanni G, Giovanni P. Do non-steroidal anti-inflammatory drugs and COX-2 selective inhibitors have different renal effects? *J Nephrol.* 2002;15(5):480–488.
2. Gurwitz JH, Field TS, Avorn J, et al. Incidence and preventability of adverse drug events in nursing homes. *Am J Med.* 2000;109(2):87–94.

3. Hanratty CG, MeGlinchey P, Johnston GD, et al. Differential pharmacokinetics of digoxin in elderly patients. *Drugs Aging.* 2000;17(5):353–362.

68. A 73-year-old man comes to the office because he awakens four to five times each night and goes to the bathroom, each time passing a small amount of urine. He is distressed by this symptom because he is afraid of falling on the way to the bathroom and is tired all day. His wife's sleep is also disrupted by these episodes. History includes hypertension, moderate obesity, and non−insulin-dependent diabetes mellitus. He takes an angiotensin-converting enzyme inhibitor and two oral hypoglycemic agents. He has no genitourinary history and no daytime urinary symptoms. He voids every 3 to 4 hours during the day.

Physical examination reveals a mildly enlarged prostate. There are no signs of heart failure. Noninvasive urinary testing reveals peak flow of 21 mL/sec (normal > 10 mL/sec) on a void of 320 mL, postvoid residual of 45 mL, and negative urinalysis. Further testing reveals normal hemoglobin A_{1C}, renal function, and prostate-specific antigen levels. He has a normal ejection fraction on cardiac echocardiography.

Which of the following is the most appropriate next step?

(A) Trial of tamsulosin, 0.4 mg twice daily
(B) Trial of desmopressin, 40 μg of nasal spray in the evening
(C) Trial of furosemide, 20 mg in the late afternoon
(D) Referral to a sleep disorders clinic
(E) Referral for urologic evaluation

ANSWER: D

This patient's history suggests a sleep disorder, either periodic leg movements during sleep or sleep apnea. Patients may complain of nocturia, but the primary problem may be awakening because of a sleep disorder. Thus, this patient should be referred for evaluation in a sleep disorders clinic. He does not need a urologic evaluation, as results of all basic testing (physical examination, prostate-specific antigen, flow rate, postvoid residual, and urinalysis) are normal.

α-Blockers, including tamsulosin, are used to treat symptoms of benign prostatic hyperplasia. Isolated nocturia in a 73-year-old man is unlikely to be due only to benign prostatic hyperplasia, and α-blockers are not very effective in treating this isolated symptom. Patients with nocturia due to volume overload (venous insufficiency with lower-extremity edema, heart failure) sometimes benefit from administration of a rapid-acting diuretic in the late afternoon. This strategy reduces the amount of fluid accumulated during the day and reduces polyuria caused by mobilization of fluid while supine during sleep. If this patient's symptoms did not suggest a sleep disorder, a trial of rapid-acting diuretic would be an appropriate next step. Oral and nasal desmopressin (DDAVP) is approved for use in children with nocturnal enuresis. Although the relationship among abnormal secretion or action of endogenous arginine vasopressin, nocturnal polyuria, and nocturia in older adults is unclear, oral DDAVP has been shown to reduce nocturia in men and is approved for this indication in several European countries. This might be a therapeutic option after a primary sleep disorder is excluded or treated.

References

1. Mattiasson A, Abrams P, Van Kerrebroeck P, et al. Efficacy of desmopressin in the treatment of nocturia: a double-blind placebo-controlled study in men. *BJU International.* 2002;89(9):855.
2. Miller M. Nocturnal polyuria in older people: pathophysiology and clinical implications. *J Am Geriatr Soc.* 2000;48(10):1321–1329.
3. Weiss JP, Blaivas JG. Nocturia. *J Urol.* 2000;163(1):5–12.

69. A 72-year-old black American woman cares for her 75-year-old black American husband with Alzheimer's disease in their own home.

Which of the following factors is the strongest predictor of whether the husband will be placed in a nursing home within the next year?

(A) The wife's age
(B) The husband's racial background
(C) The wife's racial background
(D) The husband's hallucinations and delusions
(E) The husband's dependence in one or more activities of daily living

ANSWER: D

Considerable research has focused on identifying risk factors for nursing-home placement. Caring for a spouse or other relative with dementia is stressful. Behavioral problems, such as asking the same question repetitively, wandering, and psychotic symptoms, appear to be particularly potent predictors of nursing-home placement. In one study, the presence of a behavior problem shortened a demented person's stay in the community by about 2 years.

Other risk factors include the caregiver's being over 75 years old, the demented person's living alone, one or more dependencies in activities of daily living, and more advanced cognitive impairment. Race and ethnicity may play a protective role in placement decisions. Black or Hispanic Americans with dementia are less likely than white Americans with dementia to be placed in a nursing home.

References

1. Phillips VL, Diwan S. The incremental effect of dementia-related problem behaviors on the time to nursing home placement in poor, frail, demented older persons. *J Am Geriatri Soc.* 2003;51(2):188–193.
2. Rymer S, Salloway S, Norton L, et al. Impaired awareness, behavior disturbance, and caregiver burden in Alzheimer disease. *Alzheimer Dis Assoc Disord.* 2002; 16(4):248–253.
3. Yaffe K, Fox P, Newcomer R, et al. Patient and caregiver characteristics and nursing home placement in patients with dementia. *JAMA.* 2002; 287(16):2090–2097.

70. Which of the following is an absolute contraindication to tilt-table testing?

    (A) Previous cerebrovascular accident
    (B) Previous myocardial infarction
    (C) Carotid artery stenosis
    (D) Inability to stand without an assistive device
    (E) Moderate to severe aortic stenosis

    ANSWER: E

    Moderate to severe aortic stenosis is an absolute contraindication to tilt-table testing, as is severe pulmonary hypertension. Both conditions are associated with a neurally mediated reflex disturbance of blood-pressure regulation that can result in profound hypotension (Bezold-Jarisch reflex). The presumed pathophysiologic mechanism occurs when rapid and forceful contraction of a relatively empty (because of venous pooling) ventricle results in a reflex

withdrawal of sympathetic tone, with resultant hypotension and bradycardia. Because of the fixed obstruction in significant aortic stenosis and severe pulmonary hypertension, the patient's ability to recover from this reflex response is significantly impaired, and thus the symptomatic hypotension can be sustained and even fatal.

A previous cerebrovascular accident is not an absolute contraindication to tilt-table testing. Although avoidance of systemic hypotension during an acute cerebrovascular accident is desirable, transient episodes of systemic hypotension in patients with a previous cerebrovascular accident have not been shown to be harmful. Similarly, tilt-table testing and even carotid sinus massage have been safely performed in patients with carotid bruits or carotid artery disease on ultrasound. The induction of syncope during tilt-table testing in itself has never been shown to be harmful. Consciousness is restored within seconds of being returned to the horizontal position. Elderly patients who are unable to stand unassisted can safely undergo tilt-table testing. A safety strap can be used, and lower angles of tilting can permit venous pooling without placing the patient in an upright position that he or she is unable to maintain.

References

1. Larmarre-Cliche M, Cusson J. The fainting patient: value of the head-upright tilt-table test in adult patients with orthostatic intolerance. *CMAJ.* 2001;164(3):372–376.
2. Sutton R, Bloomfield DM. Indications, methodology, and classification of results of tilt-table testing. *Am J Cardiol.* 1999;84(8A):10Q–19Q.

71. A 75-year-old woman comes to the office because of pain and swelling of the right forefoot that have progressed over the past 3 weeks. She relates going on a 2-mile walk prior to the onset of symptoms. The symptoms began as a mild ache but have become increasingly intense with her usual walking. Two weeks ago she visited the local emergency department for the pain; radiographs demonstrated normal metatarsophalangeal joints and no fractures. She has tried nonsteroidal anti-inflammatory agents, ice, and warm compresses without relief.

On physical examination, vital signs are normal. She has good pedal pulses and normal sensation. The right foot is tender to palpation at the midshaft of the second metatarsal. There is no pain with range of motion to the second metatarsophalangeal joint. There is callus on the plantar aspect of the second metatarsophalangeal joint. Ankle joint range of motion is less than 5 degrees with maximal dorsiflexion. A moderate hallux valgus and bunion are present.

What is the most likely diagnosis?

(A) Stress fracture
(B) Gout
(C) Morton's neuroma
(D) Ganglion cyst
(E) Degenerative joint disease

ANSWER: A

In 95% of cases, stress fracture appears in the lower extremities, is generally the sequelae of overuse, and occurs when repetitive, subthreshold stress exceeds the bones' reparative capacity. In the foot, stress fractures affect the second to fourth metatarsals approximately 90% of the time. Postmenopausal women often have osteoporosis or osteopenia. As a result, women are more likely than men to have stress fractures.

The hallmark finding is pinpoint tenderness on the affected metatarsal with surrounding edema. Initial radiographs are often normal; abnormal findings may not be evident until 3 to 6 weeks after injury. When present, the typical radiographic changes are a linear cortical lucent region with periosteal and endosteal thickening. Fractures that occurred several weeks earlier will also have bone callus formation about the fracture site. A three-phase bone scan is the gold standard for diagnosis when radiographs are normal. Hallux valgus deformities suggest lack of normal weight-bearing force under the first metatarsal and often result in increased pressure to the adjacent lesser metatarsals, as manifested in this patient by the plantar callus under the second metatarsophalangeal joint. Additionally, an Achilles tendon contracture induces "toe-walking" and subsequent increased forefoot pressure. The increased weight-bearing pressure, along with prolonged repetitive stress, increases risk for stress fracture.

Gout affects joints and would induce pain with toe range of motion. Morton's neuroma elicits pain with palpation in the intermetatarsal space and not the bone. It can also cause shooting, burning pain to the distal toes to which it provides innervation. A ganglion cyst rarely is painful and would be visible as a soft palpable mass. Degenerative joint disease, like gout, is painful with range of motion.

References

1. Haverstock BD. Stress fractures of the foot and ankle. *Clin Podiatr Med Surg.* 2001;18(2):273–284.
2. Weinfeld SB, Haddad SL, Myerson MS. Metatarsal stress fractures. *Clin Sports Med.* 1997;16(2):319–338.

72. A 70-year-old woman is concerned about a marked decrease in libido and near complete loss of interest in being sexually active with her partner. This has occurred gradually over 4 years. She previously had intercourse 1 to 2 times per week but stopped having sexual fantasies about 1 year ago. She has hypertension and osteoporosis. She takes hydrochlorothiazide, enalapril, and alendronate. The patient stopped estrogen-progesterone therapy 7 years ago when her hot flushes ceased. She has vaginal lubrication with stimulation, and her relationship with her partner remains strong. Physical examination is unremarkable, and she has no signs or symptoms of depression.

Which of the following may improve libido for this patient?

(A) Estrogen
(B) Growth hormone
(C) Progesterone
(D) Testosterone
(E) Cortisol

ANSWER: D

In women, androgen levels (testosterone) are linked to libido and sexual thoughts. Androgen production occurs in the ovaries and adrenal, and tends to decrease with age. Use of hormone replacement therapy tends to increase sex hormone–binding globulin, which results in lower levels of bioavailable testosterone. Defining normal androgen levels in women is difficult because of poor assay sensitivity for free and bioavailable testosterone, and because few women over age 65 have been included in studies setting normative values. Studies using testosterone implants, intramuscular testosterone, and estrogen plus methyltestosterone show increased sexual activity, sexual desire (libido), and fantasies; however, none of these formulations of testosterone is approved by the Food and Drug Administration for use in postmenopausal women with low libido. Long-term use of testosterone in women has not been well studied. Adverse effects, such as acne, hirsutism, and fluid retention, may occur, and 17α preparations are associated with hepatic toxicity. When considering testosterone treatment in women, discussion of risks and benefits is essential, as is acknowledgement of the limited amount of information available.

Growth hormone has no relationship to libido. Estrogen and progesterone may relieve vasomotor and vaginal symptoms of menopause, but are not directly involved in libido. Administration of cortisol will lower adrenocorticotropic hormone concentration and further reduce adrenal output of androgen.

References

1. Burger HG, Davis SR. The role of androgen therapy. *Best Pract Res Clin Obstet Gynaecol.* 2002;16(3):383–393.
2. Guay AT, Jacobson J. Decreased free testosterone and dehydroepiandrosterone-sulfate (DHEA-S) levels in women with decreased libido. *J Sex Marital Ther.* 2002;28(Suppl 1):129–142.
3. Lobo RA. Androgens in postmenopausal women: production, possible role, and replacement options. *Obstet Gynecol Surv.* 2001;56(6):361–376.
4. Lobo RA, Rosen RC, Yang HM, et al. Comparative effects of oral esterified estrogens with and without methyltestosterone on endocrine profiles and dimensions of sexual function in postmenopausal women with hypoactive sexual desire. *Fertil Steril.* 2003;79(6):1341–1352.

73. A 75-year-old man is brought to the emergency department because he has had fever, chills, and cough for the past 36 hours. He is visiting his daughter and grandchildren, two of whom were being treated for ear infections when he arrived.

On examination, his blood pressure is 128/70 mm Hg, pulse is 102 per minute, respiratory rate is 25 per minute, and oxygen saturation is 93% by pulse oximetry. His posterior pharynx is mildly erythematous without exudates. He has shotty cervical adenopathy. Coarse crackles are heard over the left lower lung field, and there is mild prolongation of expiration bilaterally. The rest of the examination is unremarkable. Laboratory studies are normal except for a leukocyte count of 14,000/μL with a left shift. Chest radiography demonstrates a left lower lobe infiltrate.

Which of the following is the most appropriate antibiotic treatment?

(A) Ticarcillin and clavulanate plus gentamicin
(B) Ceftriaxone
(C) Ampicillin and sulbactam
(D) Moxifloxacin
(E) Vancomycin

ANSWER: D

Community-acquired pneumonia is the fifth leading cause of death in people 65 and older. *Streptococcus pneumoniae* is involved in 48% of patients age 60 and older. In this patient, it is the most likely pathogen, especially since he was with children recently treated for otitis media. Pneumococcal polysaccharide immunization and influenza immunization remain the mainstay of prevention. The selection of initial treatment regimen and decision to hospitalize are important clinical decisions. Sputum cultures influence treatment, although the use of pneumococcal urinary antigen is gaining popularity for its sensitivity and specificity, as well as ease of use in a population where it can be difficult to obtain adequate sputum samples.

This patient is seriously ill (increased pulse and respiratory rate, and decreased oxygen saturation) and should be admitted to the hospital. Bacteremic pneumococcal pneumonia carries a mortality rate of 6% to 20%. Guidelines from the Infectious Disease Society of America, American Thoracic Society, and Canadian Infectious Diseases Society recommend a macrolide and β-lactam regimen or a respiratory fluoroquinolone for empiric treatment of patients admitted to the hospital for community-acquired pneumonia. Ticarcillin and clavulanate plus gentamicin would not be appropriate in this patient. Ceftriaxone alone is inadequate. Vancomycin would not adequately cover typical organisms in community-acquired pneumonia. Therefore, moxifloxacin, a respiratory quinolone, is the best choice for monotherapy in this patient.

References

1. Mandell LA, Bartlett JG, Dowell SF, et al.; Infectious Diseases Society of America. Update of practice guidelines for the management of acquired pneumonia in immunocompetent adults. *Clin Infect Dis.* 2003;37(11):1405–1433. Available at http://www.journals.uchicago.edu/IDSA/guidelines (accessed September 2005).
2. Niederman MS, Mandell LA, Anzueto A, et al.; American Thoracic Society. Guidelines for the management of adults with community-acquired pneumonia: diagnosis, assessment of severity, antimicrobial therapy, and prevention. *Am J Respir Crit Care Med.* 2001;163(7):1730–1754.

74. A 75-year-old man returns to the office for a follow-up visit after a 6-week trial of St. John's wort 300 mg two to three times daily. At the initial visit, he met criteria for major depressive disorder but denied having recurrent thoughts of death or suicidal ideation. He has a history of hypertension, which is well controlled on a low-salt diet and hydrochlorothiazide 12.5 mg daily, and osteoarthritis, for which he occasionally takes acetaminophen. He has no history of mental health problems. He was reluctant to take a prescription antidepressant but suggested trying St. John's wort. At follow-up, there is no apparent improvement in his depression, and he now agrees to begin treatment with sertraline.

Which of the following is the best recommendation with respect to the St. John's wort?

(A) Continue St. John's wort and begin sertraline.
(B) Discontinue St. John's wort and begin sertraline after 4 weeks.
(C) Discontinue St. John's wort and begin sertraline the next day.
(D) Discontinue St. John's wort and begin sertraline in 1 week.

ANSWER: D

St. John's wort inhibits neuronal reuptake of serotonin, norepinephrine, and dopamine. Case reports of St. John's wort used concurrently with a selective serotonin-reuptake inhibitor (SSRI) describe symptoms characteristic of central serotonin excess. In one case, a patient developed nausea, anxiety, restlessness, and irritability after taking St. John's wort for 2 days with ongoing sertraline treatment. Another patient became incoherent, groggy, and lethargic following a single dose of paroxetine 20 mg added to ongoing use of St. John's wort 600 mg per day. The patient had previously been treated with paroxetine for 8 months without adverse effect.

The active constituents of St. John's wort are thought to be hypericin and hyperforin. The elimination half-lives of hypericin and hyperforin are 43 hours and 9 hours, respectively. Since it takes five half-lives to eliminate about 95% of a medication, the risk of developing central serotonin excess may be minimized by waiting 7 to 10 days before starting an SSRI following use of St. John's wort.

References

1. Ang-Lee MK, Moss J, Yuan C. Herbal medicines and perioperative care. *JAMA.* 2001;286(2):208–216.
2. Henderson L, Yue QY, Bergquist C, et al. St John's wort (*Hypericum perforatum*): drug interactions and clinical outcomes. *Br J Clin Pharmacol.* 2002;54(4):349–356.
3. Izzo AA, Ernst E. Interactions between herbal medicines and prescribed drugs: a systematic review. *Drugs.* 2001; 61(15):2163–2175.

75. An 82-year-old man is admitted with acute right upper quadrant pain and an impacted gall stone. An open cholecystectomy is planned once the patient has been stabilized and fully assessed.

The patient resides at home with his wife. His past medical history includes: a 50-pack-per-year cigarette history and current smoking; chronic obstructive pulmonary disease for 5 years, stable on an ipratropium-albuterol metered-dose inhaler and occasional short courses of oral corticosteroids. He has no prior cardiac history and is taking no medications other than his pulmonary drugs.

On physical examination he has a body mass index (kg/m^2) of 34, blood pressure 132/78 mm Hg, heart rate 88, respiratory rate 18; he is afebrile. Lung examination shows distant breath sounds with end expiratory wheezes throughout both lung fields. The remainder of his examination is unremarkable.

Other assessments show:

FEV$_1$	30% of predicted
Electrocardiogram	normal
Chest x-ray	hyperlucent lung fields, no infiltrates, and no changes of the cardiac silhouette
Arterial blood gas (room air)	pH 7.42, PCO_2 48 mm Hg, PO_2 68 mm Hg, HCO$_3$ 31 mEq/L
Blood urea nitrogen	34 mg/dL
Serum albumin	2.9 gm/dL

What conveys the greatest risk for postoperative respiratory failure in this patient?

(A) Age greater than 69 years
(B) History of chronic obstructive pulmonary disease
(C) Obesity
(D) Upper abdominal surgery
(E) Albumin less than 3.0 mg/dL

ANSWER: D

Respiratory failure is a recognized postoperative complication for older patients undergoing surgery, but age alone is not a major risk factor for postoperative pulmonary complications. The relative risk for pulmonary complication related to advanced age is approximately doubled. Comorbidities and the type of surgery to be performed play a much larger role in predicting postoperative pulmonary complications. Smoking multiplies the relative risk by approximately 3 and chronic obstructive pulmonary disease by 3 to 4. Obesity has not been found to be a risk factor for postoperative pulmonary complications in older patients; however, the presence of obesity-associated obstructive sleep apnea may confer added risk. Albumin levels less than 3.0 gm/dL increase the risk by 2.5 and blood urea nitrogen greater than 30 mg/dL by 2.3.

The strongest predictor of postoperative respiratory failure remains the type of surgery being performed. Upper abdominal surgery confers a 4.2-fold increased risk of respiratory failure during the postoperative period. Repair of an abdominal aneurysm increases the risk of postoperative respiratory failure by 14, thoracic surgery by 8. Emergency surgery also adds significantly to the risk of postoperative respiratory failure.

The risk of postoperative respiratory failure can be predicted in men undergoing noncardiac surgery by using the Arozullah Multifactorial Risk Index. This index assigns points on the basis of the type of surgery, emergent versus nonemergent surgery, albumin, blood urea nitrogen, functional status, history of chronic obstructive pulmonary disease, and age. Patients are assigned to one of five postoperative respiratory risk categories on the basis of total points. By the use of criteria set forth in the Arozullah Index, the patient in this case would score a total of 34 points, which would assign a 10.1% risk of postoperative respiratory failure.

References

1. Arozullah AM, Daley J, Henderson EG, et al. Multifactorial risk index for predicting postoperative respiratory failure in men after major noncardiac surgery. The National Veteran Administration Surgical Quality Improvement Program. *Ann Surg.* 2000;232(2):242–253.
2. Gupta RM, Parvizi J, Hanssen AD, et al. Postoperative complications in patients with obstructive sleep apnea syndrome undergoing hip or knee replacement: a case-control study. *Mayo Clin Proc.* 2001;76(9):897–905.
3. Liu LL, Leung JM. Predicting adverse postoperative outcomes in patients aged 80 years or older. *J Am Geriatr Soc.* 2000;48(4):405–412.
4. Smetana GW. Preoperative pulmonary assessment of the older adult. *Clin Geriatr Med.* 2003;19(1):35–55.

76. An 84-year-old woman comes to the office because she has "a weak bladder." For over 15 years she has had occasional leakage of urine with coughing, sneezing, and laughing. Over the last 3 years she has had gradually worsening symptoms of overactive bladder; she now voids about eight times daily and awakens three to four times each night to void. She uses adult diapers because she has five to six episodes of urge incontinence per 24-hour period. She has gastroesophageal reflux and glaucoma; her medications are a proton-pump inhibitor and timolol eye drops.

On physical examination, she has a moderately large cystocele and reduced rectal sphincter tone that she cannot voluntarily increase. Cough test for stress incontinence is negative; after voiding 250 mL, her postvoid residual is 35 mL. Urinalysis is negative.

Which of the following is the most appropriate initial management?

(A)   Trial of extended-release oxybutynin, 5 mg daily
(B)   Trial of long-acting tolterodine, 4 mg daily
(C)   Topical estrogen cream and instructions on pelvic muscle exercises
(D)   Referral to a gynecologist for consideration of surgical intervention
(E)   Biofeedback for bladder training with pelvic muscle exercises

ANSWER: E

This patient has symptoms typical of mixed incontinence, which is common in older women. Usually, the overactive bladder symptoms are more frequent and bothersome than the stress incontinence. The most appropriate initial treatment for this patient is bladder training with pelvic muscle exercises taught using biofeedback.

Topical estrogen may be appropriate for older postmenopausal women with urinary incontinence and severe vaginal atrophy or atrophic vaginitis. However, recent data suggest that systemic estrogen may not be effective for stress, urge, or mixed stress and urge urinary incontinence. Instructions on pelvic muscle exercises can be effective in older women (in most studies the average age is in the early to mid-60s) for symptoms of stress, urge, or mixed incontinence. Many older women, however, especially those who cannot identify their sphincter muscles on pelvic examination, require biofeedback-assisted training in order to identify and strengthen pelvic muscle.

A trial of a bladder-relaxant drug as initial treatment in this patient would be less appropriate than nonpharmacologic therapy, especially since this patient's glaucoma and gastroesophageal reflux could be exacerbated by an anticholinergic drug.

Though surgery can be very effective in well-selected patients with pure stress incontinence, it would not help with the overactive symptoms this woman experiences.

References
1. Burgio KL, Goode PS, Locher JL, et al. Behavioral training with and without biofeedback in the treatment of urge incontinence in older women: a randomized controlled trial. *JAMA.* 2002;288(18):2293–2299.
2. Burgio KL, Locher JL, Goode PS, et al. Behavioral vs drug treatment for urge urinary incontinence in older women: a randomized controlled trial. *JAMA.* 1998;280(23):1995–2000.
3. Hendrix SL, Cochrane BB, Nygaard IE, et al. Effects of estrogen with and without progestin on urinary incontinence. *JAMA.* 2005;293(8):935–948.
4. Roe B, Williams K, Palmer M. Bladder training for urinary incontinence in adults. *Cochrane Database Syst Rev.* 2000;(2):CD001308.

77. A 76-year-old man comes to the emergency department following the abrupt onset of rectal bleeding. He has a history of coronary heart disease, heart failure, renal insufficiency, gastroesophageal reflux disease, and degenerative joint disease. Daily medications include metoprolol, furosemide, potassium chloride, simvastatin, celecoxib, and lansoprazole. The bleeding stops spontaneously. Diagnostic colonoscopy, performed after oral cleansing with polyethylene glycol and electrolyte solution, demonstrates residual blood in the ascending colon, scattered diverticula in the sigmoid colon, and multiple, 5-mm, flat cherry-red lesions in the cecum.

What is the most likely cause for bleeding in this patient?

(A)   Angiodysplasia
(B)   Nonspecific colitis
(C)   Aortoenteric fistula
(D)   Upper gastrointestinal lesion

ANSWER: A

The incidence of lower gastrointestinal bleeding increases more than 200-fold between ages 20 and 80. Angiodysplasia, also called *arteriovenous malformation* or *vascular ectasia*, is the source of lower gastrointestinal bleeding in up to 20% of older patients and occurs with equal frequency in men and women. Two thirds of cases are found in persons older than age 70. More than half are located in the cecum and proximal ascending colon, but they may occur throughout the gastrointestinal tract, usually are multiple, and are 5 to 10 mm wide. They are dilated, thin-walled vessels in the mucosa and submucosa that are lined by endothelium or by smooth muscle. In more than 90% of cases, bleeding stops spontaneously. Typically, diagnosis is by direct visualization by colonoscopy, but mesenteric angiography is more sensitive than colonoscopy and can detect angiodysplasia deep in the submucosa that may not be visible grossly.

Diverticular disease is the cause in up to 37% of older patients with brisk rectal bleeding. The prevalence of diverticular disease is age dependent, increasing to 30% by age 60 and to 65% by age 85. Diverticula occur at weak points in the bowel wall, usually in the sigmoid colon, where blood vessels penetrate the circular muscle of the bowel. Diverticular bleeding is usually painless and self-limited, and it rarely coexists with acute diverticulitis.

Diverticular bleeding and angiodysplasia are responsible for almost 60% of cases of lower gastrointestinal bleeding in older adults. Other sources of bleeding include colorectal neoplasms, an upper gastrointestinal source, colitis (from ischemia, inflammation, infection, or radiation), solitary rectal ulcers, and hemorrhoids. Aortoenteric fistula is a less common cause.

Approximately 10% of cases of major lower intestinal bleeding and 20% of cases of minor bleeding in elderly persons are caused by benign or malignant neoplasm. In 15% of older adults, the source of lower gastrointestinal bleeding is in the upper gastrointestinal tract. Upper intestinal endoscopy may be necessary to reveal the source of bleeding.

An infectious cause should be excluded in an older patient with acute bloody diarrhea. *Salmonella* organisms and *Escherichia coli* O157:H7 serotypes are common in elderly patients. *Clostridium difficile*–induced diarrhea rarely causes bleeding.

Nonsteroidal anti-inflammatory agents have been implicated as a cause of nonspecific colitis, exacerbation of idiopathic inflammatory bowel disease, and diverticular bleeding.

References

1. Coppola A, De Stefano V, Tufano A, et al. Long-lasting intestinal bleeding in an old patient with multiple mucosal vascular abnormalities and Glanzmann's thrombasthenia: 3 year pharmacological management. *J Intern Med.* 2002;252(3):271–275.
2. Farrell JJ, Friedman LS. Gastrointestinal bleeding in the elderly. *Gastroenterol Clin North Am.* 2001;30(2):377–407.
3. Junquera F, Quiroga S, Saperas E, et al. Accuracy of helical computed tomographic angiography for the diagnosis of colonic angiodysplasia. *Gastroenterology.* 2000;119(2):293–299.

78. A 68-year-old woman comes to the office for follow-up management of a 2.5-cm left adrenal gland mass. The mass was detected 1 month ago on computed tomography (CT) done as part of an emergency department evaluation for abdominal pain. The abdominal pain has since resolved, and she is asymptomatic. She has no history of malignancy. On physical examination, body mass index (kg/m^2) is 31, blood pressure is 145/90 mm Hg, and pulse rate is 72 per minute. There are no signs of hirsutism or virilization.

What is the most appropriate next step?

(A) CT-guided fine-needle aspirate of the mass
(B) Laboratory tests for hormone hypersecretion
(C) Excision of the mass via laparoscopy
(D) Spironolactone, 25 mg daily
(E) Repeat CT scan in 6 months

ANSWER: B

This patient's adrenal mass was found incidentally. In autopsy studies, an adrenal mass is present in at least 3% of persons over age 50. Most cause no health problems, but approximately 1 of every 4000 adrenal tumors is malignant. Size appears to be the greatest risk factor for malignancy.

The first step in the evaluation of an adrenal gland mass is to assess for hormone hypersecretion. Either a 1-mg overnight dexamethasone-suppression test or a 24-hour urinary free cortisol level is obtained to assess for Cushing's syndrome. Either 24-hour fractionated urinary catecholamine or plasma free metanephrine level is measured to exclude the possibility of pheochromocytoma. In patients with hypertension, serum potassium, plasma aldosterone concentration, and plasma renin activity should be measured to assess for primary hyperaldosteronism (Conn's syndrome).

Excluding Cushing's syndrome, pheochromocytoma, and hyperaldosteronism is particularly relevant in this case since the patient is overweight and hypertensive. A hormonally active tumor should be excluded before limiting management to a program of diet and exercise. Since her hypertension is mild, pharmacotherapy may be safely deferred until the diagnostic evaluation has been completed, especially since spironolactone will alter the aldosterone-to-renin ratio.

In general, CT-guided fine-needle aspiration biopsy is reserved for patients with a history of cancer (particularly lung, breast, and kidney) with no other signs of metastasis, or for when an adrenal mass appears heterogeneous with high attenuation (more than 20 Hounsfield units) on noncontrast CT. Pheochromocytoma should always be excluded before fine-needle aspiration or surgery is attempted to avoid the possibility of a hypertensive crisis.

A repeat CT scan would be inappropriate as it is necessary to assess for hormone hypersecretion.

Surgery is generally recommended for patients with hormonally active adrenal tumors or with tumors greater than 6 cm.

Reference

1. Grumbach MM, Biller BM, Braunstein GD, et al. Management of the clinically inapparent adrenal mass ("incidentaloma"). *Ann Intern Med*. 2003;138(5):424–429.

79. A 70-year-old Hispanic woman whose medical care has been limited to primary care medical follow-up has found reading more difficult in the past month. When reading, she is unable to follow the text and find the next line. She rarely leaves her home. She has hypertension and peripheral vascular disease, and she has lived with her family since having a stroke 7 years ago. Open-angle glaucoma was diagnosed 20 years ago. She has received no follow-up care.

Which of the following is the most likely cause of her reading disability?

(A) New stroke
(B) Macular degeneration
(C) Retinal hemorrhage
(D) Open-angle glaucoma
(E) Retinal detachment

ANSWER: D

In a recent study of a large Hispanic population in Arizona, open-angle glaucoma was found to be the leading cause of bilateral blindness. Chronic open-angle glaucoma is asymptomatic until there is progressive loss in the field of vision. This patient has not been followed by an eye care specialist who would assess her optic nerve, intraocular pressure, and visual fields. Therefore, glaucoma may have progressed without symptoms until now. Advanced visual field loss is associated with a loss of central field fixation and constriction of the field. This makes it difficult to follow reading material from line to line. As she rarely leaves the familiar surroundings of her home, the patient may not have noticed a loss of peripheral field vision.

A stroke would cause a more sudden loss of vision, such as a bilateral field cut. A retinal hemorrhage would be more acute, and the patient would complain of a new and large floater. Macular degeneration would cause a loss of central vision, usually with some distortion, and the patient would have blurring rather than an inability to follow text. Retinal detachment presents suddenly with decreased vision. However, if the vision is good in the unaffected eye, she may not notice the decreased visual function.

References

1. Brodie SE. Aging and disorders of the eye. In: Tallis RC, Fillit HM, eds. *Brocklehurst's Textbook of Geriatric Medicine and Gerontology*. 6th ed. London: Churchill Livingston; 2003:735–747.
2. Coleman AL, Brigatti L. The glaucomas. *Min Med*. 2001;92(5):365–379.
3. Rodriguez J, Sanchez R, Munoz B, et al. Causes of blindness and visual impairment in a population-based sample of U.S. Hispanics. *Ophthalmology*. 2002;109(4):737–743.

80. An 81-year-old female resident of an assisted-living facility comes to the emergency department with complaints of fatigue, nausea, and frequent urination. She has a history of hypertension, osteoporosis with spine compression fractures, osteoarthritis, and macular degeneration. The patient has previously been independent in instrumental activities of daily living, except for medications, and she uses a walker for ambulation. She is admitted to an Acute Care for the Elderly (ACE) unit with urosepsis.

Which of the following is a component of this type of intervention?

(A) An environment that promotes mobility and orientation
(B) A care map to outline her current medications
(C) A protocol outlining the length of stay for urosepsis
(D) A discussion with her family about the need for restorative care
(E) A teaching session on health promotion interventions

ANSWER: A

This patient was fortunate to have an Acute Care for the Elderly (ACE) unit in her area. In several major hospital studies, ACE units show promise in preserving activities of daily living. These units focus on multidisciplinary approaches to care of the hospitalized older adult. Components of an ACE unit include an environment that promotes mobility and orientation, nursing initiated protocols for independent self-care, strong interdisciplinary planning with early social work screening, and medical care review to promote optimal regimens. Some studies suggest that ACE units are associated with less functional decline in activities of daily living at discharge and a trend toward decreased length of hospitalization. However, it has also been shown that admission to an ACE unit early on in the hospital course is important, as there is little benefit once a patient has been stabilized on another unit. The multidisciplinary nature of the care and the emphasis on function as well as disease have made ACE units a unique model for the care of hospitalized older adults.

References
1. Counsell SR, Holder CM, Liebenauer LL, et al. Effects of a multicomponent intervention on functional outcomes and process of care in hospitalized older patients: a randomized controlled trial of Acute Care for Elders (ACE) in a community hospital. *J Am Geriatr Soc.* 2000;48(12):1572–1581.
2. Inouye SK, Bogardus ST Jr, Baker DI, et al. The Hospital Elder Life Program: a model of care to prevent cognitive and functional decline in older hospitalized patients. *J Am Geriatr Soc.* 2000;48(12):1697–1706.

81. The most commonly overlooked aspect of the care for hip fracture patients upon discharge from a subacute unit and arrival in the rehabilitation setting is:

(A) Deep-vein thrombosis prophylaxis
(B) Delirium prevention
(C) Osteoporosis treatment
(D) Nutritional support

ANSWER: C

The medical consultation for patients with hip fractures is multifaceted, and its emphasis depends on the patient's phase of illness. One neglected area has been the evaluation and treatment of osteoporosis. Several studies suggest that few patients with hip fracture receive evaluation and adequate treatment for osteoporosis, even though they are at risk for another osteoporotic fracture. Only 12% to 24% of hip fracture patients report having had dual radiographic absorptiometry. Vitamin D and calcium were reported to be prescribed in only 3% to 27% of fracture patients. Antiresorptive agents were used more frequently (12% to 79% of patients) than vitamin D and calcium, although fewer than 10% of patients received bisphosphonates. Up to 40% of hip fracture patients received no osteoporosis therapy, and only 13% received therapy that followed guidelines of the National Osteoporosis Foundation. A system to ensure evaluation and management of osteoporosis appears to be needed.

Venous thromboembolism prevention, delirium prevention, and nutritional support should be addressed during the acute phase of the hospital stay. These issues should have been resolved before discharge from a subacute setting.

References

1. Bellantonio S, Fortinsky R, Prestwood K. How well are community-living women treated for osteoporosis after hip fracture? *J Am Geriatr Soc.* 2001;49(9):1197–1204.
2. Harrington JT, Broy SB, Derosa AM, et al. Hip fracture patients are not treated for osteoporosis: a call to action. *Arthritis Rheum.* 2002;15;47(6):651–654.
3. Kamel HK, Hussain MS, Tariq S, et al. Failure to diagnose and treat osteoporosis in elderly patients hospitalized with hip fracture. *Am J Med.* 2000;109(4):326–328.

82. An 83-year-old woman comes to the office for a follow-up examination. She has a history of hypertension, osteoporosis, and mild osteoarthritis, and she had a duodenal ulcer bleed 10 years ago. She states that she feels fine. She does light housework and can walk about two blocks, being limited by arthritis in her right knee. Current medications include hydrochlorothiazide, losartan, ranitidine, calcium, vitamin D, and ibuprofen as needed.

On physical examination, she is alert and fully oriented. She has an irregular heart rate of 85 per minute. Blood pressure is 150/80 mm Hg. Neck veins are flat and there is no thyromegaly. Lungs are clear. Cardiac auscultation reveals an irregular rhythm with no murmurs or gallops. Abdominal examination is unremarkable, and there is no peripheral edema.

Electrocardiography (ECG) reveals atrial fibrillation with moderate ventricular response rate, left ventricular hypertrophy, and a nonspecific ST-T abnormality; the atrial fibrillation did not appear on an ECG obtained 1 year earlier. Echocardiography reveals left ventricular hypertrophy with normal ejection fraction and mild diastolic dysfunction, mild left atrial enlargement, and mild thickening of the aortic valve. Transesophageal echocardiography shows no clot. Thyroid function and serum electrolytes are normal.

What is the most appropriate treatment for this patient's atrial fibrillation?

(A) Aspirin
(B) Warfarin
(C) Warfarin for 3 to 4 weeks followed by cardioversion
(D) Immediate cardioversion
(E) Amiodarone

ANSWER: B

Atrial fibrillation is a potent risk factor for the development of stroke and other arterial thromboembolic events, and the risk of stroke attributable to atrial fibrillation increases with age. Five large prospective randomized trials have shown that long-term anticoagulation with warfarin (international normalized ratio maintained between 2.0 and 3.0) reduces the risk of stroke by about two thirds, and warfarin[OL] is recommended for all older adults with atrial fibrillation and no contraindications. Aspirin is less effective than warfarin in reducing stroke risk but is an acceptable alternative to warfarin in older patients with contraindications to systemic anticoagulation, such as active bleeding or frequent falls. A remote history of a peptic ulcer bleed is not a contraindication to anticoagulation. Cardioversion and antiarrhythmic drug therapy have not been shown to reduce stroke risk or mortality in the absence of significant symptoms and may be associated with an increased risk of hospitalization.

References

1. Fuster V, Ryden LE, Asinger RW, et al. ACC/AHA/ESC guidelines for the management of patients with atrial fibrillation: executive summary. *Circulation.* 2001;104(17):2118–2150.
2. Wolf PA, Abbott RD, Kannel WB. Atrial fibrillation as an independent risk factor for stroke: the Framingham Study. *Stroke.* 1991;22 (8):983–988.
3. Wyse DG, Waldo AL, DiMarco JP, et al. A comparison of rate control and rhythm control in patients with atrial fibrillation. *N Engl J Med.* 2002;347(23):1825–1833.

[OL] Not approved by the U.S. Food and Drug Administration for this use.

83. A 70-year-old woman comes to the office for management of osteoporosis. She has a history of nephrolithiasis. She went through menopause approximately 18 years ago and takes the following medications daily: alendronate 10 mg, medroxyprogesterone acetate 2.5 mg, calcium carbonate 1500 mg, and vitamin D 800 IU. She drinks three glasses of milk and several servings of yogurt and cheese daily. Her bone mineral density, as measured by dual energy x-ray absorptiometry (DEXA), reveals a T score of –3.0 at the hip and –2.5 at the lumbar spine.

Laboratory studies:

Ionized calcium	6.1 mEq/L ↑
Phosphorus	2.7 mg/dL ↓
Parathyroid hormone	62 pg/mL →
Serum creatinine	0.9 mg/dL
Thyrotropin	2.1 µU/mL

What is the most likely cause of this patient's hypercalcemia?

(A) Primary hyperparathyroidism
(B) Milk-alkali syndrome
(C) Humoral hypercalcemia of malignancy
(D) Granulomatous disease

ANSWER: A

The patient's history of nephrolithiasis coupled with her fairly severe bone loss (despite intake of alendronate, calcium, and vitamin D) raises concern for secondary causes of osteoporosis, such as hyperthyroidism, hyperparathyroidism, Cushing's syndrome, or glucocorticoid therapy. This patient has evidence of hypercalcemia. In the ambulatory care setting, the most common cause of hypercalcemia is primary hyperparathyroidism. Primary hyperparathyroidism is more common in women, and the prevalence increases with age (the incidence in postmenopausal women is fivefold higher than in the general population).

The serum parathyroid hormone level is the key to diagnosis of primary hyperparathyroidism. In this case, the parathyroid hormone level is inappropriately normal, in the context of hypercalcemia. The low serum phosphorus level also suggests hyperparathyroidism.

Although this patient's high intake of calcium supplements and dairy products suggests milk-alkali syndrome, the preserved renal function and the high-normal parathyroid hormone level do not support this diagnosis (parathyroid hormone would be suppressed in milk-alkali syndrome). Similarly, humoral hypercalcemia of malignancy and granulomatous disease are unlikely, since the parathyroid hormone level would be low or undetectable in these conditions.

References

1. Bilezikian JP. Primary hyperparathyroidism: when to observe and when to operate. *Endocrinol Metab Clin North Am.* 2000;29(3):465–478.
2. Favus M, ed. *The American Society for Bone and Mineral Research Primer on Metabolic Bone Diseases and Disorders of Mineral Metabolism.* 4th ed. New York: Lippincott Williams and Wilkins; 1999.

84. A 78-year old woman with moderate Alzheimer's disease is admitted to a nursing home with a dementia unit because she is no longer able to live alone. Her insurance coverage is traditional Medicare Parts A and B. Her only source of income is her monthly $847 ($10,164 per year) check from Social Security. At the time of admission to the nursing home, her life savings are $58,000, and she has no family, friends, or other assets as sources of financial support.

Assuming that the patient lives in the nursing home for the next 5 years, what is the principal source of payment for her stay?

(A) Medicare Part A
(B) Medicare Part B
(C) Medicaid
(D) Medigap insurance
(E) Her life savings

ANSWER: C

Long-term nursing-home care is principally financed through out-of-pocket expenses and Medicaid. The average cost for a semiprivate nursing-home bed in the United States in 2004 was $61,685 per year, according to the annual MetLife Market Survey on Nursing Home and Home Care Costs. In this case, the patient's life savings would be consumed at a rate of at least $51,521 per year ($61,685 – $10,164). After her financial resources were depleted, she would qualify (criteria vary from state to state) for Medicaid, which would be the main source of funding for her long-term care. Medicare Part A provides limited coverage for skilled nursing-home care for rehabilitative services following a 3-day hospital stay. Medicare Part B and Medigap policies, a form of supplemental insurance, do not cover custodial nursing-home care other than physician fees. Supplemental insurance policies covering long-term nursing-home care are purchased by the rare individual and are usually expensive.

References

1. Centers for Medicare and Medicaid Services home page. Available at http://www.cms.hhs.gov (accessed September 2005).
2. The MetLife Market Survey on Nursing Home & Home Care Costs: September 2004. Available at http://www.metlife.com/WPSAssets/16651817681106065148V1FNursing%20Home%20Home%20Care%20Costs.pdf (accessed September 2005).

85. Which of the following is true regarding cochlear implants in older adults?

(A) They should have profound hearing loss (no residual hearing) to benefit optimally from an implant.

(B) They are not good operative candidates for implants

(C) Those with severe hearing loss are excellent candidates for an implant.

(D) They are not candidates for implants because of the high risk of meningitis.

(E) They need to pay for the procedure out of pocket as Medicare does not cover implants.

ANSWER: C

The cochlear implant is a surgically implanted prosthetic device that consists of two parts: the body of the implant and the electrode array. The body of the implant is placed in a depression made in the mastoid bone of the skull; the electrode array is placed within the cochlea. The electrodes stimulate the remaining auditory nerve fibers in the cochlea to produce sound electronically. Electrical sound information is sent through the auditory system to the brain. Because the technology has advanced, more people are now candidates for implants than a few years ago; candidates can have more residual hearing (be less deaf) than in the past.

The hearing loss can be severe to profound, and word recognition scores (with binaural hearing aids) can be as high as 60%. Individuals who receive an implant often combine it with a hearing aid, as this improves speech understanding.

Clinical data suggest that persons with severe hearing loss (that is, with some residual hearing) perform better with cochlear implants than persons with profound hearing loss and no residual hearing. In persons with residual hearing, the auditory nerve remains viable, allowing the brain-stem auditory pathways and the brain to receive auditory information.

Age is no longer a major consideration in choosing candidates for cochlear implants, and there is no specific upper age limit for eligibility. More important than chronologic age is medical status. Healthy persons in their 80s have done well with implants. The average cost of a cochlear implant in the United States is between $45,000 and $50,000. The cochlear implant surgery is covered under Part A or Part B of Medicare (depending on whether the surgery is performed on an inpatient or outpatient basis).

In July 2002 the Food and Drug Administration announced a possible link between bacterial meningitis and cochlear implantation. Many patients had preexisting risk factors, such as history of pre-implant meningitis, congenital inner-ear deformity, and basilar skull fracture. In reported cases the symptoms appeared as soon as 24 hours to more than 6 years after surgery. Most cases in the United States have been in children younger than 7 years. The Food and Drug Administration has identified the following groups as being at risk: children under 5 years old, elderly persons with congenital malformations of the cochlea that predispose them to meningitis, persons with immune deficiency, and persons who have been deafened by meningitis.

References

1. Florian J. As candidacy criteria loosen up, use of cochlear implants grows rapidly. *The Hearing Journal.* 2003;56:4.
2. Spitzer JB. Cochlear Implants and Options for Persons with Profound Hearing Impairment. Last revision January 1999. Available at: http://www.vard.org/mono/ear/spitzer.htm (accessed September 2005).

3. U.S. Food and Drug Administration. FDA Public Health Web Notification: Risk of Bacterial Meningitis in Children with Cochlear Implants. July 24, 2002; updated September 25, 2003. Available at: http://www.fda.gov/cdrh/safety/cochlear.html (accessed September 2005).

86. An 87-year old woman comes to the office because of short-term memory loss persisting for several months, which is getting worse according to her husband. She has some college education. She has a history of hypertension, which is well controlled with hydrochlorothiazide, 25 mg daily. She is otherwise in good health. She sleeps and eats normally and has no day-to-day problems except for occasional difficulty locating her car in the parking lot. Physical and neurologic examination reveal nothing remarkable. There is no evidence of sadness or anhedonia. She scores 25 of 30 points on the Mini–Mental State Examination, losing 3 points on recall and 2 on orientation.

What is the most likely cause of the memory complaint?

(A) Benign senescent forgetfulness
(B) Mild cognitive impairment
(C) Dementia
(D) Minor depression
(E) Major depression

ANSWER: B

This patient complains of memory loss that, according to her husband, appears to be worsening. There are no other cognitive complaints, and there are no other obvious medical problems. She continues to show a reasonable level of day-to-day functioning. Examination reveals abnormalities on the Mini–Mental State Examination (MMSE), especially the inability to recall three objects. There is no evidence of depressive symptoms. Given the absence of depressive or other psychiatric symptoms and the absence of a medical problem to explain the memory loss, the differential diagnosis focuses on age-related benign memory loss, mild cognitive impairment, and a dementia syndrome.

Mild cognitive impairment is most likely since the patient has a subjective memory complaint that is confirmed by an informant, and she has measurable memory impairment on the MMSE. The memory decline cannot be ascribed to aging alone, even in an 87-year-old woman, given her good health and level of education. She does not meet criteria for dementia because the cognitive decline affects only memory and she is functionally intact. Although the type of cognitive impairment can be determined on clinical grounds, identifying the cause may require a limited laboratory and imaging work-up, even though in most similar cases laboratory (thyroid tests, vitamin B_{12}, and metabolic panel) and brain imaging studies are normal.

Diagnosing mild cognitive impairment and differentiating it from usual aging are important for two reasons. First, since mild cognitive impairment progresses to Alzheimer-type dementia at the rate of about 10% to 15% per year, patients should be followed closely for further decline (especially if they drive), and appropriate treatment should be instituted as needed. Second, ongoing clinical trials are examining the efficacy of several medications in preventing progression of mild cognitive impairment to dementia. Already, in some memory clinics, patients with mild cognitive impairment are treated with cholinesterase inhibitors and vitamin E, although current data do not yet support this practice.

References
1. Petersen RC. Mild cognitive impairment as a diagnostic entity. *J Intern Med.* 2004;256(3):183–194.
2. Rabins PV, Lyketsos CG, Steele CD. *Practical Dementia Care.* New York: Oxford University Press; 1999.

87. A 68-year-old man comes to the office for follow-up management after external-beam radiation treatment to his prostate for a moderately differentiated adenocarcinoma (Gleason grades 3 and 4). Bone scan is negative for metastatic lesion. Before treatment, his prostate-specific antigen (PSA) level had increased from 3.0 to 21 over 3 years. After radiation treatment, his PSA level falls to 4.0, but over the next 6 months it increases to 7.0. He begins combined androgen blockade with flutamide and leuprolide, as prescribed by his urologist.

Which of the following may additionally benefit the patient now?

(A) Orchiectomy
(B) Ketoconazole
(C) Zoledronic acid RECLAST
(D) Cyclophosphamide CYTOXAN

ANSWER: C

In many cases, prostate cancer progresses slowly and can be considered more as a chronic illness than a life-threatening disease. This patient is at high risk for metastases, since he had a pretreatment PSA level above 20 and a combined Gleason grade of 7. Despite treatment with external-beam radiation, the PSA level increased, suggesting residual disease. Residual or recurrent disease can be treated by salvage surgery or androgen ablation. Since the patient was started on combined androgen ablation with flutamide and leuprolide, orchiectomy is not currently needed. Ketoconazole and chemotherapy should be considered only if androgen ablation fails.

The role of bisphosphonates such as zoledronic acid and pamidronate in prostate cancer is expanding. Bisphosphonates may help prevent osteoporosis and bone metastases and may improve bone pain. Osteoporosis is a complication of androgen-deprivation therapy in men with prostate carcinoma. Androgen deprivation, from bilateral orchiectomy or treatment with a gonadotropin-releasing hormone agonist, decreases bone mineral density and increases fracture risk. Other factors, including diet and life style, may contribute to bone loss. Intravenous pamidronate, a second-generation bisphosphonate, prevents bone loss during androgen-deprivation therapy. Zoledronic acid, a more potent third-generation bisphosphonate, prevents bone loss and increases bone mineral density during androgen deprivation-therapy. Its use for prevention of bone metastases from prostate cancer is off label.

In addition, bisphosphonates may have a direct antitumor effect, possibly related to inhibition of tumor cell adhesion and spread to bone, induction of apoptosis, anti-angiogenic properties, or increased T-cell counts. Although data are limited, both pamidronate and zoledronic acid have been shown to decrease skeletal-related events in prostate cancer patients. More research is needed before bisphosphonates are used for their anticancer properties. The role of bisphosphonates in treating bone pain in metastasis is more controversial, since some data suggest that they are not as effective as chemotherapy or targeted radiation therapy.

Treatment with cyclophosphamide[OL] is well tolerated in prostate cancer but response rates are low.

References

1. Santini D, Vespasiani Gentilucci U, et al. The antineoplastic role of bisphosphonates: from basic research to clinical evidence. *Ann Oncol.* 2003;14(10):1468–1476.
2. Smith MR. Diagnosis and management of treatment-related osteoporosis in men with prostate carcinoma. *Cancer.* 2003;97(3 Suppl):789–795.
3. Smith MR. Osteoporosis during androgen deprivation therapy for prostate cancer. *Urology.* 2002;60(3 Suppl 1):79–85; discussion 86.

88. A 75-year-old woman comes to the office for a routine visit. She has a history of hypertension, osteoporosis, chronic obstructive pulmonary disease, osteoarthritis, and insomnia. Two months ago she began celecoxib 100 mg daily for arthritis and diphenhydramine at bedtime for sleep. Other medications include lisinopril 40 mg daily, hydrochlorothiazide 25 mg daily, salmeterol two inhalations twice daily, ipratropium three inhalations four times daily, atenolol 75 mg daily, calcium carbonate 500 mg three times daily, alendronate 10 mg daily, and a multivitamin daily.

On examination, blood pressure is 162/82 mm Hg; this is consistent with home readings the patient has taken over the past month. At office visits 3 and 6 months ago, systolic blood pressure was between 148 and 152 mm Hg, and diastolic pressure was between 80 and 85 mm Hg.

Which of the following is the most appropriate intervention?

[OL] Not approved by the U.S. Food and Drug Administration for this use.

(A) Substitute furosemide for hydrochlorothiazide.
(B) Substitute acetaminophen for celecoxib.
(C) Increase atenolol.
(D) Substitute ramipril for lisinopril.
(E) Substitute zolpidem for diphenhydramine.

ANSWER: B

The recent addition of celecoxib is the most likely cause of her increased blood pressure. Traditional (nonselective) nonsteroidal anti-inflammatory drugs (NSAIDs) can increase blood pressure, especially in patients with hypertension. Emerging data indicate that cyclooxygenase-2 selective agents such as celecoxib may increase blood pressure to a similar extent as nonselective NSAIDs. Since this patient's hypertension is uncontrolled despite three medications, it would be prudent to initiate a different pain medication.

Hydrochlorothiazide is less effective in patients with kidney disease (creatinine clearance under 30 mL/min), but since this patient has no signs of kidney disease, changing hydrochlorothiazide to furosemide will likely not improve blood-pressure control. In addition, furosemide is a less potent antihypertensive than the thiazide diuretics. Since angiotensin-converting enzyme inhibitors have similar efficacy at equipotent doses, substituting ramipril for lisinopril would not be effective. Increasing the atenolol dose may improve blood-pressure control. But, because this patient has chronic obstructive pulmonary disease, it would be prudent to keep the β-blocker dosage low to avoid loss of β_1 selectivity that may occur with higher doses.

Although diphenhydramine may have adverse effects in elderly persons (dry mouth, constipation, urinary retention particularly in men with benign prostatic hyperplasia), it is not likely that stopping the diphenhydramine will improve her blood-pressure control.

References

1. Johnson DL, Hisel TM, Phillips BB. Effect of cyclooxygenase-2 inhibitors on blood pressure. *Ann Pharmacother.* 2003;37(3):442–446.
2. Whelton A. COX-2-specific inhibitors and the kidney: effect on hypertension and oedema. *J Hypertens.* 2002;20 Suppl 6:S31–S35.

89. An 85-year-old man is hospitalized for 6 days for lobar pneumonia, after which he is discharged to a nursing home for physical and pulmonary rehabilitation for 15 days. When he returns home, he requires outpatient in-home physical and respiratory therapy twice weekly for 3 weeks to restore physical strength and pulmonary functioning. He takes five prescription medications and sees a primary care physician monthly for follow-up.

The patient's only medical insurance coverage is traditional Medicare Parts A and B. The total hospital bill is $4,000. The total nursing-home bill is $3,000. The physical and respiratory therapy sessions are $160 per week for 3 weeks. His outpatient prescription medications cost $120 per month.

Beginning with the time of his hospitalization, which of the following services will cost the patient most in out-of-pocket expenses over 3 months?

(A) Hospitalization
(B) Nursing-home stay
(C) Home physical and respiratory therapy
(D) Outpatient prescription medications

ANSWER: A

This case illustrates the complex array of premiums, deductibles, and coverage options that characterizes the Medicare system and often bewilders its enrollees. Part A requires a significant deductible ($912 per 90-day benefit period in 2004) before its coverage is activated. Enrollees must either pay out-of-pocket or take out supplemental insurance to cover the deductible. In this case, all of the deductible would be used up (and paid out-of-pocket by the enrollee) during the hospital stay. Part A provides 100% coverage for hospital services after the deductible is paid for up to 60 days per benefit period. Part A also provides 100% coverage for the first 20 days of postacute rehabilitation in a nursing home if it is preceded by a hospital stay of at least 3 days' duration in the prior days. In this case, since the patient had the 6-day hospitalization, he would have no out-of-pocket expense for the rehabilitative nursing-home stay.

Part B covers 80% of outpatient services, such as physical and respiratory services, after a

$100 deductible is paid first by the enrollee. For this patient, the 3-month bill for these services is $480; his out-of-pocket contribution for these services would be $100 (for the Part B deductible) plus 20% of the remaining $380, or $176.

Since Medicare Parts A and B do not cover outpatient prescription medications, the patient's out-of-pocket expense for these would be $120 each month for 3 months, or $360.

References

1. Centers for Medicare and Medicaid Services. Medicare: The Official U.S. Government Site for People with Medicare page. Available at http://www.medicare.gov (accessed September 2005).
2. Centers for Medicare and Medicaid Services. *Your Medicare Benefits.* Baltimore, MD: US Department of Health and Human Services; July 2004. CMS Publications No. 10116. Available at http://www.medicare.gov/Publications/Pubs/pdf/10116.pdf (accessed September 2005).

90. A 66-year-old woman comes to the emergency department with severe abdominal pain, abdominal distention, low-grade fever, and tachycardia. She describes a history of postprandial abdominal pain that usually occurs 10 to 15 minutes after eating, gradually increases in severity, and plateaus before abating over 3 hours. She has lost 6.8 kg (15 lb) in the previous 4 months. Findings on physical examination include bilateral carotid bruits, regular tachycardia, systolic bruit in the upper abdomen, and a soft distended abdomen with few audible bowel sounds and mild, diffuse tenderness.

Which test is most helpful in confirming the diagnosis?

(A) Upper gastrointestinal and small bowel series
(B) Splanchnic angiography
(C) Abdominal magnetic resonance imaging
(D) Abdominal computed tomography
(E) Stool for occult blood

ANSWER: B

Chronic mesenteric ischemia should be considered when a patient reports postprandial generalized abdominal pain complicated by weight loss. Initially, the pain may be minimal and occur only after a large meal, but as the disease progresses the pain can become incapacitating after smaller meals and can lead to fear of eating. It usually reflects advanced systemic atherosclerosis, with generalized signs or symptoms such as carotid, coronary, or peripheral vascular disease. Serious complications include acute thrombosis and consequent bowel infarction. Physical findings are nonspecific; a systolic bruit is heard in the upper abdomen of approximately half the patients, but similar bruits are heard in 15% of healthy patients and are not diagnostic of chronic mesenteric insufficiency. Laboratory tests are also nonspecific; steatorrhea develops in approximately half of affected persons.

The diagnosis is based on the typical clinical symptoms and arteriographic demonstration of an occlusive process of the splanchnic vessels (celiac artery, superior mesenteric artery, and inferior mesenteric artery), as well as exclusion of other gastrointestinal diseases. Conventional radiologic examination of the gastrointestinal tract is helpful in excluding inflammatory or neoplastic processes that might mimic the disorder.

Because a rich collateral vascular supply forms, symptoms are often not evident until there is severe stenosis or complete obstruction of at least two of the three major splanchnic arteries. Angiography has shown stenosis or occlusion of at least two major vessels in 91% of patients, and involvement of all three vessels in 55%.

Duplex ultrasonography can be used to demonstrate the expected normal increase in postprandial splanchnic blood flow. Findings differ in patients with chronic mesenteric insufficiency. Doppler ultrasonography may demonstrate a marked decrease in or absence of blood flow in the major mesenteric arteries, or an inadequate or absent postprandial increase in splanchnic blood flow. Magnetic resonance angiography or oximetry and intestinal oxygen consumption are indirect measures of splanchnic blood flow and alone cannot be used to diagnose chronic mesenteric insufficiency.

Surgical revascularization offers long-term symptom-free survival for most patients. Selected patients may benefit from percutaneous transluminal mesenteric angiography with angioplasty, alone or in combination with insertion of a stent.

References

1. Greenwald DA, Brandt LJ, Reinus JF. Ischemic bowel disease in the elderly. *Gastroenterol Clin North Am.* 2001;30(2):445–473.
2. Lefkowitz Z, Cappell MS, Lookstein R, et al. Radiologic diagnosis and treatment of gastrointestinal hemorrhage and ischemia. *Med Clin North Am.* 2002;86(6):1357–1399.
3. Sreenarasimhaiah J. Diagnosis and management of intestinal ischemic disorders. *BMJ.* 2003; 326(7403):1376.

References

1. Hilton M, Pinder D. The Epley maneuver for benign paroxysmal positional vertigo—a systematic review. *Clin Otolaryngol.* 2002;27(6):440–445.
2. Magnusson M, Karlberg M. Peripheral vestibular disorders with acute onset of vertigo. *Curr Opin Neurol.* 2002;15(1):5–10.
3. Parnes LS, Agrawal SK, Atlas J. Diagnosis and management of benign paroxysmal positional vertigo (BPPV). *CMAJ.* 2003;169(7):681–693.
4. Serra A, Leigh RJ. Diagnostic value of nystagmus: spontaneous and induced ocular oscillations. *J Neurol Neurosurg Psychiatry.* 2002;73(6):615–618.

91. What type of nystagmus will be seen when a patient with benign paroxysmal positional vertigo is placed with the affected ear hanging down? (Latency is a delay in onset of nystagmus from the time of onset of positioning.)

    (A) No latency, torsional upbeat nystagmus lasting less than 1 minute
    (B) Latency, pure upbeat nystagmus lasting less than 1 minute
    (C) Latency, pure downbeat nystagmus persisting until position is changed
    (D) No latency, pure torsional upbeat nystagmus persisting until position is changed
    (E) Latency, torsional upbeat nystagmus lasting less than 1 minute

ANSWER: E

In benign paroxysmal vertigo, the features of nystagmus provide an important clue to whether the vertigo has a peripheral cause (otoconia debris in the posterior semicircular canal) or central cause (such as a cerebellar lesion). Features that are consistent with a peripheral cause are latency; duration less than 1 minute (usually about 15 seconds); fatigability with repeated positioning in the head-hanging (Dix-Hallpike) position; and a torsional, geotropic (beats toward the ground when placed with affected ear down), upbeat nystagmus. Nystagmus with a peripheral cause is never purely upbeat or downbeat. A central cause is likely if the nystagmus is purely upbeat or downbeat, and if it persists longer than 1 minute in the head-hanging position. Benign paroxysmal positional vertigo is less likely if the patient does not get better with repeated maneuvers.

92. A 75-year-old man is admitted to the hospital after he has a small left parietal stroke. The patient lives independently in the community. He does not drink or smoke. He has well-controlled hypertension on hydrochlorothiazide 25 mg daily. Routine posteroanterior and lateral chest radiographs demonstrate left upper lobe fibrocalcific changes suggestive of old tuberculosis infection. The patient denies ever having had tuberculosis or contact with persons with known active disease. Induration after purified protein derivative test measures 7 mm. Stain for acid-fast bacillus on each of three sequential early-morning sputum samples is negative.

What do current tuberculosis guidelines recommend?

    (A) Clinical observation with chest radiographs repeated at 6-month intervals for the next 2 years
    (B) Clinical observation with annual chest radiographs
    (C) A multidrug regimen to treat presumed active pulmonary tuberculosis
    (D) Therapy for latent tuberculosis bacillus infection

ANSWER: D

Tuberculosis is prevalent in almost one third of the world's population. Most affected persons have latent infection (previously termed *exposed*) rather than active disease. In the United States, the yearly incidence of active tuberculosis is approximately 5 to 10 cases per 100,000 persons. Many more patients have latent tuberculosis bacillus infection; active tuberculosis may develop in as many as 10% of them. Aging, medical comorbidity, and immunosuppression increase the risk of progression from latent to active disease. A purified protein derivative (PPD) test is considered positive when induration is greater than 5 mm in patients with fibrotic changes on chest radiograph consistent with prior tuberculosis. The American Thoracic Society recommends treatment for latent tuberculosis bacillus infection in patients who do not have active disease but have a positive PPD result and radiographically stable lesions suggestive of prior tuberculosis. Accepted regimens include a 3-month course of isoniazid, a 2-month course of combination therapy with rifampin and pyrazinamide, or rifampin alone for 4 months.

The other strategies are not consistent with the standard of care supported by the American Thoracic Society.

References

1. American Thoracic Society. Targeted tuberculin testing and treatment of latent tuberculosis infection. *MMWR Recomm Rep.* 2000; 49(RR-6):1–51.
2. Jasmer RM, Snyder DC, Chin DP, et al. Twelve months of isoniazid compared with four months of isoniazid and rifampin for persons with radiographic evidence of previous tuberculosis: an outcome and cost-effectiveness analysis. *Am J Respir Crit Care Med.* 2000;162(5):1648–1652.
3. Joint Statement of the American Thoracic Society (ATS) and the Centers for Disease Control and Prevention (CDC). Targeted tuberculin testing and treatment of latent tuberculosis infection. *Am J Respir Crit Care Med.* 2000;161(4 Pt 2):S2221–S2247.

93. A 78-year old man is admitted to the coronary care unit with a myocardial infarction. The patient develops heart failure with hypoxemia which improves with diuretics and mechanical ventilator support. Past medical history includes hypertension and elevated lipids, treated with hydrochlorothiazide and lovastatin. Prior to admission he functioned independently.

    On physical examination the patient appears alert, cooperative, and in no distress. His vital signs are normal, and he has scant bibasilar rales. His Confusion Assessment Method of the Intensive Care Unit (CAM-ICU) score is abnormal, and the rest of the examination is unremarkable.

Which of the following diagnoses is most likely?

(A) Depression
(B) Delirium
(C) Vascular dementia
(D) Low educational level
(E) Sundowning

ANSWER: B

In studies, 40% of calm, cooperative older mechanically ventilated patients are found to be delirious after careful evaluation. Several instruments have been developed to assess patients, including ventilated patients, who are unable to speak. The CAM-ICU has been validated and is being used increasingly in intensive care units to detect delirium. Studies show that nurses, with training, can administer the screen rapidly and accurately in the ICU.

Although depression increases in older persons in association with many illnesses, the patient has no prior history of depression. With independence in advanced activities of daily living and instrumental activities of daily living, the patient's history does not support a prior diagnosis of dementia. A rapid development of dementia, from normal function prior to admission, could be seen in association with a large stroke or acute injury, such as hypoxemia. However, the history and physical examination here do not support a significant injury. Low educational level would not cause this score. Sundowning is a syndrome of increased confusion in patients with dementia, in association with the evening hours. It was first described in nursing-home patients who changed rooms. With acute illness, severe illness, and an abnormal CAM-ICU, delirium is the most likely diagnosis.

Sudden changes in mental status in acutely ill elderly patients are most often due to delirium.

References

1. Ely EW, Inouye SK, Bernard GR, et al. Delirium in mechanically ventilated patients: validity and reliability of the Confusion Assessment Method of the Intensive Care Unit (CAM-ICU). *JAMA.* 2001; 286(21):2703–2710.

2. Ely EW, Margolin R, Francis J, et al. Evaluation of delirium in critically ill patients: validation of the Confusion Assessment Method for the Intensive Care Unit (CAM-ICU). *Crit Care Med.* 2001;29(7):1370–1379.
3. Hart RP, Best AM, Sessler CN, et al. Abbreviated cognitive test for delirium. *J Psychosom Res.* 1997;43(4):417–423.
4. Hart RP, Levenson JL, Sessler CN, et al. Validation of a cognitive test for delirium in medical ICU patients. *Psychosomatics.* 1996;37:533–546.
5. Truman B, Ely EW. Monitoring delirium in critically ill patients: using the Confusion Assessment Method for the Intensive Care Unit. *Crit Care Nurs.* 2003;23(2):25–36.

94. A 65-year-old woman with a 30-year history of rheumatoid arthritis requires deep dental cleaning and extraction of two posterior teeth. She received methotrexate for 20 years and corticosteroids intermittently for 5 years. She currently takes aspirin 325 mg twice daily and several herbal supplements, including *Ginkgo biloba* and garlic. Her blood pressure is 130/80 mm Hg and pulse is 60 per minute.

Which of the following statements is most accurate?

(A) She has no contraindications for dental treatment.
(B) She should discontinue all medications 1 day before dental treatment.
(C) She should discontinue all medications 7 days before dental treatment.
(D) She should take prophylactic antibiotics for the procedure.

ANSWER: C

Aspirin, *Ginkgo biloba,* and garlic can all cause prolonged bleeding time during or after dental procedures and should be discontinued. Adequate hemostasis after dental treatment is critical. Aspirin has weak antiplatelet activity, with platelet inhibition lasting for the lifetime of the affected platelets (about 7 to 10 days). If discontinuing the aspirin will not harm the patient's medical status, it should be stopped 1 week prior to the procedure.

Often patients do not disclose their use of herbal agents to physicians, so it is important to ask specifically about these and other nonprescription medications. The combination of *Ginkgo biloba* and aspirin may cause additive antiplatelet effects, such that the bleeding time may need to be checked prior to treatment. Other medications with antiplatelet effects include garlic, feverfew, ginger, ginseng, licorice, and chamomile.

Patients with rheumatoid arthritis do not need prophylactic antibiotics. Because 45% to 75% of patients with rheumatoid arthritis have temporomandibular joint involvement and may have limited or painful jaw function, a useful strategy is to recommend short dental visits.

References
1. Little JW, Falace DA, Miller CS, et al. Arthritic diseases. In: *Dental Management of the Medically Compromised Patient.* 6th ed. New York: Mosby/Elsevier; 2002:478–500.
2. Lockhart PB, Gibson J, Pond SH, et al. Dental management considerations for the patient with acquired coagulopathy. Part 2: coagulopathies from drugs. *Br Dent J.* 2003;195:495–500.
3. Teranishi K, Apitz-Castro R, Robson SC, et al. Inhibition of baboon platelet aggregation in vitro and in vivo by the garlic derivative, ajoene. *Xenotransplantation.* 2003;10(4):374–379.
4. Tesch BJ. Herbs commonly used by women: an evidence-based review. *Am J Obstet Gynecol.* 2003;188(5 Suppl):S44–S55.

95. An 82-year-old nursing-home resident is hospitalized with pneumonia. She has a history of hypertension and is functionally impaired from a debilitating stoke. On admission, the nurses note her to be pleasant, alert, and oriented to person, place, and time. On examination on her second hospital day, vital signs are stable and physical examination is consistent with pneumonia and old stroke. She awakens when called by name but closes her eyes for prolonged periods during conversation. She complains of feeling tired and does not want to talk much. She is distracted by the voices in the hallway, so that questions must be repeated several times. She slurs her words more than before and has significant difficulty with word finding. An antibiotic for the pneumonia is the only new medication.

Which of the following best explains her symptoms?

(A) Alzheimer's disease
(B) Dementia with Lewy bodies
(C) Delirium
(D) Depression
(E) Stroke

ANSWER: C

This patient has an acute change in cognition with fluctuating signs. Her inattention, lethargy, and change in cognition or speech are the cardinal features of delirium, which can often be identified by careful observation. A cognitive assessment, such as the Mini–Mental State Examination, should be completed to formally assess her cognitive status, and a delirium tool can be used to confirm the diagnosis. The Confusion Assessment Method is simple and widely used for detection of delirium in hospitalized older persons. It assesses for presence of an acute change in mental status with a fluctuating course, inattention, and presence of either disorganized thinking or altered level of consciousness.

The patient has no history of dementia, and inattention and lethargy are generally not features of dementia.

In hospitalized persons with lethargy and psychomotor retardation, delirium is often misdiagnosed as depression. Many studies show that among the majority of hospital psychiatric consultations for depression, the true diagnosis is delirium. The recognition of delirium is poor among nurses and physicians, especially if baseline cognitive and functional status is not available.

Although a second stroke may explain the word-finding difficulties and lethargy, there are no other overt neurologic signs to indicate stroke.

References

1. Farrell KR, Ganzini L. Misdiagnosing delirium as depression in medically ill elderly patients. *Arch Intern Med*. 1995;155(22):2459–2464.
2. Inouye SK, Foreman MD, Mion LC, et al. Nurses' recognition of delirium and its symptoms. *Arch Intern Med*. 2001;161(20):2467–2473.
3. McNicoll L, Pisani MA, Ely EW, et al. Detection of delirium in the intensive care unit: comparison of confusion assessment method for the intensive care unit with confusion assessment method ratings. *J Am Geriatr Soc*. 2005;53(3):495–500.
4. Schuurmans MJ, Duursma SA, Shortridge-Baggett LM. Early recognition of delirium: review of the literature. *J Clin Nursing*. 2001;10(6):721–729.

96. A patient's daughter asks about options in caring for her mother, who recently had a stroke and is unable to ambulate. The mother has mild cognitive deficits and is on several medications for other medical problems. The daughter lives in a different part of the country, and her mother refuses nursing-home placement. She is willing to go to adult day care, but her privately hired, longstanding, 24-hour caregivers do not drive. The home-care physical therapy is completed, but the daughter believes her mother would benefit from further rehabilitation.

Which of the following is the most appropriate suggestion for the daughter?

(A) Convince her mother to enter a nursing home.
(B) Hire 24-hour caregivers who can drive.
(C) Refer her to the Program of All-Inclusive Care for the Elderly (PACE) in her community.
(D) Obtain an in-home safety evaluation through a certified home-care agency.

ANSWER: C

Programs of All-Inclusive Care for the Elderly (PACE) are developing in communities throughout the United States. Originally introduced as a demonstration program under Medicare, these programs were made a permanent provider under Medicare in 1997. Older adults are eligible if they otherwise would qualify for nursing-home placement. The program uses capitated funds that can be used in a flexible manner to keep participants in the community for as long as possible. At the center of PACE are day programs where patients have access to medical, rehabilitation, and social services. Meals and transportation are also provided. An older adult must relinquish her or his community-based physicians and receive all medical care under the direction of the PACE team.

If there is no PACE program in her community, you could refer the daughter to an adult day care program. Many of these programs will provide transportation for participants.

Placing this woman in a nursing home would not be the best choice because she does not wish it. Changing her longstanding 24-hour caregivers is also not the best choice, as she is familiar with her current caregivers. Evaluation for safety by a home-care agency might be helpful, but it would not provide the ongoing care or cover the needs of this chronically ill woman.

References

1. Lee W, Eng C, Fox N, et al. PACE: a model for integrated care of frail older patients: Program of All-inclusive Care for the Elderly. *Geriatrics*. 1998;53(6):62–74.
2. Wieland D. Lamb V, Wang H, et al. Participants in the Program of All-Inclusive Care for the Elderly (PACE) demonstration: developing disease-impairment-disability profiles. *Gerontologist*. 2001;40(2):218–227.

97. An 82-year-old man is hospitalized because he has sudden onset of right-sided weakness and mild expressive aphasia. Computed tomographic scan of the brain reveals a 2-cm ischemic infarct in the middle cerebral artery distribution. Follow-up magnetic resonance imaging at 48 hours shows the same 2-cm infarct with no bleeding or tumor. Rehabilitation begins on the third day after the stroke. On the fourth day he has a tonic-clonic seizure that lasts 2 minutes. For 1 hour after the seizure his sensorium is decreased, but then his sensorium and neurologic defects return to post-stroke baseline. There are no other new symptoms.

Which of the following is most appropriate?

(A) Repeat magnetic resonance imaging of the brain.
(B) Discontinue rehabilitation until medically stable.
(C) Reassure the patient and caregivers.
(D) Start treatment with phenytoin.
(E) Order electroencephalography.

ANSWER: C

Seizures after a stroke are relatively uncommon. Early seizure, arbitrarily defined as within 2 weeks of stroke, has been reported in 2% to 6% of strokes and is a predictor of recurrent seizures. Acute stroke has been reported to cause 22% of all cases of status epilepticus in adults. The frequency of early seizures varies by stroke subtype and location. Deep infarcts have the lowest rate of seizures, and hemorrhages have the highest; superficial infarcts have mid-range risk. Diabetes mellitus, hypertension, current smoking, alcohol use, age, sex, and race or ethnicity are not significant determinants of early seizure. After accounting for stroke severity, early seizure is not a predictor of 30-day case fatality.

A single seizure within the first 2 weeks after a stroke probably does not require further treatment. According to the Seizures After Stroke Study Group, 2.5% of stroke patients who are followed for 9 months developed recurrent seizures. Some experts recommend prophylactic anticonvulsant therapy for patients who have a hemorrhagic stroke. The patient and caregiver should be educated about the risks and instructed to report any further seizures. Treatment with phenytoin has inherent risks, particularly in the older patient. In addition, phenytoin may inhibit neurologic recovery in post-traumatic seizures; this risk has not been studied in seizures after stroke.

Magnetic resonance imaging or computed tomography would probably not be helpful if there are no new neurologic findings. Imaging is indicated if the patient has atrial fibrillation or other reasons for recurrent emboli, or if there is evidence of new localizing findings.

It is not necessary to interrupt rehabilitation if the patient's status is stable. In fact, mobilization will decrease the risk of other complications, such as deep-vein thrombosis or deconditioning.

Electroencephalography would probably be nonfocal and, because the risk of seizure recurrence is small, would not guide treatment decisions. In addition, many older people have background slowing, which may lead to unnecessary investigations.

References

1. Bladin CF, Alexandrov AV, Bellavance A, et al. Seizures after stroke: a prospective multicenter study. *Arch Neurol*. 2000;57(11):1617–1622.
2. Labovitz DL, Hauser WA. Preventing stroke-related seizures: when should anticonvulsant drugs be started? *Neurology*. 2003;60(3): 365–366.

3. Labovitz DL, Hauser WA, Sacco RL. Prevalence and predictors of early seizure and status epilepticus after first stroke. *Neurology.* 2001;57(2):200–206.

98. A 67-year-old man comes to the office with his family to obtain an additional medical opinion. He has lost 18.2 kg (40 lb) in the past 6 months, is weak, spends most of his time in bed, has given up participating in family activities, and is no longer interested in watching sporting events on television. His family is concerned that he has a serious, undiagnosed medical problem. He tends to sit quietly and let his family answer questions, but when pressed, he indicates that he cannot swallow solids or liquids because his throat is blocked. His family reports that he eats and drinks small amounts. He believes he has cancer that the doctors have yet to find. According to the medical records he provides, radiography and computed tomography of the chest are normal, and upper endoscopy is unremarkable. Several sets of blood work have been obtained, none of which indicate dehydration, anemia, or hepatic or renal dysfunction.

Which of the following is the most likely explanation for these findings?

(A) Occult lung cancer
(B) Vascular dementia
(C) Alzheimer's disease
(D) Major depression with psychotic features
(E) Panic disorder

ANSWER: D

In older persons, the presentation of major depression with psychotic features is often masked by concomitant physical symptoms. Although major depression can coexist with panic disorder, panic disorder involves multiple acute episodes of physical symptoms with intense fear of impending doom. In contrast, this patient has a sustained conviction of a physical abnormality not supported by medical evidence. The patient's conviction alone, however, is not sufficient to make the diagnosis of major depression with psychotic features. Patients with occult malignancy can present with weight loss and poorly articulated physical complaints. An important diagnostic clue is the presence of other signs and symptoms suggesting major depression: psychomotor retardation, loss of interest, loss of energy, social withdrawal, and increased time in bed. These symptoms are more likely to reflect depression than physical impairment, since he has lost interest in activities (for example, watching sports on television) that are unaffected by physical limitation from weight loss and weakness. A primary psychiatric concern is also suggested by his delusional belief that he cannot swallow. This is contradicted by the family, as well as by his examination.

Recognizing the presence of psychosis (somatic delusion) in this patient has important implications for further management. Major depression with psychotic features responds poorly to pharmacotherapy with an antidepressant alone, requiring the addition of an antipsychotic agent. However, the addition of an antipsychotic does not always enhance efficacy and has the potential to increase side effects. Although it has limited availability and less acceptability to patients, electroconvulsive therapy is the treatment of choice for older patients who have major depression with psychotic features.

There is no history to suggest cognitive impairment, and thus vascular dementia and Alzheimer's disease are unlikely.

References
1. Mulsant BH, Sweet RA, Rosen J, et al. A double-blind randomized comparison of nortriptyline plus perphenazine versus nortriptyline plus placebo in the treatment of psychotic depression in late life. *J Clin Psychiatry.* 2001;62(8):597–604.
2. Tew JD Jr, Mulsant BH, Haskett RF, et al. A randomized comparison of high-charge right unilateral electroconvulsive therapy and bilateral electroconvulsive therapy in older depressed patients who failed to respond to a 5-8 moderate-charge right unilateral treatments. *J Clin Psychiatry.* 2002;63(12):1102–1105.

99. The daughter of a 91-year-old patient who saw an article on the Internet requests a physical therapy referral for progressive resistance training to help her mother stay independent.

Which of the following statements is true regarding progressive resistance training?

(A) Physical disability, as measured by standardized scales, will improve.
(B) Gains in strength are common.
(C) Health-related quality of life improves.
(D) Injury due to the exercises is rare.
(E) The patient's advanced age is a contraindication.

ANSWER: B

Muscle weakness is common in old age and is associated with physical disability and an increased risk of falls. Progressive resistance training exercises (that is, movements performed against a specific external force that is regularly increased during training) are designed to increase strength in older people.

In almost 70 trials with nearly 4000 subjects, progressive resistance training was found to have a large positive effect on strength. Some measures of functional limitation, such as gait, showed modest improvements. However, there is no evidence that progressive resistance training has an effect on health-related quality-of-life measures or on physical disability as measured by standardized scales. In most of the studies, musculoskeletal injuries were detected.

Patients at advanced age may benefit from exercise interventions. The patient's underlying health status is a better determinant of outcome than age. Extremely disabled patients may not gain much in terms of functional improvement, and healthy persons may not need such exercises. However, other patients, especially those with deconditioning, are likely to see some benefits.

References

1. Fiatarone MA, Marks EC, Ryan ND, et al. High-intensity strength training in nonagenarians: effects on skeletal muscle. *JAMA.* 1990;263(22):3029–3034.
2. Latham N, Anderson C, Bennett D, et al. Progressive resistance strength training for physical disability in older people. *Cochrane Database Syst Rev.* 2003;(2):CD002759.
3. Thomas VS, Hageman PA. Can neuromuscular strength and function in people with dementia be rehabilitated using resistance-exercise training? Results from a preliminary intervention study. *J Gerontol A Biol Sci Med Sci.* 2003;58(8):746–751.

100. Which of the following antidepressant agents has the best profile to avoid a cytochrome P-450 pharmacokinetic drug-drug interaction?

(A) Escitalopram
(B) Fluoxetine
(C) Fluvoxamine
(D) Paroxetine
(E) St. John's wort

ANSWER: A

Several antidepressant medications can inhibit the cytochrome P-450 isoenzymes extensively involved in drug metabolism and can result in significant drug-drug interactions. Citalopram, escitalopram, and sertraline have minimal inhibition of cytochrome P-450 isoenzymes and are unlikely to be involved in clinically significant pharmacokinetic drug-drug interactions.

Fluoxetine, fluvoxamine, and paroxetine strongly inhibit several cytochrome P-450 isoenzymes and have been implicated in many drug-drug interactions. For example, fluoxetine and paroxetine strongly inhibit cytochrome CYP2D6, thereby interfering with metabolism of β-blockers, codeine, dextromethorphan, dextropropoxyphene, ethylmorphine, galantamine, meperidine, omeprazole, and tricyclic antidepressants. Fluvoxamine inhibits cytochrome 1A2, 2C9 or 2C19, and 3A4, thereby interfering with metabolism of acetaminophen, alprazolam, caffeine, galantamine, methadone, olanzapine, theophylline, verapamil, and warfarin. St. John's wort, used by many older persons to treat depression, is a potent inducer of cytochrome 3A4, thus resulting in diminished clinical effectiveness for cytochrome 3A4 substrates, or at least 50% of all marketed medications, including alprazolam, cortisol, cyclosporine, diltiazem, dexamethasone, felodipine, lovastatin, oxycodone, tamoxifen, and tacrolimus.

References

1. DeVane CL, Pollock BG. Pharmacokinetic considerations of antidepressant use in the elderly. *J Clin Psychiatry.* 1999;60 (Suppl 20):38–44.
2. Markowitz JS, Donovan JL, DeVane CL, et al. Effect of St John's wort on drug metabolism by induction of cytochrome P450 3A4 enzyme. *JAMA.* 2003; 290(11):1500–1504.

3. Solai LK, Mulsant BH, Pollock BG. Selective serotonin reuptake inhibitors for late-life depression: a comparative review. *Drugs Aging.* 2001;18(5):355–368.
4. von Moltke LL, Greenblatt DJ, Giancarlo GM, et al. Escitalopram (S-citalopram) and its metabolites in vitro: cytochromes mediating biotransformation, inhibitory effects, and comparison to R-citalopram. *Drug Metab Dispos.* 2001;29(8):1102–1109.

101. A 72-year-old woman with mild osteoarthritis comes to the emergency department because of pain in her right lower leg. Her only medication is acetaminophen. She reports no recent trauma, prolonged travel, or history of deep-vein thrombosis.

On physical examination, the lower leg is erythematous from the knee to the ankle, with tenderness over the lateral aspect of the calf. Cellulitis is suspected. Testing for D-dimer using an enzyme-linked immunosorbent assay is negative.

Which of the following should be done next to exclude deep-vein thrombosis?

(A) Bilateral impedance plethysmography
(B) Computed tomographic angiography
(C) Bilateral compression duplex ultrasonography
(D) Contrast venography
(E) No further testing is required

ANSWER: E

D-dimer testing has simplified diagnosis of deep-vein thrombosis (DVT). Enzyme-linked immunosorbent assay (ELISA) for D-dimer is highly sensitive for DVT and can be used to help exclude the diagnosis when results are negative. This patient's pretest probability for DVT is low to moderate in the absence of significant risk factors other than advanced age and cellulitis. Impedance plethysmography, compression ultrasonography, computed tomographic angiography, or contrast venography is excellent for making or excluding the diagnosis of DVT in symptomatic patients. However, each is unnecessary and excessive in the presence of a negative D-dimer done with a high-sensitivity assay in a patient with low to moderate pretest probability for disease.

References
1. Bates SM, Kearon C, Lynkins L, et al. A diagnostic strategy involving a quantitative latex D-dimer assay reliably excludes deep venous thrombosis. *Ann Intern Med.* 2003;138(10):787–794.
2. Becker DM, Philbrick JT, Bachhuber TL, et al. D-dimer testing and acute venous thromboembolism: a shortcut to accurate diagnosis? *Arch Intern Med.* 1996;156(9):939–946.
3. Ginsberg JS. Management of venous thromboembolism. *N Engl J Med.* 1996;335(24):1816–1828.
4. Lee AY, Ginsberg JS. The role of D-dimer and the diagnosis venous thromboembolism. *Curr Opin Pulm Med.* 1997;3(4):275–279.

102. A 65-year-old woman comes to the office with her husband because she has had behavioral changes over the past year. Her husband complains of her increasingly odd behavior, such as eating full boxes of cookies at one sitting, giggling, making rude comments to strangers, and opening drawers and cabinets in friends' apartments. She has no history of hypertension or diabetes mellitus and is on no medication.

Physical examination is normal. On mental status examination, there is decreased spontaneous speech and occasional inappropriate laughter but no obvious delusions or hallucinations. She scores 28 of 30 on the Mini–Mental State Examination, losing points for delayed recall and repetition. She places numbers correctly on a clock, but when asked to set the hands at 10 minutes past 11, she draws a straight line between the numerals 10 and 11. She names only 6 animals in 1 minute and demonstrates significant perseveration when drawing multiple loops.

Which of the following is the most likely cause of her behavioral change?

(A) Alzheimer's disease
(B) Mania
(C) Frontotemporal dementia
(D) Vascular dementia
(E) Dementia with Lewy bodies

ANSWER: C

This person likely has frontotemporal dementia. Affected patients often have behavioral and personality changes prior to development of cognitive and functional impairment. The behaviors she demonstrates include hyperorality and hypermetamorphosis (manifested by her excessive tendency to explore the environment), which, along with hypersexuality and visual agnosia, are findings associated with Klüver-Bucy syndrome. Her cognition is notable for a near normal score with significantly impaired word list generation and perseveration, which are evidence of executive dysfunction.

The behavioral changes are too marked and the cognitive deficits too mild (especially in memory and orientation) to be typical for Alzheimer's disease. Manic patients can present with elated, inappropriate affect and disinhibition, but this patient does not have other symptoms such as grandiosity, talkativeness, racing thoughts, and decreased need for sleep.

It is possible for patients with vascular dementia to present with similar symptoms if lesions are located primarily in the frontal lobes. However, this patient's young age and lack of vascular risk factors are more consistent with frontotemporal dementia.

In dementia with Lewy bodies, patients can present initially with behavioral problems, though these are more likely to be psychotic in nature (especially visual hallucinations), and depression. She also has no signs of parkinsonism, which is commonly associated with dementia with Lewy bodies.

References

1. Bathgate D, Snowden JS, Varma A, et al. Behaviour in frontotemporal dementia, Alzheimer's disease and vascular dementia. *Acta Neurol Scand.* 2001;103(6):367–378.
2. Mendez MF, Perryman KM. Neuropsychiatric features of frontotemporal dementia: evaluation of consensus criteria and review. *J Neuropsychiatry Clin Neurosciences.* 2002; 14(4):424–429.
3. Snowden JS, Neary D, Mann DM. Frontotemporal dementia. *Br J Psychiatry.* 2002; 180:140–143.

103. A 66-year-old nonverbal man comes for a follow-up visit accompanied by his residential program manager for the agency that has been his payee for 20 years. Over the past 4 weeks he has had escalating self-injurious behavior, disrupted sleep, diminished appetite, and agitation. He has a history of autism and unspecified mental retardation. He has no other psychiatric or medical diagnoses and has never been on psychotropic medications. No family history is available. His caregiver reports that he participates in a sheltered workshop. The patient is his own guardian. Recent disruptions in his residential setting include the retirement of a long-time caregiver and the need for emergency care of a peer. Two weeks ago he had a thorough medical examination, which identified a 10-lb weight loss and mild dehydration. At that time, alprazolam, 0.25 mg twice daily, was prescribed, but it has not improved his behavior. During the current appointment he sits quietly rocking and humming in his chair until the last 10 minutes, during which he becomes visibly agitated and suddenly slams his fist against his nose twice.

Which of the following is the most appropriate intervention?

(A) Begin an antidepressant.
(B) Increase the alprazolam dose.
(C) Begin low-dose risperidone.
(D) Begin an antiepileptic drug.
(E) Institute a behavior support plan.

ANSWER: E

This patient is having increased behavioral symptoms coinciding with disruptions in his home environment. In response to a significant change in their lives, persons with autism commonly demonstrate more self-injurious behaviors, non–self-injuring stereotypic behavior, aggression, and agitation. The best initial choice would be to involve a behavioral specialist to create a support plan that includes reducing stressors and using calming techniques effective for persons with autism.

An antidepressant agent, particularly a selective serotonin-reuptake inhibitor, may be reasonable given the diagnostic uncertainty and the evidence of weight loss and mild dehydration. However, the clear relationship to change in the environment suggests that behavioral intervention may be more relevant.

Alprazolam was presumably begun to decrease perceived anxiety. Stereotypic movement disorders, including self-injurious behavior, are sometimes considered part of the obsessive-compulsive spectrum disorders. Nevertheless, a benzodiazepine is not among the best choices for this patient and would probably make him less responsive to appropriate nonpharmacologic interventions.

Although some early research has focused on risperidone for challenging behaviors in persons with autistic spectrum disorders, there is no clear reason to begin this option now. If symptoms become more severe, antipsychotic medication might be used to quickly suppress dangerous behaviors.

The use of an antiepileptic drug[OL] to reduce aggression and agitation frequently involves ongoing monitoring of serum concentrations, liver enzymes, or blood cell counts. Many persons with mental retardation do not tolerate having their blood drawn, which makes this choice less than ideal.

References

1. Janssen CG, Schuengel C, Stolk J, et al. Understanding challenging behaviour in people with severe and profound intellectual disability: a stress-attachment model. *J Intellect Disabil Res.* 2002;46(Pt 6):445–453.
2. McClintock K, Hall S, Oliver C. Risk markers associated with challenging behaviours in people with intellectual disabilities: a meta-analytic study. *J Intellect Disabil Res.* 2003;47(Pt 6):405–416.
3. Tsiouris JA, Mann R, Patti PJ, et al. Challenging behaviours should not be considered as depressive equivalents in individuals with intellectual disability. *J Intellect Disabil Res.* 2003;47(Pt 1):14–21.

OL- Not approved by the U.S. Food and Drug Administration for this use.

104. A 74-year-old man comes to the office because he has a 3-month history of generalized itching. The itching has worsened as the weather has gotten colder. The patient states that this happens every winter. History includes hypertension, for which he has taken lisinopril for the past 4 years. He does not take any other agents or over-the-counter medications. He has been using a moisturizing cream with little relief. On examination, there is diffuse skin involvement with dry scaling on the trunk and extremities. The shins resemble "cracked porcelain" with red fissures that form an irregular reticular pattern.

Which of the following is the most likely cause of the itching?

(A) Drug eruption
(B) Xerosis
(C) Scabies
(D) Psoriasis
(E) Contact dermatitis

ANSWER: B

Xerosis (dry skin) is the most common cause of generalized itching in older patients. Clinically the skin is dry and scaly; in more severe cases the skin becomes inflamed, with fissuring and cracking of the stratum corneum that resembles cracked porcelain (erythema craquelé; in French *craquelé* means "marred with cracks"). Xerosis gets worse in winter, with low environmental humidity. It can be reduced by using a humidifier in the bedroom, decreasing the frequency of baths, using warm instead of hot water, and using only mild and moisturizing soaps (eg, Dove, Basis, Aveeno) or avoiding soaps altogether. The patient should be instructed in the use of emollients on wet skin, especially with lactic acid (5% or 12%) and urea (10% to 20%), which loosen retained layers of stratum corneum and decrease the scaliness. Ammonium lactate cream 5% contains urea and is available over the counter; the 12% formulation requires a prescription. Oils in the bath prolong hydration of the stratum corneum, but they are not advisable for older patients as they make the tub surface slippery and may increase the risk of falling. A mild topical corticosteroid may be helpful in some cases.

In an older patient with generalized pruritus, it is important to exclude other causes, including drug eruptions, scabies, systemic disease (diabetes mellitus or liver and kidney disorders), or lymphoproliferative disease (lymphoma or leukemia). Drug eruptions can present with all kinds of rashes and should be in the differential diagnosis of any symmetric eruption. They usually occur within the first week of initiating a new drug, although reactions to penicillins can be delayed. It is important to get a good drug history, including over-the-counter drugs and food additives. This patient's history of rash with cold weather makes xerosis more likely than drug eruption.

Scabies is a skin infestation by mites. It is characterized by burrows: gray or skin-colored ridges, 0.5 to 1.0 cm long, that end with a minute papule or vesicle. There may be secondary urticarial papules, eczematous plaques, excoriations, and superimposed bacterial infection. In psoriasis, the lesions are well-demarcated erythematous plaques with adherent silvery scales, and they usually involve elbows, knees, scalp, and trunk (extensor surfaces). Contact dermatitis is a type IV hypersensitivity reaction after contact with an antigen and is characterized by pruritus and burning of the skin. It causes inflammation of the skin and can be acute, subacute, or chronic. The acute form presents with erythematous patches with vesicles, erosions, and crusts. Subacute contact dermatitis presents with patches of mild erythema, dry scales, and sometimes small papules. Chronic contact dermatitis may have patches of lichenification (thickening) with satellite small papules, excoriation, or mild erythema. In contact dermatitis there is a history of exposure to an external agent, rather than a seasonal predilection.

References

1. Freeman A, Gordon M. Dermatologic diseases and problems. In: Cassel CK, Leipszig RM, Cohen HJ, et al., eds. *Geriatric Medicine: An Evidence-Based Approach.* 4th ed. New York: Springer-Verlag; 2003:869–881.
2. Part I: Disorders presenting in the skin and mucous membranes. Section 2: Eczema dermatitis. Asteatotic dermatitis. In: Fitzpatrick TB, Johnson RA, Wolf K, et al., eds. *Color Atlas and Synopsis of Clinical Dermatology.* 4th ed. New York: The McGraw-Hill Companies; 2001.

105. Which of the following statements regarding calorie restriction is correct?

(A) Calorie restriction has been shown consistently to increase life span in mice.
(B) Animal studies have demonstrated positive effects of calorie restriction on fertility.
(C) Calorically restricted rodents, nonhuman primates, and healthy men demonstrate lower fasting insulin levels and lower body temperature.
(D) Calorie restriction is most beneficial when initiated late in life.
(E) Calorically restricted mice live longer, are more fit, and are more likely to reproduce than control mice with unlimited access to food.

ANSWER: C

Calorie restriction has been shown to slow aging and extend life span in yeast, flies, worms, rats, and mice. Animals on a calorically restricted diet receive a well-balanced diet, yet eat less than control animals allowed unlimited access to the same food. Although most calorically restricted animals live longer, the impact of calorie restriction varies considerably in mice. For example, calorie restriction increases the life span of C57BL/6 mice, but not DBA/2 mice. The physiologic effects of calorie restriction are complex. Although restricted animals seem more fit, are more active, develop fewer tumors, and have fewer of the neurologic and endocrine abnormalities typically observed in control animals with unlimited access, they are more susceptible to bacterial infections and have reduced fertility. Human calorie restriction is probably unrealistic, yet two of the most robust markers of calorie restriction in rodents (reduced body temperature and reduced plasma insulin) have also been observed in calorie-restricted rhesus monkeys and in older men studied as part of the Baltimore Longitudinal Study of Aging. Studies of *Drosophila* spp. indicate that the life span can be extended even if calorie restriction is instituted late in life.

References

1. Forster MJ, Morris P, Sohal RS. Genotype and age influence the effect of caloric intake on mortality in mice. *FASEB J.* 2003; 17(6):690–692.

2. Roth GS, Lane MA, Ingram DK, et al. Biomarkers of caloric restriction may predict longevity in humans. *Science* 2002; 297(5582):811.

3. Vaupel JW, Carey JR, Christensen K. Aging: it's never too late. *Science*. 2003; 301(5640):1679–1681.

106. A 69-year-old man comes to the office because of difficulty swallowing solids and liquids. The dysphagia has progressed slowly over 8 months, and he has lost 20 pounds. He reports no pain. Barium radiograph demonstrates a narrowed distal esophageal segment 4.1 cm long and no dilated esophageal segment proximal to this narrowed portion. Esophageal manometry demonstrates failure of the lower esophageal sphincter to relax with swallowing, and aperistalsis of the esophageal body.

Which diagnostic procedure should be performed first?

(A) Esophagoscopy
(B) Endoscopic ultrasonography
(C) Computed tomography
(D) Chest magnetic resonance imaging
(E) Laparotomy

ANSWER: A

Achalasia is an esophageal motor disorder characterized clinically by dysphagia to liquids and solids, radiographically by esophageal dilatation with smooth "bird beak" distal narrowing, and manometrically by incomplete or absent relaxation of the lower esophageal sphincter and aperistalsis of the esophageal body. Most affected patients have primary or idiopathic achalasia, a disorder of unknown cause characterized pathologically by myenteric lymphocyte inflammation with injury to and progressive depletion of myenteric ganglion cells. However, some patients have pseudoachalasia associated with malignancy, which has clinical, radiographic, and manometric findings often indistinguishable from primary achalasia.

The peak incidence of pseudoachalasia is between ages 60 and 80 (initial onset of primary achalasia has a nearly uniform age distribution between ages 10 and 70). In older adults, recent-onset dysphagia, findings of achalasia on barium studies, and a narrowed distal esophageal segment longer than 3.5 cm with little or no proximal dilatation are highly suggestive of pseudoachalasia caused by an occult malignancy, even in the absence of other suspicious radiographic findings. The most common mechanism for pseudoachalasia is direct involvement of the esophageal myenteric plexus by neoplastic cells. Rarely, a distant neoplasm may cause this syndrome as a paraneoplastic process. Pseudoachalasia is most often associated with adenocarcinoma of the gastroesophageal junction. It has also been associated with malignancy of the esophagus, lung, liver, prostate, breast, and pancreas, as well as with lymphoma and mesothelioma.

Esophagoscopy detects mucosal or structural abnormalities of the esophagus and proximal stomach. It is useful for detection of pseudoachalasia, placement of manometry catheters, and dilatation of peptic strictures. All patients with achalasia should have esophagoscopy with biopsy of any suspicious area. Large endoscopic biopsies may not demonstrate the presence of malignancy. If endoscopic biopsy is nondiagnostic, endoscopic ultrasound, computed tomography, and laparotomy may be appropriate.

Pneumatic dilatation, thought to cause a controlled tear of the lower esophageal sphincter by vigorous stretching, is successful in 70% to 90% of patients. Generally, if there is no durable response after three treatments, an alternative therapy should be attempted. Surgical management consists of myotomy of the abnormal lower esophageal sphincter. Success rates approach 90% for relief of dysphagia.

References
1. Adler DG, Romero Y. Primary esophageal motility disorders. *Mayo Clin Proc.* 2001;76(2):195–200.

2. Liu W, Fackler W, Rice TW, et al. The pathogenesis of pseudoachalasia: a clinicopathologic study of 13 cases of a rare entity. *Am J Surg Pathol.* 2002;26(6):784–788.

3. Woodfield CA, Levine MS, Rubesin SE, et al. Diagnosis of primary versus secondary achalasia: reassessment of clinical and radiographic criteria. *Am J Roentgenol.* 2000; 175(3):727–731.

4. Zuccaro G Jr. Esophagoscopy and endoscopic esophageal ultrasound in the assessment of esophageal function. *Sem Thorac Cardiovasc Surg.* 2001;13(3):226–233.

107. A preoperative medical consultation is requested for an obese 72-year-old man admitted for coronary artery bypass grafting scheduled for the next day. He has known three-vessel coronary artery disease. He has been complaining of a headache but is otherwise considered a good candidate for the procedure.

On examination, he has tenderness over the right temporal artery and a right carotid bruit. Laboratory studies reveal a Westergren sedimentation rate of 82 mm/hr. Giant cell (temporal) arteritis is suspected.

Which of the following is the most appropriate initial step?

(A) High-dose corticosteroids
(B) Etanercept
(C) Temporal artery biopsy
(D) Coronary artery bypass graft
(E) Methotrexate

ANSWER: A

Temporal arteritis is characterized by intense inflammation that can compromise blood flow to critical structures in the head and neck, and can result in headache and visual impairment. Although the head and neck can be investigated with vascular imaging (such as magnetic resonance imaging or ultrasound), biopsy is the diagnostic procedure of choice to detect arteritis in cranial vessels. Further, the type of arteritis (giant cell, polyarteritis) can be distinguished only by biopsy and has important therapeutic implications. Clinical subtypes of giant cell arteritis can be distinguished by the predominant anatomic involvement: cranial giant cell arteritis with ischemic complications in the eye, the face, and the central nervous system; large-vessel giant cell arteritis with occlusions in the subclavian or axillary vessels; and aortic giant cell arteritis. Arteritis can also involve coronary arteries, and giant cell arteritis can result in ostial lesions.

The appropriate initial step is treatment with high-dose corticosteroids, even before definitive diagnosis with temporal artery biopsy. Methotrexate and etanercept are anti-inflammatory agents more appropriately used as disease-modifying agents in rheumatoid arthritis. Surgery should be delayed until the disease is well controlled.

References

1. Hoffman GS, Cid MC, Hellmann DB, et al. A multicenter, randomized, double-blind, placebo-controlled trial of adjuvant methotrexate treatment for giant cell arteritis. *Arthritis Rheum.* 2002;46(5):1309–1318.
2. Nordborg E, Nordborg C. Giant cell arteritis: strategies in diagnosis and treatment. *Curr Opin Rheumatol.* 2004;16(1):25–30.
3. Pfadenhauer K, Weber H. Duplex sonography of the temporal and occipital artery in the diagnosis of temporal arteritis: a prospective study. *J Rheumatol.* 2003;30(10):2177–2181.
4. Proven A, Gabriel SE, Orces C, et al. Glucocorticoid therapy in giant cell arteritis: duration and adverse outcomes. *Arthritis Rheum.* 2003;49(5):703–708.

108. An 88-year-old woman comes to the office for a follow-up visit. She has poorly controlled stage 2 hypertension, gastroesophageal reflux disease, depression, and hypothyroidism. She has lived alone since her husband's death 2 years ago. Medications include hydrochlorothiazide 50 mg daily, lisinopril 10 mg twice daily, diltiazem 30 mg four times daily, esomeprazole 20 mg daily, citalopram 40 mg daily, levothyroid 0.1 mg daily, and aspirin 81 mg daily. Metoprolol 50 mg twice daily was added to her regimen 2 months ago, when her blood-pressure reading was 168/81 mm Hg. She has no new symptoms and has had no blood-pressure readings since her visit 2 months ago.

On physical examination, blood pressure is found to be 165/78 mm Hg and heart rate is 88 per minute. There are no orthostatic blood-pressure changes. She has grade 1 hypertensive retinopathy and a laterally displaced point of maximal impulse with an apical fourth heart sound. A screening cognitive assessment is done today; she recalls only 1 of 3 objects at 3 minutes and performs a normal clock-drawing test. She reports three positive responses on the Geriatric Depression Scale. Echocardiogram shows left ventricular hypertrophy. Recent laboratory studies demonstrate normal electrolytes and renal function (calculated creatinine clearance is 43 mL/min) and thyrotropin level of 10.8 µU/mL.

Which of the following best explains the persistence of her poorly controlled blood pressure?

(A) Pseudohypertension
(B) Nonadherence to medication
(C) Pheochromocytoma
(D) Hyperaldosteronism
(E) Renovascular hypertension

ANSWER: B

Resistant hypertension is defined in the Seventh Report of the Joint National Committee on Prevention, Detection, Evaluation, and Treatment of High Blood Pressure as "failure to reach goal blood pressure in patients who are adhering to full doses of an appropriate three-drug regimen that includes a diuretic." Causes of resistant hypertension include inaccurate blood-pressure measurement (pseudohypertension), volume overload, drug-induced effect, inadequate dosing of antihypertensive drugs, and incorrect combinations of therapies, as well as secondary causes of hypertension (eg, renovascular disease, sleep apnea, hyperaldosteronism, chronic kidney disease, and pheochromocytoma). Several clues suggest that this patient's poorly controlled blood pressure persists because she does not adhere to the medication regimen. She has several risk factors for nonadherence: multiple medications are administered at different times throughout the day, she may have short-term memory impairment (forgetfulness is a major contributor to nonadherence), she has a history of depression, and she lives alone. Her physical examination does not reflect the reduction in heart rate that would be expected following the addition of the β-blocker at her last visit. Laboratory evidence of inadequate thyroid hormone replacement suggests nonadherence to the thyroid medication.

Although pseudohypertension needs to be considered in older patients with resistant hypertension, the constellation of physical (hypertensive retinopathy) and echocardiographic findings indicates target-organ damage from established hypertension. Renovascular hypertension is the most common of the secondary causes of hypertension among older patients. This patient's pattern of hypertension is not consistent with this possibility: She has normal renal function and no evidence of or risk factors for coronary or peripheral vascular disease. The normal electrolyte pattern makes hyperaldosteronism unlikely. Pheochromocytoma is a rare cause of secondary hypertension, and the patient has none of the symptoms that would typically accompany this condition.

References

1. Chobanian AV, Bakris GL, Black HR, et al. The Seventh Report of the Joint National Committee on Prevention, Detection, Evaluation, and Treatment of High Blood Pressure: the JNC 7 report. *JAMA.* 2003;289(10):2560–2572.
2. Hamilton GA. Measuring adherence in a hypertension clinical trial. *Eur J Cardiovasc Nurs.* 2003;2(3):219–228.

109. A 76-year-old man comes to the office because he is preoccupied by physical sensations, including dizziness, pressure in his head, chest discomfort, and generalized shakiness. He acknowledges that the symptoms may be due to his "nerves" and reports feeling anxious, worried, irritable, and restless. The physical sensations occur throughout the day and tend to be most severe in the morning. He had a left hemispheric stroke 2 months before the symptoms began. On additional probing, the patient also reveals depressed mood, lack of pleasure in life, loss of appetite, middle insomnia, daytime fatigue, and feelings of hopelessness.

Which of the following is the most likely diagnosis?

(A) Adjustment disorder
(B) Hypochondriasis
(C) Major depression
(D) Panic disorder
(E) Somatization disorder

ANSWER: C

This man has concurrent symptoms of generalized anxiety and major depression. The fourth edition of the *Diagnostic and Statistical Manual of Mental Disorders* does not allow for a separate diagnosis of generalized anxiety disorder if the anxiety occurs exclusively during the course of a mood disorder. The most parsimonious explanation of this man's symptoms is that the generalized anxiety is symptomatic of the depressive episode. Case-level generalized anxiety occurs in approximately 25% of patients within the first year following a stroke; usually the anxiety is symptomatic of a depressive illness. Generalized anxiety is characterized by excessive worry accompanied by motor tension and hypervigilance. Autonomic hyperarousal, a feature of generalized anxiety, may account for this patient's physical symptoms.

Anxious mood and somatic symptoms can be a feature of panic disorder, hypochondriasis, and somatization disorder. In panic disorder, the symptoms occur as discrete episodes that develop abruptly, reach a peak within 10 minutes, and then abate. This patient's symptoms are ongoing. The increased severity of physical complaints in the morning is consistent with a depression-associated diurnal variation of symptoms.

Individuals with hypochondriasis misinterpret their physical symptoms as evidence of a severe disease such as cancer, and the preoccupation persists despite appropriate medical evaluation and reassurance. This man acknowledges the possibility that his physical symptoms are associated with anxiety and he does not attribute them to severe disease.

Somatization disorder usually starts before age 30 years. It is characterized by physical complaints in several organ systems, and the symptoms persist for several years. This patient's age at onset of symptoms and their 2-month duration are not consistent with somatization disorder. Adjustment disorder is diagnosed if clinically significant emotional and behavioral symptoms occur within 3 months of a stressful event and the symptoms do not meet criteria for another psychiatric disorder, such as major depression or anxiety. Although this man's affective symptoms started 2 months after a significant stressor, a diagnosis of adjustment disorder is excluded because he fulfills criteria for major depression.

References

1. Kimura M, Tateno A, Robinson RG. Treatment of poststroke generalized anxiety disorder comorbid with poststroke depression. *Am J Geriatr Psychiatry*. 2003;11(3):320–327.
2. Lenze EJ, Rogers JC, Martire LM, et al. The association of late-life depression and anxiety with physical disability: a review of the literature and prospectus for future research. *Am J Geriatr Psychiatry*. 2001;9(2):113–135.
3. Leppavuori A, Pohjasvaara T, Vataja R, et al. Generalized anxiety disorders three to four months after ischemic stroke. *Cerebrovasc Dis*. 2003;16(3):257–264.

110. An 89-year-old woman, recently admitted to a nursing facility, is found to be frequently incontinent of urine and occasionally incontinent of stool, on initial assessment for the Minimum Data Set. She has Alzheimer's disease and lumbosacral spinal stenosis and has been taking a cholinesterase inhibitor and acetaminophen. The patient's family states that her incontinence has gradually worsened over the past 5 years, and its current severity was an important factor in placing her in the facility. The patient is unable to give a detailed history and denies bladder problems. Observations by the nursing staff suggest a diagnosis of overactive bladder with urge incontinence.

Examination reveals no evidence of severe atrophic vaginitis, pelvic prolapse, or fecal impaction. Catheterization a few minutes after an episode of incontinence reveals a residual volume of 40 mL. Urinalysis of a specimen obtained by catheterization shows 3+ bacteria and 5 to 10 leukocytes per high-power field, and the culture grows over 100,000 colony-forming units of *Escherichia coli*.

Which of the following is the most appropriate next step for managing her incontinence?

(A) A trial of oxybutynin, 2.5 mg three times daily
(B) A trial of long-acting tolterodine, 4 mg daily
(C) A 7- to 10-day course of ciprofloxacin
(D) Initiation of a prompted voiding program
(E) Simple cystometric testing

ANSWER: D

The most appropriate intervention for this patient is a trial of prompted voiding. From 25% to 40% of similar patients respond well to this behavioral protocol, and responsiveness can generally be determined within 3 to 5 days. Some patients benefit from the addition of a bladder-relaxant drug such as oxybutynin or tolterodine, but, because of potential adverse effects, these drugs should be used as an adjunct to a toileting program. Bladder-relaxant drugs may worsen cognitive impairment or precipitate delirium in patients with dementia. They should therefore be used only in patients who have bothersome overactive bladder symptoms that do not respond to a toileting program alone. Eradicating bacteriuria, even in the presence of pyuria, does not improve the severity of incontinence in chronically incontinent nursing-home patients who have no other symptoms of infection. Moreover, treating asymptomatic bacteriuria is not recommended in the nursing home. Simple cystometry would not benefit the patient, as it would not change the initial approach to management.

References

1. Burgio KL, Locher JL, Goode PS, et al. Behavioral vs drug treatment for urge urinary incontinence in older women: a randomized controlled trial. *JAMA.* 1998; 280(23):1995–2000.
2. Fantl JA, Newman DK, Colling J, et al. *Urinary Incontinence in Adults: Acute and Chronic Management.* Clinical Practice Guideline No. 2, AHCPR Publication No. 96-0682. Public Health Service, Agency for Health Care Policy and Research, Rockville, MD; 1996 Update.
3. Roe B, Williams K, Palmer M. Bladder training for urinary incontinence in adults. *Cochrane Database Syst Rev.* 2000;(2):CD001308.

111. A 70-year-old man describes a 6-month history of severe insomnia and fatigue. He has initial insomnia and interrupted sleep with multiple awakenings throughout the night. The insomnia began shortly after his wife died and has gradually worsened. He also describes fatigue, loss of energy, poor concentration, and anxiety, and he is now less active at home and in the community. He is generally in good health and has no history of sleep or psychiatric disturbance. Physical examination is normal.

Bedtime administration of which of the following agents is most likely to help him?

(A) Melatonin, 2 mg sustained release
(B) Mirtazapine, 15 mg
(C) Red wine, 6 oz
(D) Temazepam, 7.5 mg
(E) Zolpidem, 10 mg

ANSWER: B

Depression is a common cause of insomnia in older adults. Untreated depression is likely to lead to insomnia; conversely, untreated insomnia may result in depression. Antidepressant medications such as mirtazapine are effective in older adults with depression and insomnia. Recently bereaved patients commonly have disturbed sleep. They may have a full depressive syndrome, accompanied by lower sleep efficiency, decreased sleep quality, early morning awakening, shorter rapid-eye-movement (REM) sleep latency, greater proportion of REM sleep, and lower rates of delta-wave sleep when compared with nondepressed bereaved adults.

The use of temazepam, zolpidem, and other hypnotics does not effectively address sleep disturbance associated with major depressive disorder. However, judicious use of a hypnotic with an antidepressant may be warranted. Both temazepam and zolpidem are reasonable choices in this regard. Melatonin does not address mood disturbance, and its hypnotic effect is unclear. Alcohol is sometimes used to induce sleepiness, but its use is accompanied by rebound awakening during the night. Alcohol abuse, as well as depression, can be responsible for early morning awakening; generally, alcohol should be avoided as a medicinal agent.

References

1. Ancoli-Israel S. Sleep disorders in older adults. *Geriatrics.* 2004;59:37–40.
2. Nowell PD, Hoch CL, Reynolds CF. Sleep disorders. In: Coffey CE, Cummings JL, eds. *Textbook of Geriatric Neuropsychiatry.* Washington, DC: American Psychiatric Press, Inc; 2000:401–413.
3. Olde Rikkert MG, Rigaud AS. Melatonin in elderly patients with insomnia. *Z Gerontol Geriatr.* 2001;34(6):491–497.
4. Riemann D, Voderholzer U. Primary insomnia: a risk factor to develop depression. *J Affective Disord.* 2003;76(1–3):255–259.

112. A 60-year-old woman is brought to the office by her daughter, who describes a 2-year history of behavioral change, with reduced attention to personal hygiene and inappropriate behavior. The patient is threatened with eviction because she stopped paying rent. She says that the landlord is trying to get her to move by infiltrating her apartment with a toxic gas through the air vents. She often smells the gas and has several times called the police, but they have not found anything. She believes that the landlord has arranged for her problems to be referred to each night by television news broadcasters, and she hears the landlord in the walls every night, discussing her problems and his plans to get rid of her. The daughter indicates that otherwise her mother's health has been good, and both deny use of alcohol or other substances. Physical examination is normal.

Which of the following is the most likely diagnosis?

(A) Alzheimer's disease
(B) Late-onset schizophrenia
(C) Delirium
(D) Major depression
(E) Delusional disorder

ANSWER: B

This patient has a sustained course of persecutory delusions, ideas of reference, and auditory and olfactory hallucinations. The bizarre nature of her delusions and the prominent auditory hallucinations point to schizophrenia rather than a delusional disorder. Up to 20% of cases of schizophrenia occur in patients older than age 45. Unlike early-onset schizophrenia, late-onset schizophrenia is more common in women than in men and is associated with better premorbid function. Limited data suggest that elderly persons with schizophrenia respond to antipsychotic treatment at lower doses than required in younger patients.

Late-onset schizophrenia can be differentiated from delirium by its sustained course, lack of visual hallucinations, and absence of an impaired sensorium. Major depression can present with psychotic features, though typically these are not bizarre, and reflect depressive themes, such as death and disability. Persons with major depression with psychotic features have other symptoms of major depression.

Differentiating late-onset schizophrenia from dementia-related psychosis can be difficult. Sustained systematized delusions and persistent auditory hallucinations are an unlikely presentation of psychosis in Alzheimer's disease. Psychotic symptoms are rare at the onset of dementia in Alzheimer's disease, more typically emerging after several years of cognitive symptoms, and they are typically characterized by simple, repetitive, nonsustained delusions, such as delusions of theft or abandonment, or delusional misidentification of caregivers. Patients with Alzheimer's disease are more likely to have visual than auditory hallucinations.

References

1. Cook SE, Miyahara S, Bacanu SA, et al. Psychotic symptoms in Alzheimer disease: evidence for subtypes. *Am J Geriatr Psychiatry.* 2003;11(4):406–413.
2. Jeste DV, Finkel SI. Psychosis of Alzheimer's disease and related dementias: diagnostic criteria for a distinct syndrome. *Am J Geriatric Psychiatry.* 2000;8(1):29–34.
3. Sable JA, Jeste DV. Antipsychotic treatment for late-life schizophrenia. *Curr Psychiatry Rep.* 2002;4(4):299–306.

113. A 75-year-old smoker who recently had a myocardial infarction comes to the office for advice on life-style changes. History includes chronic obstructive pulmonary disease with a moderately impaired FEV_1.

In such patients, smoking cessation is associated with which of the following?

(A) Improved cognition
(B) Cessation of a decline in FEV_1
(C) Reduction in all-cause mortality
(D) Lung cancer risk that is the same as a nonsmoker

ANSWER: C

Although most smokers who have a myocardial infarction want to quit, after 4 years half will still be smoking. Several studies have demonstrated a 25% to 50% reduction in all-cause mortality in older adults who quit smoking. Other retrospective studies show that the risk of recurrent coronary artery disease in a smoker who quits equals that of a nonsmoker 3 years after cessation of smoking.

No evidence indicates that current smokers who quit will have less cognitive decline. FEV$_1$ will continue to decline, but rates of decline will be similar to those of persons who have never smoked. In persons who quit smoking, deaths due to chronic obstructive pulmonary disease have been shown to statistically increase, but deaths due to all causes (including cardiovascular and cancer) decrease. Men without coronary disease who quit at age 65 years gain an average of 1.4 to 2 years of life; women gain 2.7 to 3.7 years of life. In the smoker who quits, the risk of lung cancer declines more slowly than the risk of coronary artery disease but approaches that of the nonsmoker by 10 years.

References

1. Appel DW, Aldrich TK. Smoking cessation and the elderly. *Clin Geriatr Med*. 2003;19(1):77–100.
2. Burns DM. Cigarette smoking among the elderly: disease consequences and benefits of cessation. *Am J Health Promot*. 2000;14(6)357–361.
3. Gosney M. Smoking cessation. *Gerontology*. 2001;47(5):236–240.
4. Rea TD, Heckbert SR, Kaplan RC, et al. Smoking status and risk for recurrent coronary event after myocardial infarction. *Ann Intern Med*. 2002;137(6):494–500.

114. Which of the following can occur with intramuscular testosterone therapy in men?

(A) Leukopenia
(B) Leukocytosis
(C) Anemia
(D) Polycythemia
(E) Thrombocytopenia

ANSWER: D

Research on use of testosterone in older men is growing. The administration of testosterone has a major benefit on libido, well-being, energy, and muscle strength. It may not, however, improve erectile capability. Testosterone improves lean body mass, decreases body fat, diminishes bone loss of aging, and enhances visual spatial memory.

The most common side effect of intramuscular testosterone therapy is polycythemia. This is neither dose nor duration dependent. Although erythropoietin may increase with testosterone administration, some aspect of the polycythemia appears to be from a direct effect on marrow precursor cells. There is no evidence that testosterone affects leukocytes or platelets. Patients treated with testosterone should have their hematocrit measured at least every 3 months. Polycythemia can have severe consequences, such as thrombotic events, including stroke. Patients with polycythemia who wish to continue testosterone therapy will require phlebotomy. Alternatively, testosterone can be stopped until the hematocrit returns to normal. These strategies should be used for a hematocrit of 53% or greater. Long-term postmarketing data regarding polycythemia is not available for the testosterone patch. Other forms of testosterone, such as implantable testosterone pellets, are infrequently used in the United States.

Other adverse effects of testosterone administration include skin rashes with the patch formulation (either scrotal or nonscrotal) and gynecomastia, due to testosterone conversion to estrogen. Gynecomastia tends to remit if the testosterone is stopped.

Liver dysfunction may occur with 17α-alkylated formulations of testosterone, which are available in the United States. Transaminase elevation and even hepatic carcinomas have been reported with 17α testosterone preparations. Testosterone undecenoate, a 17β testosterone, is not available in the United States.

Users of testosterone gel must be careful not to transfer the testosterone to another person via skin-to-skin contact. Although testosterone can accelerate prostate growth, there is little evidence that this occurs in the aging male. Prostate cancer tends to occur in the setting of low testosterone levels, not elevated levels, in the aging male.

References

1. Hajjar R, Kaiser FE, Morley JE, et al. Outcomes of long-term testosterone replacement in older hypogonadal males: a retrospective analysis. *J Clin Endocrinol Metab*. 1997;82(11):3793–3796.
2. Matsumoto A. Fundamental aspects of hypogonadism in the aging male. *Rev Urol*. 2003; 5(Suppl 1):S3–S10.

3. Morales A, Johnston B, Heaton JP, et al. Testosterone supplementation for hypogonadal impotence: assessment of biochemical measures and therapeutic outcomes. *J Urol.* 1997;157(3):849–854.
4. Oettel M, Hubler D, Patchev V. Selected aspects of endocrine pharmacology of the aging male. *Exp Gerontol.* 2003;38(1–2):189–198.

115. A 75-year-old man cares for his wife, who has Alzheimer's disease, in their own home. Because his wife needs increasing help with activities of daily living, the husband reluctantly decides to place her in a nursing home.

Which of the following factors predicts a more successful transition for the husband after his wife enters the nursing home?

(A) An ambivalent marital relationship
(B) The husband's anticipating loneliness after placement
(C) The husband's having a sense of identity outside of his caregiving role
(D) The husband's volunteering at the nursing home at which his wife resides

ANSWER: C

The decision to place a family member in a nursing home is almost always wrenching. Even when the patient has significant functional deficits, difficult-to-manage behavioral problems, or other features that increase the likelihood of placement, caregivers usually have some doubt or guilt about the decision they have made.

Caregivers display a continuum of reactions to the transition. Some seem to make the transition less traumatically than others. Once the person with dementia is out of the home, the caregiver may not know what to do with the sudden increase in free time and may have a sense of guilt or obligation to visit the person in the nursing home. In some situations, the well spouse spends virtually all of his or her waking time at the nursing home, with little or no social life beyond the facility. Other spouses seem to avoid the facility, sometimes out of guilt or worry that their presence will kindle uncomfortable questions from the demented person about why he or she cannot "go home."

Of the options given, a sense of identity outside of the caregiving role has the most support in the literature for predicting a successful transition for the caregiver. This sense

of identity can take a number of forms, such as involvement in civic groups, volunteering, or assisting others who are caring for loved ones with dementia.

References
1. Grant I, Adler KA, Patterson TL, et al. Health consequences of Alzheimer's caregiving transitions: effects of placement and bereavement. *Psychosom Med.* 2002; 64(3): 477–486.
2. Hagen B. Nursing home placement: factors affecting caregivers' decisions to place family members with dementia. *J Gerontol Nurs.* 2001;27(2):44–53.

116. A 68-year-old obese woman with a history of diabetes mellitus was recently treated with an antibiotic for a urinary tract infection. She now has vulvar pruritus with a white, clumpy vaginal discharge.

Which of the following is the most likely cause of her symptoms?

(A) Bacterial vaginosis
(B) Contact irritation
(C) Candidiasis
(D) Lichen sclerosus
(E) Atrophic vaginitis

ANSWER: C

Common vulvovaginal disorders in postmenopausal women include atrophic vaginitis, vaginal candidiasis, lichen sclerosus, and squamous cell hyperplasia. Bacterial vaginosis is the most common cause of vaginitis in women of childbearing age.

Candidiasis accounts for approximately one third of vaginitis cases. Factors that predispose to symptomatic infection include antibiotic use, obesity, and diabetes mellitus. Vulvar pruritus is the most common symptom; other symptoms include dysuria, irritation, and dyspareunia. Discharge may be present and is typically white and clumpy, resembling cottage cheese. Physical examination often reveals erythema of the vulva and vaginal epithelium. Diagnosis is made via microscopy by visualizing budding yeast and hyphae in vaginal discharge treated with 10% potassium hydroxide. Treatment is with either a single dose of oral fluconazole 150 mg or topical clotrimazole or nystatin.

Noninfectious causes of vaginitis include irritants such as pads, soaps, and perfumes that produce a contact hypersensitivity reaction. The clinical features—pruritus, irritation, burning, and vaginal discharge—are similar to those of vaginitis caused by infection. It is a diagnosis of exclusion. Management comprises identifying and eliminating the offending agent.

Atrophic vaginitis is a consequence of estrogen deficiency and is common in postmenopausal women who are not on hormone replacement therapy. Symptoms include loss of vaginal secretions, burning, dyspareunia, vulvar pruritus, urinary urgency and frequency, and dysuria. Clinically, the vaginal epithelium is thin, pale, and smooth with few or no vaginal folds. Inflammation may be present with patchy erythema and increased friability. Introital stenosis and decreased vaginal depth may be seen. Treatment consists of estrogen given topically or in a hormone-releasing ring.

Lichen sclerosus usually occurs in postmenopausal women. Vulvar pruritus is its hallmark. Clinically, the labia minora may fuse with the labia majora. The vulvar skin becomes thin, white, and wrinkled. Vulvar biopsy with immunofluorescent staining confirms the diagnosis. Treatment consists of highly potent topical corticosteroids, such as clobetasol 0.05 mg or halobetasol propionate 0.05 mg daily for 6 to 12 weeks and then one to three times per week for maintenance.

References

1. Bachman GA, Nevadunsky NS. Diagnosis and treatment of the atrophic vaginitis. *Am Fam Physician.* 2000; 61(10):3090–3096.
2. Powell JJ, Wojnarowska F. Lichen sclerosis. *Lancet.* 1999;353(9166):1777.
3. Sobel JD, Faro S, Force RW, et al. Vulvovaginal candidiasis: epidemiological, diagnostic, and therapeutic considerations. *Am J Obstet Gynecol.* 1998;178:203–211.

117. Which of the following statements linking mutations with extended longevity is true?

(A) Dwarf flies and mice with mutations that decrease the activity of insulin or insulin-like growth factor-1 pathways have longer life spans.
(B) Low-expressing insulin-like growth factor-1 receptor alleles are under-represented among older individuals.
(C) Hypopituitary dwarf mice live longer than appropriate wild-type controls.
(D) Persons with untreated isolated growth hormone deficiency live longer than their unaffected siblings.

ANSWER: C

A number of conserved genes regulate longevity in fruit flies and mice. For example, mutations that decrease the activity of the fly insulin or insulin growth factor (IGF)-1-like pathway (eg, chico or insulin-like receptor) cause dwarfism and nearly double longevity. Similarly, deficits in IGF-1 signaling in mice (eg, Prop-1 or Pit-1) result in dwarves that live 25% to 65% longer than wild-type mice. At least some of the effects of these mutations appear to be mediated via declines in plasma growth hormone levels. Human subjects with low-expressing IGF-1 receptor alleles have lower levels of free plasma IGF-1 levels, and these alleles are more highly represented among longer-lived individuals. Mutant dwarf mice with a deficiency in growth hormone–binding protein or mice with a combined deficiency in growth hormone, prolactin, and thyrotropin live longer than wild-type controls. In contrast, the life span of individuals with untreated isolated growth hormone deficiency is shorter than that of their siblings or normal human population-based averages.

References

1. Bartke A, Coschigano K, Kopchick J, et al. Genes that prolong life: relationships of growth hormone and growth to aging and life span. *J Gerontol A Biol Sci Med Sci.* 2001; 56(8):B340–B349.
2. Bonafe M, Barbieri M, Marchegiani F, et al. Polymorphic variants of insulin-like growth factor I (IGF-I) receptor and phosphoinositide 3-kinase genes affect IGF-I plasma levels and human longevity: cues for an evolutionarily conserved mechanism of life span control. *J Clin Endocrinol Metab.* 2003; 88(7):3299–3304.

3. Longo VD, Finch CE. Evolutionary medicine: from dwarf model systems to healthy centenarians? *Science.* 2003; 299(5611):1342–1346.

118. A 67-year-old right-handed man comes to the office because he has pain in his neck and left shoulder, sometimes radiating to the left hand. The pain has been present for the past year, and in the past several months he has also noted some difficulty walking, with stiffness in both legs. Neurologic examination is significant for hypesthesia in the left thumb and index fingers, absent left biceps and brachioradialis reflexes, bilateral hyperactive patellar reflexes, and impaired vibratory perception in both feet.

Which of the following is the most likely diagnosis?

(A) Anterior spinal artery occlusion
(B) Parasagittal meningioma
(C) Left median neuropathy
(D) Cervical spondylosis
(E) Syringomyelia

ANSWER: D

This man has cervical spondylosis with a consequent cervical spondylotic myelopathy and radiculopathy. Magnetic resonance imaging of the cervical spine will identify the spondylosis and cord compression. Cervical spondylosis is characterized by intervertebral disk degeneration with consequent disk herniation, vertebral injury, and osteophyte formation. The osteophytes can then produce both cord and nerve root compression, often at multiple levels. The clinical features of cervical spondylotic myelopathy and radiculopathy typically develop slowly, although sometimes a stepwise pattern is evident. Pain in the neck, shoulder, or arm is often the initial symptom. Patients then develop the characteristic combination of radiculopathic features in the upper extremities (a C6 radiculopathy in this patient) and myelopathic features in the lower extremities (spasticity, patellar hyperreflexia, and posterior column dysfunction in this patient). Bowel and bladder dysfunction may be present.

Anterior spinal artery occlusion typically develops and produces symptoms over several hours or less. Pain in the neck or back, sometimes with a radicular component, is accompanied by loss of pain and temperature sensation at levels below the lesion, while posterior column function is preserved. Bilateral lower extremity weakness is usually present, initially with flaccidity and hyporeflexia, later with spasticity and hyperreflexia. Parasagittal meningiomas, which form in the fissure between the cerebral hemispheres, produce bilateral lower extremity weakness and spasticity, but not cervical radiculopathy. Median neuropathy produces weakness of wrist and finger flexion and of some intrinsic hand muscles, but it is not accompanied by loss of either biceps or brachioradialis reflexes (the biceps muscle is innervated by the musculocutaneous nerve; the brachioradialis muscle is innervated by the radial nerve). The sensory distribution of the median nerve typically encompasses the thumb, index, and middle fingers, along with the median half of the ring finger and the corresponding portions of the palm of the hand. Syringomyelia is characterized by cavitation of the spinal cord, most frequently in the cervicothoracic region. Sensory loss classically is in a "cape" distribution as a consequence of interruption of decussating pain and temperature fibers, with preservation of posterior column function, producing a dissociated pattern of sensory impairment. Muscle weakness in the upper extremities, with atrophy and loss of reflexes, may develop. Myelopathy due to corticospinal tract involvement is also seen, with resultant spasticity and hyperreflexia in the lower extremities.

References

1. Byrne TN, Benzel EC, Waxman SG. *Diseases of the Spine and Spinal Cord.* Oxford: Oxford University Press;2000:134–143.
2. Schmidt MH, Quinones-Hinojosa A, Rosenberg WS. Cervical myelopathy associated with degenerative spine disease and ossification of the posterior longitudinal ligament. *Semin Neurol.* 2002;22(2):143–148.
3. Young WF. Cervical spondylotic myelopathy: a common cause of spinal cord dysfunction in older persons. *Am Fam Physician.* 2000;62(5):1064–1070.

119. A generally healthy 74-year-old woman returns to the office for follow-up of incontinence. She is physically active and extremely bothered by the incontinence. Her symptoms include continuous dribbling and urgency with incontinence during most activities. In the past 15 years, she has had two bladder suspension surgeries that only transiently improved her symptoms of stress incontinence.

On examination she has a positive cough test for stress incontinence, both standing before voiding and supine after voiding. Mild vaginal atrophy and a moderate cystocele are noted on pelvic examination. Postvoid residual urine is 30 mL, and urinalysis is negative. During the last 6 months she underwent a course of biofeedback and has been regularly using pelvic muscle exercises and bladder-training techniques. She uses estrogen vaginal cream twice weekly. She tolerated oxybutynin 2.5 mg three times daily with no amelioration of symptoms; when the dosage was raised to 5 mg three times daily, she had dry mouth, dry eyes, and constipation with no improvement in symptoms.

Which of the following is the most appropriate next step for this patient?

(A) Refer her to a urogynecologist for consideration of surgical intervention.
(B) Increase the estrogen cream to 5 times per week.
(C) Add vaginal cones to enhance her pelvic muscle exercises.
(D) Begin long-acting tolterodine, 4 mg daily.
(E) Begin pseudoephedrine, 30 mg three times daily.

ANSWER: A

This patient's history and physical examination findings are most compatible with a diagnosis of intrinsic sphincter deficiency (type 3 stress incontinence), with an additional component of overactive bladder. Patients with intrinsic sphincter deficiency typically have a history of one or more lower urinary tract surgeries, report nearly continuous leakage of urine while active, and have a positive cough test for stress incontinence—sometimes even in the supine position with only a small amount of urine in the bladder. Although symptoms may improve with conservative therapy consisting of topical estrogen, pelvic muscle exercises, and bladder training, along with a bladder relaxant for overactive bladder, patients with intrinsic sphincter deficiency generally require surgical intervention. Some patients benefit from periurethral injections of collagen, but many require a pubovaginal sling procedure.

This patient will not benefit from a higher dose of topical estrogen, as the dose she has been on for 6 months has probably had its effect on the vaginal and urethral epithelium. Furthermore, it may be that estrogen is not effective for stress, urge, or mixed urge-stress urinary incontinence. Vaginal cones can be effective, but there is no evidence that they add benefit to a well-performed and practiced pelvic muscle exercise program. Some patients respond better to one bladder relaxant than another, and long-acting tolterodine has fewer adverse effects than short-acting oxybutynin. However, this patient's predominant problem is probably intrinsic sphincter deficiency, not overactive bladder. Thus, a trial of a different bladder relaxant would unlikely benefit her most bothersome symptoms. Symptoms of overactive bladder are relieved in some patients after surgery for stress incontinence. Adding the α-agonist pseudoephedrine may benefit patients with stress incontinence, but it is unlikely to have a major impact in a patient with intrinsic sphincter deficiency.

References

1. Harvey MA, Baker K, Wells GA. Tolterodine versus oxybutynin in the treatment of urge urinary incontinence: a meta-analysis. *Am J Obstet Gynecol.* 2001;185(1):56–61.
2. Hendrix SL, Cochrane BB, Nygaard IE, et al. Effects of estrogen with and without progestin on urinary incontinence. *JAMA.* 2005;293(8):935–948.
3. Leach GE, Dmochowski RR, Appell RA, et al. Female Stress Urinary Incontinence Clinical Guidelines Panel summary report on surgical management of female stress urinary incontinence. The American Urological Association. *J Urol.* 1997;158(3 Pt 1):875–880.

120. A 72-year-old man comes to the office for a physical examination, which is normal except for a flat, tan skin lesion on the back of his neck. The lesion measures 1.5 cm and is somewhat asymmetric, with uneven edges and dark brown or black areas. The patient does not know how long the lesion has been there or if it has grown. His wife recalls that a doctor noted a skin lesion on the back of his neck about 5 years ago.

Which of the following should be performed?

(A) Shallow shave biopsy
(B) Cryosurgery
(C) Excisional biopsy
(D) Electrocautery

ANSWER: C

Characteristics suggesting a malignant skin lesion include asymmetry, irregular border, color variance, and large diameter (ABCD mnemonic). Asymmetry can be assessed by comparing one half of the skin lesion to the other half to determine if the two are alike. A lesion is more likely to be cancerous if its border is irregular, notched, scalloped, or indistinct, or if it has color variation (such as different shades of browns, blues, reds, whites, and blacks), or if its diameter is larger than 6 mm.

Approximately 70% of melanomas are superficial spreading type, originating in a nevus. Between 15% and 30% are nodular. Nodular melanoma is much more aggressive, usually does not start from a mole, and tends to occur on the trunk, head, and neck in middle age. Acral lentiginous melanoma is found in only 2% to 8% of white patients but accounts for up to 60% of melanomas in dark-skinned patients; it often presents on the soles of feet or as a subungual lesion. Fewer than 10% of melanomas are lentigo maligna type, which occurs in older persons and is most likely in this patient. Lentigo maligna lesions develop from a precursor lesion, called Hutchinson's freckle, and can be present for 5 to 15 years before invasion. The lesion is also called *malignant lentigo of elderly people*, *junctional nevus*, and *melanoma in situ*. Most authors currently refer to it as *lentigo maligna* when it is confined to the epidermis, and *lentigo maligna melanoma* when it penetrates the dermis.

Excisional biopsy, incisional biopsy by elliptic excision, and punch biopsy are used to diagnose melanoma. Superficial skin biopsy by shaving, scissors excision, or curettage does not allow for assessment of tumor thickness, which is important for melanoma staging, prognosis, and treatment planning. An excisional biopsy with a narrow margin of normal-appearing skin can usually be performed on lesions unless the result would be disfiguring, in which case incisional biopsy is reasonable. Incisional biopsy also is indicated for lesions that are too large for complete excision. The specimen should include a portion of subcutaneous fat to ensure accurate microstaging.

Given the appearance of this lesion, it is necessary to obtain tissue to make a diagnosis. Cryosurgery and electrocautery are not appropriate choices, as they do not provide tissue.

References

1. Arca MJ, Biermann JS, Johnson TM, et al. Biopsy techniques for skin, soft-tissue, and bone neoplasms. *Surg Oncol Clin N Am.* 1995;4(1):157–174.
2. Balch CM, Buzaid AC, Soong SJ, et al. New TNM melanoma staging system: linking biology and natural history to clinical outcomes. *Semin Surg Oncol.* 2003;21(1):43–52.
3. Jemal A, Devesa SS, Hartge P, et al. Recent trends in cutaneous melanoma incidence among whites in the United States. *J Natl Cancer Inst.* 2001;93(9):678–683.

121. An 81-year-old woman who sustained a right intertrochanteric fracture yesterday evening needs preoperative clearance for intraoperative reduction and internal fixation of the fracture. The patient resides in an assisted-care facility. She has systolic hypertension, hyperlipidemia, and mild dementia. She has never smoked. Current medications include aspirin, hydrochlorothiazide, atorvastatin, donepezil, and calcium with vitamin D. She previously walked without assistance and was able to perform activities of daily living. Her advance care plan includes treatment of reversible problems.

On physical examination, the patient is mildly confused. Pulse rate is 82 per minute, respiratory rate is 20 per minute, and blood pressure is 162/84 mm Hg. She has severe pain on movement of the right leg, and the rest of the examination is within normal limits. Complete blood cell count, basic metabolic panel, and chest radiograph are normal. Electrocardiogram shows normal sinus rhythm without ischemic changes and is unchanged from previous tracings.

Which of the following decisions regarding preoperative management of this patient is most appropriate?

(A) Postpone surgery until the confusion has cleared.
(B) Postpone surgery until pharmacologically induced stress testing can be performed.
(C) Postpone surgery until blood pressure is controlled.
(D) Institute β-blocker therapy and proceed with surgery.
(E) Proceed with surgery.

ANSWER: D

Hip fracture remains an important cause of death and functional decline in older adults. For Medicare recipients, the 1-year mortality rate is 14%. Among survivors, only 54% walk unaided after 1 year. The timing of operative intervention affects patient outcome: A delay can diminish functional recovery, but failure to manage medical conditions may increase perioperative complications. Evidence from most cohort studies indicates that, for stable patients who do not have active comorbid illnesses, surgical repair within the first 24 to 48 hours is associated with better return of function and reduced mortality.

Postoperative myocardial infarction in patients having noncardiac surgery is a significant problem. In recent studies, overall rates of postoperative myocardial infarction or cardiac death range from 1% to 5% among patients undergoing noncardiac surgery. In patients with cardiovascular risk factors, the rate of postoperative myocardial infarction or cardiac death may be 20% to 40%. Perioperative β-blocker administration in appropriately risk-stratified patients reduces the risk of death up to 2 years after noncardiac surgery and lowers in-hospital mortality as well.

This patient has no contraindication to β-blocker therapy and has cardiac risk factors: age, postmenopausal status, hypertension, and hyperlipidemia. She is an appropriate candidate for immediate surgical correction with perioperative β-blocker use to a target heart rate of 70 per minute.

The patient's hypertension is not a contraindication to surgery and should not postpone surgery. Pain control with analgesic and operative repair, along with the institution of a β-blocker, may be sufficient to control her elevated blood pressure. If not, antihypertensive agents can be added. Similarly, the patient has mild dementia, which is a strong host-related risk factor for developing delirium. Management should minimize external risk factors for delirium (eg, metabolic abnormalities, medications, restraints, poor nutrition) but should not delay surgery in the absence of acute medical illness.

References

1. Auerbach AD, Goldman L. Beta-blockers and reduction of cardiac events in noncardiac surgery: clinical applications. *JAMA*. 2002:287(11):1435–1444.
2. Gilbert K, Larocque BJ, Patrick LT. Prospective evaluation of cardiac risk indices for patients undergoing noncardiac surgery. *Ann Intern Med*. 2000;133(5):356–359.
3. Lichtblau S. Hip fracture: surgical decisions that affect medical management. *Geriatrics*. 2000;55(4):50–56.
4. Mangano DT, Layug EL, Wallace A, et al. Effect of atenolol on mortality and cardiovascular morbidity after noncardiac surgery. Multicenter Study of Perioperative Ischemia Research Group. *N Engl J Med*. 1996;335(23):1713–1720.

122. A 69-year-old woman who lives alone wants to quit drinking. She was a moderate drinker until her retirement 10 years ago, when her drinking increased. She was diagnosed with alcohol dependence. She has quit drinking twice, with minimal withdrawal symptoms. Both times she participated in a 12-step self-help group, and on the second attempt she also took naltrexone but stopped after developing a hypersensitivity reaction. After each attempt she relapsed and returned to heavy regular drinking. She wants to try again and asks for a different medication to help reduce the likelihood of relapse.

Which of the following is the most appropriate pharmacologic treatment for this patient?

(A) Ondansetron
(B) Disulfiram
(C) Acamprosate
(D) Nalmefene

ANSWER: C

Acamprosate became available in the United States in January 2005 after being available for several years in Europe. A synthetic derivative of the amino acid homotaurine, it has been proven effective for maintaining abstinence in alcohol-dependent people who have already stopped drinking. It appears to suppress glutamatergic excitation that occurs in alcohol withdrawal and early abstinence. However, few studies to date have included older people. Because it is not metabolized significantly by the liver and is eliminated by the kidneys, it can be used in patients with liver disease. In persons with moderate renal impairment (creatinine clearance of 30 to 50 mL/min), half of the normal dose is recommended.

Some evidence supports the effectiveness of disulfiram for treatment of alcohol dependence, but it is not used routinely in older patients because the disulfiram-ethanol reaction may pose risks to the cardiovascular system.

Ondansetron is approved by the Food and Drug Administration for treatment of chemotherapy-induced emesis. It is a selective serotonin-receptor antagonist that has been found effective in increasing abstinent days in early-onset alcohol dependence. However, results in persons who developed dependence later in life, like this patient, were no different than results obtained with placebo.

Nalmefene, an opioid antagonist approved by the Food and Drug Administration for reversal of postoperative opioid depression and opioid overdose, is effective for treatment of alcohol dependence but is contraindicated in patients with a history of hypersensitivity to naltrexone.

References

1. Barrick C, Connors GJ. Relapse prevention and maintaining abstinence in older adults with alcohol-use disorders. *Drugs Aging.* 2002;19(8):583–594.
2. Overman GP, Teter CJ, Guthrie SK. Acamprosate for the adjunctive treatment of alcohol dependence. *Ann Pharmacother.* 2003;37:1090–1099.
3. Sattar SP, Petty F, Burke WJ. Diagnosis and treatment of alcohol dependence in older alcoholics. *Clin Geriatr Med.* 2003;19:743–761.

123. An elderly male patient is brought to the emergency department in an acute confusional state. He is combative and refusing all treatment. He has been living with a son who is out of town and temporarily was being taken care of by a cousin. It is difficult to get a clear medical history, and the covering physician for his regular physician does not know him. The cousin does know that at baseline he has lung disease that limits his mobility at home. For example, his cousin reports he gets short of breath going from his bed to the bathroom and sometimes has difficulty eating because of shortness of breath. He uses oxygen at home. He has a tendency "to repeat things" but has no known dementia.

Over the past 24 hours he developed a productive cough and has become increasingly incoherent. In the emergency department he is hypoxic, hypercarbic, and is approaching the need for intubation. Given the radiographic picture of severe bullous emphysema with probable pneumonia, it is likely that he will have a great deal of difficulty coming off of a ventilator once he is intubated.

You do not know his prior wishes or if he has any advance directives. You should do which of the following?

(A) Not intubate on the basis of your judgment of benefits versus burdens.
(B) Intubate and sort out the consequences later.
(C) Not intubate on the basis of prognosis that is based on an APACHE III score.
(D) Intubate with an agreement to extubate in 24 hours if there is no improvement.
(E) Await intubation until the son can be reached.

ANSWER: B

When a patient clearly has lacked decisional capacity before becoming acutely ill, then a surrogate decision maker will need to make decisions even in emergency situations. If the patient had decisional capacity before an acute illness and his or her wishes were known, then they would determine treatment.

In this case the patient's decisional capacity before becoming delirious is unknown, as are any prior directives he may have made. The person available is not the appropriate surrogate. Therefore, the situation must be temporized until issues can be clarified. Since a decision to refrain from instituting life-saving therapy or waiting until a surrogate is found could result in life-threatening deterioration that would preclude the possibility of further clarifying the patient's mental status, all therapies that would sustain either life or function should be instituted in this emergency situation. This is done with the understanding that once the situation is clarified, any or all interventions may be discontinued.

References

1. Drickamer MA. Assessment of decisional capacity and competency. In: Hazzard WR, Blass JP, Halter JB, et al., eds. *Principles of Geriatric Medicine and Gerontology*. 5th ed. New York: McGraw-Hill, 2003:121–125.
2. The Hastings Center. *Guidelines for the Termination of Life-Sustaining Treatment and the Care of the Dying*. Briarcliff Manor, NY: Hastings Center; 1987.

124. A 75-year-old man comes to the office for a routine examination. He has a history of hypertension controlled by medication. He smoked two packs of cigarettes daily for 30 years but quit 20 years ago. His last dental examination was 2 years ago.

On physical examination, blood pressure is 140/85 mm Hg and pulse is 75 per minute and regular. He has moderate periodontitis, some defective restorations, and a 2 × 2-cm indurated ulcer on the left lateroventral border of the tongue adjacent to a broken filling. The patient notes that the ulcer is not painful except when he eats acidic and spicy foods. He does not remember when it started.

Which of the following is the best management strategy for this patient?

(A) Restoration of the filling.
(B) Biopsy of the lesion.
(C) Topical anesthetic gel.
(D) Assure the patient that the ulcer will resolve in 7 to 10 days.

ANSWER: B

Oral cancer causes approximately 10,000 deaths in the United States each year; most cases occur in persons over age 40, especially in those with a history of smoking. Most cases (96%) are of squamous cell carcinoma that is usually preceded by dysplasia. It presents as white epithelial lesions on the oral mucosa (leukoplakia), red and white lesions (erythroplakia), or a nonhealing ulcer. Because early diagnosis and treatment markedly improve outcome and survival, this patient should be referred immediately for biopsy.

Although defective restoration could have contributed to the initiation of the ulcer, the clinical appearance of the ulcer with induration indicates a precancerous or cancerous (squamous cell carcinoma) lesion. Thus, repair of the restoration alone is not adequate. An over-the-counter topical anesthetic gel is not effective in treating precancerous or cancerous lesions, or any other oral lesion. It temporarily relieves pain by numbing the area but does not treat the underlying condition. The description of this lesion is not consistent with that of a canker sore, which is a shallow ulcer covered by a yellowish-white removable fibrinous membrane and surrounded by an erythematous halo. Canker sores are usually of short duration (7 to 10 days) and heal spontaneously.

References

1. Allergies and immunologic diseases. In: Neville BW, Damm DD, Allen CM, et al. *Oral and Maxillofacial Pathology*. 2nd ed. Philadelpia, PA: W.B. Saunders Company; 2002: 285–308.
2. Braakhuis BJ, Tabor MP, Leemans CR, et al. Second primary tumours and field cancerization in oral and oropharyngeal cancer: molecular techniques provide new insights and definitions. *Head and Neck*. 2002;24(2):198–206.
3. Reibel J. Prognosis of oral pre-malignant lesions: significance of clinical, histopathological, and molecular biologic characteristics. *Crit Rev Oral Biol Med*. 2003;14(1):47–62.

125. An 80-year-old man is transferred from the intensive care unit to a medical step-down unit. The patient was admitted to the hospital 6 weeks earlier with pneumonia complicated by respiratory failure, requiring several weeks of ventilator support. Before this hospitalization, the patient had no known health problems; he weighed 72 kg (158 lb). Because of the pneumonia and, later, urosepsis, the patient had been on intravenous antibiotics during most of his hospital stay. One day ago, he was switched to oral antibiotics. One week before transfer, a percutaneous enteral gastrostomy tube was placed and a 1.2-kcal per cc polymeric feeding solution was started at full strength. The feeding rate has remained at 25 cc per hour because diarrhea, gastric bloating, and high gastric residuals developed when faster rates were attempted. The patient has no desire to eat and chokes on soft foods when fed.

He weighs 74.5 kg (164 lb; body mass index 25 [kg/m^2]). On examination, he is very weak. There are scattered rhonchi and wheezes in both lung fields, but no crackles. Jugular venous pressure is 5 cm, and heart sounds are normal, with no S$_3$. There is anasarca with 2+ edema of both legs extending up his back.

Laboratory studies:

Albumin	1.6 g/dL
Pre-albumin	6 mg/dL (normal, 18–45 mg/dL)
Serum sodium	144 mEq/L
Urea nitrogen	36 mg/dL
Creatinine	0.8 mg/dL
Phosphate	3.0 mg/dL (normal, 2.5–4.9 mg/dL)
Hemoglobin	10.4 g/dL
Leukocyte count	7800/μL

In addition to ordering a swallowing evaluation, which of the following would best improve the patient's nutritional status at this point?

(A) Prescribe diphenoxylate with atropine.
(B) Begin total parenteral nutrition.
(C) Ask the nurses to hand-feed the patient.
(D) Begin peripheral hyperalimentation.
(E) Place a jejunostomy.

ANSWER: D

Given his presenting problems and the long duration of nutritional deprivation, this patient likely has serious nutritional deficits. His nutrient intake should be increased to at least 25 kcal per kg body weight (ideally, 35 kcal per kg body weight) as soon as possible. Of the choices provided, the best way to accomplish this goal is to start peripheral alimentation as an adjunct to enteral feedings, with close monitoring for volume overload.

None of the other choices is optimal for the patient at this time. Antimotility agents may control diarrhea associated with enteral feeding but should not be used until antibiotic-associated *(Clostridium difficile)* pseudo-membranous colitis is excluded. The combination of diphenoxylate and atropine must be used with caution as it can cause delirium. Even with an antimotility agent, this patient is unlikely to tolerate a rapid increase in rate of enteral feedings, given his poor gastric motility and profound hypoalbuminemia.

Total parenteral alimentation through a central line is also not optimal; unless there are contraindications or other insurmountable obstacles, patients should be fed enterally. It is premature to conclude that this patient will not tolerate enteral feedings, so they should not be abandoned.

Unless the swallowing study identifies contraindications to oral feeding, the patient can be started on an appropriate oral diet. However, it will probably be several weeks before he can consume an adequate amount of nutrients orally. A jejunostomy tube would bypass the stomach and thus eliminate the problem with high gastric residuals. However, other methods of resolving high gastric residuals should be considered before jejunostomy.

References

1. Anderson AD, Palmer D, MacFie J. Peripheral parenteral nutrition. *Br J Surg.* 2003;90(9):1048–1054.
2. Culkin A, Gabe SM. Nutritional support: indications and techniques. *Clinical Medicine.* 2002;2(5):395–401.
3. de la Torre AM, de Mateo Silleras B, Perez-Garcia A. Guidelines for nutrition support in the elderly. *Public Health Nutr.* 2001;4(6A):1379–1384.
4. Mentec H, Dupont H, Bocchetti M, et al. Upper digestive intolerance during enteral nutrition in critically ill patients: frequency, risk factors, and complications. *Crit Care Med.* 2001;29(10):1955–1961.

126. A 68-year-old man comes to the office for a physical examination. His only medical problem is hypertension. He has no family history of coronary artery disease, peripheral vascular disease, or stroke. He does not smoke. He has not had his cholesterol measured in more than 5 years. On examination, blood pressure is 132/70 mm Hg.

Laboratory studies (fasting):
Total cholesterol	240 mg/dL
Low-density lipoprotein	160 mg/dL
High-density lipoprotein	50 mg/dL
Triglycerides	120 mg/dL

In addition to dietary modification and exercise, which of the following is the most appropriate recommendation for this patient?

(A) Retest in 3 months.
(B) Retest in 1 year.
(C) Initiate statin therapy now.
(D) Retest in 3 years.
(E) Initiate therapy with niacin now.

ANSWER: A

Primary prevention of coronary heart disease (CHD) by lowering cholesterol begins with modification of diet and exercise. If the low-density lipoprotein (LDL) goal is not attained in 3 months, then drug therapy is introduced. The guidelines of the National Cholesterol Education Program Adult Treatment Panel III recommend treatment of older adults who are at risk for CHD without defining an age limit. Guidelines for persons with CHD or equivalent risk (eg, diabetes mellitus) should be treated to a target goal of LDL at least below 100 mg/dL and perhaps as low as 70.

In order to determine the appropriate LDL goal for this patient, his risk factors for CHD must be assessed. Risk factors that modify LDL goals are cigarette smoking, hypertension or treatment with antihypertensive medication, high-density lipoprotein level below 40 mg/dL, heart disease in a first-degree male relative before age 55 or female relative before age 65, and patient age (men aged 45 or older, women aged 55 or older).

If two or more risk factors for CHD are present, the Framingham scoring system is used to determine the risk for CHD over the next 10 years and to determine the intensity of therapy indicated. Risk factors in this scoring system include age, total cholesterol, high-density lipoprotein level, systolic blood pressure, treatment for hypertension, and cigarette smoking. In this case, the patient has a moderate risk for CHD, with a 10-year risk of 20% for myocardial infarction and coronary death, and the LDL goal is 130 mg/dL or below. If the LDL remains above 130 mg/dL after 3 months of life-style intervention, then a lipid-lowering agent such as an HMG Co-A reductase inhibitor (statin) is initiated. Older adults should be monitored for possible drug-drug interactions and altered drug metabolism.

As not all older adults at risk of CHD benefit from intensive treatment, a more conservative approach may be indicated.

References

1. Expert Panel on Detection, Evaluation, and Treatment of High Cholesterol in Adults. Executive Summary of the Third Report of the National Cholesterol Education Program (NCEP) Expert panel on detection, evaluation and treatment of high cholesterol in adults (Adult Treatment Panel III). *JAMA*. 2001;285(19):2486–2497.
2. Grundy SM, Cleeman JI, Bairey Merz CN, et al. Implications of recent clinical trials for the National Cholesterol Education Program Adult Treatment Panel III Guidelines. *Circulation*. 2004;110(2):227–239.
3. Morgan JM, Capuzzi DM. Hypercholesterolemia. The NCEP Adult Treatment Panel III Guidelines. *Geriatrics*. 2003;58(8):33–38.

127. A daughter comes with her mother to her mother's clinic appointment and requests that you fill out conservatorship papers. The mother is an 84-year-old woman who has been living on her own since the death of her husband 7 years ago. You have followed her for the past 3 years in your office for non–insulin-dependent diabetes, atrial fibrillation (for which she receives an anticoagulant), and moderate aortic stenosis. During this time you have noted an increase in nonadherence with her medication regimen. She had a hospital admission 1 month ago for dehydration, partially due to hyperglycemia, and her INR was noted to be 1.2. She was unclear as to whether she had been taking her pills correctly when in hospital. Now she assures you that she has that "all taken care of" but does not give you specifics on how she obtains her medications nor how she remembers to take them. She does know that she needs to get tested for her warfarin regularly. The daughter states that her mother does not eat correctly, rarely showers, and refuses to allow others to help her.

Her Folstein Mini–Mental State Examination (MMSE) score is 25 (errors were in recall, orientation, and the three-step command). Her Executive Interview (EXIT 25) score of 9, demonstrating difficulty with sequencing, intrusions, perseveration, and self-monitoring, suggests mild to moderate impairment in executive functioning.

The most important aspect of this patient and her examination that would persuade you that she may or may not need a conservator is which of the following?

(A) The EXIT 25 score of 9
(B) The MMSE score of 25
(C) The daughter's concern
(D) The functional ability of the patient
(E) The hospitalization

ANSWER: D

The most important factor in assessing this (or any other) patient for the need for a conservator is whether her decisions place her at significant risk. If she has the decisional capacity to understand the risks and benefits of her decisions, then she is competent to make these decisions. If she does not have this decisional capacity and makes decisions that place her at risk, then conservatorship is warranted. Although specific neuropsychologic testing can clarify the areas of deficit and support the need for a conservator, a person's demonstrated inability to care for him or herself is the gold standard for legal action.

The MMSE is a good indicator of decreased cognitive function in key areas that may affect decisional capacity, such as memory and language, but only when it demonstrates severe impairment (MMSE score of 10 or less) can it be said to demonstrate cognitive function below which the person is highly unlikely to still have the ability to safely make decisions and care for him or herself.

For tests of executive function, the correlation with impaired decision making may be higher, but even then, a score of 15 or higher on the EXIT 25 is needed in order to have a high predictive value for incompetence.

The mere fact of hospitalization is not sufficient evidence. There may have been problems causing both temporary mental status problems and dehydration, such as an infection, which could explain her medication nonadherence. The daughter's opinion, although important, should not be the sole determinant for this decision. Both of these factors may be used to correlate with other evidence to support the decision.

References

1. Grisso T, Appelbaum PS. *Assessing Competence to Consent to Treatment: A Guide for Physicians and Other Health Professionals.* 6th ed. New York: Oxford University Press; 1998.
2. Holzer JC, Gansler DA, Moczynski NP, et al. Cognitive functions in the informed consent evaluation process: a pilot study. *J Am Acad Psychiatry Law.* 1997;25(4):531–540.
3. Marson DC. Loss of competency in Alzheimer's disease: conceptual and psychometric approaches. *Int J Law Psychiatry.* 2001;24(2–3):267–283.

128. A 74-year-old man moved to a new residential care facility 2 weeks ago. He has poorly controlled type 2 diabetes mellitus and hypertension, has no history of smoking, and is sedentary. Evaluation shows blood pressure of 160/90 mm Hg and a serum glucose level of 220 mg/dL. On examination, the patient has several teeth missing on both upper and lower jaws and is wearing upper and lower partial dentures.

Which oral condition is most likely to be found?

(A) Salivary stones
(B) Xerostomia
(C) Squamous cell carcinoma
(D) Stomatitis

ANSWER: B

Diabetes mellitus increases the risk of salivary gland dysfunction, periodontitis, fungal diseases, and caries. From 40% to 80% of diabetic patients suffer from xerostomia because of salivary gland dysfunction. Diabetic patients may have a predisposition to fungal infections and caries as a result of xerostomia and elevated salivary glucose levels.

Since the patient has no history of smoking, his risk for getting oral cancer is low. Further, no association between oral cancer and diabetes is reported. The causes of salivary stones (sialoliths) are unknown, and the condition is not increased in diabetics. Stomatitis, a gray-white pallor of the hard palate with punctate red spots is commonly seen in cigarette, pipe, and cigar smokers. It occurs in response to the heat generated by smoking.

References

1. Lalla RV, D'Ambrosio JA. Dental management considerations for the patient with diabetes mellitus. *J Am Dent Assoc.* 2001;132(10):1425–1432.
2. Matthews DC. The relationship between diabetes and periodontal disease. *J Can Dent Assoc.* 2002;68(3):161–164.

129. A 88-year-old nursing-home resident with advanced Alzheimer's disease is evaluated for weight loss. Her weight had been stable since admission to the facility 5 years ago, but she has lost nearly 5.5 kg (12 lb; 9% of her weight) over the past 6 months. She has not had any hospitalizations, acute infections, or other serious medical problems in the past 18 months. Since her move to the nursing home, her cognitive function has slowly and steadily declined. She is now dependent in all activities of daily living and has required feeding assistance for the last 4 months. She is on an 1800-kcal regular diet that was modified to include finger foods and nightly snacks. The nurses state that she has become progressively more withdrawn and less dynamic over the past year and now participates much less in her own care and feeding.

Which of the following is the best next step to address the patient's weight loss?

(A) Prescribe 1 can (240 mL) of a polymeric oral supplement with each meal.
(B) Arrange for placement of percutaneous enteral gastrostomy tube.
(C) Change to a 2000-kcal pureed diet.
(D) Perform comprehensive evaluation for weight loss.
(E) Start mirtazapine, 30 mg orally each day.

ANSWER: D

There are many possible reasons as to why this resident is not consuming an adequate amount of nutrients to maintain her weight. Before her diet is changed or other nutritional intervention is provided, the patient should have a comprehensive evaluation to identify potentially reversible causes of weight loss. Several published protocols can serve as guidelines for the evaluation. Subsequent interventions should be directed at resolving any problem identified.

If nutrient intake remains low after correctable causes are excluded, a polymeric oral supplement can be added to her diet. However, supplements are generally most effective when offered between, rather than with, meals. Nothing in the patient's history suggests the need for a pureed diet. If the assessment provides evidence that the patient is depressed, a trial of an antidepressant may improve nutrient intake.

References

1. American Medical Directors Association. *Altered Nutritional Status.* Columbia, MD: American Medical Directors Association; 2001.
2. Corbett CF, Crogan NL, Short RA. Using the minimum data set to predict weight loss in nursing home residents. *Appl Nurs Res.* 2002;15(4):249–253.
3. Goldberg RJ. Weight change in depressed nursing home patients on mirtazapine. *J Am Geriatr Soc.* 2002;50(8):1461.
4. Rigler SK, Webb MJ, Redford L, et al. Weight outcomes among antidepressant users in nursing facilities. *J Am Geriatr Soc.* 2001;49(1):49–55.
5. Thomas DR, Ashmen W, Morley JE, et al. Nutritional management in long-term care: development of a clinical guideline. Council for Nutritional Strategies in Long-Term Care. *J Gerontol A Biol Sci Med Sci.* 2000;55(12):M725–M734.

130. A 79-year-old man comes to the office for a follow-up visit. He lives at home with his son, who moved in last year to care for his father in exchange for room and board. In response to questions about his home situation, he reports that his son "treats me pretty rough sometimes." The patient does not want to be separated from his son and does not want to move out of his own house. The son works full time and drinks heavily at home. Sometimes he does not provide dinner for his father and has left him for prolonged periods without helping him change his clothes or ensuring that he has food. The patient has a history of severe osteoarthritis of the knees and left hip, heart failure, and diabetes mellitus. He ambulates using a walker with moderate assistance from another person, is unable to transfer independently, and is afraid of falling.

Physical examination reveals significant peripheral neuropathy and multiple bruises on his forearms. Heart rate is 80 per minute and regular. He has crackles at the bases of both lungs. Cognitive examination is normal, but he is depressed. His diaper is wet, and the skin in his perianal area is covered with dried feces.

Which of the following is the most appropriate next step in assisting this patient?

(A) Admit him to a nursing home.
(B) Notify Adult Protective Services of possible mistreatment.
(C) Request visiting nurse services for home safety evaluation.
(D) Initiate therapy with a selective serotonin-reuptake inhibitor.
(E) Request meals-on-wheels.

ANSWER: B

This patient is being neglected by his son. The son assumed responsibility for providing care when he moved into his father's house with the promise that he would help him in exchange for housing and food. He therefore has an obligation to ensure that his father's basic needs are met. Although not all states have mandatory reporting requirements, all states have a mechanism by which a health care provider may report possible mistreatment. The agency that takes this report (Adult Protective Services) is required to investigate and assess for abuse. It is not the clinician's role to determine whether abuse or neglect has occurred; rather, the clinician makes a report when he or she has reasonable suspicion of mistreatment. The Adult Protective Service worker will then go to the victim's home and attempt to interview both the alleged victim and perpetrator. The worker may find that the patient is eligible for home-health services such as meals-on-wheels, a home-health aide or homemaker, and other community-based programs that will allow him to remain clean and safe. Since the patient is cognitively intact and understands his situation, he will decide upon his living situation for himself and cannot be admitted to a nursing home against his will.

In this scenario, risk factors for neglect include the patient's physical dependence and depression. As a person becomes more dependent on another for care, the risk of neglect rises. Some have theorized that depression is linked to neglect because depression may impair executive function and therefore interfere with the victim's ability to make good decisions. Neglect may also be a causative factor in depression. Depression should be treated, but not before the safety of the patient's circumstances are more thoroughly probed. There is conflicting information as to whether gender and race are associated with neglect. Many victims of neglect are also cognitively impaired.

Few studies have examined risk factors that make a caregiver more likely to be abusive. One small study examined characteristics of caregivers who were known to actively abuse or passively neglect an older person who was dependent on them. The older persons were physically dependent but did not have dementia. Of the nine caregivers who were proven to be physical abusers, seven used alcohol heavily, which indicates that it is important to identify alcoholism in the caregiver. In the present case, it may be appropriate to refer the son to a program such as Alcoholics Anonymous, but the more immediate need is to protect the patient.

References

1. Dyer CB, Pavlik VN, Murphy KP, et al. The high prevalence of depression and dementia in elder abuse or neglect. *J Am Geriatr Soc.* 2000;48(2):205–212.
2. Lachs MS, Williams C, O'Brien S, et al. Risk factors for reported elder abuse and neglect: a nine-year observational cohort study. *Gerontologist.* 1997;37(4):469–474.
3. Reay AM, Browne KD. Risk factor characteristics in carers who physically abuse or neglect their elderly dependents. *Aging Ment Health.* 2001;5(1):56–62.

131. Which of the following is the strongest predictor for failure to achieve independent ambulation after surgical repair of a hip fracture?

    (A) Cognitive status
    (B) Age
    (C) Incontinence
    (D) Premorbid functional status
    (E) Depression

    ANSWER: D

Functional status before the fracture is the best predictor of rehabilitation outcomes: if the patient did not walk independently before the fall, it is unlikely he or she will walk independently after the fracture repair, even with rehabilitation.

Advanced age is a known risk factor for poor outcome. However, studies in patients over age 90 have shown that outcomes in this group can be good. Age probably serves as a marker for more serious functional deficits, rather than as an independent risk factor.

The presence of dementia or cognitive impairment is generally considered a negative predictor of rehabilitation outcomes, but some studies have shown that rehabilitation can improve functional performance in patients who can follow at least one-step commands.

Incontinence is a common secondary effect of immobility and may cause falls. However, it does not appear to be as significant as premorbid mobility in determining dependence in other activities of daily living.

Depression is a common sequela of disabling conditions and is known to affect rehabilitation outcomes. However, it is treatable when recognized, and treatment leads to improved rehabilitation outcomes. Depression is not as strong a risk factor as premorbid functional status.

References

1. Eastwood EA, Magaziner J, Wang J, et al. Patients with hip fracture: subgroups and their outcomes. *J Am Geriatr Soc.* 2002;50(7):1240–1249.
2. Huusko TM, Karppi P, Avikainen V, et al. Randomised, clinically controlled trial of intensive geriatric rehabilitation in patients with hip fracture: subgroup analysis of patients with dementia. *BMJ.* 2000;321(7269):1107–1111.
3. Patrick L, Knoefel F, Gaskowski P, et al. Medical comorbidity and rehabilitation efficiency in geriatric inpatients. *J Am Geriatr Soc.* 2001;49(11):1471–1477.
4. Tanaka J, Tokimura F, Seki N, et al. Outcomes of hip fracture surgery in patients aged > or = 90 years. *Orthopedics.* 2003;26(1):55–58.

132. A 72-year-old man is accompanied by his wife to the emergency department after he has his second episode of syncope in 2 weeks. Each episode occurs while he is standing and is characterized by a brief prodrome of feeling flushed, a rapid sense of dizziness, and then abrupt loss of consciousness. He rapidly returns to consciousness and is not disoriented after the event. He has no preceding chest pain, palpitations, shortness of breath, nausea, vomiting, or diaphoresis. He has coronary artery disease and a 20-year history of well-controlled hypertension. His most recent exercise thallium stress test 2 months ago was normal.

On physical examination, supine blood pressure is 130/80 mm Hg, heart rate is 56 per minute, and respiratory rate is 16 per minute. Standing blood pressure is 127/75 mm Hg after 1 minute, and he denies any dizziness. He has a soft, early-peaking II/VI systolic murmur at the base with an intact second heart sound. The rest of the physical examination is unremarkable. Electrocardiogram demonstrates sinus bradycardia with nonspecific T-wave flattening in the lateral leads. Echocardiogram demonstrates normal left ventricular size and function and normal wall motion. A 24-hour Holter monitor test shows sinus rhythm with rates 50 to 70 and occasional premature ventricular contractions.

Which of the following is the most appropriate next diagnostic test?

(A) Carotid Doppler ultrasonography
(B) Electroencephalography
(C) Computed tomographic scan of the head
(D) Tilt-table test

ANSWER: D

Although this patient has a clear history of cardiovascular disease, there is no evidence of cardiovascular syncope. He had excellent functional capacity and no inducible ischemia on a recent stress test, and echocardiography shows normal left ventricular function with no segmental wall motion abnormality. This patient has syncope of unknown cause. In such cases, provocative tests (electrophysiologic study, tilt-table test, and carotid sinus massage) are more likely to yield a definitive diagnosis than observational testing strategies.

Testing for cerebrovascular causes of syncope, including use of carotid Doppler ultrasound, computed tomography of the head, and electroencephalography, is of little diagnostic utility in the absence of a history of neurologic disease or focal neurologic findings. In most cases, test results will be negative, and positive findings are difficult to attribute directly as the cause of the syncope. Although 24- or 48-hour Holter monitoring is routinely performed for evaluation of syncope, most findings are nonspecific and, if not directly accompanied by an episode similar to that which led to presentation, nondiagnostic. Further, arrhythmias leading to syncope are often separated by long time intervals. Short-term cardiac monitoring is relatively unlikely to uncover a symptom-correlated event and is not necessarily reassuring if no arrhythmias are found.

References

1. Ammirati F, Colivicchi F, Santini M. Diagnosing syncope in clinical practice: implementation of a simplified diagnostic algorithm in a multicentre prospective trial—the OESIL 2 study (Osservatorio Epidemiologico della Sincope nel Lazio). *Eur Heart J*. 2000;21(11):935–940.
2. Kapoor WN. Current evaluation and management of syncope. *Circulation*. 2002;106(13):1606–1609.
3. Kenny RA. Syncope in the elderly: diagnosis, evaluation, and treatment. *J Cardiovasc Electrophysiol*. 2003;14 (9 Suppl):S7–S77.
4. Sarasin FP, Louis-Simonet M, Carballo D, et al. Prospective evaluation of patients with syncope: a population-based study. *Am J Med*. 2001;111(3):177–184.

133. Which of the following statements is true with regard to assisted-living facilities?

(A) Meals, laundry service, housekeeping, and skilled nursing services are usually provided.
(B) Rates at assisted-living facilities average $200 a day.
(C) Medicare pays for individuals to reside at assisted-living facilities.
(D) Long-term-care insurance may cover the cost of assisted living.

ANSWER: D

A wide range of services are available for residents of assisted-living facilities. Some of the services that may be included are three meals a day served in a community dining area, housekeeping services, transportation, assistance with activities of daily living, access to medical services, 24-hour staffing, emergency alert systems in each domicile, health promotion and exercise classes, medication management, laundry service, and social and recreational activities. These services may be included in the daily rate or cost extra, or they may not be available, as determined by each facility. Skilled nursing services are not provided. In contrast, at nursing homes, skilled nursing services, meals, laundry services, housekeeping, and medical services are usually provided.

Medicare does not pay for assisted-living facilities; financing is the responsibility of the individual or his or her family. Daily rates range from $15 to $200. Private long-term-care insurance policies may cover the cost of assisted-living facilities or personal services, such as home-health aides. Although the number of policies sold is increasing rapidly, few persons, in absolute numbers, currently carry long-term-care insurance.

References

1. Assisted Living Federation of America. What is assisted living? Available at http://www.alfa.org/public/articles/details.cfm?id=126 (accessed September 2005).
2. Tanner RC. Long-term care issue brief: assisted living: year end report—2004. *Issue Brief Health Policy Track Serv.* 2004;Dec 31:1–21.

134. A 72-year-old man comes to the emergency department because of constant right lower quadrant abdominal pain that has been present for almost 48 hours. He has nausea and anorexia but no fever, chills, vomiting, diarrhea, hematochezia, hematuria, or dysuria.

On physical examination his abdomen is soft to palpation and tender in the right lower quadrant, with voluntary guarding. Bowel sounds are hypoactive. Rectal examination is negative for occult blood.

Laboratory values include hemoglobin of 12.6 g/dL and leukocyte count of 14,800/μL (neutrophils 88%, bands 7%, monocytes 4%, lymphocytes 8%). Amylase and liver chemistries are normal. Abdominal radiograph reveals a nonspecific gas pattern.

What is the most appropriate next step to establish the diagnosis?

(A) Ultrasound of the abdomen
(B) Gastrografin (meglumine diatrizoate) enema
(C) Computed tomography of abdomen
(D) Small bowel series
(E) Colonoscopy

ANSWER: C

Appendicitis accounts for 5% of all acute abdominal conditions in patients aged 60 years and older. Older patients often have delayed and atypical presentations, leading to increased incidence of perforation and intra-abdominal infection. Perforation occurs in up to 72% of older patients, possibly because of delayed diagnosis or more rapid progression of disease. Comorbidity in older patients increases the operative risks and postoperative complications. Often there is no fever and no or minimal pain.

The incidence of appendicitis in the growing older population seems to be increasing. Approximately 10% of patients with appendicitis are elderly, but this age group accounts for more than 50% of deaths associated with appendicitis and for a disproportionately high rate of postoperative morbidity.

The most common reasons for delay in diagnosis include delayed patient presentation to the physician (often more than 2 days after symptoms begin), systemic disease masking symptoms of acute appendicitis, mild and less specific symptoms, lack of leukocytosis, and failure to include appendicitis in the differential diagnosis. Misdiagnosis occurs in up to 50% of cases. Conditions that are confused with appendicitis include bowel obstruction, diverticulitis, cecal carcinoma, Meckel's diverticulitis, typhlitis, Crohn's disease (which has a second peak incidence in older patients), acute cholecystitis, pancreatitis, obstructing urolithiasis, and perforated duodenal ulcer (which rarely presents with right lower quadrant pain).

Abdominal radiographs are not sensitive in the emergency department evaluation of adult patients with nontraumatic abdominal pain. Computed tomography has 90% to 98% sensitivity for detecting acute appendicitis and may help in distinguishing between appendicitis and inflammatory and neoplastic conditions with which it might be confused. Ultrasonography has a sensitivity of only 53%. Gastrografin enema, small bowel series, and colonoscopy would not be the most appropriate next step in this clinical scenario. Each of these would not help diagnose the condition and may be associated with complications, including perforation.

References
1. Hui TT, Major KM, Avital I, et al. Outcome of elderly patients with appendicitis: effect of computed tomography and laparoscopy. *Arch Surg*. 2002;137(9):995–998.
2. Lee JF, Leow CK, Lau WY. Appendicitis in the elderly. *Aust N Z J Surg*. 2000;70(8):593–596.
3. Storm-Dickerson, Horattas MC. What have we learned over the past 20 years about appendicitis in the elderly? *Am J Surg*. 2003;185(3):198–201.

135. During a routine office visit, a 75-year-old man complains of erectile dysfunction. He had a myocardial infarction 8 years ago. He has a history of well-controlled hypertension for 15 years, rare episodes of angina with severe exertion, hyperlipidemia, and benign prostatic hyperplasia. Medications are enalapril, hydrochlorothiazide, doxazosin, aspirin, lovastatin, and nitro paste daily. Physical examination is notable for blood pressure of 130/80 mm Hg and somewhat decreased peripheral pulses. There is no evidence of Peyronie's disease.

Which of the following is the best treatment for erectile dysfunction for this patient?

(A) Intracavernosal injections of alprostadil
(B) Oral yohimbine
(C) Oral sildenafil
(D) Intramuscular testosterone every 2 weeks
(E) Vacuum tumescent device

ANSWER: E

Given the clinical and medication history of this patient, the best option is a vacuum device because of its safety profile. The disadvantages of a vacuum device are relative lack of spontaneity, penile reddening, and cooler penile temperature in some patients.

Sildenafil, vardenafil, and tadalafil are phosphodiesterase inhibitors for the treatment of erectile dysfunction. Although these agents have not been directly compared, they seem to have different durations of effect, with tadalafil lasting 24 to 36 hours. Phosphodiesterase inhibitors are contraindicated in patients on regular or intermittent nitrate therapy because they can potentiate fatal episodes of hypotension. The concurrent use of phosphodiesterase inhibitors with α-blockers is complicated. Use of sildenafil with α-blockers is listed as a precaution, vardenafil is absolutely contraindicated, and tadalafil is contraindicated except with tamsulosin 0.4 mg. Headache, flushing, and changes in color vision may also occur with these agents.

Intracavernosal injection of alprostadil (10 to 20 μg) is effective in producing erections, but it can be associated with penile pain, burning, and hematomas. It would not be the first choice of therapy for this patient because his aspirin use puts him at risk for hematomas or bleeding.

Yohimbine (5 to 25 mg), an α_2 blocker, can be associated with elevated blood pressure, which this patient already has, as well as nausea and dizziness. In randomized, double-blind controlled trials, it has not been found to work better than placebo.

Testosterone replacement (200 mg) may benefit patients with low libido but may not restore erectile function. Adverse effects can include polycythemia, gynecomastia, and fluid retention. It should not be administered to men with prostate cancer but does not seem to exacerbate symptoms of benign prostatic hyperplasia.

References
1. Ansong KS, Lewis C, Jenkins P, et al. Help-seeking decisions among men with impotence. *Urology*. 1998;52(5):834–837.
2. Gruenewald DA, Matsumoto AM. Testosterone supplementation therapy for older men: potential benefits and risks. *J Am Geriatr Soc*. 2003;51(1):101–115.
3. Guay AT, Spark RF, Bansal S, et al. American Association of Clinical Endocrinologists medical guidelines for clinical practice for the evaluation and treatment of male sexual dysfunction: a couple's problem: 2003 update. *Endocr Pract*. 2003;9(1):77–95.
4. Rosen RC, Kostis JB. Overview of phosphodiesterase inhibition in erectile dysfunction. *Am J Cardiol*. 2003;92(9A):9M–18M.

136. A 67-year-old man comes to the office because of pain between his rectum and scrotum that has been worsening for the past 6 to 8 months. Initially, the pain was intermittent but present most days of the week. It is now constant and increasing in severity; he rates it as moderate. He reports urinary urgency and discomfort during urination. He has had no problems with sexual intercourse, change in urinary frequency, or nocturia, and he has not seen blood in his urine. The patient has been married for over 40 years and denies sexual experience outside his marriage. He currently has intercourse about three to four times per month. Physical examination is normal except that the digital rectal examination reveals a 20-g prostate without asymmetry, nodule, or induration, but with mild tenderness on palpation.

Urinalysis obtained before digital rectal examination is normal; after the examination the urine has moderate leukocytes, no bacteria, and 2 to 3 erythrocytes per high-power field. Cultures of the urine before and after digital rectal examination are negative.

What is the most appropriate next step in evaluation?

(A) Video urodynamics study
(B) Urine cytology
(C) Computed tomography scan of the pelvis
(D) Intravenous pyelography
(E) Transrectal ultrasonography

ANSWER: B

This patient has chronic nonbacterial prostatitis (chronic prostatitis or chronic pelvic pain syndrome), a difficult-to-treat condition seen in 13% of men aged 65 or older. The diagnosis is largely clinical, with a limited number of recommended tests to exclude other causes. The characteristic symptoms, physical examination findings, and results of a simple lower urinary tract localization test make acute or chronic bacterial prostatitis or upper tract disease (such as renal tuberculosis) unlikely. Urine cytology to screen for bladder cancer is recommended by the Third International Prostatitis Collaborative as part of the work-up of chronic nonbacterial prostatitis with hematuria or irritative symptoms. Video urodynamics, computed tomography scan of the pelvis, and transrectal ultrasound are used primarily when the presentation is atypical or there is evidence to suggest a concomitant process. Intravenous pyelography would not be helpful because it provides information on upper but not lower urinary tract anatomy.

References

1. Nickel JC. Clinical evaluation of the man with chronic prostatitis/chronic pelvic pain syndrome. *Urology.* 2002;60(Suppl):20–22.
2. Schaeffer AJ, Landis JR, Knauss JS, et al. Chronic Prostatitis Collaborative Research Network Group. Demographic and clinical characteristics of men with chronic prostatitis: the National Institutes of Health Chronic Prostatitis Cohort study. *J Urol.* 2002;168(2):593–598.

137. According to a randomized controlled trial, which of the following may delay progression of Alzheimer's disease?

(A) Antioxidants, including vitamin E
(B) HMG coenzyme-A reductase inhibitors
(C) Nonsteroidal anti-inflammatory agents
(D) Estrogen, with or without progesterone
(E) Prednisone

ANSWER: A

Data from clinical trials regarding efforts to delay progression of Alzheimer's disease are disappointing. Observational epidemiologic studies suggest that various medications are associated with a reduced incidence of Alzheimer's disease, including estrogen, antioxidants (vitamins E and C), statins, and anti-inflammatory agents. The case for anti-inflammatory agents has been bolstered by findings of inflammatory changes in brains of patients with Alzheimer's disease. However, clinical trials targeted at patients with dementia have shown a lack of efficacy for agents from these classes, with no positive studies; in fact, some studies, including one with prednisone, report that patients with Alzheimer's disease do worse. The exception is a single trial of high-dose vitamin E, 2000 IU daily, which reported delays in the progression of dementia to one of four predefined endpoints, relative to placebo. That study has not been replicated and had methodologic problems, so the use of vitamin E is not universally recommended, although widely practiced in some memory disorder centers. Despite the lack of evidence, patients with dementia or their families often ask to be placed on these agents, even though some may be harmful. Although the agents do not appear to be effective for treating Alzheimer's dementia, they may prove effective in the mild cognitive impairment phase or in the preclinical phase of Alzheimer's disease. Epidemiologic studies support this possibility, since many show that earlier and longer use of these agents may reduce the incidence of Alzheimer's disease. Clinical trials are under way to test these hypotheses. In one recent prospective clinical trial of asymptomatic women over age 65, estrogen alone or in combination did not reduce the incidence of dementia or mild cognitive impairment.

References

1. Aisen PS, Schafer KA, Grundman M, et al.; Alzheimer's Disease Cooperative Study. Effects of rofecoxib or naproxen vs placebo on Alzheimer disease progression: a randomized controlled trial. *JAMA.* 2003;289(21):2819–2826.
2. Sano M, Ernesto C, Thomas RG, et al. A controlled trial of selegiline, alpha-tocopherol, or both as treatment for Alzheimer's disease. The Alzheimer's Disease Cooperative Study. *N Engl J Med.* 1997;336(17):1216–1222.
3. Schneider LS. Estrogen and dementia: insights from the Women's Health Initiative Memory Study. *JAMA.* 2004;291(24):3005–3007.
4. Shumaker SA, Legault C, Kuller L, et al. Conjugated equine estrogens and incidence of probable dementia and mild cognitive impairment in postmenopausal women: Women's Health Initiative Memory Study. *JAMA.* 2004;291(24):2947–2958.
5. Tabet N, Birks J, Grimley Evans J. Vitamin E for Alzheimer's disease. *Cochrane Database Syst Rev.* 2000;(4):CD002854.

138. An 84-year-old woman comes to the office because she has fatigue and weakness, especially in the morning. At times she finds herself stumbling and veering while walking, and she has to sit to recover her equilibrium. She has twice had to sit down to avoid falling, but she denies feeling lightheaded. History includes hypertension, urinary incontinence, and osteoarthritis. Medications include hydrochlorothiazide 25 mg daily, oxybutynin 10 mg at bedtime, lisinopril 10 mg daily, calcium carbonate 500 mg three times daily, and acetaminophen 1000 mg three times daily.

On examination, blood pressure while sitting is 118/70 mm Hg in her right arm; pulse is 80 and regular. Her movements are slow. She has a mild resting tremor in her hands, right greater than left. She rises from a chair slowly but without using her arms. She walks stooped forward, with decreased arm swing. She turns carefully, but without losing balance. She is unable to stand on one leg.

Which of the following is most likely to yield information that would help reduce her risk of falling?

(A) Testing her visual acuity
(B) Administering the Berg balance test
(C) Measuring her blood pressure when she is lying down and standing
(D) Ordering magnetic resonance imaging of the brain

ANSWER: C

This patient has nonspecific symptoms of fatigue and weakness; she feels unsteady when walking, and sitting helps her regain her equilibrium. This presentation suggests orthostatic hypotension. Many older people with orthostatic blood-pressure changes do not have dizziness or lightheadedness. Findings on examination (bradykinesia, a stooped gait, decreased arm swing, and asymmetric tremor) suggest Parkinson's disease. Autonomic dysfunction may be present in Parkinson's disease or in a variant, Shy-Drager syndrome, and may cause orthostatic hypotension. The patient takes hydrochlorothiazide, oxybutynin, and lisinopril, which may contribute singly or in combination to reducing her standing blood pressure. Only her sitting blood pressure is reported, and it is low. Measuring her blood pressure when she is lying down and standing may demonstrate a significant orthostatic change, namely, a drop in systolic blood pressure of 20 mm Hg or more after 3 minutes. Reducing her orthostatic hypotension may improve her symptoms and reduce her risk for falls.

Testing her visual acuity is important in evaluating her overall risk for falls. However, her symptoms and examination do not suggest significant vision impairment.

The Berg balance test would be helpful in characterizing the patient's residual balance impairment, but only after the possibility of orthostatic hypotension is resolved. The Berg Balance Scale measures a person's ability to do 14 common balance activities, ranging from transfers to turns and stepping on a step. Each activity is scored from 0 to 4, and the total possible score is 56. It is used by physical therapists to evaluate balance. It is particularly useful for patients who have balance and mobility impairment because it can be measured before and after a therapy intervention to assess improvement.

Magnetic resonance imaging of the brain may be helpful in diagnosing cerebrovascular disease or previous strokes that might contribute to her gait abnormality. However, diagnosing and treating orthostatic hypotension is more likely to reduce this patient's risk of falling.

References

1. American Geriatrics Society, British Geriatrics Society, and American Academy of Orthopaedic Surgeons Panel on Falls Prevention. Guideline for the prevention of falls in older persons. *J Am Geriatr Soc*. 2001;49(5):664–672.
2. Mukai S, Lipsitz LA. Orthostatic hypotension. *Clin Geriatr Med*. 2002;18(2):253–268.

139. Which of the following is true regarding osteoporosis in older men?

   (A) Androgen levels have been correlated to bone mass and fractures in older men.
   (B) Estrogen levels have been shown to be an important determinant of osteoporosis in men.
   (C) Osteoporosis is more likely to be primary or idiopathic in older men than in older women.
   (D) No treatment benefit has been documented for alendronate in older men with idiopathic osteoporosis.
   (E) Outcome after hip fracture is better for older men than older women.

ANSWER: B

Osteoporosis is an important problem for older men. Hypogonadism can be associated with increased fracture risk, and androgen replacement in hypogonadal men can delay loss of bone mass. However, androgen levels do not predict risk of fracture in older men. The Framingham cohort demonstrated that hypogonadism related to aging has little

influence on bone mineral density, but serum estradiol levels have a strong and positive association with bone mineral density. Clinical studies have further shown that levels of estradiol and estrone in older men are related to osteoporosis. Men with lower levels appear more susceptible to lower bone mineral density, and estrogen appears to have an independent effect in this regard when multivariate analyses are performed.

Men with osteoporosis should undergo evaluation for secondary causes. In 40% to 60% of cases, a contributing factor can be identified (such as hypogonadism, glucocorticoid therapy, gastrointestinal disease); this identification seems to be greater than in studies of women. Older men with osteoporosis can benefit from treatment with a number of modalities, including bisphosphonates. For reasons that are not entirely clear, the mortality associated with hip fracture is higher among older men than among older women. In one report of 363 patients with hip fractures, the 12-month mortality was 32% in men and 17% in women.

References

1. Amin S, Zhang Y, Sawin CT, et al. Association of hypogonadism and estradiol levels with bone mineral density in elderly men from the Framingham study. *Ann Intern Med*. 2000;133(12):951–963.
2. Finkelstein JS, Hayes A, Hunzelman JL, et al. The effects of parathyroid hormone, alendronate, or both in men with osteoporosis. *N Engl J Med*. 2003;349(13):1216–1226.
3. Khosla S, Melton LJ 3rd, Atkinson EJ, et al. Relationship of serum sex steroid levels and bone turnover markers with bone mineral density in men and women: a key role for bioavailable estrogen. *J Clin Endocrinol Metab*. 1998;83(7):2266–2274.
4. Kiebzak GM, Beinart GA, Perser K, et al. Undertreatment of osteoporosis in men with hip fracture. *Arch Intern Med*. 2002;162(19):2217–2222.

140. A 65-year-old woman comes to the office for a physical examination, during which a 2 × 2−cm smooth, ovoid nodule is palpated in the left lobe of the thyroid gland. The nodule moves easily with swallowing and is not associated with cervical lymphadenopathy. She has no history of radiation exposure to the head or neck. Serum thyrotropin and serum free thyroxine levels are normal.

Which of the following is the most appropriate next step?

(A) Fine-needle aspiration biopsy
(B) Left thyroid lobectomy
(C) Thyroid uptake and scan
(D) Reexamination in 6 months

ANSWER: A

Palpable thyroid nodules occur in up to 7% of the general adult population. The prevalence is higher in women and older patients. The clinical challenge is to distinguish the few nodules that are malignant (and require surgical resection) from the vast majority that are benign.

In addition to measurement of serum thyrotropin level, fine-needle aspiration biopsy is well established as the initial procedure of choice for evaluating a thyroid nodule. It is an outpatient procedure with 85% sensitivity and 90% specificity for malignant thyroid lesion when an adequate specimen is interpreted by an experienced cytopathologist. Repeat biopsy is indicated if the initial aspirate is not diagnostic.

Radioisotope imaging studies (such as iodine 123 thyroid uptake scan) lack sensitivity and accuracy. The iodine scan separates cold nodules, which are more likely to be malignant, from hot nodules, which are rarely malignant. Imaging would not add much in this case, as the normal serum thyrotropin level suggests that the nodule is cold, thus requiring further evaluation by fine-needle aspiration.

References

1. Kim N, Lavertu P. Evaluation of a thyroid nodule. *Otolaryngol Clin North Am.* 2003;36(1):17–33.
2. Ko HM, Jhu IK, Yang SH, et al. Clinicopathologic analysis of fine needle aspiration cytology of the thyroid: a review of 1,613 cases and correlation with histopathologic diagnoses. *Acta Cytol.* 2003;47(5):727–732.
3. Welker MJ, Orlov D. Thyroid nodules. *Am Fam Physician.* 2003;67(3):559–566.

141. A 79-year-old man comes to the office because he has had a generalized, throbbing, almost constant headache for the past 3 weeks. He has no previous history of headache. No obvious factor precipitated the headache, although the patient notes that chewing food seems to accentuate jaw pain. Two days ago he lost vision in his left eye for 5 minutes; this resolved spontaneously. Earlier today he suddenly lost hearing in his left ear. His current medications include aspirin and folic acid. Neurologic examination is normal except for the hearing loss.

Which of the following is the most appropriate treatment?

(A) Azathioprine
(B) Clopidogrel
(C) Heparin
(D) Phenytoin
(E) Prednisone

ANSWER: E

This man has characteristic symptoms of giant cell (temporal) arteritis, a disorder primarily seen in persons above age 50. Headache is the most common presenting symptom; it is typically throbbing and may be most prominent in the temporal region. Various neurologic complications can develop in the setting of giant cell arteritis, including sudden vision loss due to anterior ischemic optic neuropathy and sudden hearing loss due to acute auditory nerve infarction. Jaw claudication is common. Prominent elevation of the erythrocyte sedimentation rate and C-reactive protein level is characteristic, and diagnosis is confirmed with temporal artery biopsy.

Treatment is initiated with high doses of oral corticosteroids, typically 40 to 60 mg of prednisone daily. Treatment with higher doses or with intravenous methylprednisolone is suggested for patients with an acute neurologic syndrome. Azathioprine is not effective in the acute management of giant cell arteritis. Medications used to treat thrombotic or embolic cerebrovascular disease, such as clopidogrel and heparin, are not appropriate for giant cell arteritis. The anticonvulsant drug phenytoin has no effect on the inflammation that characterizes giant cell arteritis.

References
1. Caselli RJ, Hunder GG. Giant cell arteritis and polymyalgia rheumatica. In: Silberstein SD, Lipton RB, Dalessio DJ, eds. *Wolff's Headache and Other Head Pain*. Oxford: Oxford University Press; 2001:525–535.
2. Nordborg E, Nordborg C. Giant cell arteritis: strategies in diagnosis and treatment. *Curr Opin Rheumatol.* 2004;16(1):25–30.
3. Penn H, Dasgupta B. Giant cell arteritis. *Autoimmun Rev.* 2003;2(4):199–203.

142. A 60-year-old man is brought to the office by his family because he has difficulty walking and is becoming increasingly confused. He has a history of alcoholism. On examination, he is unable to move his eyes horizontally, and he has upbeat nystagmus, dysmetria of the extremities, and severe ataxia.

Which of the following vitamins is most likely to be deficient in this patient?

(A) Vitamin B_1
(B) Vitamin B_6
(C) Vitamin B_{12}
(D) Vitamin E
(E) Vitamin K

ANSWER: A

Wernicke's encephalopathy is associated with ocular motor abnormalities (often inability to move the eyes), nystagmus, ataxia, global confused state, vestibular paresis, hypotension, and hypothermia. It occurs secondary to deficiency in vitamin B_1 (thiamine). Older patients are at risk for Wernicke's encephalopathy especially if there is a history of alcohol abuse or malnutrition. Other conditions that place patients at risk are prolonged intravenous feeding, intravenous hyperalimentation, hyperemesis gravidarum, anorexia (which can be associated with dementia or depression), prolonged fasting, refeeding after starvation, and gastric plication. Treatment consists of intravenous thiamine. Often the nystagmus and eye abnormalities resolve with treatment, and there may be some resolution of the gait imbalance, but the confusion and memory deficit may remain. The other vitamins are not usually deficient in patients with alcoholism.

References
1. Furman JM, Cass SP. *Vestibular Disorders: A Case-Study Approach.* Oxford: Oxford University Press; 2003.
2. Kunze K. Metabolic encephalopathies. *J Neurol.* 2002;249(9):1150–1159.
3. Thomson AD. Mechanisms of vitamin deficiency in chronic alcohol misusers and the development of the Wernicke-Korsakoff syndrome. *Alcohol Alcohol Suppl.* 2000;35 (Suppl 1):2–7.

143. A 76-year-old woman who lives with her husband in a retirement community comes to the office because she has nearly fallen on three occasions during the previous 6 months. In each instance she averted the fall by grabbing hold of something. She has moderate visual impairment due to macular degeneration and osteoarthritis involving several joints, especially the left hip and knee. She takes pride in not having to take any medications. She has 1 mixed drink before dinner almost every day, while socializing with other residents, and has a glass of wine with dinner 2 to 3 times each week. Alcohol, combined with impaired vision and the effects of arthritis on balance and gait, is suspected as a possible cause of the near-falls. She has not been treated previously for an alcohol-use disorder.

Which of the following is the most appropriate first step in the care of this patient?

(A) Treat with naltrexone, 50 mg once daily for 12 weeks.
(B) Treat with disulfiram, 200 mg once daily until drinking is reduced.
(C) Provide information about risks and advise her to reduce her drinking.
(D) Refer to an age-specific residential treatment center.
(E) Refer to a self-help group such as Alcoholics Anonymous.

ANSWER: C

Brief intervention is effective and can be conducted in primary care settings. It typically involves informing patients about potential problems associated with their drinking and specifically advising them to reduce consumption of alcohol.

Naltrexone, an opioid antagonist, reduces craving and the emotional response to the pleasurable effects of alcohol. Naltrexone has been shown to decrease alcohol use by social drinkers, including those at risk of harm from their drinking. Its greatest benefit may be for social drinkers who have not responded to nonpharmacologic therapy or who regularly drink heavier amounts. Outcomes are best when naltrexone is given as an adjunct to a comprehensive treatment plan, rather than as monotherapy. This patient has not received previous treatment for drinking, and her drinking is limited to about 7 to 10 alcoholic beverages per week. Moreover, she takes pride in the fact that she does not take any medications.

This patient can be described as a drinker at risk for harm from her drinking; it is unlikely that she is alcohol dependent. The American Society of Addiction Medicine regards residential treatment centers as an appropriate option for treating alcohol dependence. Such centers are not usually necessary for the management of nondependent drinking, even when it places a person at risk for harm, in part because the centers focus on overcoming dependence and preventing relapses. Self-help groups such as Alcoholics Anonymous focus on helping participants overcome dependence and maintain sobriety.

Disulfiram is recommended only for treatment of alcohol dependence. Moreover, it is not used routinely in older patients because the disulfiram-ethanol reaction may pose cardiovascular risks.

References

1. Barrick C, Connors GJ. Relapse prevention and maintaining abstinence in older adults with alcohol-use disorders. *Drugs Aging*. 2002; 19:583–594.
2. Blow FC, Barry KL. Older patients with at-risk and problem drinking patterns: new developments in brief interventions. *J Geriatr Psych Neurol*. 2000;13:115–123.
3. Gordon AJ, Conigliaro J, Maisto SA, et al. Comparison of consumption effects of brief interventions for hazardous drinking elderly. *Subst Use Misuse*. 2003;38:1017–1035.
4. Sattar SP, Petty F, Burke WJ. Diagnosis and treatment of alcohol dependence in older alcoholics. *Clin Geriatr Med*. 2003;19:743–761.

144. A 71-year-old woman with Alzheimer's dementia and hypertension treated with a β-blocker resides in a skilled nursing facility. After a fall while walking, she appears uncomfortable but is unable to communicate the source of her pain. Bone radiographs of both hips are originally read as normal, but repeat films after 3 days of bed rest reveal a nondisplaced fracture of the left femoral neck.

On admission to the hospital the patient's physical examination and laboratory assessment are unremarkable except for swelling of the left hip. She is treated with hydration, warfarin, intermittent pneumatic compression stockings, and surgery under general anesthesia for internal fixation, and her β-blocker is continued.

Two days postoperatively the patient becomes acutely anxious and tachypneic. Her pulse oximetry is 88% on room air and improves to 90% with 4 liters of nasal oxygen. White blood cell count is 12,500/uL (70% segmented neutrophils and band forms). Her lung sounds are clear to auscultation, and there is no dullness over the chest to percussion. Heart sounds are crisp with a normal S1 and S2, without gallops. The surgical site shows erythematous edges and no purulent drainage. Blood chemistries are normal and her INR is 1.8. Chest radiograph is normal and electrocardiogram is unchanged.

Which of the following is the best next step?

(A) Barium swallow
(B) Echocardiogram
(C) Blood and wound cultures
(D) Cardiac catheterization
(E) Computerized tomographic angiogram of chest

ANSWER: E

Older patients are uniquely predisposed to the development of venous thromboembolic disease. Risk factors for deep-vein thrombosis include venous stasis (secondary to immobility, heart failure, or deep venous insufficiency), inflammation or trauma to vasculature, and a hypercoagulable state secondary to malignancy, autoimmune, and other inflammatory processes. An older patient immobilized without benefit of anticoagulation for 3 or more days has a markedly increased risk of developing venous thromboembolic disease. Patients undergoing hip surgery have a 54% risk of venous thromboembolic complications if not treated prophylactically with an anticoagulant. Early initiation of anticoagulation with adjunct therapy (sequential compression devices) helps reduce the risk of venous thromboembolism. In hip surgery, the risk can be reduced by 60% to 70% through the early initiation of warfarin or low-molecular-weight heparin therapy. Although unfractionated heparin is helpful in preventing venous thromboembolism in patients undergoing abdominal and gynecologic surgeries as well as in hospitalized medical patients, it is distinctly inferior to warfarin and low-molecular-weight heparin in prevention for patients undergoing hip surgeries. Aspirin is also inferior. Three days of immobility without venous thromboembolism prophylaxis greatly increased this patient's risk of developing a venous thromboembolic complication prior to hospitalization and a subsequent pulmonary embolism after admission.

The findings on examination and radiographic studies show no evidence of pulmonary aspiration or wound site infections. Nor are the physical findings or electrocardiogram consistent with pericardial tamponade, pulmonary edema, or an acute coronary syndrome. In this patient, initiating heparin for possible pulmonary embolism while awaiting the result of a computerized tomographic angiographic study of the chest, or a ventilation-perfusion scan, is the most appropriate next step. In the future, recombinant hirudin and other new products may offer safer and more effective therapies.

References

1. Geerts WH. Prevention of venous thromboembolism. The Seventh ACCP Conference on Antithrombotic and Thrombolytic Therapy. *Chest.* 2004; 126(3 Suppl):338S–400S.
2. Pulmonary Embolism Prevention (PEP) Trial Collaborative Group. Prevention of pulmonary embolism and deep vein thrombosis with low dose aspirin. Pulmonary Embolism Prevention (PEP) trial. *Lancet.* 2000;355(9212):1295–1302.
3. Rosenthal RA, Kavic SM. Assessment and management of the geriatric patient. *Crit Care Med.* 2004;32(4 Suppl):S92–S105.

145. In the United States, which of the following statements concerning women and aging is true?

(A) As more women enter the work force, they have a reduced role as caregivers for elderly persons.
(B) The number of women aged 65 and over living alone is approximately equal to the number of men of that age living alone.
(C) In the year 2000, there were more men per 100 women in the age group 85 years and over than in the age group 65 to 74 years.
(D) The numbers of elderly men and women residing in institutions are similar until the oldest old age groups are considered.

ANSWER: D

Women traditionally assume the role of caregiver for elderly persons. As greater numbers of women enter the work force, a potential consequence could be a decrease in the availability of women as caregivers. However, several studies have found that women in the work force are as likely as women who stay at home to act as caregivers for elderly persons.

Many aging women in developed countries live alone. In the United States and Canada, older women are more likely than men to live alone, in part because they are much more commonly widowed.

In the year 2000, there were 82 men per 100 women in the age group 65 to 74, and only 41 men per 100 women in the group aged 85 years and over.

The numbers of elderly men and women residing in institutions are similar until the oldest age groups are considered. Among persons aged 75 and older, more women than men are institutionalized. One explanation is that elderly men are more likely to be married and their wives provide needed care. Also, there are greater absolute numbers of women in the oldest age groups (older than 90 years), and members of this group are most likely to require care.

References

1. *The 65 Years and Over Population: 2000.* Census 2000 Brief. U. S. Department of Commerce, Bureau of the Census; October 2001.

2. Velkoff VA, Lawson VA. *International Brief Gender and Aging: Caregiving.* U.S. Department of Commerce, Economics and Statistics Administration, Bureau of the Census; December 1998.

146. A 68-year-old woman comes to the office for a second opinion regarding a rash on her breast. She states that she has had problems with her right breast for about 1 year. Initially the nipple was itchy and burning, but there was no rash. Later the nipple became red with some yellowish exudate. The rash then extended to the surrounding area. Her physician prescribed topical antibiotic creams with only temporary improvement. Her history includes hypertension, osteoarthritis, and diabetes mellitus. A mammogram obtained 9 months ago was normal.

On examination, the right breast has a demarcated erythematous area involving the nipple, areola, and surrounding skin. There is slight scaling, oozing of serous liquid, and superficial induration. There is no palpable mass and no axillary adenopathy. The left breast is normal.

Which of the following is the most appropriate next step?

(A) Repeat mammogram.
(B) Do culture swab of the rash.
(C) Do wedge biopsy of the nipple.
(D) Do potassium hydroxide stain on scraping of the rash.
(E) Prescribe a topical corticosteroid.

ANSWER: C

In patients with a unilateral eczematous rash of the nipple, Paget's disease of the breast should be suspected until proven otherwise. Paget's disease of the breast is the local cutaneous spread from an intraductal carcinoma of the breast. It accounts for 1% of all cases of breast cancer in women and 1% of all cases of breast cancer in white men. This carcinoma involves the nipple and areola with a rash that can be erythematous, eczematous, scaly, raw, vesicular, or ulcerated. Spontaneous improvement of the rash can occur and should not be taken as an indication that the patient does not have Paget's disease of the breast. A palpable breast mass is present in about 50% of cases, but it is often located more than 2 cm from the nipple-areolar complex. A palpable mass tends to be found in

more advanced cases and is associated with lower survival. Mammography will show an abnormality in about 20% of cases. In about 25% of cases there is no mass or mammographic abnormality; these patients are more likely to have noninvasive breast carcinoma and a favorable prognosis. In less than 5% of cases of Paget's disease of the breast, there is no palpable mass, no mammographic abnormality, and no underlying parenchymal breast cancer. Management depends on the stage of the underlying breast cancer and may include surgery, radiotherapy, or chemotherapy.

A topical corticosteroid would be used to treat simple eczema of the nipple and areola. Eczema of the nipple and areola is typically bilateral, but can be unilateral. However, temporary improvement of eczematous changes are seen with Paget's disease of the breast, and thus a full-thickness wedge or punch biopsy should be done before treating it as possible eczema. As this is unlikely to be a bacterial or fungal infection, given its location and appearance, potassium hydroxide preparation and culture are not appropriate next steps.

References
1. Freeman A, Gordon M. Dermatologic diseases and problems. In: Cassel CK, Leipzig RM, Cohen HJ, et al., eds. *Geriatric Medicine: An Evidence-Based Approach.* 4th ed. New York: Springer-Verlag; 2003:869–881.
2. Kothari AS, Beechey-Newman N, Hamed H, et al. Paget disease of the nipple: a multifocal manifestation of higher-risk disease. *Cancer.* 2002;95(1):1–7.
3. Sheen-Chen SM, Chen HS, Chen WJ, et al. Paget disease of the breast—an easily overlooked disease? *J Surg Oncol.* 2001;76(4):261–265.

147. A 76-year-old woman is undergoing treatment for major depression that began 6 months after her husband died. She has had three episodes of depression since age 58. Her previous most recent episode was 4 years ago, when her husband was diagnosed with colon cancer. At that time she tolerated and responded to sertraline 50 mg daily; this regimen is resumed for the current episode of depression. After 3 weeks of treatment she feels significantly better, and after 4 months she reports that she is back to normal. She has no significant side effect.

Which of the following is most appropriate in management of this patient?

(A) Discontinue sertraline and monitoring her closely.
(B) Taper sertraline slowly over the next few months.
(C) Continue sertraline at half the current dose.
(D) Continue sertraline at the current dose.

ANSWER: D

In most older patients, depression should be managed as a chronic relapsing and remitting illness that requires treatment for acute episodes and prophylaxis to prevent relapse or recurrence. In younger and older patients with recurrent depression, maintenance of antidepressant treatment at full therapeutic dose is necessary to prevent recurrence. Older patients with a first episode of depression (late-onset depression) are also likely to have recurrence, and most need long-term treatment. Even in younger patients with a first episode of depression, AHCPR-AHRQ guidelines recommend a minimum of 3 months of acute treatment followed by 6 to 9 months of continuation treatment before discontinuation is attempted under close monitoring.

This patient has been treated for 4 months and tolerates the antidepressant well. It would be inappropriate to discontinue her medication, even if it were done slowly to prevent discontinuation symptoms or rebound relapse. In studies comparing long-term use of antidepressants given at half the dose or at the full dose required for initial remission, older patients treated with half the dose had more brittle remission with more residual symptoms. Similarly, trials to prevent recurrence show weaker benefits with long-term individual psychotherapy than with long-term antidepressant medications. No data support the belief that it is safer to discontinue antidepressant medications in patients in whom reactive depression is associated with a psychosocial stressor (for example, grief associated with a spouse's death) than in a patient who appears to have an endogenous depression. The contrast between reactive and endogenous depression is flawed: recent research has shown that patients genetically predisposed to depression tend to react more negatively to psychosocial stressors. Conversely, antidepressant medication appears to buffer these patients against the impact of stressors.

References

1. Dew MA, Reynolds CF 3rd, Mulsant B, et al. Initial recovery patterns may predict which maintenance therapies for depression will keep older adults well. *J Affect Dis.* 2001;65(2):155–166.
2. Flint AJ, Rifat SL. Maintenance treatment for recurrent depression in late life: a four-year outcome study. *Am J Geriatr Psychiatry.* 2000;8(2):112–116.
3. Reynolds CF 3rd, Frank E, Perel JM, et al. Nortriptyline and interpersonal psychotherapy as maintenance therapies for recurrent major depression: a randomized controlled trial in patients older than 59 years. *JAMA.* 1999;281(1):39–45.
4. Reynolds CF 3rd, Perel JM, Frank E, et al. Three-year outcomes of maintenance nortriptyline treatment in late-life depression: a study of two fixed plasma levels. *Am J Psychiatry.* 1999;156(8):1177–1181.

148. An 84-year-old woman is referred for evaluation of anemia. The patient has a history of anemia, hypertension, osteoarthritis, and renal insufficiency. Her hemoglobin was 10 g/dL until 9 months ago, when it dropped to 6.8 g/dL. At that time there was no evidence of bleeding, and ferritin, serum iron, iron-binding capacity, and B_{12} and folic acid levels were normal. With transfusion, her hemoglobin stabilized between 9 and 10 g/dL. The patient has no history of weight loss, hematochezia, melena, or hematuria. She complains of pain in her neck, knees, and wrists. Medications include enalapril and acetaminophen. Physical examination is within normal limits.

Laboratory tests:

Hemoglobin	8.9 g/dL
Mean corpuscular volume	87 fL
Leukocyte count	3700/μL
Platelet count	150,000/μL
Westergren erythrocyte sedimentation rate	77 mm/h
Reticulocyte count	0.9%
Folic acid	1.3 ng/mL (normal)
Thyrotropin	2.1 μU/mL
Iron	89 μg/dL
Iron-binding capacity	234 μg/dL
Serum calcium	9.2 mg/dL
Serum albumin	4.0 g/dL
Blood urea nitrogen	32 mg/dL
Serum creatinine	1.8 mg/dL

Which of the following is the most appropriate next step?

(A)   Serum erythropoietin level
(B)   Chest radiograph and liver function tests
(C)   Serum and urine protein electrophoresis and immunofixation
(D)   Bone marrow biopsy

ANSWER: C

Anemia is best considered in terms of the bone marrow, the organ of erythropoiesis. Anemia may be due to hypoproliferative erythropoiesis, ineffective erythropoiesis, or a consumptive (hemolytic) process. The laboratory tests most useful in identifying the cause are mean corpuscular volume and corrected reticulocyte count. A reticulocyte count in the normal range cannot be considered normal in the setting of anemia, where the normal bone marrow can increase erythrocyte production by a factor of 10. Therefore, the reticulocyte count must be corrected for the degree of anemia. In this case, the corrected reticulocyte count is the product of the uncorrected reticulocyte percentage and the patient's hemoglobin divided by normal hemoglobin (11.5 in a woman). This would equal 0.69, which is an inadequate erythroid response. In this case, the patient has a reticulocytopenic anemia that is normocytic; that is, the mean corpuscular volume is in the normal range. These two findings indicate that the anemia is hypoproliferative. This is the most common type of anemia in elderly persons, and it is most commonly caused by iron deficiency or anemia of chronic inflammation. Other causes include chronic kidney failure, pure erythrocyte aplasia, marrow-infiltrative disorders, and multiple myeloma.

Several features in this case suggest multiple myeloma, most obviously the longstanding history of mild renal insufficiency. The patient's arthritic symptoms may represent bone disease or, less likely, amyloidosis. The initial laboratory findings also support a diagnosis of multiple myeloma, given the high erythrocyte sedimentation rate and the normal serum calcium level despite renal insufficiency. Thus, it would be appropriate to pursue a diagnosis of multiple myeloma. Erythropoietin level, liver function tests, and chest radiography are not appropriate tests for multiple myeloma. Bone marrow biopsy may not lead to the diagnosis, since the disease is often patchy; a negative bone marrow biopsy does not exclude multiple myeloma. Serum and urine protein electrophoresis and immunofixation are positive in 85% to 90% of persons with multiple myeloma. False-negative studies in the serum and urine do not exclude the diagnosis, but occur in only 10% to 15% of patients. Urine and serum studies are necessary since, in some patients, only light chains are produced, and these would be detected in the urine as Bence-Jones protein rather than in the serum as monoclonal immunoglobulin.

References

1. Kyle RA, Gertz MA, Witzig TE, et al. Review of 1027 patients with newly diagnosed multiple myeloma. *Mayo Clin Proc.* 2003;78(1):21–33.
2. Rodon P, Linassier C, Gauvain JB, et al. Multiple myeloma in elderly patients: presenting features and outcome. *Eur J Haematol.* 2001;66(1):11–17.

149. A 77-year-old right-handed woman comes to the emergency department because she has an unusual tingling sensation involving her right face and arm, as if they are "asleep." The sensation began several hours earlier. She has no other symptoms. Neurologic examination is normal except for impaired sensation involving the right side of the body, including the face.

Which artery is most probably occluded?

(A) Anterior choroidal
(B) Middle cerebral
(C) Lenticulostriate
(D) Posterior inferior cerebellar
(E) Thalamoperforate

ANSWER: E

This woman's symptoms fit the description of pure (isolated) sensory stroke, a classic lacunar syndrome. Most often, the responsible lesion is in the posterior-ventral thalamus and is due to occlusion of one of the thalamoperforate or thalamogeniculate arteries, which are penetrating branches that typically arise from the posterior cerebral artery. Lacunes account for approximately 10% of all symptomatic strokes; they are often associated with hypertension and diabetes mellitus.

Occlusion of the anterior choroidal artery can produce infarction involving the optic tract and portions of the internal capsule, thalamus, basal ganglia, and optic radiations. Consequent signs may include contralateral hemiparesis, hemisensory deficit, homonymous hemianopia, dysarthria, and behavioral abnormalities. Middle cerebral artery occlusion produces a combination of contralateral hemiparesis, hemisensory loss, homonymous hemianopia, and, depending on the side involved, either aphasia or neglect and other nondominant parietal lobe features. Lenticulostriate arteries are penetrating branches off the middle cerebral artery that supply the internal capsule and portions of the basal ganglia. Occlusion produces pure motor hemiparesis, the most common of the lacunar syndromes. The posterior inferior cerebellar artery supplies the inferior cerebellum and a portion of the dorsal medulla. Occlusion of this artery produces a combination of cerebellar and brain-stem symptoms.

References

1. Adams HP Jr, Hachinski V, Norris JW. *Ischemic Cerebrovascular Disease*. Oxford: Oxford University Press;2001:57–102.
2. Caplan LR. Posterior circulation disease. In: *Clinical Findings, Diagnosis and Management*. Cambridge, MA: Blackwell Science;1996:381–443.
3. Inzitari D, Lamassa M. Small-vessel disease with lacunes. *Adv Neurol*. 2003;92:141–146.

150. An 83-year-old woman comes to the office because she has had intermittent lower back pain for 18 months. It bothers her when she moves from lying to sitting positions, when she bends, and particularly when she is bumped or has a sudden unguarded movement. The pain resolves after several minutes. The pain does not affect her ability to stand for long periods or to walk up to 1½ miles daily.

On physical examination, she has moderate spasm of the paravertebral muscles of the lumbar spine. There is asymmetric immobility of the spine, with pain on side flexion to the right and forward flexion. Bilateral straight leg raise tests are normal. There is mild weakness of the right great toe extensor, right hip abductor, and right hip extensor. There is pain when going from the flexed to extended position of the lumbar spine.

Plain radiograph of the lumbar spine reveals an area of marked joint space narrowing with vertebral endplate sclerosis at L-4, L-5 with facet space narrowing, and osteophytosis at L-4, L-5. Magnetic resonance imaging of the lumbar spine reveals moderate to severe lumbar spinal stenosis at L-4, L-5 and L-5, S-1.

What is the most appropriate next step in the management of this patient?

(A) Administer an epidural corticosteroid injection.
(B) Prescribe isometric abdominal strengthening exercises and back protection maneuvers.
(C) Obtain surgical consultation.
(D) Obtain electromyography and nerve conduction studies.
(E) Obtain a bone scan.

ANSWER: B

This patient's intermittent lower back pain occurring with movement of the lumbar spine is a typical presentation for instability of the lumbar spine. Affected patients have brief episodes of severe pain, particularly on sudden unguarded movements. They often have one focal area of disk space and facet joint abnormalities. Ongoing pain from the flexed to extended position is typical. Stabilization of the lumbar spine with isometric abdominal strengthening exercises is a reasonable management approach.

Lumbar spinal stenosis is seen on magnetic resonance imaging in up to 20% of asymptomatic persons aged 60 or older and does not in itself indicate that spinal stenosis is the cause of the patient's back pain. The clinical presentation of lumbar spinal stenosis is pain on extending the spine that is relieved when the spine is flexed. Thus, pain develops after prolonged standing and walking, and it is relieved with sitting. Brief back pain when going from lying to sitting positions and during bending is not the clinical presentation of lumbar spinal stenosis. Magnetic resonance imaging should not be pursued in the absence of typical clinical features.

Administration of epidural corticosteroids has not been demonstrated to be helpful for back pain alone and should be considered only in patients with sciatic pain. The patient's 18-month history of intermittent and positional pain is not consistent with a diagnosis of cancer.

As most mechanical lower back pain occurs in the lower lumbar spine and the spinal cord ends at approximately L-1, significant neurologic weakness is unusual with mechanical lower back pain. This patient has signs of L-4, L-5 and L-5, S-1 involvement with weakness of the great toe extensor, hip abductor, and hip extensor. Electromyography and nerve conduction studies are unnecessary in this case, as the physical examination has documented the L-4, L-5 and L-5, S-1 weakness.

References

1. Atlas SJ, Deyo RA. Evaluating ad managing acute low back pain in the primary care setting. *J Gen Intern Med*. 2001;16(2):120–131.
2. Jarvik JG, Deyo RA. Diagnostic evaluation of low back pain with emphasis on imaging. *Ann Intern Med*. 2002;137(7):586–597.
3. Jensen MC, Brant-Zawadzki MN, et al. Magnetic resonance imaging of the lumbar spine in people without back pain. *N Engl J Med*. 1994;331(2):69–73.

151. Which of the following is the most common pattern of hearing loss in the United States among older persons with presbycusis?

(A) Asymmetric unilateral conductive hearing loss
(B) Bilateral symmetric low-frequency sensorineural hearing loss
(C) Bilateral symmetric high-frequency sensorineural hearing loss
(D) Bilateral symmetric high-frequency conductive hearing loss
(E) Bilateral symmetric mixed sensorineural and conductive hearing loss

ANSWER: C

Asymmetric unilateral hearing loss means that the hearing loss is in one ear only; in symmetric bilateral hearing loss, the loss is in both ears and is comparable in severity, configuration, and type.

The hearing loss typical of presbycusis is symmetric, bilateral, and mildly to moderately severe. It primarily involves high-frequency sound because the degenerative changes occur in the basal end of the cochlea. The cochlea is tonotopically organized such that the basal end is most responsive to high frequencies; the apical end responds to low frequencies. The hearing loss is sensorineural, rather than conductive, as it is due to degenerative changes within the sensory and neural structures of the cochlea and auditory nerve. Conductive hearing loss arises from disease of the middle ear that interferes with sound conduction from the outer to the inner ear. In conductive hearing loss, hearing is normal for bone-conducted stimuli, but abnormal for sound entering the ear via air conduction.

Mixed hearing loss describes loss for bone- and air-conducted stimuli, with air conduction more affected than bone conduction. Mixed hearing loss may occur in an older adult with presbycusis and transient otitis media. Once the conductive component (middle-ear disease) is resolved, the hearing loss reverts to being entirely sensorineural.

References

1. Bogardus ST, Yueh B, Shekelle PG. Screening and management of adult hearing loss in primary care: clinical applications. *JAMA.* 2003;289:1986–1990.
2. Gates GA, Murphy M, Rees TS, et al. Screening for handicapping hearing loss in the elderly. *J Fam Practice.* 2003;52:56–62.
3. Weinstein B. *Geriatric Audiology.* New York: Thieme Medical Publishers, Inc; 2000.
4. Willott J. Anatomic and physiologic aging: a behavioral neuroscience perspective. *J Am Acad Audiol.* 1996;7(3):141–151.
5. Yueh B, Shapiro N, MacLean CH, et al. Screening and management of adult hearing loss in primary care: scientific review. *JAMA.* 2003;289:1976–1985.

152. A 72-year-old woman comes to the office as a new patient. She is overweight and has a history of hypertension, diabetes mellitus, hyperlipidemia, hypertensive heart disease, atrial fibrillation, diastolic dysfunction, and hypothyroidism. She had a wrist fracture 5 years ago. Medications include atorvastatin, warfarin, furosemide, hydrochlorothiazide, and levothyroxine.

Which of her medications may have the added benefit of increasing bone mass and reducing fracture risk?

(A) Atorvastatin
(B) Warfarin
(C) Furosemide
(D) Hydrochlorothiazide
(E) Levothyroxine

ANSWER: D

Thiazide diuretics are widely used for managing hypertension and sometimes used as adjunctive therapy for refractory heart failure. Epidemiologic studies suggest that thiazides also reduce fracture risk, and prospective studies suggest improved bone mass in patients taking thiazide diuretics[OL]. These agents spare calcium at the renal level and could plausibly have beneficial effects on calcium and bone homeostasis. Although thiazides are not approved for treatment of osteoporosis, their use would seem prudent in patients who both need a diuretic agent and have or are at risk for osteoporosis. Conversely, loop diuretics such as furosemide increase renal calcium loss and lead to negative calcium balance. There is no reason to believe that furosemide favorably affects bone mass or fractures.

The evidence on the skeletal benefits of statins remains controversial and is not as consistent as the evidence for thiazides. In the Women's Health Initiative Observational Study, statin use was not found to improve fracture risk or bone density over a median follow-up of 3.9 years. Vitamin K may play a beneficial role in bone metabolism. Antagonizing vitamin K with anticoagulants such as warfarin may produce adverse effects on bone mass and may predispose the person to fractures. Data are conflicting about a negative role for warfarin with regard to skeletal integrity. Warfarin has not consistently been shown to benefit bone or reduce fracture risk. Thyrotoxicosis is known to cause osteoporosis. Excess thyroid hormone from exogenous administration can also lead to reduced bone mass. Thyroid replacement in geriatric patients should be monitored and prolonged thyroid excess avoided.

References

1. LaCroix AZ, Cauley JA, Pettinger M, et al. Statin use, clinical fracture, and bone density in postmenopausal women: results from the Women's Health Initiative Observational Study. *Ann Intern Med.* 2003; 39(2):97–104.
2. LaCroix AZ, Ott SM, Ichikawa L, et al. Low-dose hydrochlorothiazide and preservation of bone mineral density in older adults: a randomized, double-blind, placebo-controlled trial. *Ann Intern Med.* 2000;133(7):516–526.
3. Pasco JA, Kotowicz MA, Henry MJ, et al. Statin use, bone mineral density, and fracture risk: Geelong Osteoporosis Study. *Arch Intern Med.* 2002;162(5):537–540.
4. Reid IR, Ames RW, Orr-Walker BJ, et al. Hydrochlorothiazide reduces loss of cortical bone in normal postmenopausal women: a randomized controlled trial. *Am J Med.* 2000;109(5):362–370.

[OL] Not approved by the U.S. Food and Drug Administration for this use.

153. A 74-year-old man with a history of longstanding hypertension, previous myocardial infarction, peripheral vascular disease, and chronic renal insufficiency was admitted to the hospital with an acute myocardial infarction. He has had a difficult course in the intensive care unit for several weeks, and his prognosis appears poor. He is not able to participate in discussions about his care. The patient's physician is about to meet with the patient's family to discuss options for treatment and an overall plan of care. The patient and his family are black American. The patient's physician, who is not black, recalls having heard about a study showing that black American patients request more life-sustaining treatments than their white counterparts.

Which of the following is the most appropriate way to communicate this information in an initial meeting with the family?

(A) The physician should reassure the family that he has read about their culture and he understands their point of view.

(B) The physician should ask the family for their observations of how the patient is doing and what their wishes are.

(C) The physician should focus his comments on the severity of illness and poor prognosis and suggest less aggressive care.

(D) The physician should avoid mentioning the possibility of treatment limitation.

ANSWER: B

Several studies have described racial differences in patient preferences for end-of-life treatments. For example, some studies have reported comparisons of preferences expressed by black American and white American patients, reporting that the black patients are more likely to request aggressive treatment. Black patients are less likely than white patients to express their wishes in an advance directive. When black Americans do express their advance preferences for end-of-life care, they are more likely to request that their physicians attempt to keep them alive no matter how ill they are. White Americans are more likely to request cessation or withholding of aggressive treatments such as cardiopulmonary resuscitation, mechanical ventilation, and kidney dialysis. Awareness of information from these studies may be useful

background, particularly for physicians who assume that everyone else has the same preferences that they have. However, it would be a serious error to assume knowledge of the preferences of any individual or family on the basis of race or ethnicity. Statistical differences by race may be found in populations studied, but these findings do not apply to every member of the population. Each individual's preferences can be known only if he or she is given an opportunity to express them.

If a physician believes in a particular situation that the correct approach is treatment limitation, he or she may be tempted to highlight the most grim aspects of the patient's condition as a way of persuading the family that it is time to withdraw care. However, selective reporting of the patient's condition is deceptive and should be avoided.

Legitimate treatment options, including treatment limitation, should be presented to family members so that they are fully informed about the range of options. A prior assumption about what the family believes is particularly harmful if it leads to withholding of information about the range of possible options that are medically appropriate.

References

1. Hallenbeck J, Goldstein MK. Decisions at the end of life: cultural considerations beyond medical ethics. *Generations: J Am Soc Aging.* 1999;23:24–29.
2. McKinley ED, Garrett JM, Evans AT, et al. Differences in end-of-life decision making among black and white ambulatory cancer patients. *J Gen Intern Med.* 1996;11(11):651–656.
3. Mebane EW, Oman RF, Kroonen LT, et al. The influence of physician race, age, and gender on physician attitudes toward advance care directives and preferences for end-of-life decision-making. *J Am Geriatr Soc.* 1999;47(5):579–591.

154. A 70-year-old man comes to the office because he has increased difficulties with urination, including poor stream, straining to void, and incontinence. History includes transient ischemic attack, hypertension, diabetes mellitus type 2 with neuropathy, and osteoarthritis. Current medications include clopidogrel 75 mg daily, lisinopril 10 mg daily, glipizide 10 mg daily, naproxen 500 mg twice daily, nortriptyline 50 mg daily (increased 2 weeks ago from 25 mg for peripheral neuropathy), and a daily multivitamin. He does not have insurance for his medications and has a history of not filling prescriptions if they "cost too much." A urinalysis performed today shows 0–5 leukocytes and is negative for bacteria and leukocyte esterase.

Which of the following is the most appropriate next intervention?

(A) Discontinue naproxen.
(B) Reduce nortriptyline.
(C) Begin oxybutynin.
(D) Assess postvoid residual urine.
(E) Order a prostate-specific antigen (PSA) test.

ANSWER: D

Urinary incontinence affects from 15% to 30% of community-dwelling older adults. Medications with anticholinergic effects, such as nortriptyline, can cause urinary retention by inhibiting contraction of the bladder. This patient most likely has overflow incontinence secondary to the increase in nortriptyline dose. Although nortriptyline has less anticholinergic activity than amitriptyline, it may still cause problems for susceptible individuals. However, this new-onset incontinence may be due to another cause, and since nortriptyline is an inexpensive option for treating peripheral neuropathy, it is worth first assessing postvoid residual urine. If the postvoid residual is normal, then nortriptyline is unlikely to be contributing to the incontinence and may be continued. Naproxen is unlikely to cause incontinence. Oxybutynin has anticholinergic and antispasmodic activity and is used to treat urinary frequency, urgency, or urge incontinence secondary to an overactive bladder. Thus, oxybutynin could worsen incontinence secondary to urinary retention. Although

ordering a PSA test may help determine if the patient has prostate cancer, it will not address his urinary symptoms.

Reference

1. Couture JA, Valiquette L. Urinary incontinence. *Ann Pharmacother.* 2000;34(5):646–655.
2. Curtis LA, Dolan TS, Cespedes RD. Acute urinary retention and urinary incontinence. *Emerg Med Clin North Am.* 2001;19:591–619.
3. Pickles T. Current status of PSA screening: early detection of prostate cancer. *Can Fam Physician.* 2004:50;57–63.

155. Which one of these supplements should be discontinued before surgery because of increased risk for bleeding?

(A) Aloe vera
(B) *Ginkgo biloba*
(C) Glucosamine
(D) Lutein

ANSWER: B

Ginkgo biloba has been used for cognitive disorders such as Alzheimer's disease and vascular dementia. It is purported to enhance memory in adults with normal cognition, but study results are conflicting. *Ginkgo biloba* inhibits platelet-activating factor and may increase the risk for bleeding complications, especially when combined with anticoagulants and platelet-inhibiting medications. Given the pharmacology of its active constituents, *Ginkgo biloba* should be discontinued at least 36 hours prior to surgery.

The risk for bleeding may be increased by other herbal therapies, including garlic and ginseng. Ephedra, kava, St. John's wort, and valerian have other pharmacokinetic and pharmacodynamic properties that can adversely affect patients undergoing surgery. As with prescribed and over-the-counter medications, the patient's use of herbal therapies should be reviewed in advance of surgery.

Aloe vera gel, glucosamine, and lutein are not known to affect coagulation.

References

1. Ang-Lee MK, Moss J, Yuan C. Herbal medicines and perioperative care. *JAMA.* 2001; 286(2):208–216.

2. Fong KC, Kinnear PE. Retrobulbar haemorrhage associated with chronic *Gingko biloba* ingestion. *Postgrad Med J.* 2003;79(935):531–532.
3. Hauser D, Gayowski T, Singh N. Bleeding complications precipitated by unrecognized *Gingko biloba* use after liver transplantation. *Transpl Int.* 2002;15(7):377–379.

156. An 86-year-old widowed white man is brought to the emergency department after a neighbor found him sleeping in his car with the engine on while it was parked in the garage. The patient's physical and cognitive examinations are unremarkable. Laboratory tests are remarkable only for slightly elevated liver function. His affect is restricted. The patient denies any suicide attempt and explains that he fell asleep after he drove back home. He refuses to allow his son, who lives out of state, to be contacted because "he does not want him to be bothered." Similarly, he refuses to talk to the psychiatric triage nurse, insisting that he should go home now.

Which of the following is the most appropriate next step in the management of this patient?

(A) Discharge with follow-up the next day with his primary care provider.
(B) Initiate involuntary psychiatric evaluation.
(C) Admit the patient to a general medical unit for further observation.
(D) Keep the patient in the emergency department for further observation.
(E) Call the patient's son to discuss your concerns.

ANSWER: B

This patient presents with a psychiatric emergency, since the circumstances and presence of several major risk factors make suicide a strong possibility. His refusal of further evaluation for depression and suicidality does not leave the physician any choice. White men 85 years and older have the highest suicide rate among all demographic groups in the United States. Widowhood and lack of social support increase the risk of suicide. In addition, this patient's blunted affect suggests depression, and his elevated liver function suggests that he may be drinking. Depression and alcoholism are strongly linked to suicide completion in late life.

It would be helpful to obtain additional clinical information from a family member, but it is inappropriate (and possibly illegal) to call the patient's son without his permission. Keeping the patient in the emergency department or admitting him to a general medical unit for further observation creates a significant risk. He may elope, try to hurt himself in the hospital, or be discharged at a later time without ever having been evaluated properly. Even if he agrees to follow-up the next day with his primary care provider, this strategy is dangerous: he may not go, or if he goes, he may deny being depressed and suicidal, and kill himself. In several psychological autopsy studies, more than two thirds of elderly persons who completed suicide had been seen by a primary care provider within 1 month of killing themselves; up to one half had been seen within 1 week, and one fourth had been seen within 24 hours.

References
1. Brown GK, Bruce ML, Pearson JL. High-risk management guidelines for elderly suicidal patients in primary care settings. *Int J Geriatr Psychiatry.* 2001;16(6):593–601.
2. Conwell Y, Duberstein PR, Caine ED. Risk factors for suicide in later life. *Biol Psychiatry.* 2002;52(3):193–204.
3. Szanto K, Gildengers A, Mulsant BH, et al. Identification of suicidal ideation and prevention of suicidal behaviour in the elderly. *Drugs Aging.* 2002;19(1):11–24.
4. Turvey CL, Conwell Y, Jones MP, et al. Risk factors for late-life suicide: a prospective, community-based study. *Am J Geriatr Psychiatry.* 2002;10(4):398–406.

157. An 82-year-old man comes to the office for evaluation of palpitations. The patient states that he has noted an occasional "skipped beat" for about 20 years; it occurs more frequently since his wife died 3 months ago. He has no other symptoms. He has a history of hypertension, peptic ulcer disease, and benign prostatic hyperplasia. His exercise tolerance is good, and he can walk 0.5 miles without difficulty. Current medications include hydrochlorothiazide 12.5 mg daily, doxazosin 4 mg daily, and omeprazole 20 mg daily.

On physical examination, heart rate is 58 per minute with occasional ectopy, and blood pressure is 130/70 mm Hg. Body mass index (kg/m^2) is 24. He has a II/VI systolic ejection murmur and S_4 is present, but no S_3. The remainder of the examination is normal.

Electrocardiography shows sinus rhythm with occasional ventricular premature beats (VPBs) and left ventricular hypertrophy with repolarization abnormality. A 24-hour Holter monitor reveals frequent VPBs, averaging 100 to 200 per hour, occasional atrial premature beats, rare ventricular couplets, and no ventricular tachycardia; the "skipped beats" reported in the patient's diary correspond with isolated VPBs. Stress echocardiography shows left ventricular hypertrophy with normal left ventricular systolic function, mild diastolic dysfunction, aortic valve sclerosis, and no ischemia. Thyroid function tests and serum electrolytes are normal.

What is the most appropriate treatment for this patient's rhythm disorder?

(A) Atenolol
(B) Sotalol
(C) Amiodarone
(D) Propafenone
(E) Reassurance

ANSWER: E

The prevalence of supraventricular and ventricular premature beats increases with age, but these arrhythmias are not associated with an adverse prognosis in the absence of documented coronary artery disease, heart failure, or impaired left ventricular systolic function. As a result, no treatment is required unless symptoms are severe and disabling. In this patient, it is possible that the stress of his wife's death resulted in an increase in symptomatic ventricular premature beats and that the frequency will decline over time. When treatment is required, β-blockers are first-line therapy. This patient's resting heart rate of 58 per minute suggests underlying sinus node dysfunction that might be exacerbated by β-blockers, resulting in symptomatic bradycardia. Antiarrhythmic agents, such as sotalol, amiodarone, and propafenone, are not indicated for treatment of frequent ventricular premature beats, and each of these drugs may precipitate life-threatening tachy- or bradyarrhythmias.

References

1. Aronow WS, Ahn C, Mercando AD, et al. Prevalence and association of ventricular tachycardia and complex ventricular arrhythmias with new coronary events in older men and women with and without cardiovascular disease. *J Gerontol Biol Sci Med Sci.* 2002;57(3):M178–M180.
2. Fleg JL. Arrhythmias and conduction disturbances in the octogenarian: epidemiology and progression. In: Wenger NK, ed. *Cardiovascular Disease in the Octogenarian and Beyond.* London: Martin Dunitz Publishers;1999:279–290.
3. Frishman WH, Heiman M, Karpenos A, et al. Twenty-four-hour ambulatory electrocardiography in elderly subjects: prevalence of various arrhythmias and prognostic implications (report from the Bronx Longitudinal Aging Study). *Am Heart J.* 1996;132(2 Pt 1):297–302.
4. Zipes DP, Ackerman MJ, Estes NA 3rd, et al. Task Force 7: arrhythmias. *J Am Coll Cardiol.* 2005;45(8):1354–1363.

158. A 70-year-old woman describes early morning awakening and daytime fatigue for the past 8 months. She is generally healthy and has no symptoms of anxiety or depression. Over the past year she has been retiring as early as 7 PM. Despite recent efforts to retire later in the evening, she continues to awaken regularly at 3 AM.

Which of the following most likely accounts for this patient's sleep disturbance?

(A) Breathing-related sleep disorder
(B) Circadian rhythm advance
(C) Periodic limb movements
(D) Restless legs syndrome
(E) Sleep apnea

ANSWER: B

Integration of circadian rhythms depends on the suprachiasmatic nucleus of the anterior hypothalamus, which deteriorates with age, particularly in women. As people age, the circadian rhythm advances so that sleepiness occurs earlier in the evening (perhaps at 7 PM or 8 PM), and awakening occurs spontaneously about 8 hours later. Most older adults try to correct the problem by retiring later in the evening, but they nevertheless wake up as core body temperature rises in the early morning hours. Another common pattern is for older adults to nap during the late afternoon or early evening and then have initial insomnia and wake up too early in the morning. Changes in circadian rhythm may also be responsible for daytime agitation in dementia patients who reside in long-term-care facilities.

Treatment of this advanced sleep phase involves delaying the sleep cycle with bright light late in the day, ideally from 7 PM to 9 PM. Also, older adults should try to be outdoors as late in the day as possible before the sun goes down. This strategy will delay the circadian rhythm, so patients will become sleepy later in the evening and sleep later in the morning. In the absence of sunlight, a bright-light box is effective for light exposure later in the day. Normal room light is not bright enough to be effective.

Sleep apnea and breathing-related disorders are more likely to produce excessive daytime sleepiness, rather than the pattern of insomnia seen in this case. Periodic limb movements and restless legs syndrome are both characterized by brief arousals throughout the night and reduced total sleep time. Early-morning awakening is not characteristic of either of these disorders.

References

1. Ancoli-Israel S, Gehrman PR, Martin JL, et al. Increased light exposure consolidates sleep and strengthens circadian rhythms in severe Alzheimer disease patients. *Behavioral Sleep Med.* 2003;1(1):22–36.
2. Avidan AY. Sleep changes and disorders in the elderly patient. *Clin Neurol Neurosci Rep.* 2002;2(2):178–185.
3. Bliwise DL. Normal aging. In: Kryger MH, Roth T, Dement WC, eds. *Principles and Practice of Sleep Medicine.* 3rd ed. Philadelphia, PA: WB Saunders Co.;2000:26–42.
4. Van Someren EJ. Circadian rhythms and sleep in human aging. *Chronobiol Int.* 2000;17(3):233–243.

159. A 72-year-old woman is admitted for an elective left hip replacement. Her medical history is significant for chronic obstructive pulmonary disease, osteoarthritis, and cigarette smoking. Two months ago she was strongly advised to quit smoking and was referred to a smoking cessation program. However, she still smokes one pack of cigarettes every 4 days. One month prior to admission she had a normal cardiac nuclear stress test. Her current medications are calcium, vitamin D, ipratropium-albuterol nebulizer treatments, and oxygen 2 liters while sleeping and with exertion. Approximately 2 months ago she received a course of oral corticosteroids for wheezing, with a good response. She now reports a chronic cough productive of yellow sputum in the morning and white or yellow sputum throughout the remainder of the day.

On examination her vital signs are unremarkable. Her pulse oximetry is 87% on room air at rest and 93% on 2 liters nasal oxygen. She has diffuse degenerative joint disease with painful and limited range of motion in both hip joints. Her lungs show prolongation of the expiratory phase with diffuse expiratory wheezes throughout both lung fields. The remainder of the examination is unremarkable.

Chest radiograph shows chronic scarring of the lung fields, plate-like atelectasis in the right lower lobe, and no infiltrates. Electrocardiogram is unremarkable.

Which of the following, in addition to oxygen therapy and ipratropium-albuterol nebulizer treatment, would you recommend to minimize the risks of postoperative pulmonary complications?

(A) Corticosteroids and chest physical therapy
(B) Corticosteroids and antibiotics
(C) Corticosteroids, antibiotics, and theophylline
(D) Chest physical therapy, antibiotics, and theophylline
(E) No additional therapy

ANSWER: A

The pulmonary status of any patient with chronic obstructive pulmonary disease should be optimized before any elective or emergent surgery. Treatment modalities are similar to those used in the outpatient setting. Smoking cessation should be recommended and achieved as early as possible, optimally at least 2 months prior to surgery. Current smoking significantly increases the risk of postoperative pulmonary complications. The relative risk of complications may be even higher for patients who quit cigarettes less than 1 month before their surgery. This increased risk may be related to the increased incidence of cough and sputum production experienced by chronic smokers during the first 4 to 8 weeks postcessation.

Bronchodilators remain the mainstay of management of chronic obstructive pulmonary disease. Ipratropium alone is beneficial to many patients, and a β-agonist can be added for symptomatic relief, as needed. Chest physical therapy is of value in preventing atelectasis and mucous plugging. Corticosteroids should be added to the medication regimen of patients demonstrating bronchospasm who have benefited from steroid use in the past.

Theophylline provides benefit in improving FEV_1 and dyspnea in patients who have not achieved maximal benefit from other therapies. Theophylline should be used with caution in older patients, as it has a narrow therapeutic window and high potential for toxicity. Antibiotics have no prophylactic benefit for preventing pulmonary complications and should be reserved for patients who demonstrate clinical or radiographic findings suggestive of a lower respiratory tract infection. Elective surgery should be delayed in any older patient with a lower respiratory tract infection and rescheduled after the infection has cleared.

References

1. Arozullah AM, Khuri SF, Henderson WG, et al. Development and validation of multifactorial risk index for predicting postoperative pneumonia after major noncardiac surgery. *Ann Intern Med.* 2001;135(10):847–857.
2. Karpel JP, Kotch A, Zinny M, et al. A comparison of inhaled ipratropium, oral theophylline plus inhaled beta-agonist, and the combination of all three in COPD. *Chest.* 1994;105(4):1089–1094.
3. Nakagawa M, Tanaka H, Tsukuma H, et al. Relationship between the duration of the preoperative smoke-free period and the incidence of postoperative pulmonary complications after pulmonary surgery. *Chest.* 2001;120(3):705–710.
4. Smetana GW. Preoperative pulmonary assessment of the older adult. *Clin Geriatr Med.* 2004;19(1):35–55.

160. An 84-year-old woman comes to the office for evaluation of elevated blood pressure. She had a reading of 178/68 mm Hg at a community health fair. She brings a diary of home blood-pressure readings that she obtained using an automatic cuff; the diary records systolic values that range from 132 mm Hg to 145 mm Hg. She takes no medications other than a daily multivitamin and a calcium supplement.

On physical examination, systolic blood pressure by palpation is found to be 178 mm Hg while she is lying down. The radial pulse heart rate is 76 per minute. Manual blood pressure is 176/64 mm Hg; there is an auscultatory gap between approximately 160 and 140 mm Hg. Her manual standing blood pressure after 1 minute of standing is 168/60 mm Hg with a heart rate of 80 per minute.

Which of the following provides the best explanation for the difference between her home and the office and health fair blood-pressure readings?

(A) "White-coat" hypertension
(B) Orthostatic hypotension
(C) Postprandial hypotension
(D) Arterial stiffness
(E) Decreased baroreflex sensitivity

ANSWER: D

Several features of this patient's presentation demonstrate arterial stiffness: the marked elevation in systolic pressure with normal diastolic readings, a markedly elevated pulse pressure, and the auscultatory gap during the systolic reading. The presence of the auscultatory gap is a cardiovascular risk marker and likely explains the discordance between the home and office readings. Automated cuffs may fail to inflate to a pressure that is high enough to detect the true systolic blood pressure. In this case, the automated cuff used at home may only inflate to 170 mm Hg; there are no Korotkoff sounds detected as the cuff deflates until the lower bound of the auscultatory gap, which the device falsely interprets as the systolic pressure. It is important to calibrate the patient's home device against a known standard to ensure its accuracy. Although this patient could possibly have "white-coat" hypertension, the presence of the auscultatory gap is the more likely explanation for the difference in blood-pressure readings.

The patient has no evidence of orthostatic hypotension on physical examination. The drop of 8 mm Hg between her supine and upright blood-pressure readings is within the normal range of postural blood-pressure response and below the 20–mm Hg difference most commonly used to define orthostatic hypotension. Similarly, there is no evidence to support postprandial hypotension in this case. Postprandial hypotension, although prevalent among residents in long-term-care settings, is uncommon in community-dwelling individuals. Affected patients most often also demonstrate orthostatic blood-pressure changes.

Decreased baroreceptor sensitivity is a common characteristic of older persons with hypertension and may contribute to the age-related increase in sympathetic nervous system activity and greater variability in blood pressure—perhaps including orthostatic and postprandial hypotension. Impaired baroreceptor sensitivity may cause variability in blood-pressure readings, but it is not likely to account for the difference between home and office blood-pressure readings observed in this patient.

References

1. Dart AM, Kingwell BA. Pulse pressure: a review of mechanisms and clinical relevance. *J Am Coll Cardiol.* 2001;37(4):975–984.
2. Jansen RW, Lipsitz LA. Postprandial hypotension: epidemiology, pathophsyiology, and clinical management. *Ann Intern Med.* 1995;122(4):286–295.
3. Lakatta EG, Levy D. Arterial and cardiac aging: major shareholders in cardiovascular disease enterprises: Part II: the aging heart in health: links to heart disease. *Circulation.* 2003;107(2):346–354.
4. Lipsitz LA. Orthostatic hypotension in the elderly. *N Engl J Med.* 1989;321(14):952–957.

161. A 72-year-old woman comes to the office for a routine physical examination. She is in generally good health. She takes aspirin 81 mg daily and occasionally she needs a stool softener. She reports feeling overwhelmed and mildly depressed from caring for her 84-year-old husband, who has mid-stage Alzheimer's disease and who needs increasing care. Over the past few months, he needs more reminders for his daily living activities, cannot be left alone, and has grown more frail. He sees a specialist in Alzheimer's disease every few months. The woman at times feels angry toward her husband, is sleeping less well, but denies being depressed.

Which of the following interventions is most likely to help this patient?

(A) Refer for a support group through the Alzheimer's Association
(B) Begin a selective serotonin-reuptake inhibitor
(C) Refer for psychotherapy
(D) Refer her husband to adult day care twice weekly
(E) Provide a one-time counseling session in the office on how to care for her husband

ANSWER: D

Many times, psychologic distress in elderly patients is related to caregiving, and Alzheimer's disease has serious effects on primary caregivers, especially spouses. This patient is in the early stages of changes that typically come on in the caregiver as the person with Alzheimer's disease declines and needs more care. If her distress is not addressed, it may worsen and lead to a decline in her overall health. In this case, the best recommendation is for a combined approach (education for the caregiver plus day care for the patient) that directly involves the person with Alzheimer's disease. Respite-type interventions that reduce the total amount of time providing care benefit the caregiver and possibly the person with Alzheimer's disease. Single interventions in the primary care setting, such as brief counseling or referral to a support group alone, do not seem to be effective, as indicated by evidence in clinical trials. Immediate treatment with antidepressant medication or referral for specific counseling is premature, although this patient should be monitored closely and referred to a counselor or psychiatrist if initial interventions are not successful.

References

1. Brodaty H, Green A, Koschera A, et al. Meta-analysis of psychosocial interventions for caregivers of people with dementia. *J Am Geriatr Soc.* 2003; 51(5):657–664.
2. Mace N, Rabins PV. *The 36-Hour Day.* Baltimore, MD: Johns Hopkins University Press; 2001.
3. Opie J, Rosewarne R, O'Connor DW, et al. The efficacy of psychosocial approaches to behavior disorders in dementia: a systematic literature review. *Aust N Z J Psychiatry.* 1999;33(6):789–799.
4. Rabins PV, Lyketsos CG, Steele CD. *Practical Dementia Care.* New York: Oxford University Press; 1999.

162. A 71-year-old woman comes to the office because she has had pain and swelling in her hands, wrists, shoulders, and knees for 6 months. She also has debilitating fatigue and joint stiffness that persists through mid-day.

On physical examination, she is found to have lost 6.9 kg (15 lb) over the past year. There is swelling, erythema, and tenderness of the metacarpophalangeal joints, wrists, and elbows. Warmth and effusions are present in the knees. Significant laboratory values include erythrocyte sedimentation rate of 64 mm/h, serum creatinine of 2.3 mg/dL, and rheumatoid factor titer of 1:640.

Which of the following is the most appropriate therapy for this patient?

(A) Celecoxib 100 mg daily
(B) Hydroxychloroquine 400 mg daily *Plaquenil*
(C) Methotrexate 10 mg orally weekly
(D) Prednisone 60 mg daily
(E) Etanercept 25 mg twice weekly *Enbrel*

ANSWER: C

Rheumatoid arthritis is an inflammatory systemic disease that deforms and destroys the peripheral joints. Although cyclooxygenase-2 (COX-2) agents reduce inflammation and pain and therefore are effective as initial agents, they do not alter the natural course of the disease. The short- and moderate-term efficacy of the lowest possible dose of corticosteroids is well accepted as a disease-altering treatment for

rheumatoid arthritis. However, there are significant adverse effects, and steroids are neither as effective nor safe as methotrexate. Methotrexate is a safe and effective disease-modifying agent for rheumatoid arthritis when properly prescribed and monitored. Hydroxychloroquine and sulfasalazine also modify disease, but with less supportive evidence in older adult patients. Cyclophosphamide, penicillamine, and gold compounds are tolerated less well. Anticytokine therapy (etanercept, infliximab) can be considered for older patients who respond suboptimally to methotrexate.

References

1. Gardner G, Furst DE. Disease-modifying antirheumatic drugs: potential effects in older patients. *Drugs Aging.* 1995;7(6):420–437.
2. Saag KG. Glucocorticoid use in rheumatoid arthritis. *Curr Rheumatol Rep.* 2002;4(3):218–225.
3. Strand V, Simon LS. Low dose glucocorticoids in early rheumatoid arthritis. *Clin Exp Rheumatol.* 2003;21(5 Suppl 31):S186–S190.

163. An 84-year-old woman is transferred from her nursing home to an acute-care hospital for treatment of pneumonia with ceftriaxone and azithromycin. She returns to the nursing home, but 5 days later watery diarrhea, cramping lower abdominal pain and tenderness, low-grade fever, and leukocytosis develop.

What is the most appropriate next step in diagnosing this condition?

(A) Stool for fecal leukocytes
(B) Abdominal computed tomography scan
(C) Stool culture
(D) Stool immunoassay for *Clostridium difficile* toxin
(E) Blood cultures

ANSWER: D

Clostridium difficile causes approximately 25% of all cases of antibiotic-associated diarrhea. All antibiotics have been associated with *C. difficile* diarrhea, most commonly clindamycin, ampicillin, amoxicillin, and the cephalosporins. Clinical presentation varies from asymptomatic colonization to mild diarrhea to severe debilitating disease with high fever, severe abdominal pain, paralytic ileus, colonic dilatation, and rarely perforation. In patients with *C. difficile* diarrhea, symptoms usually begin soon after colonization. The incubation period for disease after colonization is likely to be less than 1 week, with a median time to onset of approximately 2 days. Colonization may occur during antibiotic treatment or during the weeks after a course of antibiotics. Commercial immunoassays for *C. difficile* infection have reasonable sensitivity (70% to 90%) and specificity (99%) and are most commonly performed for diagnosis. Stool and blood cultures would not reveal the *C. difficile* infections.

As *C. difficile* diarrhea is the most likely cause of this patient's diarrhea, given the clinical course and presentation, the other choices are not appropriate as the next steps in diagnosis. A stool culture is unlikely to reveal a pathogen in this case. Abdominal imaging tests may show only nonspecific findings.

References

1. Kyne, L, Farrell RJ, Kelly CP. Clostridium difficile. *Gastroenterol Clin North Am.* 2001;30(30):753–777.
2. Mylonakis E, Ryan ET, Calderwood SB. Clostridium difficile–associated diarrhea: a review. *Arch Intern Med.* 2001;161(4):525–533.
3. Yassin SF, Young-Fadok TM, Zein NN, et al. Clostridium difficile–associated diarrhea and colitis. *Mayo Clin Proc.* 2001;76(7):725–730.

164. An 87-year-old man who is an established patient comes to the office because over the past year he has noted increasing shortness of breath with activity. He reports that 2 years ago he could easily walk 1 mile, but now he has to stop and rest after walking one block. He also becomes "winded" after climbing one flight of stairs. He has no chest discomfort or palpitations but often becomes lightheaded when he stands up, and he felt as though he was going to "pass out" on at least two occasions. History includes type 2 diabetes mellitus and depression. He does not smoke or drink alcohol. He is the primary caregiver for his wife, who is disabled with advanced Parkinson's disease. Current medications include glyburide, aspirin, atorvastatin, and paroxetine.

On physical examination, heart rate is 70 per minute and regular, blood pressure is 140/60 mm Hg, respiratory rate is 18 per minute, and body mass index (kg/m^2) is 25. He has a flat affect. Examination of the neck shows no jugular venous distention, normal thyroid, and delayed carotid upstrokes bilaterally. He has a III/VI late-peaking systolic ejection murmur and S$_4$ gallop, with no S$_3$. His Mini–Mental State Examination score is 28 of 30, with no focal deficits.

Laboratory studies:

Hemoglobin	13.8 g/dL
Hematocrit	41%
Leukocyte count	6500/μL
Platelet count	180,000/μL
Creatinine	1.0 mg/dL
Blood urea nitrogen	22 mg/dL
Albumin	3.8 g/dL

Electrocardiography shows sinus rhythm and left ventricular hypertrophy with repolarization abnormality. Echocardiography shows moderate left ventricular systolic dysfunction (ejection fraction 35%) and a heavily calcified aortic valve (estimated area 0.6 cm^2).

Which of the following is the most appropriate management for this patient?

(A) Aortic valve replacement
(B) Balloon aortic valvuloplasty
(C) Percutaneous coronary angioplasty, if indicated
(D) Angiotensin-converting enzyme inhibitor and titration to tolerance
(E) Digoxin

ANSWER: A

This patient has severe symptomatic aortic stenosis with moderate left ventricular dysfunction. The only effective treatment for this condition is aortic valve replacement (AVR). Early and long-term results of AVR in older persons are excellent, with significant improvement and restoration of normal age-adjusted life expectancy for most patients. Angiography is indicated before AVR to exclude significant coronary artery disease, which is common even in asymptomatic patients. If present, coronary bypass grafting should be performed at the time of AVR. Contraindications to AVR include moderate or severe dementia, advanced chronic lung disease, or other terminal illness.

Balloon aortic valvuloplasty provides short-term palliation for some patients with severe aortic stenosis, but restenosis occurs within 6 to 12 months in most cases and long-term outcomes are poor. Coronary angioplasty is an effective therapy for obstructive coronary artery disease but has no impact on the prognosis of patients with severe aortic stenosis. Angiotensin-converting enzyme inhibitors and digoxin may provide palliation for patients with severe aortic stenosis, but these and other medications do not alter the natural history of the disease, which is characterized by progressive clinical deterioration following the onset of symptoms.

References

1. ACC/AHA guidelines for the management of patients with valvular heart disease: a report of the American College of Cardiology/American Heart Association. Task Force on Practice Guidelines (Committee on Management of Patients with Valvular Heart Disease). *J Am Coll Cardiol.* 1998;32(5):1486–1588.
2. Dauterman KW, Michaels AD, Ports TA. Is there any indication for aortic valvuloplasty in the elderly? *Am J Geriatr Cardiol.* 2003;12(3):190–196.
3. Sedrakyan A, Vaccarino V, Paltiel AD, et al. Age does not limit quality of life improvement in cardiac valve surgery. *J Am Coll Cardiol.* 2003;42(7):1208–1214.
4. Sundt TM, Bailey MS, Moon MR, et al. Quality of life after aortic valve replacement at the age of > 80 years. *Circulation.* 2000;102(Suppl 3):III70–III74.

165. Which of the following is the best approach to treat psychosis in dementia with Lewy bodies?

    (A) Haloperidol
    (B) Clozapine   *Clozaril*
    (C) Quetiapine   *Seroquel*
    (D) Diazepam

ANSWER: C

Dementia with Lewy bodies is often associated with an increased likelihood of adverse events, in particular extrapyramidal side effects, during treatment with antipsychotic agents. Because of this sensitivity, conventional antipsychotics such as haloperidol[OL] are contraindicated as first-line treatment for dementia with Lewy bodies. The atypical antipsychotic agent quetiapine[OL] has a lower risk of extrapyramidal symptoms in patients with dementia with Lewy bodies. Clozapine[OL] also has a lower risk of extrapyramidal symptoms, but it requires weekly monitoring of leukocyte counts because of its age-related incidence of agranulocytosis. Low-dose benzodiazepines with a short half-life, such as lorazepam[OL], may be useful in short-term management of agitation in patients with dementia. Benzodiazepines with a long-half life, such as diazepam[OL], are contraindicated in elderly persons because they increase the risk of falls and injury.

References

1. Kinderman SS, Dolder CR, Bailey A, et al. Pharmacological treatment of psychosis and agitation in elderly patients with dementia: four decades of experience. *Drugs and Aging.* 2002;19(4):257–276.
2. Richards SS, Sweet RA. Treating psychosis in Alzheimer's disease. *Alzheimer's Disease Management Today.* 2000;2(3):3–9.

166. A 75-year-old woman comes to the office because she has had repeated episodes of profound dizziness and near loss of consciousness, along with at least two episodes in which she found herself on the floor but was unaware of how she fell. She denies any confusion after the episode or any significant trauma. She has hypertension, and her daily medication is amlodipine 5 mg.

    On physical examination, blood pressure is 152/84 mm Hg and heart rate is 76 per minute when she is supine. In upright posture, blood pressure is 146/86 mm Hg and heart rate is 86 per minute. There is no jugular venous distension or carotid bruit. Lungs are clear. There is a slightly delayed carotid upstroke and a II/VI systolic murmur at the base with an intact S_2 but no gallop.

    Which of the following is the most appropriate next step in the evaluation of this patient to stratify her risk for adverse outcomes?

[OL] Not approved by the U.S. Food and Drug Administration for this use.

Geriatrics Review Syllabus, 6th Edition   **125**

(A) Blood tests
(B) Electrocardiography
(C) Holter monitoring
(D) Event monitor
(E) Tilt-table test

ANSWER: B

Risk stratification is an essential initial step in management of the patient with unexplained syncope. The most important risk factor is the presence of structural heart disease as identified through history, physical examination, electrocardiography, or echocardiography. Electrocardiography is the most likely of the options given to aid in risk stratification, and thus prognosis and diagnosis. Although the electrocardiogram is most commonly normal after a syncopal episode, it may reveal a definitive diagnosis, such as Mobitz type II second- or third-degree atrioventricular block, alternating left and right bundle branch block, ventricular tachycardia, pacemaker malfunction, paroxysmal supraventricular tachycardia, sinus bradycardia, sinoatrial block, or pauses, if associated with symptoms. Such findings occur in fewer than 5% of patients, as arrhythmias resulting in syncope are often self-limited, but other electrocardiographic rhythm and conduction abnormalities or the presence of pathologic Q waves can indicate a myocardial infarction and thus structural heart disease that will guide further evaluation.

Blood tests have an extremely low yield for patients with unexplained syncope. For example, hypoglycemia does not result in a transient loss of consciousness, but rather requires intervention in order to reverse the metabolic derangement that could be contributing to symptoms. Unless it uncovers frequent ventricular ectopy or nonsustained ventricular tachycardia, short-term continuous electrocardiographic monitoring, such as telemetry or Holter monitor or an event monitor, is not useful for identifying the cause of syncope, since weeks, months, or even years may pass before the next arrhythmia-related event. Also, most arrhythmias detected in patients with syncope are brief and result in no symptoms.

Triage decisions and management should be based on preexisting cardiac disease or electrocardiographic abnormalities, which are important predictors of arrhythmic syncope and

mortality, rather than on symptoms. A tilt-table test would be an appropriate evaluation only after structural heart disease has been excluded.

References

1. Kapoor WN, Cha R, Peterson JR, et al. Prolonged electrocardiographic monitoring in patients with syncope: importance of frequent or repetitive ventricular ectopy. *Am J Med.* 1987;82(1):20–28.
2. Kenny RA. Syncope in the elderly: diagnosis, evaluation, and treatment. *J Cardiovasc Electrophysiol.* 2003;14(9 Suppl):S74–S77.
3. Meyer MD, Handler J. Evaluation of the patient with syncope: an evidence based approach. *Emerg Med Clin North Am.* 1999;17(1):189–201.
4. Oh JH, Hanusa BH, Kapoor WN. Do symptoms predict cardiac arrhythmias and mortality in patients with syncope? *Arch Intern Med.* 1999;159(4):375–380.
5. Pires LA, Ganji JR, Jarandila R, et al. Diagnostic patterns and temporal trends in the evaluation of adult patients hospitalized with syncope. *Arch Intern Med.* 2001;161(15):1889–1895.

167. A 69-year-old man comes to the office because for the past several weeks he has had recurrent spells of room-spinning vertigo that last for about 4 minutes. The spells occur spontaneously, are unassociated with positional changes, and are accompanied occasionally by double vision and sometimes by weakness on the right side. Several times, he has had sudden drop attacks, after which he has mild weakness of both legs lasting several minutes. He has a history of diabetes mellitus and coronary artery disease.

Which of the following is the most likely cause of the vertigo?

(A) Vestibular neuronitis
(B) Vertebrobasilar insufficiency
(C) Labyrinthitis
(D) Migraine-associated vertigo
(E) Ménière's disease

ANSWER: B

Transient ischemia within the vertebrobasilar system is a common cause of spontaneous attacks of vertigo in older patients. Typically, the vertigo begins abruptly, lasts several minutes, and is often associated with other neurologic symptoms. In any older patient with brief episodes of vertigo, and especially in patients with risk factors for cerebrovascular disease (such as diabetes mellitus, hypertension, hypercholesterolemia, peripheral vascular disease, coronary artery disease), transient ischemic attacks must be excluded. Diplopia, unilateral or bilateral weakness, and drop attacks (sudden falls without loss of consciousness) are also signs of posterior circulation insufficiency; other signs and symptoms include visual hallucinations, vision loss, visceral sensations, headache, dysarthria, and ataxia. Magnetic resonance imaging, magnetic resonance angiography of the brain and neck (to look for evidence of cerebrovascular atherosclerotic disease) if possible, and diffusion-weighted imaging (to look for evidence for an ischemic infarct) are appropriate. Management could include antiplatelet drugs such as clopidogrel[OL], combination aspirin and slow-release dipyridamole[OL], or warfarin[OL] if there is evidence for emboli.

MRI/MRA

Vestibular neuronitis produces a spontaneous episode of vertigo that lasts for several days and crescendos over several hours, often with nausea and vomiting. It is thought to occur secondary to viral infection of the eighth cranial nerve. The term *labyrinthitis* is sometimes used by clinicians interchangeably with *vestibular neuronitis*, but it can also refer to a bacterial infection that extends from the middle ear (for example, otitis media or cholesteatoma). It is unusual for migraine-associated vertigo to present first in older age, and with several focal neurologic complaints. Ménière's disease is associated with hearing loss, aural fullness, tinnitus, and episodic rotational vertigo usually of about 20 minutes' to several hours' duration.

References

1. Baloh RW. Clinical practice: vestibular neuritis. *N Engl J Med*. 2003;348(11):1027–1032.
2. Baloh RW, Honorubia V. *Clinical Neurophysiology of the Vestibular System*. 3rd ed. New York: Oxford University Press; 2001.
3. Caplan LR. Vertebrobasilar disease. *Adv Neurol*. 2003;92:1131–1140.
4. Cloud GC, Markus HS. Diagnosis and management of vertebral artery stenosis. *QJM*. 2003;96(1):27–54.

[OL] Not approved by the U.S. Food and Drug Administration for this use.

168. An 80-year-old woman comes to the office because she recently has had difficulty eating and swallowing solid foods. She notes that when she prepares to swallow, the food scrapes her cheeks and roof of her mouth. The patient has hypertension, diabetes mellitus, a recent history of kidney stones, and depression. Current medications include hydrochlorothiazide and metformin. For the first time in many years, her last dental examination revealed several cavities, located at the roots of the teeth.

Which of the following is the most likely cause of her symptoms?

(A) Aging
(B) Salivary duct stones
(C) Metformin
(D) Hydrochlorothiazide

ANSWER: D

Saliva has multiple functions in the oral cavity: It is a protective cleanser with antibacterial activity, a buffer that inhibits demineralization, a lubricant, and a transport medium to taste sensors. These functions are seriously altered in xerostomia. Although older adults are likely to have a decreased amount of active glandular tissue, numerous clinical studies have demonstrated that salivary flow does not decrease significantly with age. Signs and symptoms of xerostomia include intra-oral dryness or burning, alterations in tongue surface, dysphagia, cheilosis, alterations in taste, difficulty with speech, and development of root caries.

The causes of salivary stones (sialoliths) are largely unknown; theories range from autoimmune to inflammatory causes. Salivary stones are unrelated to kidney stones. Salivary stones do not cause severe xerostomia, as the stones are usually local, affecting one gland (commonly the submandibular gland). Sialoliths usually occur unilaterally, so saliva is still present in other major and minor salivary glands.

Many conditions and treatments may contribute to xerostomia, including radiation, chemotherapy, psychologic stressors, endocrine disorders, and nutritional disorders. Xerostomia is a side effect of more than 200 commonly used drugs. Antihypertensive medications (especially diuretics) and antidepressants (especially tricyclic antidepressants) reduce saliva flow. Metformin is not known to decrease salivary flow.

Treatment for patients with xerostomia includes scrupulous oral hygiene, with use of a soft toothbrush and fluoride rinses, reduced consumption of alcohol, frequent intake of water, saliva substitutes, and avoidance of highly acidic foods.

References

1. Chiappelli F, Bauer J, Spackman S, et al. Dental needs of the elderly in the 21st century. *Gen Dent.* 2002;50(4):358–363.
2. Ghezzi EM, Wagner-Lange LA, Schork MA, et al. Longitudinal influence of age, menopause, hormone replacement therapy, and other medications of parotid flow rates in healthy women. *J Gerontol A Biol Sci Med Sci.* 2000;55(1):M34–M42.

169. A 78-year-old man with no significant medical history comes to the emergency department with severe chest pain of 3 hours' duration associated with shortness of breath and diaphoresis. Initial electrocardiogram demonstrates 4- to 5-mm ST segment elevation in precordial leads V_2-V_5 and 1- to 2-mm ST depression in limb leads II, III, and aVF. Emergency cardiac catheterization reveals 100% occlusion of the left anterior descending artery just after the first large septal branch. Percutaneous coronary angioplasty with insertion of a stent into the left anterior descending artery is successful. Peak troponin I level is 8.6 ng/mL (normal 0 to 0.4 ng/mL). The hospital course is complicated by mild heart failure that resolves with diuresis. Predischarge echocardiography reveals anteroapical hypokinesis with mildly decreased left ventricular systolic function and an estimated ejection fraction of 45%.

Lipid profile (obtained on
day of admission):

Total cholesterol	186 mg/dL
High-density lipoprotein	47 mg/dL
Low-density lipoprotein	113 mg/dL
Triglycerides	130 mg/dL

In addition to aspirin, a statin, and clopidogrel, which of the following are appropriate discharge medications for this patient?

(A) β-Blocker and long-acting nitrate
(B) β-Blocker and spironolactone
(C) Nondihydropyridine calcium antagonist and angiotensin receptor blocker
(D) β-Blocker and angiotensin-converting enzyme inhibitor
(E) Nondihydropyridine calcium antagonist and long-acting nitrate

ANSWER: D

Aspirin and β-blockers have been shown to reduce mortality following acute myocardial infarction in patients of all ages, and clopidogrel is also indicated for at least 6 to 9 months after acute coronary intervention. An angiotensin-converting enzyme inhibitor is appropriate in patients with acute myocardial infarction complicated by heart failure, even when left ventricular systolic function is preserved. Studies have also shown that statins reduce the risk of recurrent events in patients after acute myocardial infarction as well as in patients with chronic coronary heart disease. Angiotensin receptor blockers have not been shown to improve outcomes after myocardial infarction in patients with preserved left ventricular systolic function, and calcium antagonists have been associated with increased mortality following acute myocardial infarction complicated by heart failure. The value of aldosterone antagonists such as spironolactone is unknown in patients with acute myocardial infarction and preserved left ventricular systolic function.

References

1. Rich MW. Therapy for acute myocardial infarction in older persons. *J Am Geriatr Soc.* 1998;46(10):1302–1307.
2. Ryan TJ, Antman EM, Brooks NH, et al. 1999 update: ACC/AHA guidelines for the management of patients with acute myocardial infarction. *J Am Coll Cardiol.* 1999;34(3):890–911.
3. Schwartz GG, Olsson AG, Ezekowitz MD, et al. Effects of atorvastatin on early recurrent ischemic events in acute coronary syndromes: the MIRACL study: a randomized controlled trial. *JAMA.* 2001;285(13):1711–1718.

4. Williams MA, Fleg JL, Ades PA, et al. American Heart Association Council on Clinical Cardiology Subcommittee on Exercise, Cardiac Rehabilitation, and Prevention. Secondary prevention of coronary heart disease in the elderly (with emphasis on patients ≥ 75 years of age). *Circulation*. 2002;105(14):1735–1743.

170. A 65-year-old black man comes for a consultation because he is concerned about prostate cancer. His father had prostate cancer for the last 5 years of his life; he recently died at age 80 of a heart attack. The patient reports some difficulty initiating his urine stream; the difficulty has progressed over the past few years. He has no other symptoms. He has mild hypertension that is well controlled on losartan 50 mg daily.

On physical examination, blood pressure is 130/70 mm Hg. The prostate is at least 30 g on digital rectal examination. There is no tenderness, asymmetry, induration, or nodule.

Which of the following approaches is the most appropriate for this patient?

(A) Annual prostate-specific antigen (PSA) screen
(B) Annual digital rectal examination
(C) No screening
(D) Transrectal ultrasonography

ANSWER: A

Because black American men and men with first-degree relatives who have prostate cancer are at greater risk for prostate cancer and because he is in good general health with a life expectancy greater than 10 years, this patient may benefit from screening with measurement of prostate-specific antigen (PSA).

Although major trials are under way, to date there are no data on the effect of digital rectal examination combined with PSA screening on prolongation of life. The evidence is insufficient for the U.S. Preventive Services Task Force to recommend for or against screening for prostate cancer for the individual with average risk. The decision to proceed with screening should therefore be made on an individual basis, but his risk status probably warrants PSA screening.

If the decision is made to proceed with screening, PSA should be measured. Digital rectal examination is less sensitive than PSA

(sensitivity of 59% to 64% versus over 73%, respectively). His obstructive urinary symptoms are not associated with increased risk of prostate cancer. Ultrasound with biopsy would be an appropriate diagnostic test should a screening PSA be elevated, but it is not an appropriate screening test.

References

1. Harris R, Lohr KN. Screening for prostate cancer: an update of the evidence for the U.S. Preventive Services Task Force. *Ann Intern Med*. 2002;137(11):917–929.
2. Holmberg L, Bill-Axelson A, Helgesen F, et al. Scandinavian Prostatic Cancer Group Study Number 4. A randomized trial comparing radical prostatectomy with watchful waiting in early prostate cancer. *N Engl J Med*. 2002;11(11);347:781–789.

171. An 87-year-old previously well woman comes to the emergency department because for the past day she has had difficulty swallowing. She also has productive cough, dyspnea, elevated blood pressure, and low-grade fever. Physical examination is consistent with consolidation in the left lower lobe. Chest radiography reveals a corresponding left lower-lobe infiltrate. On bedside testing, she immediately sputters and coughs after drinking a small amount of water from a cup. There are no other neurologic findings. She is mildly dehydrated and has a slightly elevated leukocyte count. Magnetic resonance scanning finds a new brain stem infarction.

Treatment for pneumonia is instituted. The next day, formal swallowing evaluation shows aspiration with most food consistencies. The patient's treatment preferences include treatments for reversible conditions.

Which of the following is the most appropriate recommendation regarding nutrition?

(A) Gastrostomy feeding
(B) Dental soft diet with thickened liquids
(C) Intravenous parenteral nutrition for 1 week
(D) Honey-thick liquids with chin-tuck and double swallowing
(E) Oral supplements between meals

ANSWER: A

This patient most likely has pharyngeal phase dysphagia as the result of a brain stem infarct. Many patients with this type of injury will have significant, if not complete, recovery within 1 year with rehabilitation and many will recover much faster. Given her good premorbid functional status and lack of serious comorbidities, she can expect substantial recovery and therefore should be encouraged to accept optimum treatment. Early gastrostomy placement with appropriate nutritional support and judicious rehabilitation will give this patient the best opportunity to return to her premorbid status.

Clinical evaluation suggests that she will not obtain adequate nutrition via an oral route at this time. Most people do not meet their nutritional needs with the highly restricted diet described in option D, and the patient has demonstrated that she cannot swallow most consistencies. Intravenous nutritional support will be inadequate, as the patient's swallowing function will take some time to improve.

References

1. Ramsey DJ, Smithard DG, Kalra L. Early assessments of dysphagia and aspiration risk in acute stroke patients. *Stroke.* 2003; 34(5):1252–1257.
2. Schindler JS, Kelly JH. Swallowing disorders in the elderly. *Laryngoscope.* 2002;112(4):589–602.
3. Verhoef MJ, Van Rosendaal GM. Patient outcomes related to percutaneous endoscopic gastrostomy placement. *J Clin Gastroenterol.* 2001;32(1):49–53.

172. A 78-year-old woman comes to the office because she has heavy vaginal bleeding after no bleeding for many years. She has been on continuous estrogen replacement therapy for the past 30 years. Physical examination, including pelvic, reveals severe arthritis. She requests evaluation with the least invasive test, as she has severe arthritis.

What is the best evaluation for this patient?

(A) Coagulopathy work-up
(B) Vaginal ultrasound to assess endometrial thickness
(C) Endometrial biopsy
(D) Hysteroscopy
(E) Dilation and curettage

ANSWER: B

Causes of postmenopausal bleeding (bleeding after 1 year of amenorrhea) include vaginal atrophy, trauma, infection, cervical cancer, endometrial cancer, endometrial or cervical polyps, and endometrial hyperplasia. Bleeding can occur with the start of continuous combined hormone replacement therapy. From 75% to 86% of women report amenorrhea after 1 year of continuous combined therapy. Endometrial assessment is recommended during the first year only if the bleeding is unusually heavy or prolonged. The endometrium should be evaluated if there is bleeding after 1 year.

Endometrial biopsy, hysteroscopy, dilation and curettage, and transvaginal ultrasonography are all effective for evaluating vaginal bleeding. Transvaginal ultrasound is the least invasive diagnostic test for endometrial hyperplasia or cancer detection. Its specificity is about 63% for women on combination hormone replacement therapy. An endometrial thickness (endometrial stripe) measuring 4 mm or less is normal. If results are abnormal, endometrial biopsy should be obtained. Endometrial biopsy is done in the office and is 85% to 95% sensitive for endometrial hyperplasia or cancer. If office-based endometrial biopsy is unobtainable as a consequence of the inability to enter the endometrial cavity (because of stenotic os) or functional impairment (such as debilitating arthritis), transvaginal ultrasound may be useful.

Dilation and curettage is the gold standard for evaluating postmenopausal bleeding. The procedure is usually done in the operating room in women with a negative or nondiagnostic endometrial biopsy or in women with abnormal ultrasound findings in whom an office endometrial biopsy is not possible.

Hysteroscopy is often performed along with dilation and curettage. It does not add to the diagnostic accuracy for endometrial hyperplasia or cancer but may increase the sensitivity for sessile or pedunculated intraluminal masses.

Coagulopathy work-up is done in addition to evaluation of vaginal bleeding only if the patient has other symptoms or signs suggesting coagulopathy.

References

1. Archer DF, Pickar JH, Bottiglioni F. Bleeding patterns in postmenopausal women taking continuous combined or sequential regimens of conjugated estrogens with medroxyprogesterone acetate. Menopause Study Group. *Obstet Ggynecol.* 1994; 83(5 Pt 1):686–692.
2. Clark TJ, Voit D, Gupta JK, et al. Accuracy of endometrial cancer and hyperplasia: a systematic quantitative review. *JAMA.* 2002;288(13):1610–1621.
3. Gull B, Carlsson MD, Karlsson B, et al. Transvaginal ultrasonography of the endometrium in women with postmenopausal bleeding: is it always necessary to perform an endometrial biopsy? *Am J Obstet Gynecol.* 2000;182(3):509–515.
4. Tabor A, Watt HC, Wald NJ. Endometrial thickness as a test for endometrial cancer in women with postmenopausal bleeding. *Obstet Gynecol.* 2002;99(4):663–670.

173. An 81-year-old woman with a history of "bad nerves" comes to the office for a second opinion because she is "tired of being sick all my life." She has a history of headaches, back pain, and joint pain, for which she had taken nonsteroidal anti-inflammatory drugs (NSAIDs) intermittently for decades. She also has nausea, bloating, and stomach ache that persisted after she discontinued NSAIDs. She cannot tolerate certain foods, has difficulty swallowing, and at times is unable to speak. She has had gastroen-terology, neurology, and rheumatology consulta-tions, and different tests were recommended, but no medications were prescribed. She sleeps and eats well, and enjoys crafts and spending time with family and friends. At this visit she appears upset and tearful.

Which of the following is most likely?

(A)   Major depressive disorder
(B)   Generalized anxiety disorder
(C)   Somatization disorder
(D)   Hypochondriasis
(E)   Pain disorder

ANSWER: C

This is a typical case of somatization disorder. Patients often present with an "organ recital," involving, at a minimum, pain in at least four areas of the body, two gastrointestinal complaints, one genitourinary or sexual and one pseudoneurologic symptom other than pain,

with a duration longer than 6 months and debut prior to age 30. In somatization disorder, multiple symptoms are not fully explained by the physical findings.

Hypochondriasis refers to preoccupation with having a disease based on misinterpretation of symptoms. Diagnosis of major depressive disorder requires depressed mood or anhedonia, and a constellation of symptoms, such as changes in sleep and appetite, that this patient does not display. Generalized anxiety disorder refers to excessive worry about multiple issues, including safety of self or others, and is associated with fatigue, restlessness, insomnia, problems concentrating, appetite change, and muscular tension. This patient is concerned about multiple somatic complaints for which no medical cause has been found. In pain disorder, pain is the only focus of clinical attention, and psychologic factors have an important role in onset, exacerbation, and maintenance of pain.

References

1. Holloway KL, Zerbe KJ. Simplified approach to somatization disorder: when less may prove to be more. *Postgrad Med.* 2000;108(6):89–92,95.
2. Sheehan B, Banerjee S. Review: somatization in the elderly. *Int J Geriatr Psychiatry.* 1999;14(12):1044–1049.
3. Sheehan B, Bass C, Briggs R, et al. Somatization among older primary care attenders. *Psychol Med.* 2003;33(5):867–877.

174. An 87-year-old resident of an Alzheimer's assisted-living unit is evaluated because she has fallen twice in the past month. She has a history of dementia, urge urinary incontinence, and hypertension. She has had no recent acute illness or changes in medication. She takes vitamin E 400 units twice daily, galantamine 8 mg twice daily, enteric-coated aspirin 81 mg daily, sustained-release tolterodine 4 mg daily, and hydrochlorothiazide 25 mg daily. Unless redirected, she spends most of the day walking. It is difficult to get her to finish her meals.

On examination, she is alert, oriented to place but not date, and thin, and she appears tired. She has normal gait speed, with normal foot clearance and arm swing, but she turns quickly and reaches for the wall to steady herself.

Which of the following would be part of a treatment plan to reduce this patient's risk of falling?

(A) Medication with quetiapine 25 mg daily
(B) Scheduled brief rest periods during the day
(C) Use of hip protectors during the day
(D) Use of a lap tray to prevent her from getting up

ANSWER: B

This assisted-living resident has dementia and walks excessively throughout the day. She becomes fatigued by this activity, and she may not be eating or drinking sufficiently. It is likely that fatigue is contributing to her risk of falls. Her difficulty getting up from a chair and turning suggests impairment of lower extremity strength and balance. Having regular rest periods throughout the day would be an important component of a treatment plan to reduce her risk of falling again. During these times, she could be offered snacks and drinks to increase her caloric intake and improve hydration. Her deficits in lower extremity strength and balance would best be addressed initially by a physical therapy evaluation and individualized treatment.

Quetiapine and other atypical antipsychotic medications are not indicated. They would not decrease her walking behavior and would be likely to increase her risk for falls as a consequence of adverse effects (postural hypotension, dizziness, and somnolence). Consistent use of hip protectors during the day may help prevent a hip fracture but would not be part of a plan to prevent falls. A regular group exercise program might be a component of a fall prevention plan for her, once she has been evaluated by physical therapy and has responded to scheduled rest periods. Although an individualized exercise program would be more likely to improve her strength and balance, a supervised group exercise program might help maintain gains and could serve as a distractor to keep her from walking during that time. The use of a lap tray is a physical restraint and should be avoided. A trial of providing food and drink during rest periods and while she is "on the go" should be attempted prior to any use of restraints.

References
1. Becker C, Kron M, Lindemann U, et al. Effectiveness of a multifaceted intervention on falls in nursing home residents. *J Am Geriatr Soc.* 2003;51(3):306–313.
2. Jensen J, Lundin-Olsson L, Nyberg L, et al. Fall and injury prevention in older people living in residential care facilities: a cluster randomized trial. *Ann Intern Med.* 2002;136(10):733–741.
3. Nowalk MP, Prendergast JM, Bayles CM, et al. A randomized trial of exercise programs among older individuals living in two long-term care facilities: the FallsFREE Program. *J Am Geriatr Soc.* 2001;49(7):859–865.

175. After viewing a television commercial about hearing aids, a 74-year-old woman comes to the office to ask whether she should purchase one. She first noticed her hearing loss about 10 years ago. It has gradually gotten worse, and she now curtails activities because she has difficulty understanding conversations.

Following an otoscopic examination, which of the following is the most appropriate test to determine whether this woman should be referred to an audiologist for possible intervention?

(A) HHIE-S (Hearing Handicap Inventory for the Elderly—Screening Version)
(B) Tympanometry test
(C) Auditory brain stem response test
(D) Rinné and Weber tests
(E) Electronystagmography

ANSWER: A

Elderly patients should regularly receive screening for hearing impairment, given the high prevalence and negative consequences of hearing loss in this population. An otoscopic examination is an important part of the routine examination of older persons who have a high prevalence of impacted cerumen as compared with younger adults.

The Hearing Handicap Inventory for the Elderly—Screening Version (HHIE–S) is a 10-item instrument that assesses self-perceived psychosocial handicap of hearing impairment in the elderly person. Its reliability and validity are well established. Scores above 8 indicate a hearing handicap requiring audiologic intervention. It is both sensitive and specific as a screening test for participation restrictions due to hearing loss.

Acoustic immittance measures, including tympanometry, are physiologic tests that yield information about middle-ear function and assist in diagnosis of retrocochlear, facial nerve, and central nervous system disorders. This testing is not recommended for older adults because they are not at high risk for development of middle-ear disease. The auditory brain-stem response waveform represents the spatial-temporal pattern of brain-stem electrical activity. Electrophysiologic recording of the response is used to differentiate cochlear from retrocochlear lesions in sensorineural hearing loss and neurologic causes of central dysfunction. The Rinné and Weber tests rely on tuning forks and have not been validated as screening tests to identify hearing impairment that restricts activity. The Weber test is more sensitive at identifying possible conduction abnormalities. Electronystagmography is a battery of electrophysiologic tests administered to help determine the cause of vertigo.

References

1. Bogardus ST, Yueh B, Shekelle PG. Screening and management of adult hearing loss in primary care: clinical applications. *JAMA*. 2003; 289:1986–1990.
2. Gates GA, Murphy M, Rees TS, et al. Screening for handicapping hearing loss in the elderly. *J Fam Practice*. 2003; 52:56–62.
3. Wiley TL, Cruickshanks KJ, Nondahl DM, et al. Self-reported hearing handicap and audiometric measures in older adults. *J Am Acad Audiol*. 2000;11(2):67–75.
4. Yueh B, Shapiro N, MacLean CH, et al. Screening and management of adult hearing loss in primary care: scientific review. *JAMA*. 2003;289:1976–1985.

176. At a routine office visit, a 72-year-old man complains of erectile dysfunction. He has a stable, warm relationship with his wife of 45 years. He had a myocardial infarction 8 years ago, and he has a history of well-controlled hypertension for the past 15 years, hyperlipidemia, occasional angina with severe exertion, and benign prostatic hyperplasia. He takes enalapril, hydrochlorothiazide, doxazosin, aspirin, lovastatin, and nitro paste daily. His erectile dysfunction preceded the initiation of these medications.

What is the most likely cause of erectile dysfunction in this patient?

(A) Vascular disease
(B) Medications
(C) Autonomic neuropathy
(D) Psychogenic causes
(E) Benign prostatic hyperplasia

ANSWER: A

Over 50% of men older than age 50 with erectile dysfunction have vascular disease as the cause of the dysfunction. In men with a history of myocardial infarction, the prevalence of erectile dysfunction is 64%. Both arterial and venous dysfunction increases with age. Atherosclerosis, hyperlipidemia, and diabetes mellitus can contribute to arterial changes. Venous "leaks" (due to intrinsic venous problems or to structural changes of the albuginea) become more common with age and alter venous compression. Therefore, both inadequate filling and inability to maintain pressure because of venous leaks contribute to erectile difficulties. Abnormal penile brachial pressure indices can even predict major cardiovascular events, such as myocardial infarction or stroke, in patients without a previous history of those diseases.

Peripheral and autonomic neuropathies can be associated with erectile problems but are less likely to be the major cause of erectile dysfunction in this patient with a clear history of vascular disorders.

Depression, anxiety, and relationship concerns should be assessed in patients with erectile dysfunction. However, this patient's history does not suggest a primary psychologic cause of difficulty. Medications are a common contributory cause to erectile dysfunction but are unlikely to be a primary cause in this patient, whose dysfunction preceded the initiation of these medications. Even though both benign prostatic hyperplasia and erectile dysfunction are common in aging men, there is no evidence of a causative link.

References

1. Bortz WN 2nd, Wallace DH, Wiley D. Sexual function in 1,202 aging males: differentiating aspects. *J Gerontol A Biol Sci Med Sci*. 1999;54(5):M237–M241.

2. Feldman HA, Goldstein I, Hatzichristou DG, et al. Impotence and its medical and psychosocial correlates: results of the Massachusetts Male Aging Study. *J Urol.* 1994;151(1): 54–61.
3. Mulligan T, Reddy S, Gular PV, et al. Disorders of male sexual function. *Clin Geriatr Med.* 2003;19(3):473–481.
4. Tariq SH, Haleem U, Omran ML, et al. Erectile dysfunction: etiology and treatment in younger and older patients. *Clin Geriatr Med.* 2003;19(3):539–551.

177. A 72-year-old woman comes to the office because she has low energy, poor sleep, and poor appetite. She also reports low mood with crying spells and hopeless thoughts about her future. She had an inferior myocardial infarction 3 weeks ago; her ejection fraction was well preserved, and she was discharged from the hospital on a regimen of metoprolol, enteric-coated aspirin, and a statin. She has a longstanding history of smoking and hypercholesterolemia. She believes that she would be better off if she had died from the heart attack, but she denies any suicidal thought, plan, or intent. Laboratory tests, including thyroid-stimulating hormone, are unremarkable.

Which of the following is most appropriate in management of this patient?

(A) Discontinue metoprolol.
(B) Discontinue the statin.
(C) Start nortriptyline.
(D) Start sertraline.
(E) Start venlafaxine.

ANSWER: D

This woman meets criteria for diagnosis of major depression, a major risk factor for death following myocardial infarction. Currently, the strongest evidence supports the safety and efficacy of selective serotonin-reuptake inhibitors (SSRIs) for treatment of major depression in patients with coronary artery disease. In particular, in a large placebo-controlled randomized study, sertraline was found to be effective and safe in patients with recent myocardial infarction or unstable angina. It would be inappropriate to discontinue metoprolol or the statin, since pharmacoepidemiologic studies have failed to confirm an association between β-blockers and depression. Similarly, no controlled data support the theoretic concerns that, by decreasing cholesterol, statins may cause depression or suicidality. Controlled studies have found a similar efficacy for tricyclic antidepressants (such as nortriptyline) and SSRIs (such as sertraline) in older persons and in patients with heart disease. However, tricyclic antidepressants are associated with deleterious effects (for example, sustained increase in heart rate, reduction in heart-rate variability) and a higher rate of adverse cardiac events. Also, in patients with ischemic heart disease, SSRIs—but not tricyclic antidepressants—are associated with beneficial inhibition of platelet activation and aggregation. Venlafaxine is a dual reuptake inhibitor, affecting the serotonin and noradrenergic neurotransmitter systems. Several studies have raised concerns regarding its cardiac safety. In the absence of controlled data establishing its safety, it should be avoided in patients with significant heart disease.

References

1. Frasure-Smith N, Lesperance F. Depression and other psychological risks following myocardial infarction. *Arch Gen Psychiatry.* 2003;60(6):627–636.
2. Glassman AH, O'Connor CM, Califf RM, et al.; Sertraline Antidepressant Heart Attack Randomized Trial (SADHEART) Group. Sertraline treatment of major depression in patients with acute MI or unstable angina. *JAMA.* 2002;288(6):701–709.
3. Oslin DW, Ten Have TR, Streim JE, et al. Probing the safety of medications in the frail elderly: evidence from a randomized clinical trial of sertraline and venlafaxine in depressed nursing home residents. *J Clin Psychiatry.* 2003; 64(8):875–882.
4. Pollock BG, Laghrissi-Thode F, Wagner WR. Evaluation of platelet activation in depressed patients with ischemic heart disease after paroxetine or nortriptyline treatment. *J Clin Psychopharmacol.* 2000;20(2):137–140.
5. Roose SP. Treatment of depression in patients with heart disease. *Biol Psychiatry.* 2003; 54(3):262–268.

178. A 72-year-old woman comes to the office as a new patient. She has a 15-year history of type 2 diabetes mellitus. She also has a history of coronary artery disease and heart failure. She began taking glipizide 8 years ago for her diabetes. Over the past 2 years she has required additional therapy. Initially, she did well on a combination of glipizide and NPH insulin at bedtime. Over the past 6 months, glipizide was stopped, and she has required twice-daily doses of NPH and regular insulin, given before breakfast and dinner. Despite increasing doses of insulin, her hemoglobin A_{1C} has increased to 9% and she now has hypoglycemia before lunch and during the night. Serum creatinine is 1.6 mg/dL.

Which of the following is the best management step?

(A) Add metformin.
(B) Add rosiglitazone.
(C) Replace the regular insulin with insulin lispro.
(D) Restart the glipizide.

ANSWER: C

This case illustrates a common problem in type 2 diabetes mellitus: over time, oral agents fail to control hyperglycemia and insulin therapy becomes necessary. As insulin deficiency progresses, more sophisticated insulin regimens are needed to control hyperglycemia while minimizing hypoglycemia.

In this patient, as the dose of insulin was increased, hypoglycemia developed and hemoglobin A_{1C} increased further. Insulin lispro is a rapidly absorbed insulin analogue. Peak serum levels after subcutaneous injection occur earlier and are shorter than with regular insulin. In both types 1 and 2 diabetes mellitus, insulin lispro is less likely than regular insulin to produce postprandial hypoglycemia. Therefore, substituting lispro for regular insulin will minimize hypoglycemia and is the best option.

The use of metformin in patients with heart failure or renal impairment (serum creatinine over 1.5 mg/dL in men or 1.4 mg/dL in women) significantly predisposes to lactic acidosis, a potentially fatal complication. Thiazolidinediones (rosiglitazone, pioglitazone) cause plasma volume expansion and may exacerbate this patient's heart failure. These drugs should not be used in persons with New York Heart Association class III or IV heart failure. Even if her volume status were carefully monitored, the addition of rosiglitazone (without modification of the insulin regimen) would not solve this patient's problem with pre-lunch and nocturnal hypoglycemia. She was previously resistant to the glipizide so restarting it would be unlikely to be effective.

References

1. American Diabetes Association. Clinical practice recommendations 2003. *Diabetes Care.* 2003;26(Suppl 1):S1–S156.
2. DeFronzo RA. Pharmacologic therapy for type 2 diabetes mellitus. *Ann Intern Med.* 1999;131(4):281–303.
3. Holleman F, Hoekstra JB. Insulin lispro. *N Engl J Med.* 1997;337(3):176–183.

179. A 65-year-old postmenopausal woman comes to the office for advice on physical activity to decrease her likelihood of having vertebral fractures and disability. Her mother has severe osteoporosis and back deformity with kyphosis.

Which of the following has been shown to reduce the likelihood of osteoporotic vertebral fractures?

(A) Daily high-intensity running program
(B) Progressive back extensor resistive exercise program 5 times each week
(C) High-intensity strength training exercises twice weekly
(D) Walking at an average pace 1 hour three times each week
(E) Household chores

ANSWER: B

Aerobic, weight-bearing, and resistance exercises all increase the bone mineral density of the spine in postmenopausal women. The best evidence comes from a well-done prospective trial on strengthening back musculature, which showed sustained reduction in fracture over 10 years. Women between the ages of 48 and 65 (mean age 55) were randomly assigned to a progressive resistive back-strengthening exercise program for 2 years or to a control group. At 10-year follow-up, the exercise group had significantly better back muscle strength and greater spine bone mineral density than the control group, and the control group had a 2.7-fold greater risk for vertebral fracture.

A prospective observational cohort study of older women showed that hip fractures were associated with higher levels of leisure time, sports activity, and household chores, and fewer hours of sitting daily. Furthermore, vertebral fractures were more likely in the moderately or vigorously active women. Total physical activity, hours of household chores per day, and hours of sitting per day were not significantly associated with wrist or vertebral fractures.

In women followed for 12 years in the Nurses Health Study, walking for at least 4 hours each week was associated with a 41% lower risk of hip fracture than walking less than 1 hour each week. However, vertebral fractures were not included in the analysis.

High-intensity strength training can increase muscle mass, muscle strength, dynamic balance, and bone density in postmenopausal women. However, fracture rates over time have not been reported, and there is no convincing evidence that high-intensity exercise (such as running) is superior to lower intensity activity (such as walking).

References

1. Bonaiuti D, Shea B, Iovine R, et al. Exercise for preventing and treating osteoporosis in postmenopausal women. *Cochrane Database Syst Rev.* 2002;(3):CD000333.
2. Feskanich D, Willett W, Colditz G. Walking and leisure-time activity and risk of hip fracture in postmenopausal women. *JAMA.* 2002; 288(18): 2300–2306.
3. Sinaki M. Nonpharmacologic interventions: exercise, fall prevention, and role of physical medicine. *Clin Geriatr Med.* 2003;19(2):337–359.
4. Sinaki M, Itoi E, Wahner HW, et al. Stronger back muscles reduce the incidence of vertebral fractures: a prospective 10 year follow-up of postmenopausal women. *Bone.* 2002; 30(6):836–834.

180. A 79-year-old woman comes to the emergency department with palpitations and shortness of breath of 2 hours' duration. She has a history of hypertension, type 2 diabetes mellitus, mild restrictive lung disease, gastroesophageal reflux disease, and positional tremor. The patient relates that she was sitting in a chair when she noted the sudden onset of "heart racing," followed a few minutes later by difficulty breathing. She reports no chest discomfort, diaphoresis, dizziness, or syncope. When the symptoms did not resolve after an hour, her son brought her to the emergency department.

On physical examination, the patient is in mild respiratory distress. Heart rate ranges from 130 to 150 per minute and is irregular, blood pressure is 140/70 mm Hg, and respiratory rate is 22 per minute. Her neck is supple, with normal jugular venous pressure and no thyromegaly. Bibasilar crackles are heard. The heart is irregularly irregular, with a II/VI systolic ejection murmur and no S_3 or S_4 gallop. She has a moderate positional tremor.

Laboratory studies:

Cardiac biomarker proteins	normal
Creatinine	0.8 mg/dL
Blood urea nitrogen	17 mg/dL
Hemoglobin	13.1 g/dL
Hemoglobin A_{1C}	7.3%
Thyrotropin	2.0 μU/mL
Total cholesterol	198 mg/dL
High-density lipoprotein	55 mg/dL
Low-density lipoprotein	113 mg/dL
Triglycerides	150 mg/dL

Electrocardiography reveals atrial fibrillation with rapid ventricular response, left ventricular hypertrophy with repolarization abnormality, and no ischemic changes. Chest radiograph shows mild cardiomegaly with mild pulmonary vascular redistribution. Adenosine-thallium stress test reveals a left ventricular ejection fraction of 67% with no evidence of ischemia. Echocardiogram demonstrates moderate left ventricular hypertrophy, mild left atrial enlargement, normal left ventricular systolic function, and mild left ventricular diastolic dysfunction.

The patient is treated with intravenous diltiazem with subsequent reversion to sinus rhythm (85 per minute). Intravenous furosemide results in a net diuresis of 1160 cc, and her shortness of breath resolves. Myocardial infarction is excluded by normal serial troponin levels.

Which of the following are appropriate discharge medications for this patient?

(A) Aspirin, warfarin, amiodarone, and angiotensin-converting enzyme inhibitor
(B) Warfarin, diltiazem, β-blocker, and angiotensin-receptor blocker
(C) Aspirin, β-blocker, angiotensin-converting enzyme inhibitor, and statin
(D) Warfarin, β-blocker, angiotensin-converting enzyme inhibitor, and angiotensin-receptor blocker
(E) Diltiazem, β-blocker, angiotensin-converting enzyme inhibitor, and statin

ANSWER: C

This patient has new-onset atrial fibrillation and heart failure with preserved left ventricular systolic function ("diastolic" heart failure), as well as a history of hypertension and diabetes. Data from the Heart Outcomes Prevention Evaluation (HOPE) study and the Heart Protection Study indicate that older adults with diabetes or vascular disease benefit from routine treatment with an angiotensin-converting enzyme (ACE) inhibitor (ramipril) and a statin (simvastatin), even when left ventricular function and fasting lipid profile are normal or near normal. In addition, despite this patient's "negative" stress test, her age and risk factors place her at moderate risk for coronary heart disease and stroke, thus justifying the addition of aspirin to her regimen. Although the value of β-blocker therapy in patients with diastolic heart failure is unproven, β-blockers are effective anti-ischemic, antihypertensive, and rate-controlling agents, and they may reduce the risk of recurrent atrial fibrillation. Warfarin is indicated in the management of chronic or paroxysmal atrial fibrillation, but long-term use of this drug following a single episode of atrial fibrillation that resolves within 24 hours is unproven. Intravenous diltiazem is an effective agent for controlling heart rate in patients with acute atrial fibrillation and rapid ventricular

response, but β-blockers are preferable for long-term treatment. Angiotensin-receptor blockers have been shown to reduce admissions but not mortality in patients with diastolic heart failure; by contrast, the ACE inhibitor ramipril reduced both mortality and morbidity in diabetic patients in the HOPE study, so ACE inhibitors are preferable to angiotensin-receptor blockers in this population. Amiodarone is not indicated in patients with transient atrial fibrillation.

References

1. Angeja BG, Grossman W. Evaluation and management of diastolic heart failure. *Circulation.* 2003;107(5):659–663.
2. Fuster V, Ryden LE, Asinger RW, et al. ACC/AHA/ESC guidelines for the management of patients with atrial fibrillation: executive summary. *Circulation.* 2001;104(17):2118–2150.
3. Heart Protection Study Collaborative Group. MRC/BHF Heart Protection Study of cholesterol lowering with simvastatin in 20,536 high-risk individuals: a randomised placebo-controlled trial. *Lancet.* 2002;360(9326):7–22.
4. Yusuf S, Sleight P, Pogue J, et al. Effects of an angiotensin-converting-enzyme inhibitor, ramipril, on cardiovascular events in high-risk patients. The Heart Outcomes Prevention Evaluation Study Investigators. *N Engl J Med.* 2000;342(3):145–153.

181. A 73-year-old woman who lives alone has restricted her activity since she tripped and fell on the sidewalk 4 months ago. The fall caused mild bruising. Fearing another fall, she now leaves the house only when necessary, hence has less social contact than before, and prefers to be accompanied by another person to appointments and shopping. She has no history of psychiatric disorder.

Which of the following is the most likely diagnosis?

(A) Agoraphobia without history of panic disorder
(B) Panic disorder with agoraphobia
(C) Posttraumatic stress disorder
(D) Social phobia
(E) Specific phobia

ANSWER: A

This patient's anxiety about leaving her home, associated with avoidance of activities outside the home, is consistent with agoraphobia. Agoraphobia in younger adults is often considered a conditioned response to panic attacks. Older people with agoraphobia, however, rarely have a history of panic attacks. When agoraphobia develops late in life, most patients attribute it to an abrupt onset of physical illness or other traumatic event, such as a fall or being mugged. Agoraphobia in late life is often associated with moderate to severe social impairment.

Exposure therapy, in which the person faces the feared situation, is the optimal treatment for patients with agoraphobia and no history of panic disorder. Exposure usually occurs in a graded fashion over several weeks. Results are best when the exposure is prolonged rather than brief, takes place in real life rather than in fantasy, and is regularly practiced by the patient.

Although this woman was traumatized by the fall, she does not report symptoms of posttraumatic stress disorder, such as distressing recollections, flashbacks, numbing of general responsiveness, or persistent increased arousal. A diagnosis of social phobia is not appropriate because her reduced social activity is secondary to phobic avoidance, not to fear of humiliation or embarrassment in a social situation. Specific phobia involves fear and avoidance of a circum-scribed stimulus, such as animals, heights, or blood. This woman's avoidance is not limited to a single situation and, therefore, is more gener-alized than that seen with specific phobia.

References

1. Bruce DG, Devine A, Prince RL. Recreational physical activity levels in healthy older women: the importance of fear of falling. *J Am Geriatr Soc.* 2002;50(1):84–89.
2. Gagnon N, Flint AJ, Naglie G, et al. Affective correlates of fear of falling in elderly persons. *Am J Geriatr Psychiatry.* 2005;13(1):7–14.
3. Legters K. Fear of falling. *Phys Ther.* 2002;82(3):264–272.

182. A home-care team initiates house calls to an 84-year-old white retired policeman who is homebound because of chronic back pain from spinal stenosis. His medications include hydrocodone plus acetaminophen (at the maximal dose). Since he became homebound, he and his wife argue frequently. He has been drinking more alcohol recently to cope with his back pain and currently drinks about two six-packs of beer daily.

Which of the following is the most urgent action to take at this time?

(A) Begin antidepressants.
(B) Make sure there are no guns in the home.
(C) Prescribe a stronger pain medication.
(D) Begin alcohol abuse counseling.

ANSWER: B

Older white men constitute the most likely demographic group to successfully complete suicide. In spite of what this man might answer on screening questions, he is at high risk for suicide. The presence of chronic pain, disability, anger, and substance abuse add to his risk. For the safety of the patient, his wife, and the home-care team, it is essential that the home be assessed for the presence of guns before in-home services commence. Any guns should be removed or, at least, ammunition should be taken away. This is often difficult and commonly involves the assistance of family members and sometimes the police.

Treatment of depression, pain relief, and alcohol abuse counseling are all important long-term interventions, but the immediate safety of everyone involved is primary.

References

1. Kaplan MS, Adamek ME, Geling O. Sociodemographic predictors of firearm suicide among older white males. *Gerontologist.* 1996;36(4):530–533.
2. Malphurs JE, Eisdorfer C, Cohen D. A comparison of antecedents of homicide-suicide in older married men. *Am J Geriatr Psychiatry.* 2001;9(1):49–57.
3. Marzuk PM, Tardiff K, Hirsch CS. The epidemi-ology of murder-suicide. *JAMA.* 1992;267(23):3179–3183.

183. A 72-year-old man comes to the office because he has had itching and burning of his feet for 2 months. He also notes a strong odor when he removes his socks. He wears shoes with rubber soles. History includes hypertension, osteoarthritis, and childhood asthma. On examination, the lateral borders of both feet show erythema and scaling in a moccasin distribution. The toe web spaces are normal.

Which of the following is the most appropriate next step?

(A) Examine skin scrapings on a saline wet mount slide.
(B) Culture skin scrapings.
(C) Examine potassium hydroxide stain of scrapings of the rash.
(D) Do a punch skin biopsy.

ANSWER: C

Scaliness in a moccasin distribution is characteristic of tinea pedis; therefore, the best approach is to demonstrate hyphae with a potassium hydroxide stain. Cultures or skin biopsy are not necessary. Tinea pedis can also present with peeling, fissures, and maceration of the web spaces. Because the web spaces can be the port of entry for skin bacteria, especially staphylococci and streptococci, it is important to look between the toes, especially in patients with diabetes mellitus or recurrent lower-extremity cellulitis. Tinea pedis of the moccasin type or chronic hyperkeratotic type is more common in atopic individuals and is most often caused by *Trichophyton rubrum*. This patient has a history of childhood asthma, which is associated with atopy.

Tinea pedis should be treated with a topical broad-spectrum antifungal preparation containing imidazoles. A cream or solution should be applied twice daily and continued for 2 weeks after the rash has resolved. Keratolytic agents (salicylic acid, lactic acid, hydroxy acid) with plastic occlusion help reduce the hyperkeratosis. Moccasin-type tinea pedis is often associated with tinea unguium of the nails, which is a source of reinfection. If there is a nail reservoir, it should be eradicated with a systemic antifungal agent, such as itraconazole or terbinafine, if contraindications or cost are not an issue for the patient.

To minimize recurrence of tinea pedis, the patient should wash his feet daily with benzoyl peroxide bar, dry between the spaces well, and avoid thick socks and shoes that increase sweating. If the patient has frequent recurrences, indefinite use of a topical antifungal agent may be needed.

Use of topical steroids alone may initially improve the rash by reducing the inflammation, but the fungal infection will continue to spread. A combination antifungal-steroid agent may be used when there is prominent inflammation, but topical steroids should be used with caution as they can cause atrophy of the skin and other complications. Allergic contact dermatitis to rubber chemicals can cause a rash of the soles, mostly on the pressure points, while the proximal parts of the toes and the toe webs are spared. This rash can be misdiagnosed as fungal infection. A potassium hydroxide stain will be negative in allergic contact dermatitis.

References

1. Disease due to microbial agents, fungal infection of skin and hair, and superficial infections. In: Fitzpatrick TB, Johnson RA, Wolf K, et al., eds. *Color Atlas and Synopsis of Clinical Dermatology*. 4th ed. New York: The McGraw-Hill Companies; 2001.
2. Weinstein A, Berman B. Topical treatment of common superficial tinea infections. *Am Fam Physician*. 2002;65(10): 2095–2102.

184. A 66-year-old man became addicted to prescription opioid analgesics 2 years ago, while being treated for chronic back pain. Clonidine was prescribed, and he underwent opioid detoxification. Although the clonidine helped control withdrawal symptoms, it was discontinued because he became hypotensive. The patient completed detoxification and began group and individual counseling. After 3 months of abstinence, he relapsed and resumed abuse of oxycodone. He expresses renewed interest in outpatient treatment and is again willing to participate in counseling after detoxification.

Which of the following is the most appropriate pharmacologic treatment for detoxification and maintenance of abstinence for this patient?

(A) Methadone
(B) Naltrexone   *Revia/Vivitrol*
(C) Levomethadyl acetate
(D) Buprenorphine   *Buprenex*

ANSWER: D

Buprenorphine, a partial μ-opiate-receptor agonist and κ-opiate-receptor antagonist, is a schedule III controlled substance approved for opioid detoxification and maintenance. It is well tolerated and reduces craving for opioids. In younger patients, its efficacy is similar to that of methadone, but few data are available on its use in older patients. A sublingual tablet formulation can be prescribed in ambulatory settings to persons who are abusing prescribed opioid analgesics. Under terms of the Drug Addiction Treatment Act of 2000, the prescribing physician must hold an addiction-related certification from the American Board of Medical Specialties, the American Osteopathic Association, or the American Society of Addiction Medicine, or must have completed at least 8 hours of training in the care of opioid-dependent patients and have registered with the Center for Substance Abuse Treatment. The Food and Drug Administration also approved a combination of buprenorphine and naloxone. Naloxone neither improves nor diminishes the efficacy of buprenorphine, but it helps deter potential misuse, as naloxone would precipitate acute withdrawal symptoms.

Methadone, a pure opioid agonist, has proven efficacy for detoxification from opioids and in programs for long-term maintenance of abstinence. However, it is a schedule II controlled substance and can be prescribed only in a strictly regulated environment, usually a clinic-based opioid treatment program, with few options for at-home dosing. These restrictions may dissuade addicted patients from seeking help.

Naltrexone is an opioid antagonist that may be an option for maintenance of abstinence. However, it is not an option for detoxification, because it produces immediate withdrawal.

Levomethadyl acetate, a longer-acting congener of methadone, has proven efficacy. It is a schedule II controlled substance, with restrictions similar to those of methadone. Because there have been several reports of prolongation of the QT interval and serious arrhythmias, its use is recommended only when other treatments fail.

References

1. Clark HW. Office-based practice and opioid-use disorders. *N Engl J Med.* 2003; 349:928–930.
2. Fiellin DA, O'Connor PG. Clinical practice: office-based treatment of opioid dependent patients. *N Engl J Med.* 2002; 347:817–823.
3. Fudala PJ, Bridge TP, Williford HS, et al. Office-based treatment of opiate addiction with a sublingual-tablet formulation of buprenorphine and naloxone. *N Engl J Med.* 2003; 349:949–958.

185. A 76-year-old man with Alzheimer's disease is brought to the office for a follow-up visit. For the past few weeks he has had difficulty staying asleep at night. He goes to bed at 9 PM, sleeps until about 2 AM, and awakens to go to the bathroom. He remains awake for several hours, during which he is often disoriented, paces the house, and wakes his wife. He and his wife are fatigued, and he is more withdrawn during the day. He requires help with instrumental activities of daily living (IADLs), needs reminders with some basic ADLs, and is independent with feeding, toileting, and ambulation. His general health is good. There is no evidence of sadness or anhedonia, and he is eating well. He has well-controlled hypertension on a diuretic and takes an oral hypoglycemic agent for mild type 2 diabetes mellitus. He had a transurethral resection of the prostate 1 year ago for prostatic hyperplasia and has had no recurrence. At his last office visit, he was counseled about sleep hygiene, but this intervention has failed.

Which of the following, given at bedtime, is the most appropriate first-line pharmacologic treatment?

(A) Zolpidem, 5 to 10 mg
(B) Melatonin, 0.3 to 5 mg
(C) Zaleplon, 5 to 10 mg
(D) Trazodone, 25 to 50 mg
(E) Lorazepam, 1 mg

ANSWER: D

Mild sleep disturbances affect up to 20% of outpatients with dementia. Usually the disturbance is not associated with depression or other psychiatric symptoms and is thus a primary sleep disorder. Most common are early insomnia and middle insomnia, as with this patient. The sleep problems often adversely affect the patient and exhaust caregivers. If left untreated, sleep problems can slowly lead to full reversal of the sleep cycle, which is difficult to treat. Sleep hygiene interventions are only modestly successful and are often difficult for the caregiver to implement. Bright-light therapy may improve sleep disturbance in patients with dementia, but the equipment is expensive and there is no third-payer support; it is also difficult to implement outside institutional settings. Therefore, pharmacologic management is often necessary. Although there are no controlled trials to guide decision making, trazodone is preferred by most experts given its low adverse-effect profile (including dizziness, excessive sedation, confusion, and hypotension), potential antidepressant activity, and low cost. Starting doses of 25 to 50 mg are recommended, and doses as high as 150 to 200 mg may be needed. Melatonin is unproven in this setting and anecdotally appears to have limited efficacy. Newer agents such as zolpidem and zaleplon, which are schedule IV agents, are best reserved as second-line agents. Benzodiazepines, such as lorazepam, and related compounds lead to disinhibition and agitation and cause falls; they are reserved for short-term treatment of more severe forms of sleep disturbance in patients with dementia. Over-the-counter medications containing the antihistamine diphenhydramine should be avoided because its anticholinergic activity can worsen dementia. Any evidence of sleep apnea, depression, psychosis, or mania should be investigated as the cause of the sleep disorder and treated. Sleep apnea in particular appears to be more common than previously thought, even in non-overweight patients with dementia. It should be assessed with a sleep laboratory study and treated appropriately with weight loss and a continuous positive airway pressure device.

References

1. McCurry SM, Ancoli-Israel S. Sleep dysfunction in Alzheimer's disease and other dementias. *Curr Treat Options Neurol.* 2003;5(3):261–272.
2. Rabins PV, Lyketsos CG, Steele CD. *Practical Dementia Care.* New York: Oxford University Press; 1999.
3. Sink KM, Holden KF, Yaffe K. Pharmacological treatment of neuropsychiatric symptoms of dementia: a review of the evidence. *JAMA.* 2005;293(5):596–608.

186. A 75-year-old man comes to the office because he has fallen repeatedly over the past 2 months. He reports that his right leg seems to collapse under him without warning. He also stumbles while climbing stairs because his right foot does not always clear the next step. The patient is right handed. Neurologic examination demonstrates right thigh atrophy, right quadriceps weakness, an absent right patellar reflex, and hypesthesia over the anterior right thigh and medial calf.

Which of the following is the most likely diagnosis?

(A) Femoral neuropathy
(B) Spinal stenosis
(C) Herniated disc at the L5–S1 level
(D) Myositis
(E) Iliac artery stenosis

ANSWER: A

This man has a femoral neuropathy, which can be caused by retroperitoneal tumor or hemorrhage, trauma, diabetes mellitus, and even errant attempts at femoral arterial puncture. Femoral neuropathy is identified by electromyography and nerve conduction studies. The femoral nerve innervates the quadriceps muscle and the iliopsoas muscle. Thus, a lesion compromising femoral nerve function will produce quadriceps atrophy and weakness, with impairment of knee extension and possibly hip flexion. The patellar reflex will also be reduced or absent. The femoral nerve also is responsible for sensation over the anterior thigh and the medial calf, the latter via its saphenous branch. The functional consequences of quadriceps weakness are considerable. The knee buckles easily, which can lead to sudden falling.

In spinal stenosis, the spinal canal narrows, with epidural compression of multiple nerve roots from midlumbar to sacral levels. Symptoms and signs are not limited to a single root or peripheral nerve pattern, and pain is prominent. A herniated disc at the L5–S1 interspace will typically impinge upon the S1 nerve root (even though it is the L5 root that exits the spinal canal through the L5–S1 foramen) and produce weakness of the gastrocnemius muscle, loss of the Achilles reflex, and hypoesthesia over the lateral aspect of the foot and the heel. Myositis, as seen in polymyositis or dermatomyositis, is an inflammatory process within muscle that produces pain and weakness but not sensory loss. Iliac artery stenosis can lead to vascular claudication, but not to neurologic deficits such as sensory and reflex loss.

References

1. Dawson DM, Hallett M, Millender LH. *Entrapment Neuropathies.* 2nd ed. Boston, MA: Little, Brown and Company; 1990:307–323.
2. Freimer M, Brushart TM, Cornblath DR, et al. Entrapment neuropathies. In: Mendell JR, Kissel JT, Cornblath DR, eds. *Diagnosis and Management of Peripheral Nerve Disorders.* Oxford: Oxford University Press; 2001:592–638.
3. Misulis KE. Lower back and lower limb pain. In: Bradley WG, Daroff RB, Fenichel GM, et al., eds. *Neurology in Clinical Practice.* 4th ed. Philadelphia, PA: Butterworth Heinemann; 2004:445–456.

187. A 70-year-old woman comes to the office for follow-up after left colectomy of a mass found on colonoscopy. Biopsy demonstrated moderately differentiated adenocarcinoma. Computed tomography of the abdomen shows no evidence of metastases or lymph node involvement, and chest radiograph is normal. The pathology report describes the tumor as invading into but not through the muscularis, with one pericolic lymph node positive for tumor involvement (T_2N_1 stage III colon cancer). The patient is otherwise well except for mild hypertension.

What is the most appropriate management for this patient?

(A) Carcinoembryonic antigen monitoring in 3 months
(B) Lymph node dissection
(C) Adjuvant chemotherapy
(D) Radiation therapy

ANSWER: C

Colorectal cancer is the third leading cause of death from cancer in both men and women. The risk of developing colorectal cancer begins to increase at age 40. About 25% of tumors extend through the bowel wall (T_4), and 50% to 60% have lymph node involvement at diagnosis. Although 75% of patients present with resectable tumors, almost half of all patients die from metastatic disease, presumably because of microscopic residual disease or circulating tumor cells.

Adjuvant chemotherapy is standard treatment for patients with resected colon cancer who are at high risk for recurrence, but risk-benefit considerations in patients over 70 years old are controversial. In a meta-analysis comparing the effects of postoperative fluorouracil plus leucovorin or levamisole with the effects of surgery alone in patients with stage II or III colon cancer, adjuvant treatment was found to have a significant positive effect on overall survival and time to tumor recurrence, regardless of patient age. The 5-year overall survival was 71% for patients who received adjuvant therapy and 64% for those treated with surgery alone.

The incidence of toxic effects (nausea or vomiting, diarrhea, stomatitis, and leukopenia) was not increased among patients older than 70 years, except for leukopenia in one study. Selected elderly patients with colon cancer receive the same benefit from fluorouracil-based adjuvant therapy as their younger counterparts, without a significant increase in toxic effects.

Lymph node dissection is not an appropriate choice, as it would not change management in this patient with known lymph node involvement.

Radiation therapy may be appropriate for rectal cancer but not for cancers of the left colon.

References

1. Hurwitz H, Fehrenbacher L, Novotny W, et al. Bevacizumab plus irinotecan, fluorouracil, and leucovorin for metastatic colorectal cancer. *N Engl J Med.* 2004;350(23):2335–2342.
2. Muss HB. Older age—not a barrier to cancer treatment. *N Engl J Med.* 2001;345(15):1127–1128.
3. Nauta RJ. Chemotherapy in the elderly. *N Engl J Med.* 2002;346(8):622–623.
4. Perrone F, Gallo C, Daniele B. Chemotherapy in the elderly. *N Engl J Med.* 2002;346(8):622–623.

5. Sargent DJ, Goldberg RM, Jacobson SD, et al. A pooled analysis of adjuvant chemotherapy for resected colon cancer in elderly patients. *N Engl J Med.* 2001;345(15):1091–1097.
6. Warren JL, Brown ML. Chemotherapy in the elderly. *N Engl J Med.* 2002;346(8):622–623.

188. A 78-year-old man comes to the office because he has lost 11.4 kg (25 lb) over the past 6 months. His appetite is good, but bloating and abdominal distension often develop soon after he eats. He passes stool, usually diarrheal, three to four times each day. He has no abdominal pain and is otherwise well. He stopped eating dairy products, but that had no effect. He has remained active throughout his illness, walking 1 to 3 miles regularly. He lives in a retirement village and drinks city water.

On physical examination, he weighs 50 kg (110 lb); he is 167.6 cm (5 ft 6 in) tall. Laboratory studies are normal except albumin is 2.7 mg/dL (total protein, 6.7 mg/dL). Malabsorption is confirmed by markedly reduced urinary excretion after ingestion of D-xylose 25 g. Stool examination for ova and parasites and stool enzyme-linked immunosorbent assay for *Giardia* infection are negative.

What is the most likely cause of the malabsorption?

(A) Giardiasis
(B) Small bowel bacterial overgrowth
(C) Intestinal ischemia
(D) Pancreatic insufficiency
(E) *Helicobacter pylori* infection

ANSWER: B

In older adults without an exposure history or underlying pancreatic disease, giardiasis and pancreatic insufficiency are unusual. Although stool examination for ova and parasites has poor sensitivity for giardiasis (previous recommendations often required a "string test" or small bowel biopsy to exclude the diagnosis), immunologic detection assays of the stool for giardiasis are sensitive (between 91% and 100%) and specific (between 89% and 100%). Thus, giardiasis is unlikely in this patient. Of the options given, the most common causes of malabsorption in older adults are intestinal ischemia and small bowel bacterial overgrowth.

Mesenteric ischemia is usually associated with postprandial pain and is more common in patients with clinically evident vascular or coronary disease. This patient has neither pain nor underlying vascular disease.

A recent study suggests 15.6% of adults over age 61 have evidence of small bowel bacterial overgrowth, probably because of the high prevalence of achlorhydria in this population. Small bowel bacterial overgrowth is associated with lower body mass index, plasma albumin level, and higher incidence of diarrhea, and it can be treated by broad-spectrum antimicrobials (such as doxycycline) that are inexpensive and well tolerated.

Helicobacter pylori infection does not cause malabsorption.

References
1. Holt PR. Diarrhea and malabsorption in the elderly. *Gastroenterol Clin North Am.* 2001;30(2):427–444.
2. Holt PR. Gastrointestinal diseases in the elderly. *Curr Opin Clin Nutr Metab Care.* 2003;6(1):41–48.
3. Parlesak A, Klein B, Schecher K, et al. Prevalence of small bowel bacterial overgrowth and its association with nutrition intake in nonhospitalized older adults. *J Am Geriatr Soc.* 2003;51(6):768–773.

189. A 75-year-old man calls the office because he has had a slight distortion in the vision in his left eye over the past 2 days. The edge of a door seems wavy, not straight. He has a history of hypertension and macular degeneration in his right eye, wears eyeglasses, and has a 50-pack-per-year smoking history. Visual acuity via Snellen distance chart is 20/40.

Which of the following is the most appropriate recommendation?

(A) See an ophthalmologist urgently for evaluation.
(B) See optometrist within 1 week for full examination.
(C) See a primary care physician urgently for blood-pressure check.
(D) See an optician at his convenience to straighten his glasses.

ANSWER: A

The sudden change in this patient's vision implies a recent change in his ocular status. Considering his history of macular degeneration in the right eye, hypertension, and smoking, new macular degeneration may have developed in the left eye. The patient needs to see an ophthalmologist urgently to evaluate his retina for subfoveal choroidal neovascularization. Early treatment with photodynamic therapy can reduce the risk of severe loss of vision and maintain essential visual function.

Although the patient notes a change, acuity tested by eye chart may not show deterioration; patients may experience subtle distortion but still demonstrate good acuity. Urgent evaluation of his retina is essential to avoid risk of significant functional vision impairment. Poor blood-pressure control and crooked glasses are unlikely to cause the symptoms he describes.

References

1. Age-Related Eye Disease Study Research Group. Risk factors associated with age-related macular degeneration. *Ophthalmology*. 2000;107(12):2224–2232.
2. American Academy of Ophthalmology. Photodynamic therapy with verteporfin for age-related macular degeneration. *Ophthalmology*. 2000;107(12):2314–2317.
3. Brodie SE. Aging and disorders of the eye. In: Tallis RC, Fillit HM, eds. *Brocklehurst's Textbook of Geriatric Medicine and Gerontology*. 6th ed. London: Churchill Livingston; 2003:735–747.
4. Mackenzie PJ, Chang TS, Scott IU, et al. Assessment of vision-related function in patients with age-related macular degeneration. *Ophthalmology*. 2002;109(4):720–729.

190. Which of the following is correct regarding the use of occlusive dressings in the treatment of pressure ulcers?

    (A) They promote a mildly alkaline pH.
    (B) They maintain a relatively high oxygen tension on the wound surface.
    (C) They are more likely than nonocclusive dressings to preserve cytokines.
    (D) They are associated with more pain from partial-thickness wounds than nonocclusive dressings.

ANSWER: C

Understanding the effect of occlusive dressings has been an important development in successful wound care. By offering an occluded, moist environment, occlusive dressings maintain a mildly acidic pH and a relatively low oxygen tension on the wound surface. The steep oxygen gradient stimulates angiogenesis, an important factor in wound healing. Low oxygen tension also provides optimal conditions for proliferation of fibroblasts and formation of granulation tissue. Cytokines encourage granulation-tissue formation and epithelialization and are more likely to be preserved in an occluded wound environment. Moisture also facilitates epidermal migration, angiogenesis, and connective-tissue synthesis. Moisture supports autolysis of necrotic material by providing the solute for enzymatic debridement. Wound desiccation should be avoided, as it leads to cell death. Occlusive dressings better limit the pain associated with partial-thickness wounds than do nonocclusive dressings.

References

1. Enoch S, Harding K. Wound bed preparation: the science behind the removal of barriers to healing. *Wounds*. 2002;15(7):213–229.
2. Lionelli GT, Lawrence WT. Wound dressings. *Surg Clin North Am*. 2003; (83):3:617–638.

191. An 85-year-old woman is evaluated because she has lost 2.7 kg (6 lb) since admission to a nursing home 1 month ago after a stroke. Her admission weight was 120 pounds and her height 64 inches. She has mild cognitive impairment. The staff reports that she takes a long time to chew her food and that she pockets food in her cheek. She denies pain with chewing or swallowing, and she is not depressed. Examination indicates that her denture fits well and that she has no oral lesions. Her gag reflex is intact.

Which of the following is the most appropriate first step?

    (A) Request swallowing evaluation.
    (B) Order a nutritional supplement.
    (C) Discuss feeding tube placement with her family.
    (D) Order mirtazapine.
    (E) Initiate therapy with megestrol acetate.

ANSWER: A

Weight loss is a clinically important sign of nutritional risk in the nursing-home population, and regular assessment of weight change is an important element of quality nursing-home care. Weight change is reported in the Minimum Data Set, and national nursing-home quality measures consider prevalence of weight loss. This resident's history of stroke places her at high risk for a swallowing disorder; the prolonged eating and pocketing of food further point toward this possibility. An intact gag reflex does not preclude the presence of a swallowing disorder. The evaluation may vary from bedside assessment to endoscopy. The tests have a wide range of sensitivity, specificity, and inter-rater reliability. Bedside assessment is generally considered the simplest and most efficient initial screen. Videofluoroscopy allows visualization of the trajectory of different types of food and liquids. Some swallowing difficulties may be resolved by change in diet consistency or patient position during feeding.

Initiating a nutritional supplement or placing a feeding tube is inappropriate in the absence of a swallowing evaluation. Recent literature has focused on the lack of evidence supporting tube feeding for persons with advanced dementia. However, this resident has mild cognitive impairment, and the cause of weight loss is most likely a swallowing disorder related to stroke. If alternative options are not effective, placement of a feeding tube may be appropriate after discussion with the resident and family. Mirtazapine may increase appetite among depressed persons but would not be the best initial choice in this nondepressed person. The evidence for efficacy of megestrol acetate in nursing homes is mixed, but it would not be considered a first-line therapy in this resident. Megestrol acetate has been associated with fluid retention, exacerbation of heart failure, adrenal suppression, and delirium.

References

1. Lind CD. Dysphagia: evaluation and treatment. *Gastroenterol Clin North Am*. 2003;32(2):553–575.
2. Ramsey DJ, Smithard DG, Kalra L. Early assessments of dysphagia and aspiration risk in acute stroke patients. *Stroke*. 2003;34(5):1252–1257.
3. Saliba D, Solomon DH, Young RT, et al. Feasibility of quality indicators for the management of geriatric syndromes in nursing home residents. *J Am Med Dir Assoc*. 2004;5(5):310–319.
4. Thomas DR, Ashmen W, Morley JE, et al. Nutritional management in long-term care: development of a clinical guideline. Council for Nutritional Strategies in Long-Term Care. *J Gerontol A Biol Sci Med Sci*. 2000;55(12):M725–M734.

192. A 70-year-old woman is concerned about vaginal discomfort and pain and occasional bleeding with intercourse. She had a hysterectomy and oophorectomy for fibroids at age 56, and estrogen receptor–positive breast cancer at age 65. The breast cancer was treated with lumpectomy and radiation, with no evidence of recurrence. She has never taken hormone replacement therapy. She is on no medications other than ibuprofen as needed for joint pains. In former years, sexual activity was mutually pleasurable to her and her husband. Her husband has recently started taking sildenafil.

Physical examination is remarkable for vaginal atrophic changes and mild difficulty introducing a regular-size speculum. No masses are present.

Which of the following is the best therapeutic choice for this patient?

(A) Oral conjugated estrogen
(B) Oral esterified estrogen and methyltestosterone
(C) Oral fluoxetine
(D) Water-soluble lubricant
(E) Intramuscular testosterone

ANSWER: D

About one third of sexually active women age 65 and older report dyspareunia. Causes include inadequate vaginal lubrication (most commonly due to estrogen deficiency), irritation and dryness of the external genitalia, vulvovaginitis, local trauma (such as from episiotomy scars), urethritis, improper intromission (often related to angle of penile entry), anorectal disease, altered anatomy of the female genital tract (such as retroverted or prolapsed uterus), and arthritis.

In women who are appropriate candidates, estrogen, either systemically or locally (in the form of a cream or estradiol-releasing vaginal ring or pellet), is the best choice, as the major cause of dyspareunia is loss of lubrication due to estrogen deficiency. Some women may require both systemic and local application of estrogen for best effect. The use of estrogen for the shortest possible duration is advisable. With this patient's history of breast cancer, however, most clinicians would hesitate to use estrogen, including locally, as topical estrogen cream can have systemic effects. The use of combined estrogen and testosterone or testosterone alone enhances libido and may improve vaginal lubrication. This patient, however, does not have low libido, and these agents may cause virilization, hepatic dysfunction, and worsened lipid parameters. In this patient, the best option with the least risk to the patient is the use of a water-soluble lubricant.

This patient has no history of depression. In addition, fluoxetine and other selective serotonin-reuptake inhibitors can cause anorgasmia and loss of libido.

References

1. Bachmann GA, Burd ID, Ebert GA. Menopausal sexuality. In: RA Lobo, J Kelsey, R Marcus, eds. *Menopause: Biology and Pathobiology.* San Diego: Academic Press; 2000:382–393.
2. Bernhard LA. Sexuality and sexual health care for women. *Clin Obstet Gynecol.* 2002; 45(4):1089–1098.
3. Morley JE, Kaiser FE. Female sexuality. *Med Clin N Amer.* 2003;87(5):1077–1090.
4. Rhodes JC, Kjerulff KH, Langenberg PW, et al. Hysterectomy and sexual functioning. *JAMA.* 1999; 282(20):1934–1941.

193. In an office setting, which of the following is the most appropriate screening strategy for hearing loss in older adults?

    (A) Rubbing fingers next to the ears
    (B) Hand-held AudioScope test
    (C) Holding a vibrating tuning fork next to the ears
    (D) Whisper test
    (E) Weber test

ANSWER: B

Hearing loss affects between 25% and 40% of adults aged 65 years and older in the United States. In patients older than 75 years, its prevalence is between 40% and 66%. Hearing loss is strongly associated with functional decline and depression. In spite of its prevalence and clinical significance, only 9% of internists offer hearing tests to patients aged 65 years and older, and only 25% of patients with hearing loss that could be improved with hearing aids actually receive hearing aids.

The AudioScope offers sensitivity of 94% and specificity between 69% and 80% for hearing loss. It is a physiologic test based on a combination otoscope and audiometer that generates a 40-dB pure tone at 500 Hz, 1000 Hz, 2000 Hz, and 4000 Hz. Minimal training is required for use. Patients unable to hear a predetermined series of tones may be referred for formal audiogram testing. An alternative to the AudioScope is the use of a standardized, self-administered 10-item questionnaire, the Hearing Handicap Inventory for the Elderly—Screening Version. This questionnaire offers reasonable sensitivity and specificity but screens for functional hearing loss, rather than for physiologic hearing loss as with the AudioScope. Because the questionnaire identifies individuals with impairment related to hearing, it may miss mild hearing loss. One study suggests that patients prefer the AudioScope to the standardized questionnaire. Another option is a single question ("Do you have a hearing problem now?"), which performed reasonably well in a recent study, and has the attraction of being very quick and easy.

Rubbing fingers next to the ears, holding a vibrating tuning fork next to the ears, and the whisper test are inexpensive and quick, and they require no special equipment other than a tuning fork. The whisper test, in which the examiner whispers a series of words or numbers from a set distance behind the patient, after full exhalation, has been perhaps the best described. Although some studies suggest that these tests offer reasonable accuracy, their reliability has not been confirmed. Nonetheless, in settings where an AudioScope or standardized questionnaire is not available, they may be preferable to no screening at all.

The Weber test, in which a vibrating tuning fork is placed on the midline skull, may help to distinguish between conductive and sensorineural hearing loss. Lateralization of the tuning fork tones suggests either ipsilateral conductive hearing loss on the side the tone is perceived to be louder or contralateral sensorineural hearing loss. However, the Weber test, often paired with the Rinne test, is most useful when hearing loss is suspected, rather than as a screening test for hearing loss.

References

1. Bogardus ST, Yueh B, Shekelle PG. Screening and management of adult hearing loss in primary care: clinical applications. *JAMA*. 2003;289(15):1986–1990.
2. Gates GA, Murphy M, Rees TS, et al. Screening for handicapping hearing loss in the elderly. *J Fam Practice*. 2003;52(1):56–62.
3. Mills JH. Age-related changes in the auditory system. In: Hazzard WR, Blass JP, Halter JB, et al., eds. *Principles of Geriatric Medicine and Gerontology*. 5th ed. New York: McGraw Hill; 2003:1239–1251.
4. Yueh B, Shapiro N, MacLean CH, et al. Screening and management of adult hearing loss in primary care: scientific review. *JAMA*. 2003;289(15):1976–1985.

194. A 70-year-old woman comes to the office because of slurred speech and deterioration in gait, balance, and coordination that has progressed over the past 2 months. Neurologic examination demonstrates truncal and limb ataxia, severe dysarthria, and nystagmus with a downbeat component. Laboratory testing is positive for anti-Yo antibodies, and magnetic resonance imaging demonstrates cerebellar atrophy.

In which of the following organs is malignancy most likely to be found?

(A) Colon
(B) Kidney
(C) Lung
(D) Ovary
(E) Thyroid

ANSWER: D

Paraneoplastic cerebellar degeneration is the most common and best characterized of the paraneoplastic syndromes involving the central nervous system. Although it is associated with several cancers, including small cell carcinoma of the lung, when anti-Yo antibodies are present the underlying cancer is almost always ovarian, endometrial, fallopian tube, or breast. In approximately two thirds of patients, recognition of cerebellar dysfunction precedes diagnosis of the underlying cancer. Symptoms of paraneoplastic cerebellar degeneration typically evolve over weeks to several months and include progressive gait ataxia, dysarthria, and oscillopsia (due to nystagmus). Vertigo and diplopia may occur.

None of the other options are associated with anti-Yo antibodies. Colon cancer does not usually metastasize to the brain, although when it does, it has a predilection for the cerebellum and can thus produce symptoms of cerebellar dysfunction. Fluorouracil, used in the treatment of colon cancer, may also produce a cerebellar syndrome. Renal carcinoma often metastasizes to the brain, and the metastatic lesions tend to be hemorrhagic. Although paraneoplastic complications have been reported with renal carcinoma, they are rare and not associated with anti-Yo antibodies. Small cell carcinoma of the lung is associated with various paraneoplastic syndromes affecting the nervous system, including Lambert-Eaton myasthenic syndrome, subacute sensory neuropathy, and subacute cerebellar degeneration. The paraneoplastic syndromes associated with small cell lung cancer are not anti-Yo positive, but may have anti-Hu, antiretinal, and antineuromuscular junction antibodies. When paraneoplastic cerebellar degeneration occurs in the setting of small cell lung carcinoma, it is antibody negative. Thyroid gland tumors have been associated with myasthenia gravis, but this disease is characterized by weakness rather than cerebellar dysfunction.

References

1. Bataller L, Dalmau J. Paraneoplastic neurologic syndromes: approaches to diagnosis and treatment. *Semin Neurol*. 2003;23(2):215–224.
2. Darnell RB, Posner JB. Paraneoplastic syndromes involving the nervous system. *N Engl J Med*. 2003;349(16):1543–1554.
3. Rosenfeld MR, Dalmau J. Paraneoplastic disorders of the nervous system. In: Bradley WG, Daroff RB, Fenichel GM, et al., eds. *Neurology in Clinical Practice*. 4th ed. Philadelphia, PA: Butterworth Heinemann; 2004:1461–1474.

195. A 76-year-old man is admitted to the intensive care unit for management of severe bacterial pneumonia with sepsis. He is treated with intravenous antibiotics, dopamine, and mechanical ventilation. Thyroid function tests are obtained. On physical examination, he does not have goiter.

Laboratory studies:

Serum thyrotropin	0.2 µU/mL	↓
Serum free thyroxine	1.1 ng/dL	←→
Serum free triiodothyronine	75 pg/dL (normal range 210–440)	↓

What is the most likely diagnosis?

(A) Hashimoto's thyroiditis with hypothyroidism
(B) Euthyroid sick syndrome *(TSH ↑↓, ↓T₃, FreeT₄ Nl)*
(C) Subacute (de Quervain's) thyroiditis *(↓TSH, ↑FreeT₄, ↑T₃)*
(D) Thyrotropinoma *(↑TSH ↑T₃ ↑free T₄)*

ANSWER: B

The euthyroid sick syndrome (also called nonthyroidal illness) refers to a constellation of changes in serum thyroid hormone and thyrotropin concentrations that occur in the context of systemic illness (such as infection, trauma, malignancy, starvation, inflammatory disease). The syndrome does not represent primary thyroid disease; rather, it results from alterations in thyroid hormone metabolism (such as decreased conversion of thyroxine to triiodothyronine) and transport that are induced by underlying systemic illness. As the underlying illness resolves, thyroid hormone concentrations return to normal. Current evidence does not support use of thyroid hormones in this condition. The most common pattern seen in the euthyroid sick syndrome is low serum triiodothyronine with a normal free thyroxine and normal thyrotropin. However, thyrotropin may be mildly depressed or elevated.

Many medications may alter thyroid function tests. Dopamine and corticosteroids suppress serum thyrotropin. The mild reduction in this patient's thyrotropin level is likely due to a combination of systemic (nonthyroidal) illness and the use of dopamine.

Response A is incorrect because the serum TSH level should be elevated in persons with untreated primary hypothyroidism. Response C is incorrect because persons with subacute thyroiditis would be hyperthyroid (eg, elevated serum concentrations of free thyroxine or triiodothyronine, or both, with a depressed serum TSH level). Response D is incorrect because a person with a thyrotropinoma (ie, TSH-secreting pituitary adenoma) would have evidence of central hyperthyroidism (eg, elevated serum concentrations of free thyroxine or triiodothyronine, or both, with an elevated serum TSH level).

References

1. Attia J, Margetts P, Guyatt G. Diagnosis of thyroid disease in hospitalized patients: a systematic review. *Arch Intern Med.* 1999;159(7):658–665.
2. Samuels MH, Pillote K, Asher D, et al. Variable effects of nonsteroidal antiinflammatory agents on thyroid test results. *J Clin Endocrinol Metab.* 2003;88(12):5710–5716.

196. Which of the following statements regarding age-associated changes in stem cells is true?

(A) The number of quiescent skeletal muscle precursor (satellite) cells declines with age.
(B) The proliferative capacity of aged satellite cells declines with aging but telomere length is unchanged.
(C) Forced activation of Notch signaling pathways can restore the regenerative potential of skeletal muscle in aged mice.
(D) Neural stem cells with the potential to produce neurons in tissue culture are present throughout the adult rodent brain
(E) Most regions of the adult mammalian brain are able to give rise to new neurons in vivo.

ANSWER: C

Satellite cells represent the endogenous source of muscle precursor cells and account for more than 99% of the regenerative potential of adult muscle. Although skeletal muscle cell regeneration is markedly impaired in old age, the role of age-related changes in satellite cell numbers or function had remained unclear until a recent study found that the numbers of satellite cells isolated from young and aged mice were similar. This study also demonstrated that satellite cells derived from aged muscle had a markedly diminished propensity to proliferate, with fewer myoblasts formed and an inadequate activation of Notch signaling. Notch is a transmembrane receptor that regulates numerous developmental decisions, and the misregulation of Notch has been linked to physiologic and developmental disorders. Although chromosomes in satellite cells lose telomere length with age, forced activation with Notch restored the regenerative potential of muscle in aged mice.

Neural stem cells have the capacity to self-renew and to give rise to the major types of cells present in the central nervous system. Recent studies indicate that neural stem cells can be isolated from most regions of rodent and human adult brains and give rise to new nerve cells in tissue culture. In contrast, clear evidence of adult neurogenesis occurring in vivo is limited to select regions (such as the subventricular zone of the lateral ventricle, or the dentate gyrus of the hippocampus).

References

1. Carlson BM. Muscle regeneration in amphibians and mammals: passing the torch. *Dev Dyn.* 2003; 226(2):167–181.
2. Conboy IM, Conboy MJ, Smythe GM, et al. Notch-mediated restoration of regenerative potential to aged muscle. *Science.* 2003;302(5650):1575–1577.
3. Lie DC, Song H, Colamarino SA, et al. Neurogenesis in the adult brain: new strategies for central nervous system diseases. *Annu Rev Pharmacol Toxicol.* 2004; 44:399–421.
4. Palmer TD, Schwartz PH, Taupin P, et al. Cell culture: progenitor cells from human brain after death. *Nature.* 2001; 411(6833):42–43.

197. A 72-year-old man comes to the office for a first visit. He runs 5 miles daily and occasionally has soreness in his knees that responds to aspirin. He takes several over-the-counter health preparations, including a multiple vitamin, calcium 500 mg, and a fish oil extract. On questioning, the patient describes an increasing sense of urinary urgency and nocturia, one or two times a night, over the past 2 years. He is bothered enough by the symptoms to consider treatment.

On physical examination, blood pressure is 110/70 mm Hg and heart rate is 60 per minute. Digital rectal examination reveals a normal prostate. Urinalysis and blood urea nitrogen and creatinine levels are normal; prostate-specific antigen level is 1.5 ng/mL.

Which of the following is most appropriate at this time?

(A) Obtain a transrectal ultrasound study.
(B) Initiate treatment with tamsulosin, 0.4 mg daily.
(C) Initiate treatment with oxybutynin, 2.5 mg three times daily.
(D) Initiate treatment with finasteride, 5 mg daily.

ANSWER: B

This patient's evaluation is consistent with mild to moderate benign prostatic hyperplasia. Further evaluation is not needed before proceeding with medical treatment or watchful waiting.

An α-blocker such as tamsulosin is the recommended initial treatment for men with small prostates and primarily irritative symptoms; symptoms may improve within several weeks. Finasteride is most effective in men with large prostates and primarily obstructive symptoms; clinical improvement takes several months. Further, a recent report suggests that treatment with finasteride may lower the overall risk of prostate cancer but increase the risk of aggressive prostate cancer. Although this risk can be managed with careful monitoring and should not preclude its use in appropriate patients, it reinforces the practice of initiating treatment with an α-blocker in men with small prostates.

This patient's symptoms are relatively mild for surgery to be considered. Oxybutynin is used for the management of urge urinary incontinence, not obstructive uropathy, and might precipitate urinary retention in this patient.

References

1. AUA Practice Guidelines Committee. AUA guideline on management of benign prostatic hyperplasia (2003). Chapter 1: diagnosis and treatment recommendations. *J Urology.* 2003:170(2 Pt 1):530–547.
2. Thompson IM, Goodman PJ, Tangen CM, et al. The influence of finasteride on the development of prostate cancer. *N Engl J Med.* 2003;349(3):215–224.
3. Wilt TJ, MacDonald R, Rutks I. Tamsulosin for benign prostatic hyperplasia. *Cochrane Database Syst Rev.* 2003;(1):CD002081.

198. A 78-year-old woman comes to the office with her husband, who notes that she has had an increase in aggressive behavior, delusions, and confusion over the past 2 weeks. History is significant for hypertension, depression, osteoarthritis, probable Alzheimer's disease, and urinary incontinence. Her score on the Mini–Mental State Examination 6 months ago was 16 of 30. Medications include acetaminophen 500 mg four times daily, donepezil 5 mg daily, hydrochlorothiazide 25 mg daily, lisinopril 10 mg daily, oxybutynin 5 mg twice daily (increased 1 month ago from 2.5 mg twice daily), and citalopram 20 mg daily (increased 2 months ago from 10 mg). Urinalysis performed today is normal.

Which of the following is the most appropriate next intervention?

(A) Start risperidone.
(B) Start lorazepam.
(C) Increase the dosage of donepezil.
(D) Discontinue oxybutynin.
(E) Reduce citalopram

ANSWER: D

This patient's symptoms are consistent with cognitive deficits or delirium induced by anticholinergic medications (in this case, oxybutynin). Patients with Alzheimer's disease are especially susceptible to the anticholinergic effects of medications because they have preexisting deficits in cholinergic transmission. In addition, it is possible that oxybutynin could interfere with the effectiveness of the cholinesterase inhibitor donepezil, reducing its ability to promote cholinergic transmission in the central nervous system.

Increasing the donepezil dosage to 10 mg daily may provide some additional cognitive benefits, but it is unlikely to improve her acute symptoms. Risperidone may be effective for treating agitation and aggressive behavior, but it may also result in an increased risk for vascular events. Lorazepam should be avoided for routine use in individuals with moderate to severe dementia since it may worsen cognition and behavior. Reducing the dose of citalopram is unlikely to affect her acute symptoms and may worsen her depression.

References

1. Katz IR, Sands LP, Bilker W, et al. Identification of medications that cause cognitive impairment in older people: the case of oxybutynin chloride. *J Am Geriatr Soc.* 1998;46(1):8–13.
2. Motsinger CD, Perron GA, Lacy TJ. Use of atypical antipsychotic drugs in patients with dementia. *Am Fam Physician.* 2003;67(11):2335–2340.
3. Sink KM, Holden KF, Yaffe K. Pharmacological treatment of neuropsychiatric symptoms of dementia: a review of the evidence. *JAMA.* 2005;293(5):596–608.
4. Tariot PN, Ryan JM, Porsteinsson AP, et al. Pharmacologic therapy for behavioral symptoms of Alzheimer's disease. *Clin Geriatr Med.* 2001;17(2):359–376.

199. A 77-year-old man comes to the office for a new patient examination. He is a pipe smoker. Examination of the oral cavity reveals a diffuse grayish-white appearance to the hard palate with multiple punctate red spots.

Which of the following is the most appropriate next step?

(A) Refer the patient for biopsy.
(B) Scrape lesion for cytology.
(C) Inform the patient that this is a smoking-related change.
(D) Initiate 10-day treatment with doxycycline.

ANSWER: C

Nicotinic stomatitis is most commonly seen in men aged 45 and over. It occurs as a response to the heat generated from cigarette, pipe, and cigar smoking. It has a characteristic diffuse grayish-white appearance of the hard palate with multiple punctate red spots that represent inflamed minor salivary duct orifices. It is not a premalignant change and is completely reversible with cessation of smoking; if it does not subside within 2 weeks, it should be biopsied. Biopsy or scraping at this time is not warranted. Antibiotic therapy would be of no benefit.

The high-risk sites for oral cancer include the lateral border of the tongue, ventral surface of tongue, floor of mouth, retromolar pads, and soft palate–tonsillar complex. The hard palate is a low-risk site for oral cancer. There are no changes to blood values from nicotinic stomatitis.

References

1. Mirbod SM, Ahing SI. Tobacco-associated lesions of the oral cavity: Part I. nonmalignant lesions. *J Can Dent Assoc.* 2000;66(5):252–256.
2. Taybos G. Oral changes associated with tobacco use. *Am J Med Sci.* 2003;326(4):179–182.

200. The daughter of a 93-year-old woman with Alzheimer's disease calls to discuss the patient's weight loss. The patient lives with her daughter and has had dementia for more than 6 years. Her average adult weight was 72.7 kg (160 lb). In recent years, she has weighed approximately 63.6 kg (140 lb); the community health nurse reports that she weighed 55.5 kg (122 lb) last week. The patient has not walked in at least 3 months and has required assistance for all of her activities of daily living, including feeding, for the past year. According to recent laboratory studies, her albumin level is 2.1 g/dL and total cholesterol is 93 mg/dL. Additional laboratory tests are unremarkable. When last examined, the patient was frail but well cared for and did not engage with you or her daughter.

What is the most appropriate response to this patient's weight loss?

(A) Prescribe nutritional supplements.
(B) Arrange for placement of a gastrostomy tube.
(C) Prescribe megestrol 400 mg oral suspension daily.
(D) Arrange swallowing evaluation.
(E) Recommend hospice care.

ANSWER: E

In this patient with end-stage dementia, the time course is consistent with adult failure-to-thrive syndrome, and no readily reversible cause of weight loss has been identified. No interventions have been shown consistently to make a significant difference in such cases. There is little harm in a trial of oral supplements, but supplements are costly. Artificial feeding and hydration via gastrostomy have adverse effects and have not been shown to improve most outcomes of interest. Careful hand feeding is usually preferable and may be more efficacious. Megestrol suspension is approved for use in AIDS wasting syndrome; one study of megestrol for long-term-care patients showed an association with deep-vein

thrombosis with its use. Other medications have not made a substantial difference for patients in this situation. It is unlikely that this patient can participate in a swallowing evaluation. As this patient likely has a prognosis of less than 6 months, it is appropriate to refer her to hospice after a plan of care is agreed upon. The most appropriate response to her weight loss is to meet with her family to clarify her goals and preferences in the context of her terminal condition.

References

1. Finucane TE, Christmas C, Travis K. Tube feeding in patients with advanced dementia: a review of the evidence. *JAMA.* 1999; 282(14):1365–1370.
2. Golden AG, Daiello LA, Silverman MA, et al. University of Miami Division of Clinical Pharmacology therapeutic rounds: medications used to treat anorexia in the frail elderly. *Am J Ther.* 2003;10(4):292–298.
3. Mackie SB. PEGs and ethics. *Gastroenterol Nurs.* 2001;24(3):138–142.
4. Mitchell SL, Buchanan JL, Littlehale S, et al. Tube-feeding versus hand-feeding nursing home residents with advanced dementia: a cost comparison. *J Am Med Dir Assoc.* 2004; 5(2):S23–S29
5. Potter JM. Oral supplements in the elderly. *Curr Opin Clin Nutr Metabol Care.* 2001;4(1):21–28.

201. A 73-year-old man fractures his hip while roller blading. He undergoes total hip arthroplasty and is discharged to a skilled nursing facility on the third postoperative day. At initial nursing evaluation, his right heel is erythematous and has a "mushy" feel to it. The physician's history and physical examination notes indicate that the extremities are "within normal limits." Three days later nursing notes document a blister on the heel. There is no notation that the physician is called. A physician progress note the following day does not document examination of the patient's extremities. Two days later the blister opens and reveals a large ulcer with necrotic tissue. The physician is called and gives treatment orders for wet-to-dry dressings. The patient's family calls the state health department and a survey is done, the results of which document a pattern of poor skin care in the facility. The patient has an extended stay in the nursing facility and is ultimately discharged to an assisted-living facility. He files a lawsuit against the hospital, doctors, and nursing facility.

Which of the following may affect the outcome of this case?

(A) Wet-to-dry dressings have not been found efficacious in recent studies.
(B) Nursing homes are rarely defendants in lawsuits related to pressure ulcers.
(C) Lack of detail about skin condition in nursing-home charts deters lawsuits.
(D) Plaintiffs have introduced survey results to show a pattern of poor care in a facility.

ANSWER: D

Since the passage of nursing-home reform legislation in 1987 and the publication of Omnibus Budget Reconciliation Act of 1987 (OBRA-87) regulations in 1992, the risk of litigation for negligent care involving pressure ulcers has increased. Although OBRA-87 has increased the awareness of good skin care and the importance of prevention of pressure ulcers, it has also helped spotlight the problem. Legislating good skin care has thus opened up opportunities for lawsuits.

Critically ill patients are among the most vulnerable for developing pressure ulcers. In pressure ulcer—related lawsuits, hospitals have been the defendants in almost one fourth of cases. In this scenario, pressure-related deep-tissue damage occurred while the patient was in the hospital but was not readily apparent without an examination. Once pressure-related deep-tissue injury was identified by nursing-home staff, the plan of care should have been modified to address this issue.

One of the most important aspects of medical malpractice involving pressure ulcers is documentation. Coordination of documentation is also important. In this case, the nurses documented evidence of a pressure ulcer, but the physician's notes did not corroborate these findings, and there was no evidence that the physician had been notified by the nursing staff.

Standard of care is essentially a legal concept that reflects common and expected practices in the community. It does not necessarily reflect the latest information offered in the literature. Despite the literature supporting moisture-retentive dressings in wound care, many clinicians still consider wet-to-dry dressings to be the standard of care.

By law, all nursing homes that accept Medicaid and Medicare payments must be surveyed by state inspectors at least every 15 months, and more frequently for cause. Survey results are public documents, and plaintiffs can easily obtain them. Plaintiffs have been successful in introducing survey results to show a pattern of poor care in a facility.

References

1. Bennett RG, O'Sullivan J, DeVito EM, et al. The increasing medical malpractice risk related to pressure ulcers in the United States. *J Am Geriatr Soc.* 2000; 48(1):73–81.
2. Dimant J. Implementing pressure ulcer prevention and treatment programs: using AMDA clinical practice guidelines. *JAMDA.* 2001;2(6):315–325.
3. Theaker C. Pressure sore prevention in the critically ill: what you don't know, what you should know and why it's important. *Intensive Crit Care Nurs.* 2003;19(3):163–168.

202. Which antihypertensive class is less effective as a single agent in black than in white Americans?

(A) Angiotensin-converting enzyme inhibitors
(B) Calcium channel blockers
(C) Centrally acting agents
(D) Diuretics

ANSWER: A

Hypertension is more prevalent and often more severe in African-descended populations living outside Africa than in any other population. Black patients generally respond well to diuretic therapy, with the fall in blood pressure exceeding that seen with monotherapy with an angiotensin-converting enzyme (ACE) inhibitor or a β-blocker. This increased efficacy of diuretics suggests an important role for volume in the genesis of hypertension in black patients and is consistent with the observation that blacks have a higher frequency of salt sensitivity (as defined by a rise in blood pressure with salt loading) than whites. Hypertension also appears to be less angiotensin II−dependent in blacks than in whites. Although black patients do not respond well to ACE inhibitors or β-blockers when these agents are given as monotherapy, either drug is effective when given in combination with a diuretic.

Black patients are also more responsive to calcium channel blockers than to monotherapy with ACE inhibitors or β-blockers. This relative advantage may apply only to the use of calcium channel blockers as monotherapy. There is no difference in the efficacy of centrally acting agents in blacks and whites.

References

1. Chobanian, AV, Bakris, GL, Black, HR, et al. The Seventh Report of the Joint National Committee on Prevention, Detection, Evaluation, and Treatment of High Blood Pressure: The JNC 7 report. *JAMA*. 2003;289(19):2560–2572.
2. Douglas, JG, Bakris, GL, Epstein M, et al. Management of high blood pressure in African Americans: consensus statement of the Hypertension in African Americans Working Group of the International Society on Hypertension in Blacks. *Arch Intern Med*. 2003; 163:525–541.
3. Lopes AA, James SA, Port FK, et al. Meeting the challenge to improve the treatment of hypertension in blacks. *J Clin Hypertens*. 2003;5(6):393–401.

203. An 89-year-old woman comes to the office complaining of feeling short of breath when climbing the stairs for the previous 2 weeks. Her lung examination is notable for bibasilar crackles. Electrocardiography showed changes of an inferior wall myocardial infarction of indeterminate age, chest radiography revealed some fluid at the bases, and echocardiography showed an ejection fraction of 35%. Her creatinine level was 2.2. She is placed on a loop diuretic, and at follow-up 2 weeks later, she is asymptomatic.

In addition to a β-blocker, which of the following classes of medication should be added at this time?

(A) Calcium channel blocker
(B) Long-acting nitrate
(C) Digoxin
(D) Angiotensin-converting enzyme inhibitor
(E) Aldactone

ANSWER: D

According to a review of randomized clinical trials on use of angiotensin-converting enzyme (ACE) inhibitors in renal insufficiency, no patient should be denied a long-term trial of ACE inhibitor therapy because of preexisting renal insufficiency. Additional diuretics are not indicated for long-term use because there is no evidence of hypervolemia, and their use may worsen the renal insufficiency. Since this patient has no signs of left ventricular diastolic dysfunction, atrial fibrillation, or ischemia, there is no indication for a calcium channel blocker, digitalis, or nitrate therapy in treatment of her heart failure. Aldactone might be beneficial after maximizing the ACE therapy.

References

1. Ahmed A, Kiefe CI, Allman RM, et al. Survival benefits of angiotensin-converting enzyme inhibitors in older heart failure patients with perceived contraindications. *J Am Geriatr Soc*. 2002;50(10):1659–1666.
2. Bakris GL, Weir MR. Angiotensin-converting enzyme inhibitor-associated elevations in serum creatinine: is this a cause for concern? *Arch Intern Med*. 2000;160(5):268–272.
3. Guyatt GH, Devereaux PJ. A review of heart failure treatment. *Mt Sinai J Med*. 2004;71(1):47–54.

204. A 75-year-old man with heart failure, diabetes mellitus, and history of stroke is admitted to the nursing home.

Which of the following should be included in admission screening for tuberculosis?

(A) Chest radiography
(B) Purified protein derivative skin test
(C) Tine tuberculin test
(D) Two-step purified protein derivative skin test
(E) Purified protein derivative skin test with three controls

ANSWER: D

Residents of institutions, including nursing homes, are considered to be at high risk for developing active tuberculosis infection. Screening with a two-step intradermal protein derivative (PPD) skin test is recommended for all new admissions to the nursing home. Tine testing is not considered accurate and is not appropriate for screening. The PPD tests for a delayed hypersensitivity reaction that manifests as a visible skin induration in persons with a history of exposure to tuberculosis. This reaction to tuberculin antigens (0.1 ml of 5 tuberculin units) peaks 48 to 72 hours after injection. Skin test conversion is defined as an increase in induration of 10 mm or more in persons not at high risk. An increase of 5 mm or more is considered positive in high-risk persons (such as persons with HIV, or persons who receive immunosuppressive therapy, who had recent close contact with infectious tuberculosis, or who have a chest radiograph consistent with prior tuberculosis infection).

In some persons, the delayed hypersensitivity reaction may wane over time, resulting in a false-negative response to a single-dose skin test. The first dose may increase the response to a subsequent dose, and persons with past infection with *Mycobacterium tuberculosis* may have significant induration on repeat testing weeks to years later ("boost" phenomenon). Because of the difficulty in determining whether an increase in induration between a first and second test reflects boosting or new infection, all nursing-home residents should undergo two-step testing. In two-step testing, tuberculin antigen is administered twice approximately 1 to 2 weeks apart.

Anergy testing, using controls, even in persons at high risk for compromised immunity, is controversial. The U.S. Preventive Services Task Force describes anergy testing as optional even in persons at increased risk for anergy. The Centers for Disease Control and Prevention recommends that chest radiography be reserved for follow-up of persons with abnormal skin test results or with symptoms strongly suggestive of active disease. If the resident has a significant skin induration or has had a prior positive PPD, active tuberculosis should be excluded by performing a history and physical examination and obtaining a chest radiograph and appropriate bacteriologic and histologic examinations.

Active tuberculosis should be treated. If active tuberculosis is not present, but the resident has a recent known new conversion or has increased risk for progression of latent tuberculosis to active tuberculosis, treatment with isoniazid is recommended. Therapy should be closely monitored since the risk for hepatotoxicity increases with age and the use of other medications. Therapy should not be started if hepatic transaminase levels are significantly elevated.

References

1. American Thoracic Society and Centers for Disease Control and Prevention. Targeted tuberculin testing and treatment of latent tuberculosis infection. *Am J Respir Crit Care Med.* 2000;161(4 Pt 2):S221–S247.
2. Cohn DL. Treatment of latent tuberculosis infection. *Semin Respir Infect.* 2003;18(4):249–262.
3. U.S. Preventive Services Task Force. *Guide to Clinical Preventive Services.* 2nd ed. Washington, DC: U.S. Department of Health and Human Services, Office of Disease Prevention and Health Promotion; 1996.
4. Zevallos M, Justman JE. Tuberculosis in the elderly. *Clin Geriatr Med.* 2003; 19(1):121–138.

205. A 68-year-old woman residing in a long-term-care facility is evaluated because of recent onset of dizziness, difficulty with ambulation, and mental status changes. History includes epilepsy, seasonal allergies, overactive bladder, recently diagnosed depression, and osteoporosis. Medications include phenytoin 300 mg daily, alendronate 10 mg daily, tolterodine 2 mg twice daily, fexofenadine 180 mg daily, and calcium carbonate 500 mg three times daily; 2 weeks ago she began fluoxetine 20 mg daily.

Laboratory studies from 1 month ago:

Phenytoin concentration	13.7 μg/mL
Sodium	138 mEq/L
Potassium	4.0 mEq/L
Urea nitrogen	15 mg/dL
Creatinine	1.0 mg/dL
Albumin	2.6 g/dL

Which of the following is the most appropriate next intervention?

(A) Obtain an unbound (free) phenytoin concentration.
(B) Discontinue tolterodine.
(C) Discontinue fexofenadine.
(D) Discontinue fluoxetine.

ANSWER: A

This patient's symptoms are consistent with phenytoin toxicity. Since phenytoin is highly bound to albumin, patients with reduced albumin may have a total plasma concentration within the therapeutic range and an elevated unbound concentration; the unbound concentration of phenytoin is what determines efficacy and toxicity. After adjustment for her low albumin, her phenytoin concentration 1 month ago was 18.3 μg/mL (corrected phenytoin level = observed phenytoin level/0.25 × albumin level + 0.1) or 13.7 / (0.25)(2.6) + 0.1 = 18.3, which is on the high side of the therapeutic range of 10 to 20 μg/mL.

Fluoxetine, which was added 2 weeks ago, can inhibit metabolism of phenytoin by its action on the cytochrome P-450 2C9 enzyme. This can lead to increased phenytoin concentrations. Thus, her total and unbound phenytoin concentration is likely to be higher than 18.3 μg/mL now. The appropriate action at this time would be to obtain an unbound (free) phenytoin concentration, or if it is not available, a total concentration and perform the adjustment for low albumin. Although fluoxetine is probably not the best antidepressant for her given its potential for interaction with phenytoin, it is premature to reduce the fluoxetine dose until her symptoms are confirmed to be due to phenytoin toxicity. In any case, a better option for this patient would be to change to any of the other selective serotonin-reuptake inhibitors that all have less of an effect on 2C9 phenytoin metabolism.

Many medications can affect the central nervous system in frail older adults and should be suspected in a person with unexplained cognitive changes. Both tolterodine and fexofenadine have minimal effect on the central nervous system but could cause problems for individual frail older patients. Given this patient's presentation, these agents would be low in the differential diagnosis as a cause for her symptoms.

References

1. Bourdet SV, Gidal BE, Alldredge BK. Pharmacologic management of epilepsy in the elderly. *J Am Pharm Assoc.* 2001;41(3):421–436.
2. Nelson MH, Birnbaum AK, Remmel RP. Inhibition of phenytoin hydroxylation in human liver microsomes by several selective serotonin re-uptake inhibitors. *Epilepsy Res.* 2001;44:71–82.
3. Spina E, Scordo MG. Clinically significant drug interactions with antidepressants in the elderly. *Drugs Aging.* 2002;19(4):299–320.

206. A 78-year-old man in an assisted-living facility has cough, shortness of breath, and pleuritic chest pain. He has a history of chronic obstructive pulmonary disease. He uses an albuterol metered-dose inhaler as needed. On examination, respiratory rate is 28 per minute and temperature is 39.2°C (102.5°F). He has crackles in the left lower lobe, and chest radiograph demonstrates an infiltrate. Community-acquired pneumonia is diagnosed, he is admitted to the hospital, and therapy with moxifloxacin is initiated.

Two hours later his condition rapidly deteriorates. He is obtunded and increasingly tachypneic, and he is excreting little urine. Blood pressure is 75/50 mm Hg; after several liters of intravenous fluid, it is 95/60 mm Hg.

Repeat chest radiograph demonstrates early acute respiratory distress syndrome and a computed tomography angiogram reveals no pulmonary embolus. His advance directive requests aggressive treatment if he has a reversible process, and he is admitted to the intensive care unit.

In addition to beginning pressor agents and broadening antimicrobial coverage, what is the most appropriate pharmacologic treatment for this patient?

(A) Enoxaparin
(B) Activated protein C
(C) Unfractionated heparin
(D) Fondaparinux
(E) Unfractionated heparin and antithrombin III

ANSWER: B

In sepsis, microbial products cause a burst of robust inflammatory responses that result in activation of the clotting cascade and end-organ failure. Enoxaparin, unfractionated heparin, antithrombin III, and fondaparinux have anticoagulant properties, and there is some rationale for their use on the basis of the pathophysiology of sepsis. However, heparin and heparin plus antithrombin III have failed in sepsis trials, probably because the thrombolytic pathways are markedly inhibited, and there are no data on fondaparinux or enoxaparin in sepsis.

Activated protein C (drotrecogin alpha) is approved by the Food and Drug Administration for use in patients with severe illness. In a large randomized trial, it was found to reduce mortality due to sepsis. A subanalysis of the Protein C Worldwide Evaluation of Severe Sepsis (PROWESS) trial of 350 patients aged 75 and over found a nonsignificant increase in bleeding complications in older adults in comparison with younger adults. Despite this trend, the survival benefits of using activated protein C were seen in adults aged 75 years and older up to 1 year later.

References

1. Bernard GR, Vincent JL, Laterre PF, et al. Efficacy and safety of recombinant human activated protein C for severe sepsis. *N Engl J Med.* 2001;344(10):699–709.

2. Ely EW, Angus DC, Williams MD, et al. Drotrecogin alfa (activated) treatment of older patients with severe sepsis. *Clin Infect Dis.* 2003;37(2):187–195.

207. A 71-year-old woman comes to the office for a routine physical examination. History includes pedal edema due to venous insufficiency, episodic insomnia due to situational anxiety, and mild acid reflux disease. She has no fatigue, poor appetite, or gastrointestinal symptoms. Medications include garlic capsules 270 mg each morning, *Ginkgo biloba* 40 mg one or two times daily, kava 150 mg one to two capsules at bedtime as needed, and valerian 1.5 g at bedtime as needed for sleep.

Physical examination is normal. Laboratory results are normal except for an alanine aminotransferase level of 210 IU/L and an aspartate aminotransferase level of 250 IU/L. Previous liver function tests were normal. The patient is advised to discontinue all supplements pending further evaluation of the transaminase abnormalities.

Of the supplements used by this patient, which one is the most likely cause of the laboratory abnormalities?

(A) Garlic
(B) *Ginkgo biloba*
(C) Kava
(D) Valerian

ANSWER: C

The Food and Drug Administration has issued a consumer advisory notice about the potential risk of hepatic toxicity associated with use of kava (also known as kava kava). Kava comes from the dried root of *Piper methysticum*. It is used for anxiety, insomnia, restlessness, and stress. Kavapyrones, the active constituents in kava, have centrally acting relaxant properties for skeletal muscle. The sale of products containing kava is restricted in several countries because of associated adverse hepatic effects. In 11 patients who developed liver failure that was associated with kava use and who underwent liver transplantation, doses (when known) ranged from 60 to 240 mg daily. Kava products may differ in the amounts and distribution of kavapyrones present. Patients with evidence of liver disease or hepatic abnormalities and patients at risk for liver disease should avoid these herbal therapies.

Garlic, *Ginkgo biloba*, and valerian have not been associated with liver function abnormalities.

References

1. Hepatic toxicity possibly associated with kava-containing products—United States, Germany, and Switzerland, 1999–2002. *MMWR Morb Mortal Wkly Rep.* 2002; 51(47):1065–1067.
2. Humberston CL, Akhtar J, Krenzelok EP. Acute hepatitis induced by kava kava. *J Toxicol Clin Toxicol.* 2003; 41(2):109–113.

208. A 73-year-old woman is brought to the emergency department because she awakened this morning completely blind. On examination, she is still unable to see and lacks light perception. However, her pupils are reactive, she has full eye movements, and she has no nystagmus, even to optokinetic testing. The rest of the physical examination is normal.

Which of the following is the most likely cause of the findings?

(A) Acute angle-closure glaucoma
(B) Bilateral occipital lobe infarction
(C) Conversion reaction
(D) Pituitary apoplexy
(E) Retinal artery occlusion

ANSWER: B

This patient has cortical blindness, which is characterized by vision loss with preservation of the pupillary light reflex. It can be seen with lesions involving the radiatio optica or occipital cortex bilaterally. This occurs because the fibers that mediate the pupillary light reflex exit the visual pathway at the lateral geniculate body to travel to the midbrain. Thus, the fibers are still fully functional in lesions of the visual pathway that are posterior to their exit.

Vision loss in lesions of visual pathways anterior to the lateral geniculate is accompanied by loss of the pupillary reaction to light, since fibers involved with pupillary function are also affected. Thus, the pupils of persons with blindness due to retinal artery occlusion or glaucoma do not react to light. Pituitary apoplexy, due to hemorrhage into or infarction of the pituitary gland, can compromise vision by

compressing the optic chiasm. This classically produces bitemporal visual field loss but may also produce complete loss of vision in one or both eyes and involvement of cranial nerves III, IV, VI, and V1. However, pupillary responses are also lost.

Cortical blindness can be difficult to differentiate from hysterical blindness (conversion reaction) because pupillary responses are intact in both. However, optokinetic nystagmus is preserved with hysterical blindness since the visual system is still functionally intact, whereas cortical blindness is not associated with nystagmus on optokinetic testing.

References

1. Devinsky O, D'Esposito M. *Neurology of Cognitive and Behavioral Disorders.* Oxford: Oxford University Press; 2004:133–134.
2. Tomsak RL. Vision loss. In: Bradley WG, Daroff RB, Fenichel GM, et al., eds. *Neurology in Clinical Practice.* 4th ed. Philadelphia: Butterworth Heinemann; 2004:177–183.
3. Trobe JD. *The Neurology of Vision.* Oxford: Oxford University Press; 2001:140–146.

209. A 75-year-old woman comes to the office because she has a painless blurring in her right eye that has progressed over the past few months. She is more sensitive to light and complains of glare and haloes. Ten years ago she had cataract surgery with intraocular lens implantations to both eyes with good results. She was recently diagnosed with type 2 diabetes, and her eye examination did not reveal any diabetic retinopathy.

Which of the following is the most likely cause of her symptoms?

(A) Vitreous hemorrhage
(B) Macular degeneration
(C) Opacified posterior lens capsule
(D) Diabetic macular edema

ANSWER: C

At the time of cataract surgery with an intraocular lens implant, the posterior capsule of the natural lens is left in place. Over time the capsule can opacify. With the styles of intraocular lens implanted 10 years ago, up to 33% opacification can occur, causing a gradual loss of vision, glare, and, in some cases, haloes around lights. Lysing the capsule with an Nd:YAG laser resolves symptoms permanently, and often instantly.

A vitreous hemorrhage occurs acutely and causes immediate symptoms of visual loss. Macular degeneration and diabetic macular edema often cause a distortion of central vision rather than a generalized blurring. Haloes and glare are not common symptoms of either.

References

1. Apple DJ, Peng Q, Visessook N, et al. Eradication of posterior capsule opacification. *Ophthalmology*. 2001;108(3):505–518.
2. Brodie SE. Aging and disorders of the eye. In: Tallis RC, Fillit HM, eds. *Brocklehurst's Textbook of Geriatric Medicine and Gerontology*. 6th ed. London: Churchill Livingston; 2003:735–747.
3. Rosenthal BP. Ophthalmology: screening and treatment of age-related and pathologic vision changes. *Geriatrics*. 2001; 56(12):27–31.

210. A 68-year-old black American woman recently moved in with her daughter and comes to the office to establish care. She states that she has been in good general health except that she may have "borderline" diabetes. She has no significant medical history and has no known risk factors for cardiac disease. She brings a copy of laboratory results from her previous physician; the results are normal except for a random blood glucose level of 212 mg/dL. Her daughter, who is a nurse, has checked her mother's blood-pressure readings on several occasions in the past month; all of these had a systolic reading above 160 mm Hg. She takes no prescribed or over-the-counter medications.

On physical examination, her sitting blood pressure is found to be 182/86 mm Hg, and heart rhythm is regular at a rate of 72 per minute. There are no orthostatic changes in heart rate or blood pressure. Her body mass index (kg/m^2) is 38. She has central obesity (waist circumference 95 cm), grade 1 hypertensive retinopathy, a laterally displaced point of maximal impulse with an apical fourth heart sound, and impaired monofilament test in the feet bilaterally. A resting electrocardiogram shows normal sinus rhythm and evidence of left ventricular hypertrophy.

Current laboratory studies:

Fasting glucose	138 mg/dL
Creatinine	1.2 mg/dL
Urine microalbumin: creatinine ratio	52 mg/g (normal < 30 mg albumin/g creatinine)

Which of the following is the most appropriate approach to initiating treatment of this patient's hypertension?

(A) Defer therapy until additional blood-pressure readings are obtained.
(B) Prescribe a 3-month trial of diet and exercise.
(C) Begin metoprolol.
(D) Begin lisinopril.

ANSWER: D

The diagnosis of hypertension should never be made on the basis of a single isolated elevated reading. This caution is especially important with older persons, who are likely to demonstrate more variability in their blood pressure, in part because of a decline in baroreflex sensitivity. This patient presents with a markedly elevated systolic blood-pressure reading at the time of her office visit. The additional home blood-pressure readings demonstrating systolic pressures above 160 mm Hg, and the physical findings (retinopathy and evidence consistent with left ventricular hypertrophy) provide sufficient evidence to establish a diagnosis of hypertension. Further, assuming that the home blood-pressure readings are accurate (which should be confirmed by validating the home cuff), the patient has stage 2 hypertension according to the staging classification of the Seventh Report of the Joint National Committee on Prevention, Detection, Evaluation, and Treatment of High Blood Pressure.

Most patients with stage 2 hypertension whose blood pressure exceeds target levels by more than 20/10 mm Hg will require two antihypertensive drugs to achieve their treatment goal. This patient's comorbidity of type 2 diabetes (as suggested by the combination of a single fasting glucose value above 125 mg/dL and a random value above 200 mg/dL) means that her target systolic blood-pressure level is below 135 mm Hg. In this situation, one of the two antihypertensive medications should be a thiazide-type diuretic. Because of the type 2 diabetes and the presence of significant microalbuminuria, the most appropriate second medication for this patient is an angiotensin-converting enzyme (ACE) inhibitor; even though ACE inhibitors tend to be less effective in black patients, they have some renoprotective effect.

Life-style interventions (sodium-restricted diet, exercise, and weight loss) should be recommended for all hypertensive patients; in this patient, these interventions will also be appropriate to help manage her type 2 diabetes. However, an initial trial of life-style interventions is appropriate only for individuals with stage 1 hypertension (systolic pressure below 160 mm Hg).

A β-blocker would not be an optimal first-line agent for this patient because monotherapy with β-blockers in black persons is less efficacious than a thiazide diuretic. In the absence of a history of underlying coronary artery disease or myocardial infarction, a thiazide-type diuretic in combination with an ACE inhibitor is the better option.

References

1. ALLHAT Officers and Coordinators for the ALLHAT Collaborative Research Group. Major outcomes in high-risk hypertensive patients randomized to angiotensin-converting enzyme inhibitor or calcium channel blocker vs diuretic: the Antihypertensive and Lipid-Lowering Treatment to Prevent Heart Attack Trial (ALLHAT). *JAMA.* 2002;288:2981–2997.
2. Chobanian AV, Bakris GL, Black HR, et al. The Seventh Report of the Joint National Committee on Prevention, Detection, Evaluation, and Treatment of High Blood Pressure: the JNC 7 report. *JAMA.* 2003;289(19):2560–2572.
3. Messerli FH, Grossman E, Goldbourt U. Are beta-blockers efficacious as first-line therapy for hypertension in the elderly? a systematic review. *JAMA.* 1998;279(23):1903–1907.
4. Snow V, Weiss KB, Mottur-Pilson C. The evidence base for tight blood pressure control in the management of type 2 diabetes mellitus. *Ann Intern Med.* 2003;138(7):587–592.

211. An 80-year-old man is admitted to the hospital from his nursing home because of mental status changes that culminated in frank coma over a 36-hour period. Other than Alzheimer's dementia, he has no chronic medical conditions. His caregiver noted increased urinary incontinence during the week preceding the hospital admission. On physical examination, pulse rate is 115 per minute and blood pressure is 90/50 mm Hg.

Laboratory studies:

Serum sodium	130 mEq/L
Serum potassium	4.0 mEq/L
Serum chloride	98 mEq/L
Serum bicarbonate	21 mEq/L
Blood urea nitrogen	79 mg/dL
Serum creatinine	3.0 mg/dL
Serum glucose	900 mg/dL

Which of the following is the most appropriate initial treatment?

(A) Restrict free water intake.
(B) Give 20-unit bolus of insulin.
(C) Begin fluid replacement with 0.9% sodium chloride.
(D) Begin fluid replacement with 0.45% sodium chloride.

ANSWER: C

This patient has nonketotic hyperosmolar syndrome, which primarily occurs in elderly persons because they have a higher prevalence of impaired thirst perception and reduced renal function. There is no prior history of diabetes mellitus in about 40% of cases. Nonketotic hyperosmolar syndrome is often precipitated by an infection (commonly gram-negative pneumonia). Other precipitants include cerebrovascular accidents, myocardial infarction, or pancreatitis. Mortality ranges from 10% to 60%.

In contrast to diabetic ketoacidosis, metabolic acidosis does not occur in nonketotic hyperosmolar syndrome because insulin is present, although at levels inadequate to prevent hyperglycemia. The hyperglycemia leads to glycosuria, osmotic diuresis, increased osmolality, and profound hypovolemia. Thus, the most important first step is volume replacement. Fluid repletion increases glucose excretion in the urine and dilutes the extracellular compartment. Since the fluid deficit can be severe (ranging from 8 to 12 L), initial fluid therapy should include isotonic (0.9%) saline because it more rapidly corrects plasma volume. Once hypotension is corrected and vital signs are stable, hypotonic (0.45%) saline may be substituted.

Insulin should not be administered before fluid resuscitation because rapid lowering of serum glucose with insulin will result in a shift of water back from the extracellular to the intracellular space and may lead to vascular collapse.

The low serum sodium level is due to osmotic shift from hyperglycemia, not syndrome of inappropriate antidiuretic hormone, so fluids should not be restricted to correct hyponatremia. In the context of hyperglycemia, the following formula can be used to ascertain the adjusted sodium level:

$$\text{Corrected sodium} = \text{Serum sodium} + \frac{1.6\,(\text{serum glucose} - 100)}{100}$$

In this case, therefore, the true sodium level is 143 meq/L.

References

1. American Diabetes Association. Clinical practice recommendations 2003. *Diabetes Care.* 2003;26(Suppl 1):S1–S156.
2. Nathan MH. Diabetic ketoacidosis and hyperosmolar coma. In: Leahy JL, ed. *Medical Management of Diabetes Mellitus.* New York: Marcel Dekker Publishers, Inc; 2000:655–686.

212. An 80-year-old man is brought to the office by his daughter because he developed difficulty walking 3 months ago. He lives alone and has trouble doing housework. It takes him longer now to shower and get dressed. He says his balance is not good, and he is worried that he will fall. He does not use a cane or walker. History includes a transient ischemic attack 4 years ago, non−insulin-dependent diabetes mellitus, hypertension, hyperlipidemia, and osteoarthritis. Medications include glyburide 5 mg daily, lisinopril 20 mg daily, atorvastatin 10 mg daily, enteric-coated aspirin 81 mg daily, and acetaminophen 1000 mg every 6 hours as needed for pain.

On examination, blood pressure is 120/70 mm Hg, with no postural change. Visual acuity is 20/100 in the left and 20/50 in the right eye (Snellen distance vision). He has arthritic changes in his fingers and knees. Ankle reflexes are absent. Sensation is intact to position and vibration but is decreased to pinprick in the feet. He has a resting tremor of his hands, right greater than left. Muscle tone is normal; strength is 4+/5 throughout. He does not exhibit a Romberg. He talks and moves slowly, and uses his arms to get up from the chair. Gait initiation is normal, but his gait is slow and wide-based, with decreased foot clearance, decreased arm swing, and abnormal turning. He reaches for the wall for support as he turns.

Which of the following is most likely to help determine the cause of his gait disturbance?

(A) Nerve conduction study
(B) Radiography of the cervical spine
(C) Radiography of the knees
(D) Magnetic resonance imaging of the brain
(E) Retinal examination

ANSWER: D

In this patient, further questioning would be useful to determine whether the difficulty walking occurred gradually or suddenly. He has a history of non−insulin-dependent diabetes mellitus, which may lead to peripheral neuropathy and is a risk factor, along with his hypertension and previous transient ischemic attack, for stroke. He has osteoarthritis that has affected his fingers and knees, decreased visual acuity, and peripheral neuropathy. His gait and movements are slow but not entirely typical of Parkinson's disease. The history and gait characteristics are most consistent with a frontal gait disorder due to cerebrovascular disease. Magnetic resonance imaging of the brain would likely show previous infarcts or periventricular white matter disease.

A nerve conduction study would confirm the diagnosis of peripheral neuropathy but would not explain the parkinsonian gait features. Radiography of the cervical spine might show osteoarthritis but would not diagnose a myelopathy. Radiography of the knees would show osteoarthritic changes, but there is no evidence from history or gait observation that knee pain or deformity is the cause of his impairment. His impaired visual acuity is possibly due to diabetic retinopathy, and a retinal examination is indicated in his general care. However, his decrease in visual acuity would not explain his abnormal gait.

References

1. Alexander NB. Gait disorders in older adults. *J Am Geriatr Soc.* 1996;44(4):434–451.
2. Whitman GT, Tang T, Lin A, et al. A prospective study of cerebral white matter abnormalities in older people with gait dysfunction. *Neurology.* 2001;57(6):990–994.

213. An 82-year-old man with bilateral hearing aids comes to the office for follow-up evaluation. During the examination, you find that cupping a hand over his right ear elicits a squealing sound but that when a hand is cupped over his left ear, there is no squealing.

What is the most appropriate next step in the assessment of this man's hearing?

(A) Turn down the volume on the right hearing aid.
(B) Make sure the right hearing aid is properly seated in the external ear canal.
(C) Check that the left hearing aid is on.
(D) Make sure that the left hearing aid is properly seated in the external ear canal.
(E) Take no further action.

ANSWER: C

Hearing loss is the third most prevalent chronic condition in older Americans, and it is strongly associated with functional decline and depression. Of patients with hearing loss that could be improved with hearing aids, only 25% actually receive hearing aids. Among patients who receive hearing aids, estimates of nonadherence are as high as 30%. In one study of patients older than 90 years, 33% to 79% had difficulty with inserting the hearing aid, changing the battery, cleaning the hearing aid, and changing the volume.

Primary care physicians and geriatricians can help assess possible reasons for improper hearing aid function, as well as reasons for failure to use them. For example, physicians can ask if the hearing aid is uncomfortable, if the patient knows how to use the hearing aid, if the hearing aid is turned on, when the battery was

last replaced, and if the patient has trouble inserting the hearing aid or changing the volume.

Usually, a physician can easily check for dead batteries, low volume, or hearing aids set in the off position by cupping a hand over the aid—a normally functioning aid will squeal. Thus, the correct answer for this question is to turn on the nonsquealing left hearing aid before assessing hearing; if the left hearing aid is already turned on, then the volume may be too low or the batteries may be dead.

Although improper fit is common, that is not a likely explanation for the squealing or the absence of squealing. Improperly adjusted volume is also common, but squealing is a normal response when a hand is cupped over the hearing aid. Taking no further action is inappropriate, as there is likely a problem with the function of the left hearing aid. In this patient who is making the effort to use his hearing aids, simple measures may help ensure optimal benefit.

References

1. Bogardus ST, Yueh B, Shekelle PG. Screening and management of adult hearing loss in primary care: clinical applications. *JAMA.* 2003;289(15):1986–1990.
2. Mills JH. Age-related changes in the auditory system. In: Hazzard WR, Blass JP, Halter JB, et al., eds. *Principles of Geriatric Medicine and Gerontology.* 5th ed. New York: McGraw Hill; 2003:1239–1251.
3. Yueh B, Shapiro N, MacLean CH, et al. Screening and management of adult hearing loss in primary care: scientific review. *JAMA.* 2003;289(15):1976–1985.

214. A 75-year-old woman comes to the office because she has fatigue, difficulty falling asleep, and frequent headaches. She has no history of hypertension. She is the primary caregiver for her 79-year-old husband; he has Alzheimer's disease (Mini–Mental State Examination score of 14 of 30) and has recently developed behavioral problems related to repetitive questions and demands. On examination, the patient's blood pressure is 168/95 mm Hg.

Which of the following is the most helpful intervention for her at this time?

(A) Prescribe a calcium channel blocker.
(B) Prescribe lorazepam.
(C) Prescribe sertraline.
(D) Refer to a psychiatrist for psychotherapy.
(E) Provide counseling about community services related to dementia caregiving.

ANSWER: E

Providing direct, daily care for a spouse with dementia is stressful and affects the mental and physical health of the caregiver. The stress is compounded when the demented spouse develops behavioral problems, such as repetitive questions, demands, threats, or physical aggression. The behavioral problems are often the turning point that leads to placement in an assisted-living facility or nursing home.

This patient's symptoms are suggestive of caregiver stress. Although treatment of specific symptoms of anxiety or depression with medication or psychotherapy is reasonable, the coincidence of her symptoms with her husband's increased behavioral problems suggests that the most helpful intervention would be to reduce her burden as a caregiver. The use of community respite programs and educational groups for caregivers have both been demonstrated to reduce the sense of burden reported by caregivers and in turn may reduce the behavioral problems exhibited by the demented spouse. If her blood pressure remains elevated, consideration of treatment is indicated.

References

1. Gaugler JE, Jarrott SE, Zarit SH, et al. Adult day service use and reductions in caregiving hours: effects on stress and psychological well-being for dementia caregivers. *Int J Geriatr Psychiatry.* 2003; 18(1):55–62.
2. Gerdner LA, Buckwalter KC, Reed D. Impact of a psychoeducational intervention on caregiver response to behavioral problems. *Nurs Res.* 2002; 51(6):363–374.
3. Herbert R, Levesque L, Vezina J, et al. Efficacy of a psychoeducative group program for caregivers of demented persons living at home: a randomized controlled trial. *J Gerontol B Psychol Sci Soc Sci.* 2003; 58(1):58–67.
4. Hooker K, Bowman SR, Coehlo DP, et al. Behavioral change in persons with dementia: relationships with mental and physical health of caregivers. *J Gerontol B Psychol Sci Soc Sci.* 2002; 75(5):453–460.

215. Several weeks ago, an urgent consultation was requested for a 77-year-old nursing-home resident after he struck another resident without provocation. Behavioral interventions and environmental modifications were suggested, but his aggression has not changed, and further management is indicated. The patient has a 5-year history of cognitive decline that necessitated nursing-home admission 2 years earlier. He has atrial fibrillation and is treated with digoxin and warfarin. His score on the Mini–Mental State Examination has declined progressively over the years and is currently 12 of 30. He has been irritable and resistive to care for a number of years. For several months before he struck the other resident, he had been aggressive, striking and kicking staff. Magnetic resonance imaging done 2 years ago demonstrated significant diffuse atrophy, periventricular white matter lesions, and lacunar infarcts in the thalamus and frontal lobes.

Which of the following regimens is the most appropriate pharmacologic intervention?

(A) Trazodone 25 mg twice daily
(B) Clonazepam 1 mg three times daily
(C) Lorazepam 1 mg as needed
(D) Buspirone 10 mg three times daily
(E) Olanzapine 5 mg daily   Zyprexa

ANSWER: E

Following appropriate assessment and attempts at nonpharmacologic interventions and recognizing that none of these interventions has a specific indication for use in dementia, treatment with psychotropic medication is appropriate for management of agitated aggressive behavior in patients with dementia. A placebo-controlled trial demonstrated that the atypical antipsychotic agent olanzapine[OL], 5 mg daily, was well tolerated and effective at decreasing agitation, aggression, and psychosis. Three large randomized controlled trials with risperidone[OL] note similar benefits at doses of approximately 1 mg daily. However, a threefold increased risk of cerebrovascular events has been

---

[OL] Not approved by the U.S. Food and Drug Administration for this use.

observed in double-blind, placebo-controlled trials of both drugs in comparison with placebo. It remains unclear to what extent other antipsychotics display this increased risk.

There is less evidence supporting the use of trazodone[OL]; the most recent study demonstrated no increased benefit in comparison with placebo. Other studies have suggested that trazodone can be effective and may also be useful in low doses as an hypnotic. Carbamazepine[OL] has been shown to be effective at decreasing agitation and aggression in patients with dementia. This patient receives warfarin, however, and an induction of hepatic metabolism could lead to decreases of the international normalized ratio. Divalproex sodium[OL] may provide similar benefits with less risk of drug interactions.

Benzodiazepines[OL] have not been well studied for agitation and aggression in dementia and carry the risk of excessive sedation, falls, and development of tolerance. The use of medication as needed for this patient might not be helpful in pre-empting aggressive behaviors. Some data support the use of buspirone[OL], but one placebo-controlled study did not demonstrate any significant benefit for the treatment of agitation.

References

1. Brodaty H, Ames D, Snowdon J, et al. A randomized placebo-controlled trial of risperidone for the treatment of aggression, agitation, and psychosis of dementia. *J Clin Psychiatry.* 2003;64(2):134–143.
2. Brodaty H, Low LF. Aggression in the elderly. *J Clin Psychiatry.* 2003;64(Suppl 4):36–43.
3. Herrmann N. Recommendations for the management of behavioral and psychological symptoms of dementia. *Can J Neurol Sci.* 2001;28(Suppl 1):S96–S107.
4. Street JS, Clark WS, Gannon KS, et al. Olanzapine treatment of psychotic and behavioral symptoms in patients with Alzheimer disease in nursing care facilities. *Arch Gen Psychiatry.* 2000;57(10):968–976.
5. Teri L, Logsdon RG, Peskind E, et al. Treatment of agitation in AD: a randomized, placebo-controlled clinical trial. *Neurology.* 2000;55(9):1271–1278.
6. Wooltorton E. Olanzapine (Zyprexa): increased incidence of cerebrovascular events in dementia trials. *CMAJ.* 2004;170(9):1395.

[OL] Not approved by the U.S. Food and Drug Administration for this use.

216. An 87-year-old woman with Alzheimer's disease comes to the office with her daughter for advice on managing care. She lives with her daughter, who works during the day. Over the past year she has become increasingly dependent in her instrumental activities of daily living. Four months ago, the daughter noticed that her mother was forgetting to eat the prepared lunch and neglecting to take her afternoon medications. She began to sleep more during the day and was awake and confused at night. The mother and daughter are committed to keeping the mother at home as long as possible. They are not willing to hire caregivers at home because they find them too unreliable.

Which of the following would be most appropriate to suggest as the next step in managing the mother's care?

(A) Nursing-home placement
(B) Enrollment in adult day care
(C) Referral to home-health care
(D) Referral to respite care
(E) Assisted-living placement

ANSWER: B

This patient does not require nursing-home care at this time. She may qualify for personal home care, but other, community-based alternatives can be offered initially. Adult day health care, where available, is an excellent alternative for older adults who need monitoring and some care during the day when primary caregivers are working or need respite. The services may range from nonskilled care, including bathing and grooming, to highly skilled care, including wound care management. Often activities are geared toward clients with dementia to keep them stimulated and awake during the day, so that they are less likely to be awake during the night. The charges for adult day health care are often based on a sliding scale. Transportation may be provided by the centers.

Home-care agencies do not provide long-term intervention or nonskilled services in the home. Respite care would only provide very short-term relief and would not be in the daughter's home. Assisted living does not make sense because it removes the patient from her daughter's home.

References

1. Hollander M, Prince MJ. *Analysis of Interfaces along the Continuum of Care*. Victoria, British Columbia: Hollander Analytic Services Inc., 2002.
2. Levine C. *Rough Crossings: Family Caregivers Odysseys Through the Healthcare System*. New York: United Hospital Fund of New York; 1998.
3. Wenger NS, Young R. Quality indicators for continuity and coordination of care in vulnerable elders. American College of Physicians, December 30, 2003. Available at www.acponline.org/sci-policy/acove (accessed April 2005; temporarily unavailable September 2005).

2. Carr D, House JS, Kessler RC, et al. Marital quality and psychological adjustment to widowhood among older adults: a longitudinal analysis. *J Gerontol B Psychol Sci Soc Sci*. 2000; 55(4):S197–S207.
3. Christakis NA, Iwashyna TJ. The health impact of health care on families: a matched cohort study of hospice use by decedents and mortality outcomes in surviving, widowed spouses. *Soc Sci Med*. 2003; 57(3):465–475.
4. Walsh K, King M, Tookman A, et al. Spiritual beliefs may affect outcome of bereavement: a prospective study. *BMJ*. 2002; 324(7353):1551.

217. A 75-year-old woman cared for her 78-year-old husband with metastatic cancer in their home until he died.

Which of the following most strongly predicts an uncomplicated course of bereavement?

(A) A high level of dependence on her husband before his illness
(B) The involvement of a hospice agency in the husband's care
(C) The wife's lack of religious belief
(D) The presence of considerable pain in the husband's final days

ANSWER: B

Research on the impact of a spouse's death has demonstrated several factors that may predict the degree of difficulty in the bereavement. Factors that predict a fairly straightforward bereavement include the surviving spouse's having religious beliefs and being less dependent on the deceased person prior to the terminal illness. Also, a death characterized by physical comfort, social support, and appropriate medical care appears to attenuate anxiety and intrusive thoughts during bereavement. Enrollment in a hospice program may alleviate some of the more disturbing symptoms of bereavement in survivors. In one large study, enrollment in a hospice program appeared to decrease the mortality rate of the surviving spouses, especially when the survivors were women.

References

1. Carr D. A "good death" for whom? quality of spouse's death and psychological distress among older widowed persons. *J Health Soc Behav*. 2003; 44(2):215–232.

218. A 90-year-old woman comes to the office because she has had blurring, pain, constant tearing, foreign body sensation, and itching in both eyes for several months. Her conjunctiva are red but without discharge.

Which of the following is the most likely cause?

(A) Blepharitis
(B) Herpes simplex
(C) Dry eye
(D) Bacterial conjunctivitis
(E) Viral conjunctivitis

ANSWER: C

Dry eye is especially common in older persons. It causes an irregular corneal surface, which produces blurred vision, and is often associated with pain and foreign body sensation. Dry eye is exacerbated in patients who have decreased blinking, as in Parkinson's disease.

Tears provide oxygen to the corneal surface and flush the eye of debris. The meibomian glands and glands of Zeis and Moll in the lids contribute a lipid layer to the tear film. The aqueous layer comes primarily from the lacrimal gland. If the lipid layer of tears is abnormal, it leads to an unstable aqueous layer. When the eye is irritated from a lack of tears, the lacrimal gland may be stimulated to release more aqueous tears and the patient may experience excessive tearing, as well as itching due to the dryness.

Tear substitutes, including preservative-free tears, are the mainstay of treatment of dry eyes. Ophthalmic ointments and gels are also available. Occluding the punctum in the eyelids can help prolong the effectiveness of the tears and tear substitute. Recently, an ophthalmic preparation of cyclosporine has been introduced to treat moderate to severe dry eye.

Blepharitis may be associated with dry eyes, but crusting of the lid margins would be present. Herpes simplex is often associated with pain and blurring but usually presents unilaterally, and fluorescein dye on the cornea would reveal a dendrite. Bacterial conjunctivitis presents with discharge and redness of the conjunctivae. Viral conjunctivitis presents acutely with redness, chemosis, tearing, and often increased preauricular lymph nodes.

References

1. Brodie SE. Aging and disorders of the eye. In: Tallis RC, Fillit HM, eds. *Brocklehurst's Textbook of Geriatric Medicine and Gerontology.* 6th ed. London: Churchill Livingston; 2003:735–747.
2. Huang FC, Tseng SH, Shih MH, et al. Effect of artificial tears on corneal surface regularity, contrast sensitivity, and glare disability in dry eyes. *Ophthalmology.* 2002;109(10):1934–1940.
3. Sall K, Stevenson OD, Mundorf TK, et al. Two multicenter, randomized studies of the efficacy and safety of cyclosporin ophthalmic emulsion in moderate to severe dry eye disease. *Ophathalmology.* 2000;107(4):631–639.

219. A 72-year-old white woman comes to the office because she has a new rash on her face and arms. The skin is burning and stinging; there is no itching. She noticed the rash after she was walking outside in the park. She did not use sunscreen because she usually does not get sunburns. She has a history of hypertension and osteoarthritis and has taken lisinopril, aspirin, and ibuprofen for several years. Two weeks earlier she was prescribed hydrochlorothiazide as well. She has not been using any cream on her skin, new soap, or other chemicals.

On physical examination, she has diffuse erythema of the face, neck, forearms, and dorsum of hands. Some edema, vesicles, and bullae are also present. There are spared areas behind the ears, upper eyelids, under the chin, above the upper lip, in neck creases, and under the watch strap. Complete blood cell count, renal panel, and urinalysis are normal.

Which of the following is the most likely cause of the rash?

(A) Sunburn
(B) Phototoxic drug-induced photosensitivity
(C) Photoallergic drug-induced photosensitivity
(D) Contact dermatitis
(E) Drug-induced lupus erythematosus

ANSWER: B

Drug-induced photosensitivity is a rash due to exposure to certain drugs and to ultraviolet radiation. Phototoxic drug-induced photosensitivity is an exaggerated sunburn response with erythema, edema, and vesicles. An eczematous reaction is not seen. It causes pruritus, burning, or stinging and is confined to areas exposed to light. Skin that is covered or in the shade is not affected (eg, areas behind the ears, upper eyelids, under the chin, above the upper lip, in neck creases, and under the watch band). Common causes for phototoxic drug-induced photosensitivity are amiodarone, thiazides, coal tar and derivatives, doxycycline, furosemide, nalidixic acid, tetracyclines, phenothiazine, nonsteroidal anti-inflammatory drugs, quinolones (especially sparfloxacin and enoxacin), and sulfonamides. Some of these drugs can also cause photoallergic reactions. It is not known why some people develop this reaction but others do not. Phototoxic drug reactions disappear after cessation of the drug.

In photoallergic drug-induced photosensitivity, the drug present in the skin forms a photo product by absorbing photons; the drug binds to a protein and forms antigen. Photoallergy depends on the individual's immunologic reactivity and is much less common than phototoxic drug reactions. The most common causes are topically applied agents that interact with sunlight, including topical local anesthetics (benzocaine), biocides added to soaps (halogenated phenolic compounds), stilbene in whiteners, and fragrances such as musk ambrette in aftershave lotions and 6-methyl coumarin in sunscreens. Systemic photoallergens such as the phenothiazine, sulfonamides, neomycin, and nonsteroidal anti-inflammatory drugs can produce photoallergic reactions, although most of their reactions are phototoxic. The rash in photoallergic drug reaction is on sun-exposed areas but may spread to adjacent nonexposed skin. The skin rash is similar to eczematous dermatitis or lichen planus–like eruptions. In chronic drug photoallergy, as in atopic dermatitis or chronic contact dermatitis, there is scaling, lichenification, and pruritus. With time, the condition becomes independent of the original photoallergen, and avoidance of the photoallergen may not resolve the problem. The condition may then worsen with each sun exposure; severe cases are treated with immunosuppression.

In this case, the rash is not likely to be sunburn as the patient has not previously developed a rash after sun exposure. Contact dermatitis is not likely as the rash is only on exposed areas. Lupus can present with a photo-sensitive rash, a malar "butterfly" rash, or a more diffuse maculopapular rash in sun-exposed areas. This patient does not have other symptoms suggestive of lupus and is not on a medication, such as procainamide or hydralazine, that is known to cause a lupus-like syndrome.

References

1. Dawe RS, Ibbotson SH, Sanderson JB, et al. A randomized controlled trial (volunteer study) of sitafloxacin, enoxacin, levofloxacin and sparfloxacin phototoxicity. *Br J Dermatol.* 2003;149(6):1232–1241.
2. Moore DE. Drug-induced cutaneous photosensitivity: incidence, mechanism, prevention and management. *Drug Saf.* 2002;25(5):345–372.
3. Part I: Disorders presenting in the skin and mucous membranes. Section 8: Photosensitivity and photo induced disorders. Drug–induced photosensitivity. In: Fitzpatrick TB, Johnson RA, Wolf K, et al., eds. *Color Atlas and Synopsis of Clinical Dermatology.* 4th ed. New York: The McGraw-Hill Companies; 2001.

220. An 86-year-old woman comes to the office because she has urinary frequency, urgency, urge incontinence, leakage of urine when bending over and climbing stairs, and a sensation of incomplete bladder emptying. She has hyper-tension and an early dementia syndrome. She takes a combination of a thiazide diuretic and angiotensin receptor blocker, and a cholinesterase inhibitor.

On physical examination, she has signs of mild atrophic vaginitis, a moderate cystocele, normal rectal sphincter tone, and no fecal impaction. A cough test for stress incontinence is positive in the standing position before voiding 100 mL; postvoid residual is 225 mL. Urinalysis is unremarkable.

Which of the following is the most likely cause of her symptoms?

(A) Stress incontinence
(B) Diuretic-induced incontinence
(C) Cholinesterase inhibitor–induced inconti-nence
(D) Detrusor hyperactivity with impaired bladder contractility
(E) Urinary retention and incontinence due to cystocele

ANSWER: D

This patient has symptoms and findings typical of detrusor hyperactivity with impaired bladder contractility. Affected patients have two simulta-neous abnormalities of bladder function: invol-untary bladder contractions and weakness of the detrusor muscle resulting in incomplete bladder emptying with the involuntary (and voluntary) bladder contractions. Detrusor hyperactivity with impaired bladder contractility can cause several different symptoms, as in this patient, and can mimic stress incontinence. Diuretics can exacerbate symptoms of detrusor hyperactivity, but a thiazide diuretic is unlikely to be the primary cause of symptoms in this patient. Cholinesterase inhibitors can theoretically increase bladder contractions, but there are no data to support this assertion. In older women with severe pelvic prolapse, urethral obstruction can cause difficulty with bladder emptying. This patient, however, does not have severe pelvic prolapse; even if she had some urethral obstruction due to the cystocele, this would not account for all of her symptoms.

References

1. Griffiths DJ, McCracken PN, Harrison GM, et al. Urge incontinence and impaired detrusor contrac-tility in the elderly. *Neurourol Urodyn.* 2002;21(2):126–131.
2. Resnick NM, Yalla SV. Detrusor hyperactivity with impaired contractile function: an unrecognized but common cause of incontinence in elderly patients. *JAMA.* 1987; 257(22):3076–3081.

221. A 77-year-old man comes to the office because of insomnia and nocturia. He lives alone in a continuing-care community that he joined 8 months ago. On a medical history form, he describes himself as a social drinker. Other than a recent hospitalization for pancreatitis, he has been healthy. Alcohol use is considered as a potential cause of or contributor to the pancreatitis and the sleep and urinary symptoms.

Which of the following is the most appropriate next step?

(A) Measurement of carbohydrate-deficient transferrin serum level
(B) Measurement of alanine and aspartate aminotransferase
(C) Close-ended questions about symptoms and consequences of drinking
(D) Close-ended questions about quantity and frequency of drinking
(E) Screening questionnaire with items on quantity, frequency, and effects of drinking

ANSWER: E

A screening questionnaire offers the best approach to assessing alcohol use disorders because it combines accuracy and convenience. The standardized wording is useful for this potentially sensitive topic and reduces the potential for biasing responses. The Michigan Alcoholism Screening Test—Geriatric Version (MAST–G) and the Alcohol-Related Problems Survey (ARPS) were both designed to identify problems in older persons. ARPS distinguishes between nonhazardous and hazardous or harmful drinking by correlating range of drinking with age-related physiologic changes, decreasing health and functional status, and medication use. Both the MAST–G and the ARPS are available in short and self-report forms. Other screening questionnaires, such as CAGE (Cut down, Annoyed by criticism, Guilty feelings about drinking, Eye-opener) or the Alcohol Use Disorders Identification Test (AUDIT), detect cases that meet *Diagnostic and Statistical Manual of Mental Disorders* (*DSM*) criteria for current or past alcohol dependence or abuse, but may not yield information about current drinking or problems not specifically defined by *DSM* criteria.

Close-ended questions about symptoms and consequences of drinking may yield some information relevant to current or past dependence or abuse. However, such questions fail to yield information about the quantity and frequency of drinking. Likewise, close-ended questions about quantity and frequency of alcohol use may yield information about current drinking, but not about symptoms or consequences of drinking. Depending on their wording, close-ended questions may also prompt denial of drinking.

Carbohydrate deficient transferrin is a marker for heavy, regular alcohol use. It is 60% to 75% sensitive and 70% to 80% specific for detecting daily use that exceeds 50 g of ethanol, and its sensitivity improves with increased alcohol consumption. However, the utility of the test may be limited in older people, in whom alcohol-related problems may develop at much lower levels of daily use. A disproportionate increase in aspartate compared with alanine aminotransferase, such that the ratio of aspartate to alanine exceeds 2.0, is suggestive of alcoholic hepatitis. However, the sensitivity and specificity of alanine and aspartate aminotransferases are lower for detecting other alcohol-related problems in older people.

References

1. Fiellin DA, Reid MC, O'Connor PG. Screening for alcohol problems in primary care: a systematic review. *Arch Intern Med*. 2000;160:1977–1989.
2. Fink A, Morton SC, Beck JC, et al. The Alcohol-Related Problems Survey: identifying hazardous and harmful drinking in older primary care patients. *J Am Geriatr Soc*. 2002;50:1717–1722.

222. On routine pelvic examination, a 72-year-old woman is found to have vaginal mucosal pallor and thinning as well as decreased vaginal folds. She notes that during sexual intercourse she experiences dyspareunia and occasional vaginal bleeding.

Which of the following is the most appropriate treatment?

(A) Topical corticosteroid cream
(B) Topical estrogen cream
(C) Topical nystatin cream
(D) Topical metronidazole cream
(E) Single-dose fluconazole, 150 mg

ANSWER: B

Vulvovaginal disorders common in postmenopausal women include atrophic vaginitis, vaginal candidiasis, squamous cell hyperplasia, and lichen sclerosus. Between 10% and 40% of postmenopausal women have symptoms of atrophic vaginitis. Reduced levels of endogenous estrogen cause a thinning of the vaginal epithelium. Genital symptoms can include loss of vaginal secretions, burning, dyspareunia, and vulvar pruritus. Urinary symptoms can include frequency, urinary tract infection, and dysuria. On physical examination, the vaginal epithelium is thin, pale, and smooth with few or no vaginal folds. Inflammation may be present, with patchy erythema and increased friability. Vaginal examination or sexual activity can result in vaginal bleeding or spotting. Treatment consists of transvaginal delivery of estrogen in the form of a topical cream or hormone-releasing ring (Estring). Nightly use of one half of an applicator of the topical cream, for 2 weeks, is usually sufficient to alleviate symptoms.

Vulvar candidiasis is associated with pruritus, burning, and occasionally dysuria and dyspareunia. It causes large patches of erythema involving the labia majora, genitocrural folds, perianal area, and inner thighs. Vaginal erythema and a cottage cheese–like discharge may be present. Treatment is either with a single oral dose of fluconazole 150 mg or with topical antimycotic creams such as clotrimazole or nystatin.

Lichen sclerosus is a pruritic vulvar condition. Dyspareunia is often a late symptom associated with introital stenosis. On physical examination, the skin of the labia minora or labia majora becomes thin, white, and wrinkled. As the disease progresses, the labia majora and minora become fused. Treatment is with a highly potent topical corticosteroid, such as clobetasol or halobetasol propionate.

Bacterial vaginosis causes an unpleasant, "fishy smelling" discharge. There is no pruritus or inflammation, and dyspareunia is rare. The diagnosis is confirmed by presence of clue cells on a saline wet mount slide. A positive whiff-amine test causes a fishy odor when 10% potassium hydroxide is added to the vaginal discharge. Treatment includes metronidazole or clindamycin administered orally or intravaginally.

References

1. Bachman GA, Nevadunsky NS. Diagnosis and treatment of the atrophic vaginitis. *Am Fam Physician*. 2000;61(10):3090–3096.
2. National guideline for the management of bacterial vaginosis. Clinical Effectiveness Group (Association of Genitourinary Medicine and the Medical Society for the Study of Venereal Diseases). *Sex Transm Infect*. 1999;75(Suppl 1):S16–S18.
3. Powell JJ, Wojnarowska F. Lichen sclerosis. *Lancet*. 1999;353(9166):1777–1783.
4. Sobel JD, Faro S, Force RW, et al. Vulvovaginal candidiasis: epidemiological, diagnostic, and therapeutic considerations. *Am J Obstet Gynecol*. 1998;178(2):203–211.

223. An 80-year-old woman comes to the emergency department with acute severe mid thoracic back pain after a fall. A thoracic vertebral fracture is diagnosed. The patient has a history of osteoporosis, for which she takes calcium, vitamin D, and a bisphosphonate. An orthopedic surgeon suggests vertebroplasty.

Which of the following is likely to result from the vertebroplasty procedure?

(A) Greater need for analgesia
(B) More rapid pain relief in comparison with traditional therapeutic measures
(C) Reduced morbidity in comparison with traditional therapeutic measures
(D) Restoration of height

ANSWER: B

The traditional management of acute osteoporotic vertebral spine fractures comprises analgesics, rest, and physical therapy, with an emphasis on resuming activity as soon as possible. Surgical approaches include vertebroplasty and kyphoplasty. Vertebroplasty is the percutaneous injection of bone cement into the vertebral body under fluoroscopic guidance. Kyphoplasty uses a balloon tamp in the fractured vertebral body for elevation of the endplates prior to fixation of the fracture, so that cement is delivered to the cavity created by the balloon, the fracture is reduced, and vertebral height is restored. The precise indications for these procedures are evolving. The procedures seem effective in controlling pain. A nonrandomized series of comparable patients with osteoporotic fractures demonstrated superior pain relief and physical function in the acute postfracture period for patients receiving vertebroplasty. Vertebroplasty could possibly relieve this patient's pain rapidly, reducing the need for analgesia. Since the procedure is percutaneous, pain from vertebroplasty should be minimal.

Long-term data on pulmonary function and mortality are not available. Vertebral height is restored with kyphoplasty, but not with vertebroplasty. Complications of these procedures are cement leakage or extravasation resulting in increased pain, and nerve damage from heat or pressure. In vertebroplasty, installation of cement under high pressure has been associated with adult respiratory distress syndrome and, rarely, death. There is concern that adjacent vertebral fractures may occur because of changes in mechanical forces after these procedures. Thus, the overall impact on morbidity in comparison with traditional treatments has yet to be established.

References

1. Cornell CN, Lane JM, Poynoton AR. Orthopedic management of vertebral and long bone fractures in patients with osteoporosis. *Clin Geriatr Med.* 2003;19(2):433–455.
2. Diamond TH, Champion B, Clark WA. Management of acute osteoporotic vertebral fractures: a nonrandomized trial comparing percutaneous vertebroplasty with conservative therapy. *Am J Med.* 2003;114(4):257–265.
3. Watts NB, Harris ST, Genant HK. Treatment of painful osteoporotic vertebral fractures with percutaneous vertebroplasty or kyphoplasty. *Osteoporos Int.* 2001;12:429–437.

224. An 85-year-old woman with known coronary artery disease, hypertension, chronic renal insufficiency, anemia, and osteoarthritis comes to the emergency department with acute shortness of breath that began when she was preparing dinner. She had no chest discomfort, diaphoresis, nausea, dizziness, or syncope. When the shortness of breath did not resolve after 15 minutes, she contacted the emergency medical service. En route to the hospital she received oxygen and nitroglycerin sublingually, with moderate improvement.

On physical examination, she is in moderate respiratory distress; respiratory rate is 24 per minute and oxygen saturation is 92% on 2 L of oxygen. Heart rate is 110 per minute and blood pressure is 190/80 mm Hg. Neck veins are flat and carotid upstrokes are normal. Bibasilar crackles are noted in the lower and middle lung fields bilaterally. Cardiac auscultation demonstrates a regular tachycardia with an S_4 gallop but no S_3 or murmurs. Abdomen is soft and nontender. Pulses are symmetric, and there is no peripheral edema.

Laboratory studies:
Arterial blood gases on
  2 L oxygen
    PO_2 61 mm Hg
    PCO_2 30 mm Hg
    pH   7.47
Creatinine   2.6 mg/dL
Blood urea nitrogen   34 mg/dL
Hemoglobin   11.1 g/dL
Troponin I   0.4 ng/mL (normal
                          0 to 0.4 ng/mL)

Repeat troponin I (6
  hours later)   1.5 ng/mL

Electrocardiography demonstrates sinus tachycardia, moderate left ventricular hypertrophy, and 2- to 3-mm downsloping ST segment depression in leads V_4-V_6. Chest radiograph shows mild cardiomegaly and moderate pulmonary congestion.

In addition to aspirin and furosemide, what is the most appropriate treatment for this patient's condition?

(A) Intravenous heparin, β-blocker, and angiotensin receptor blocker
(B) Low-molecular-weight heparin, diltiazem, and angiotensin-converting enzyme inhibitor
(C) Low-molecular-weight heparin, β-blocker, and nitroglycerin infusion
(D) Glycoprotein IIb/IIIa inhibitor, β-blocker, and urgent coronary angiography
(E) Intravenous heparin, diltiazem, and urgent coronary angiography

ANSWER: C

On the basis of this patient's history, physical findings, and laboratory data, the most likely diagnosis is an acute non−ST-elevation myocardial infarction. Optimal treatment includes antithrombotic therapy, anti-ischemic medication, blood-pressure control, and, in selected cases, urgent coronary angiography and revascularization. Low-molecular-weight heparin (LMWH) has been associated with outcomes superior to those with intravenous unfractionated heparin in older patients, and recent studies indicate that, with proper dosing, impaired kidney function is not a contraindication to LMWH. A β-blocker is indicated to control heart rate and to help lower blood pressure, and nitroglycerin is warranted as an anti-ischemic agent as well as for its effects in lowering blood pressure and reducing pulmonary congestion. Glycoprotein IIb/IIIa inhibitors are associated with increased bleeding risk in older adults and are contraindicated in the presence of severe renal insufficiency. Angiotensin-converting enzyme inhibitors and angiotensin-receptor blockers have not been shown to be efficacious in the acute phase of non−ST-elevation myocardial infarction, and diltiazem is contraindicated in patients with overt heart failure. Urgent catheterization and revascularization have been associated with improved outcomes in several studies, but none have included very elderly patients with advanced renal insufficiency, who are at substantially increased risk for procedure-related complications.

References

1. Braunwald E, Antman EM, Beasley JW, et al. ACC/AHA 2002 guideline update for the management of patients with unstable angina and non-ST-segment elevation myocardial infarction—summary article. *J Am Coll Cardiol.* 2002;40(7):1366–1374.
2. Braunwald E, Antman EM, Beasley JW, et al. ACC/AHA guidelines for the management of patients with unstable angina and non-ST-segment elevation myocardial infarction. *J Am Coll Cardiol.* 2000;36:970–1062.
3. Cannon CP, Weintraub WS, Demopoulos LA, et al. Comparison of early invasive and conservative strategies in patients with unstable coronary syndromes treated with the glycoprotein IIb/IIIa inhibitor tirofiban. *N Engl J Med.* 2001;344(25):1879–1887.
4. Nagge J, Crowther M, Hirsh J. Is impaired renal function a contraindication to the use of low-molecular-weight heparin? *Arch Intern Med.* 2002;162(22):2605–2609.

225. An 82-year-old man comes to the office for a routine physical examination. He has a history of hypertension and atrial fibrillation. He reports episodes of dizziness and has occasional diarrhea but no melena or hematochezia. Medications include atenolol, digoxin, and warfarin. He was the primary caregiver for his wife; she died 1 year ago after a long struggle with cancer. He admits to being fatigued and to having a poor appetite, but he does not think that he is depressed. On examination, blood pressure and heart rate are well controlled; his blood pressure is 138/70 mm Hg, pulse is 60 per minute, respiratory rate is 14 per minute, and temperature is 36.7°C (98°F). He has lost 6.4 kg (14 lb; 6% of his body weight) over the past 6 months. The rest of the physical examination shows no substantial changes from the previous visit.

Which of the following is most likely to reveal the cause of this man's weight loss?

(A) Fecal occult blood testing
(B) Serum digoxin level
(C) Geriatric depression screen
(D) Home visit
(E) Chest radiography

ANSWER: B

Anorexia, fatigue, diarrhea, and dizziness are common effects of digoxin toxicity and may result in significant weight loss. Other adverse effects include bradycardia, ventricular arrhythmias, apathy, nausea, confusion, visual disturbances, and depression. There is some controversy surrounding digoxin levels, as some patients may have toxicity at laboratory-established normal levels. Higher levels correlate with more adverse reactions. Clinically, if subacute digoxin toxicity is suspected, a trial of tapering off the drug without testing may also be reasonable.

Medication review should be part of the assessment of weight loss. Fecal occult blood testing to screen for malignancy or hemorrhage is reasonable, but these diagnoses are not as likely as digoxin toxicity. The Geriatric Depression Scale may be positive, but depression should not be considered endogenous until digoxin toxicity is excluded. Depression will likely be refractory until the toxicity resolves. A home visit may determine if the patient is caring for himself and has quality nutritional resources available. However, any poor home conditions may be due to digoxin-related fatigue and apathy. There is little in this case to suggest that chest radiography will be helpful.

References

1. Abad-Santos F, Carcas AJ, Ibanez C, et al. Digoxin level and clinical manifestations as determinants in the diagnosis of digoxin toxicity. *Ther Drug Monit.* 2000;22(2):163–168.
2. Canas F, Tanasijevic MJ, Ma'luf N, et al. Evaluating the appropriateness of digoxin level monitoring. *Arch Intern Med.* 1999;159(4):363–368.
3. Onder G, Penninx BW, Landi F, et al. Depression and adverse drug reactions among hospitalized older adults. *Arch Intern Med.* 2003; 163(3):301–305.

226. A 90-year-old resident of a skilled nursing facility has fallen three times in the past month. She has a history of dementia, hypertension, atrial fibrillation, osteoarthritis, and transient ischemic attacks. She walks with a walker. Medications include hydrochlorothiazide 25 mg daily, atenolol 50 mg daily, warfarin 2 mg daily, celecoxib 100 mg daily, calcium carbonate 600 mg twice daily, a multivitamin daily, donepezil 10 mg daily, and lorazepam 0.25 mg twice daily as needed.

Which of the following should be done first to assess her risk for future falls?

(A) Order 24-hour cardiac monitoring.
(B) Measure her blood pressure when she is lying down, sitting, and standing.
(C) Review the circumstances of her falls.
(D) Ask the physical therapist to evaluate her gait, transfers, and walker.

ANSWER: C

The first step in investigating falls by nursing-home residents is to review the circumstances of the fall. Given this patient's dementia, it is likely that she does not remember the falls. Nursing staff should be asked about times and locations of the falls, her activity at the time of the falls, whether any environmental hazards were involved, and whether the patient lost consciousness. The circumstances of the falls will direct further investigation and treatment of risk factors. For example, if the patient falls after going to bed because side rails are raised, the management would be to leave the side rails down or place the bed on the floor.

If there was loss of consciousness, the physician and staff would be directed toward a work-up of syncope, including 24-hour heart monitoring. If there was no apparent loss of consciousness, then other risk factors should be investigated.

A major risk factor for falls is taking four or more medications on a regular basis. Classes of high-risk medications include anticholinergics, antipsychotic medications, antidepressants, sedatives, narcotic pain medications, medications for anxiety, antihypertensives, and diuretics. Medications are more likely to cause problems when a new one has been added, the patient has an acute illness or change in condition, or the patient has been recently discharged from the hospital. Reviewing and, if possible, reducing the number or dosage of medications should be done regularly.

Symptomatic or asymptomatic orthostatic hypotension may occur in more than 50% of frail elderly nursing-home residents and may have contributed to this patient's falls. In evaluating her fall risk, the clinician should measure her blood pressure when she is measured lying down, sitting, and standing and should do this several times during the day to check for postural changes. A drop in systolic pressure of 20 mm Hg or more 3 minutes after standing is positive. Measurement of the patient's blood pressure would be a useful step after exploring the circumstances of her falls, which may reveal solely an environmental cause.

Decreased mobility with abnormal gait and transfers is another important risk factor for falls. Physical therapy, followed by regular supervised exercise, can help nursing-home residents improve mobility. After a fall, assistive devices (canes, walkers, wheelchairs) should be checked to make sure they are in good repair. Nonetheless, evaluation by physical therapy would not be the first action to evaluate this patient's fall risk.

References

1. American Geriatrics Society, British Geriatrics Society, and American Academy of Orthopaedic Surgeons Panel on Falls Prevention. Guideline for the prevention of falls in older persons. *J Am Geriatr Soc.* 2001;49(5):664–672.
2. Mukai S, Lipsitz LA. Orthostatic hypotension. *Clin Geriatr Med.* 2002;18(2):253–268.

227. A man inquires about whether his 80-year-old aunt can receive house calls for her medical care. She lives by herself in a second-floor apartment in a building with no elevator. She has morbid obesity, coronary artery disease, heart failure, adult-onset diabetes mellitus, hyperlipidemia, asthma, and chronic back pain. She is independent in activities of daily living, but can walk only 10 feet with a walker. She cannot negotiate steps, which constitute the only access to her apartment; she never leaves her apartment, other than when she is hospitalized. Her nephew brings her meals and assists in other instrumental activities of daily living. For health coverage, she has traditional Medicare Parts A and B and no supplemental insurance.

How would Medicare compensate for a house call to this patient?

(A) Medicare Part A would pay on a capitation basis.
(B) Medicare Part A would pay on a fee-for-service basis.
(C) Medicare Part B would pay on a capitation basis.
(D) Medicare Part B would pay on a fee-for-service basis.
(E) Medicare would not pay for physician home visits.

ANSWER: D

Medicare considers patients to be homebound if they have medical conditions that make leaving their home a "considerable and taxing effort." Homebound patients are normally unable to leave home for nonmedical reasons. Thus, this patient would be eligible for home-care coverage. Part A compensates home-care agencies for nonphysician home services on a fixed-fee basis. Part B reimburses physicians on a fee-for-service basis for home visits. A physician may also bill an additional monthly for oversight of the care plan if he or she documents spending at least 30 minutes each month on overseeing all the home care provided to the patient. Traditional Medicare is not a capitation program.

References

1. Centers for Medicare and Medicaid Services. Home Health Information Resource for Medicare page. Available at http://www.cms.gov/providers/hha/default.asp? (accessed September 2005).
2. Centers for Medicare and Medicaid Services. Medicare Glossary page. Available at http://www.medicare.gov/Glossary/search.asp?SelectAlphabet=H&Language=English (accessed September 2005).

228. A 72-year-old woman is referred for evaluation of erythrocytosis. She reports no fevers, chills, sweats, pruritus, visual or auditory disturbance, headache, or dyspnea. She had two episodes of dizziness a few months ago that resolved after several minutes. She is of Ashkenazi Jewish background, but there is no family history of hematologic disease. She is a former cigarette smoker (1 pack daily for 25 years) but she quit smoking 20 years ago.

On physical examination, she appears plethoric, but she is in no acute distress. Temperature is 36.2°C (97.2°F), blood pressure is 166/98 mm Hg, pulse is 91 per minute, and respiratory rate is 14 per minute. The spleen is identifiable by percussion and just palpable at the costal margin. Otherwise, the physical examination is unremarkable.

Laboratory studies 1 year ago included hemoglobin, 16.4 g/dL; erythrocyte count, 5 × 10^6/μL; leukocyte count, 10,600/μL. Last month, hemoglobin was 17.0g/dL.

Current laboratory tests:

Hemoglobin	18.2 g/dL
Leukocyte count	13,000/μL
Platelet count	454,000/μL
Erythropoietin level	< 2 (5–36 μ/L)
Serum iron	30 μg/dL
Iron-binding capacity	324 μg/dL
Oxygen saturation on room air	94%

Which of the following is true of this patient?

(A) She is likely to die in 5 years from fibrosis.
(B) She is likely to have prolonged survival with therapeutic phlebotomy.
(C) She is likely to have a major thrombotic complication such as stroke or Budd-Chiari syndrome.
(D) She is likely to die in 5 years from acute leukemia.

ANSWER: B

This patient has polycythemia vera, which can be confirmed by measurement of red cell mass, but this test is no longer easily obtained in most departments of nuclear medicine. The diagnosis therefore rests on identification of primary erythrocytosis. In this case, many potential secondary causes have been excluded. Levels of erythropoietin are typically low in polycythemia vera on the basis of independent erythrocyte production. A so-called normal level, or an overtly elevated level, suggests erythrocytosis secondary to hypoxemia, hypercapnia, shunting, or tumor. Despite a suggestive history, this patient has relatively normal oxygen saturation and a markedly depressed erythropoietin level, consistent with diagnosis of primary erythrocytosis, or polycythemia vera.

The course of polycythemia vera is generally prolonged. Minor thrombotic complications are common and not completely ameliorated by therapeutic phlebotomy, but major complications, such as stroke or Budd-Chiari syndrome, are rare. Evolution to acute leukemia, in the absence of therapy with radioactive phosphorus or alkylating agents (now contraindicated), is rare. In one third of patients, polycythemia evolves to myelofibrosis. Marrow fibrosis should be suspected in a patient in whom there is spontaneous normalization of hemoglobin, increasing splenomegaly, and features of splenic sequestration. This complication occurs after more than a decade of polycythemia vera, though rarely progression to fibrosis is rapid.

References

1. Pearson TC. The risk of thrombosis in essential thrombocythemia and polycythemia vera. *Semin Oncol.* 2002;29(3 Suppl 10):16–21.
2. Ruggeri M, Tosetto A, Frezzato M, et al. The rate of progression to polycythemia vera or essential thrombocythemia in patients with erythrocytosis or thrombocytosis. *Ann Intern Med.* 2003;139(6):470–475.
3. Tefferi A. A contemporary approach to the diagnosis and management of polycythemia vera. *Curr Hematol Rep.* 2003;2(3):237–241.

229. Which of the following structures is most susceptible to age-related histopathologic changes that result in sensorineural hearing loss and dizziness?

(A) Inner ear
(B) Central auditory system
(C) Ossicles
(D) Tympanitic membrane
(E) External auditory canal

ANSWER: A

The inner ear contains the vestibular (balance) and auditory systems and lies in the petrous portion of the temporal bone. The neuronal and sensory cells in the balance and hearing mechanisms of the inner ear are nonmitotic; they are highly differentiated cells that cannot reproduce during adulthood. Their life span is determined by the ability to maintain structural organization within their environment. Degenerative changes occur throughout the auditory and vestibular systems of the inner ear. Age-related changes are especially prominent in the sensory receptors of the vestibular system, namely, the cristae of the semicircular canals and the maculae of the saccule and utricle. Further, there is a reduction in the hair cell population of the semicircular canals and the utricular and saccular maculae. The vasculature of the vestibular system also appears to change with age. The organ of Corti is the inner-ear structure most susceptible to age-related histopathologic changes. The basilar membrane, upon which the sensory hair cells of the inner ear lie, runs through the cochlea from its base to the apex. Degenerative changes are greatest along the basilar membrane, most notably the basal section that is responsive to high frequencies, thus contributing to the high-frequency hearing loss related to age.

There is also an age-associated loss of nerve fibers and ganglion cells, which is most pronounced in the basal turn of the cochlea.

The central auditory system relays information from the cochlea and eighth nerve to the auditory cortex. The central auditory system undergoes degenerative changes, but it is responsible for auditory processing, not balance.

The middle ear consists of the tympanic membrane, the tympanic cavity (an air-filled space containing a chain of three ossicles—the malleus, incus, and stapes), and the eustachian tube. Hearing loss due to damage to middle-ear structures is conductive, not sensorineural.

The eustachian tube connects the tympanic cavity to the nasopharynx. The outer ear comprises the external auditory meatus or canal and the pinna. Excessive build-up of cerumen in the external auditory canal is common in older adults and can result in conductive, not sensorineural, hearing loss.

References

1. Schuknecht H. *Pathology of the Ear.* 2nd ed. Philadelphia, PA: Lea and Febiger; 1993.
2. Willott J. Anatomic and physiologic aging: a behavioral neuroscience perspective. *J Am Acad Audiol.* 1996;7(3):141–151.

230. A 73-year-old man comes to the office because of shortness of breath. He has a 40 pack-year history of smoking. On physical examination, he has decreased breath sounds at the left base. Chest radiograph demonstrates moderate left pleural effusion; diagnostic thoracentesis is consistent with adenocarcinoma. Over the next week, computed tomographic scan of the chest and abdomen are performed and show no abnormalities other than the malignant pleural effusion. During this period, his shortness of breath worsens and therapeutic thoracentesis is performed. Stage IIIB non−small cell lung cancer is diagnosed. The patient states that quality of life is more important to him than life expectancy.

In addition to discussing the likely need for pleurodesis, what is the most appropriate management for this patient?

(A) Surgery
(B) Referral to hospice
(C) Radiation
(D) Chemotherapy

ANSWER: D

Surgery is the primary treatment in stages I and II non−small cell lung cancer and may be of benefit in stage IIIA, but it is not an option for stage IIIB. In this case, the disease is inoperable because there is malignant pleural effusion. Patients with malignant pleural effusion have a poor prognosis, and their disease course is similar to that of patients with metastases or stage IV lung cancer. Although radiation is useful for local control, it does not have much efficacy when used for fluid-filled cavities.

The benefits of hospice (best supportive care) and chemotherapy on quality of life were compared in the Elderly Lung Cancer Vinorelbine Italian Study (ELVIS), which randomly assigned 171 patients to either best supportive care or best supportive care with chemotherapy (vinorelbine). Patients who received chemotherapy had longer median survival, better quality of life, improved global health status, and improved physical, cognitive, and social functioning. Pain and shortness of breath were reduced. Although patients on chemotherapy had more nausea, vomiting, and neuropathy, adverse effects related to chemotherapy may be more tolerable than the symptoms of progressing untreated lung cancer, making a net benefit for chemotherapy on quality of life.

There is some controversy regarding benefit of single-agent and combined chemotherapy. Some trials, such as the Multicenter Italian Lung Cancer in the Elderly Study (MILES), have not shown a benefit to polychemotherapy (vinorelbine plus gemcitabine) over single-agent use (vinorelbine or gemcitabine), whereas other trials looking at carboplatin and paclitaxel have shown a benefit from polychemotherapy.

References

1. Bunn PA Jr, Lilenbaum R. Chemotherapy for elderly patients with advanced non-small-cell lung cancer. *J Natl Cancer Inst.* 2003;95(5):341–343.

2. Gridelli C. The ELVIS trial: a phase III study of single-agent vinorelbine as first-line treatment in elderly patients with advanced non-small cell lung cancer. Elderly Lung Cancer Vinorelbine Italian Study. *Oncologist*. 2001;6 (Suppl 1):4–7.
3. Gridelli C, Perrone F, Gallo C, et al. Chemotherapy for elderly patients with advanced non-small-cell lung cancer: the Multicenter Italian Lung Cancer in the Elderly Study (MILES) phase III randomized trial. *J Natl Cancer Inst*. 2003;95(5):362–372.

231. A 92-year-old woman is being treated with paroxetine for major depression following successful surgery for uncomplicated hip fracture. Her overall physical and cognitive status is otherwise good. She has mild hypertension and osteoarthritis, and she takes a thiazide diuretic and acetaminophen. Ten days after paroxetine is started, the patient's daughter calls to report that her mother is lethargic and confused.

Which of the following metabolic disturbances is the most likely cause of this patient's delirium?

(A) Hyponatremia
(B) Hypernatremia
(C) Hypoglycemia
(D) Hyperglycemia

ANSWER: A

Hyponatremia is a frequent, under-recognized, and potentially serious complication of treatment with selective serotonin-reuptake inhibitors (SSRIs) or venlafaxine in older patients. It is typically due to a transient syndrome of inappropriate antidiuretic hormone secretion (SIADH). During the first 2 weeks of treatment with an SSRI, plasma sodium concentrations decrease in almost half of older depressed patients, and 10% to 20% may become hyponatremic. Increased risk of SSRI-induced SIADH and hyponatremia is associated with older age, being female, lower baseline sodium level, lower body mass index, and concurrent use of a diuretic medication. Many affected patients are asymptomatic; symptomatic patients have nausea, anorexia, fatigue, or confusion, which can be mistaken for depressive symptoms or medication side effects. In patients at risk, it is prudent to monitor sodium before and 1 or 2 weeks after initiating treatment with an SSRI. At minimum, sodium level should be obtained in all elderly patients who exhibit abrupt changes in mental status (such as lethargy or confusion) upon initiation of an SSRI.

Hypernatremia or an acute change in glucose level is highly unlikely to be associated with SSRI treatment.

References
1. Barclay TS, Lee AJ. Citalopram-associated SIADH. *Ann Pharmacother*. 2002;36(10):1558–1563.
2. Fabian TJ, Amico JA, Kroboth PD, et al. Paroxetine-induced hyponatremia in older adults: a twelve-week prospective study. *Arch Intern Med*. 2004;164(3):327–332.
3. Finfgeld DL. SSRI-related hyponatremia among aging adults. *J Psychosocial Nurs Ment Health Serv*. 2003;41(4):12–16.
4. Kugler JP, Hustead T. Hyponatremia and hypernatremia in the elderly. *Am Fam Phys*. 2000;61(12):3623–3630.

232. An 86-year-old woman comes to the office because she has pelvic pressure, especially when moving her bowels. She has class III heart failure. On pelvic examination, she is found to have grade III uterine prolapse.

Which of the following is the most appropriate next step in her management?

(A) Refer for hysterectomy.
(B) Prescribe Kegel's exercises.
(C) Put a pessary in place.
(D) Prescribe topical estrogen.
(E) Prescribe a stool softener.

ANSWER: C

Genital prolapse is a downward displacement of one or all pelvic organs. The most common symptoms and signs include pelvic pressure, difficulty with rectal emptying, and a palpable mass. There may also be voiding dysfunction. Grade I prolapse involves extension of the cervix to the mid-vagina; in grade II prolapse the cervix approaches the hymenal ring; in grade III prolapse the cervix is at the hymenal ring; and in grade IV prolapse the cervix is beyond the ring.

Grades I and II prolapse can be treated with topical estrogen cream and Kegel's exercises to strengthen the pelvic floor musculature. Surgery, typically with general anesthesia, can be considered for more severe prolapse. Pessaries can be used to delay or avoid surgery in patients who have comorbid medical conditions or who do not want surgery. Patients must be fitted with a pessary. There are several types, including a ring pessary for mild to moderate prolapse, a Gellhorn pessary for moderate to severe prolapse, and a cube pessary for women in whom perivaginal muscle tone cannot support other types of pessaries. The cube pessary must be removed daily to prevent infection and erosions; the other types may be left in place for weeks, as they allow for drainage of vaginal secretions. The patient should be seen within 1 week of insertion and then regularly, depending on individual circumstances and the pessary type.

Topical estrogen cream alone does not help in the management of genital prolapse. Kegel's or pelvic muscle exercises are likely to have little effect in patients with grade III prolapse. Stool softeners and laxatives have no role in management of genital prolapse.

References

1. Bash KL. Review of vaginal pessaries. *Obstet Gynecol Surv.* 2000; 55(7):455–460.
2. Davila GW. Vaginal prolapse management with nonsurgical techniques. *Postgrad Med.* 1996; 99(4):171–176,181,184–185.

233. A 65-year-old woman has had symptoms of generalized anxiety since she was a teenager. At age 56, she had an episode of major depression with associated panic attacks. The depression and panic attacks resolved after she started taking hormone replacement therapy (HRT). She took HRT for 8 years; during that time, symptoms of generalized anxiety continued, but she did not have depression or panic attacks. She stopped HRT because of concerns about its cardiovascular risk. Four months later, she suffered a recurrence of panic attacks, but not depression. She is unwilling to take psychotropic medication, but would participate in psychologic treatment of the panic disorder.

Which of the following would be most beneficial for her?

(A) Cognitive-behavioral therapy
(B) Interpersonal psychotherapy
(C) Psychoanalytic psychotherapy
(D) Supportive psychotherapy

ANSWER: A

Cognitive-behavioral therapy is the psychologic treatment of choice for panic disorder. The premise of the cognitive model is that anxiety is caused not by events per se, but by the person's expectation and interpretation of events. According to this model, anxious persons overestimate the danger inherent in a situation, thereby activating autonomic and behavioral manifestations of anxiety. They then misinterpret these sensations as a further source of threat, leading to a vicious cycle that maintains or exacerbates the anxiety disorder. The goal of cognitive-behavioral therapy is to change the thoughts and behaviors that help to maintain the anxiety. It is at least as effective as pharmacologic treatment of panic disorder and appears to have more lasting effects following termination of treatment. Cognitive-behavioral therapy for panic disorder usually involves a combination of cognitive restructuring (that is, changing anxious thoughts, interpretations, and predictions into more rational, less anxious thoughts), exposure to feared objects and situations, and relaxation training. The therapy is highly structured, occurs over 6 to 20 sessions, and is usually conducted by a psychologist or psychiatrist who is trained in the procedure. It can be delivered in a group format or on an individual basis.

Cognitive-behavioral therapy is also the psychologic treatment of choice for generalized anxiety disorder. Generalized anxiety disorder is a risk factor for development or recurrence of depression. Thus, in addition to alleviating panic attacks and generalized anxiety, a goal of cognitive-behavioral therapy in this woman would be to reduce the risk of future episodes of depression.

Most studies have found that cognitive-behavioral therapy is more effective than supportive therapy in panic disorder. Since psychoanalytic psychotherapy and interpersonal psychotherapy have not been evaluated in a controlled fashion as treatment for panic disorder, neither can be recommended as an alternative to cognitive-behavioral therapy.

References

1. Bruce SE, Machan JT, Dyck I, et al. Infrequency of "pure" GAD: impact of psychiatric comorbidity on clinical course. *Depress Anxiety*. 2001;14(4):219–225.
2. Flint AJ, Gagnon N. Diagnosis and management of panic disorder in older patients. *Drugs Aging*. 2003;20(12):881–891.
3. Stanley MA, Novy DM. Cognitive-behavior therapy for generalized anxiety in late life: an evaluative overview. *J Anxiety Disord*. 2000;14(2):191–207.
4. Swales PJ, Solfvin JF, Sheikh JI. Cognitive-behavioral therapy in older panic disorder patients. *Am J Geriatr Psychiatry*. 1996;4(1):46–60.

234. A 78-year-old man comes to the office for a 6-month follow-up visit. He has a history of well-controlled stage 1 hypertension, benign prostatic hyperplasia, and osteoarthritis. His prostate and musculoskeletal symptoms are stable. Medications are lisinopril 10 mg daily, hydrochlorothiazide 25 mg daily, ibuprofen 200 mg three times daily (begun at his last visit), and saw palmetto.

On physical examination, his blood pressure is found to be 152/78 mm Hg, and heart rate is 82 per minute with a regular rhythm. He has joint deformities in both hands consistent with osteoarthritis; there is no acute inflammation. He has 1+ bilateral lower extremity edema to the mid-shin; the edema was not evident at his last visit.

Which of the following is the best approach to management of this patient's findings?

(A) Recommend compression stockings.
(B) Discontinue ibuprofen.
(C) Increase the hydrochlorothiazide.
(D) Begin a loop diuretic.
(E) Increase the lisinopril dosage.

ANSWER: B

Many agents can directly or indirectly increase blood pressure, including sympathomimetic agents, corticosteroids, nonsteroidal anti-inflammatory drugs (NSAIDs), selective cyclooxygenase (COX)-2 inhibitors, excessive alcohol use, and some alternative and over-the-counter drugs (decongestants and ephedra). Although secondary causes of hypertension are uncommon in older persons (more than 90% develop essential hypertension), the effect of medications on blood pressure should always be considered, even in patients who are receiving antihypertensive medications for established hypertension. There are no reported effects of saw palmetto on blood pressure, nor any interactions with antihypertensive medications.

Renal prostaglandins regulate renal hemodynamics, sodium excretion, and renin release. The blood-pressure−elevating effects of NSAIDs are well established and believed to be due to the renal effects of decreasing prostaglandin production, resulting in sodium retention and a decrease in glomerular filtration rate. Although reports are conflicting, most clinical studies have demonstrated blood-pressure increases during chronic COX-2 inhibitor therapy that are comparable to the increases observed with NSAID use. Since most antihypertensive drugs (except calcium channel antagonists) require the production of vasodilating renal prostaglandins, the blood-pressure−elevating effects of COX-2 inhibitors have been reported more commonly in patients also receiving ACE inhibitors or β-blockers.

Increasing the thiazide-type diuretic or increasing the lisinopril dosage should not be considered until the effect of discontinuing the NSAID is clear. Lower extremity edema could be managed by compression stockings or a loop diuretic, but given the likelihood that it developed as a consequence of the NSAID, discontinuing the medication is the best initial approach.

References

1. Cheng HF, Harris RC. Cyclooxygenases, the kidney, and hypertension. *Hypertension*. 2004;43(3):525–530.
2. Cheng HR, Harris RC. Renal effects of non-steroidal anti-inflammatory drugs and selective cyclooxygenase-2 inhibitors. *Curr Pharm Des*. 2005;11(14):1795–804.
3. Solomon DH, Schneeweiss S, Levin R, et al. Relationship between COX-2 specific inhibitors and hypertension. *Hypertension*. 2004;44(2):140–145.

235. A healthy 68-year-old man has no history of heart disease and currently walks about 20 minutes twice a day. He also works in his garden. He plans to begin an exercise program consisting of upper and lower extremity resistance exercises, stair climbing, and brisk walking 3 days per week.

Which of the following statements describes the long-term effects of increased physical activity on this patient's risk for coronary artery disease (CAD) and mortality?

(A) His increased activity will not result in further risk reduction of CAD or mortality.
(B) His increased activity will result in further risk reduction of CAD or mortality.
(C) His increased activity will improve his CAD risk but not overall mortality risk.
(D) His increased activity will improve his overall mortality risk but not CAD risk.

ANSWER: B

Physical activity has important health benefits, particularly in reducing the risk of CAD and all-cause mortality. The mortality benefit is large. Some studies report that inactive adults have mortality rates that are twice as high as those of active adults.

The greatest benefits are seen in sedentary persons who begin regular moderate physical activity, such as brisk walking (3 to 4 mph, at an intensity of 3 to 6 metabolic equivalents). This patient already is exercising at a moderate level, meeting the recommendation for 30 minutes of moderate physical activity at least 5 days per week. Persons who exceed the recommendation for moderate activity or those who engage in vigorous activity have lower CAD and all-cause mortality risks. There is no evidence that vigorous activity increases all-cause mortality. Individuals willing to start with a low-intensity, short-duration exercise program that gradually increases in intensity and duration do not need pre-exercise program cardiac testing. Physician-supervised treadmill-exercise electrocardiography is recommended for previously sedentary persons aged 50 and over who want to begin a vigorous exercise program and who are unlikely to start with a low-intensity, short-duration program that gradually increases in duration and intensity.

References

1. Evans WJ. Exercise training guidelines for the elderly. *Med Sci Sports Exerc.* 1999;31(1):12–17.
2. Nied RJ, Franklin B. Promoting and prescribing exercise for the elderly. *Am Fam Phys.* 2002;65(3):419–426.
3. Taylor AH, Cable NT, Faulkner G, et al. Physical activity and older adults: a review of health benefits and the effectiveness of interventions. *J Sports Sci.* 2004;22(8):703–725.

236. A 65-year-old man comes to the office because his family has noticed increasing forgetfulness and confusion over the past few months. For example, he now gets lost on his way home from familiar places. He has been widowed for 10 years and dates occasionally. He has no significant comorbidities and is on no medications. His family is concerned that he may have symptoms of early Alzheimer's disease.

Physical examination is normal except for the neurologic component, which reveals slowing of rapid finger and toe tapping, short-term memory deficits, and an inability to do relatively simple calculations. There are no metabolic or endocrine abnormalities, and rapid plasma reagent is negative. Enzyme-linked immunoassay and Western blot tests are positive for human immunodeficiency virus (HIV) antibodies and remain positive on repeat testing.

Which of the following is most likely over 3 years if this is an HIV-associated dementia and the patient takes antiretroviral therapy?

(A) Improvement or arrest in dementia progression and improved survival rate
(B) Improvement or arrest in dementia progression and unaltered survival rate
(C) Progression of dementia and improved survival rate
(D) Progression of dementia and unaltered survival rate

ANSWER: A

One of every 11 new diagnoses of HIV is in persons over age 50. In the United States, older adults are the cohort least likely to practice safe sex; most cases of HIV infection in older adults are acquired through sexual activity. Older adults are more likely than young adults to meet criteria for acquired immune deficiency syndrome (AIDS) at the time of HIV diagnosis, perhaps because nonspecific symptoms such as weight loss, dementia, and failure to thrive are more common in older adults and because, untreated, AIDS progresses faster in older adults. However, older adults with HIV are as likely to benefit from anti-HIV therapy as young adults, with regard to both survival and immunologic recovery. Arrest and even reversal of HIV-associated dementia are widely described and expected with combinations of antiretroviral drugs that penetrate the central nervous system. Although hyperlipidemia, accelerated atherosclerosis, and other metabolic complications occur in patients on antiretroviral therapies, these effects do not offset the marked benefit of therapy. If treated, this patient should expect marked improvement in his memory, and he has better than an 80% chance of surviving at least 3 years. He should be counseled regarding safe sex and routes of transmission. All his recent (within 5 years) sexual partners should be tested for HIV.

References

1. Perez JL, Moore RD. Greater effect of highly active antiretroviral therapy on survival in people aged > or = 50 years compared with younger people in an urban observational cohort. *Clin Infect Dis.* 2003;36(2):212–218.
2. Price RW. Neurologic disease. In: Dolin R, Masur H, Saag MS, eds. *AIDS Therapy.* New York: Churchill Livingstone; 2003:737–757.
3. Wellons MF, Sanders L, Edwards LJ, et al. HIV infection: treatment outcomes in older and younger adults. *J Am Geriatr Soc.* 2002;50(4):603–607.

237. A 72-year-old man with hypertension and kidney failure has had a stable renal allograft for the past 5 months. He has a history of scrutinizing his doctor's recommendations, inquiring in detail about mechanisms of action, side effects, and treatment alternatives; this tendency has increased since the kidney transplant. Despite being scheduled for a 3-month return visit, he calls or comes by the office daily, without an appointment. He is furious at his cardiologist for recommending aspirin for stroke prophylaxis, because "it is against the rules the nephrologist established: aspirin and acetaminophen might damage the kidney." He keeps his own records of medical information and brings them every time, spending much of the visit looking up what he recorded previously. The patient's wife states that none of the routines at home have changed and that he has a pattern of "wanting things his way."

In addition to adjustment disorder with anxiety, this presentation is most likely an exacerbation of which of the following?

(A) Delirium due to chronic kidney failure
(B) Obsessive-compulsive disorder
(C) Generalized anxiety disorder
(D) Delusional disorder with late onset (paraphrenia)
(E) Obsessive-compulsive personality disorder

ANSWER: E

This patient's pervasive preoccupation with rules and details and his rigidity and stubbornness are characteristic of obsessive-compulsive personality disorder. His ego-syntonic beliefs differ from the ego-dystonic beliefs seen in obsessive-compulsive disorder, in which obsessions or compulsions are recognized as irrational, creating a high level of distress to the patient.

Generalized anxiety disorder is characterized by excessive worry occurring almost daily for 6 months about various events. The worry is recognized by the patient as difficult to control, and it is associated with fatigue, restlessness, insomnia, decreased concentration, irritability, and muscle tension. This patient is anxious, but his concerns extend beyond those of generalized anxiety disorder.

Although his beliefs about following certain rules are inflexible, the beliefs are not false or delusional in intensity; thus, delusional disorder is unlikely. Chronic kidney failure is unlikely since nothing in the history points to a new medical issue, and the patient has a stable allograft.

References

1. Gabbard GO. *Psychodynamic Psychiatry in Clinical Practice*. 3rd ed. Arlington, VA: American Psychiatric Press, Inc., 2000:547–560.
2. Sadock B, Sadock V. *Kaplan and Sadock's Synopsis of Psychiatry*. 9th ed. Philadelphia, PA: Lippincott Williams and Wilkins; 2003:814–816.

238. In *Cruzan v. Director, Department of Health of Missouri* the Supreme Court ruled:

(A) Patients have the right to request and refuse therapy.
(B) Patients do not have a constitutional right to physician-assisted suicide.
(C) Patients have a right to refuse only currently proposed therapies.
(D) Patients do not have the right to demand therapy.
(E) Patients have the right to refuse any therapy.

ANSWER: E

Nancy Cruzan was a woman who had been in a persistent vegetative state for several years. Her parents had made the decision to discontinue her tube feedings and argued that their daughter would not wish to have her life prolonged under these circumstances. The Missouri Department of Health challenged their right to make this decision, citing the state's obligation to protect life.

In ruling in this case, the Supreme Court had to first establish that there is a constitutional right to refuse unwanted interventions, including the right to influence those decisions even when no longer capable of making the decision oneself. The court went on to say that each state could set its own standards for the degree of evidence needed to affirm that the individual would not have wanted the intervention.

The court did not state that persons have the right to demand interventions. It only dealt with the right to decline or discontinue treatments.

The *Cruzan* case did not raise the issue of physician-assisted suicide. The Supreme Court did rule, in two 1997 cases, that there is not a constitutional right to physician-assisted suicide but left it up to states to decide the legality in each jurisdiction.

References

1. Annas GJ, Arnold B, Aroskar M, et al. Bioethicists' statement on the U.S. Supreme Court's Cruzan decision. *N Engl J Med.* 1990;323(10):686–687.
2. Burt RA. The Supreme Court speaks—not assisted suicide but a constitutional right to palliative care. *N Engl J. Med.* 1997;337(17):1234–1236.
3. *Cruzan v Harmon*, 760 S.W.2d 408 (1988), affirmed, 110 Sup. Ct. 2841 (1990).
4. *Vacco v. Quill*, 117 Sup. Ct. 2258 (1997).
5. *Washington v. Glucksberg*, 117 Sup. Ct. 2293 (1997).

239. An 82-year-old man comes to the office because of gradually worsening "bladder trouble." He is bothered by severe urgency, frequency every 1 to 2 hours, and three to four episodes of nocturia every night. He is only rarely incontinent. He has occasional hesitancy, a slow urinary stream, and an intermittent sense of incomplete bladder emptying, but these symptoms do not bother him. He had a transurethral resection of the prostate at age 73 but has no other genitourinary history. He has hypertension, for which he takes an angiotensin-converting enzyme inhibitor and a β-blocker.

Physical examination is normal, and noninvasive testing reveals peak urinary flow of 18 mL/sec (normal > 10 mL/sec) on a void of 175 mL, postvoid residual volume of 20 mL, and negative urinalysis. Prostate-specific antigen level is normal.

Which of the following is the most appropriate next step?

(A) A trial of terazosin, starting at 1 mg at bedtime
(B) A trial of bethanechol, 10 mg three times daily
(C) A trial of oxybutynin, 2.5 mg twice daily and at bedtime
(D) Referral for cystoscopy and complex urodynamics
(E) Referral for repeat transurethral resection of the prostate

ANSWER: C

A diagnosis of obstruction or prostate cancer cannot be excluded on the basis of this patient's symptoms and prostate size and contour. However, peak urinary flow faster than 10 mL/sec with low postvoid residual volume effectively excludes obstruction in men age 75 and older. Thus, referral for repeat transurethral resection of the prostate is not appropriate. The normal prostate-specific antigen level indicates that cancer is unlikely.

The patient's most bothersome symptoms are related to overactive bladder. A trial of short-acting oxybutynin, with careful monitoring for development of urinary retention and other anticholinergic adverse effects, is the best choice listed. Terazosin and other α-blockers are commonly prescribed for symptoms of benign prostatic hyperplasia, but they probably are more effective for voiding difficulty than for the overactive bladder component. These drugs can cause postural hypotension in older patients, especially in those who are already taking antihypertensive agents. Tamsulosin may have less effect on blood pressure than other α-blockers. Bethanechol is a cholinergic agent and would not be appropriate for this patient. Cystoscopy and complex urodynamic testing would not change the initial treatment regimen for this patient and are not appropriate at this point.

References

1. Diokno AC, Appell RA, Sand PK, et al. Prospective, randomized, double-blind study of the efficacy and tolerability of the extended-release formulations of oxybutynin and tolterodine for overactive bladder: results of the OPERA trial. *Mayo Clin Proc.* 2003;78(6):687–695.

2. Johnson, TM, Jones, K, Williford WO, et al. Changes in nocturia from medical treatment of benign prostatic hyperplasia: secondary analysis of the Department of Veterans Affairs Cooperative Study Trial. *J Urol.* 2003;170(1):145–148.
3. Staskin D, Wein A. New perspectives on the overactive bladder. *Urology.* 2002;60(5A Suppl):1–104.

240. A 73-year-old woman comes to the office because of pain in her right shoulder for the past 6 weeks. The pain is often worse when she wakes up in the morning and with prolonged sitting and standing; lying down relieves the pain. She feels spasm and notes tenderness in her right shoulder. It bothers her particularly when she backs her car out of the driveway in the morning. She has had no weight loss, fatigue, general malaise, or other systemic symptoms.

On physical examination, there is good mobility of the right shoulder with no pain. She has moderate spasm and tenderness in the right trapezius region, asymmetric loss of movement of the cervical spine, and mild weakness of the right elbow extensor and right finger abductors.

What is the most likely cause of this patient's pain?

(A) Fibromyalgia
(B) Metastatic cancer affecting the right scapula
(C) Rotator cuff tendonitis of the right shoulder
(D) Acromioclavicular disease of the right shoulder
(E) Cervical disk disease

ANSWER: E

The trapezius area is the site of referred pain from the C-6, C-7 and C-7, C-8 cervical spine regions. Spasm of the trapezius muscle often occurs when the cervical spine is irritated. Asymmetry of motion (rotation to the right, rotation to the left, flexion, and extension) indicates mechanical displacement in the cervical spine. The elbow extensor and finger abductors are both innervated by C-7, C-8. The site of this person's pain, along with the asymmetric loss of range of motion of the cervical spine and weakness in the C-7, C-8–innervated muscle of the arm, suggests cervical disk disease.

This patient's physical findings indicate that there is a mechanical cause of her trapezius muscle spasm. Fibromyalgia refers to diffuse musculoskeletal pain without a clear mechanical or inflammatory cause. Significant fatigue occurs in 90% of patients with fibromyalgia, and sleep disturbances, lightheadedness, dizziness, and other systemic symptoms are common.

Although the scapula can be a site for metastatic cancer, a patient with cancer is likely to have gradually worsening persistent pain that is unrelated to position and movement.

A patient with rotator cuff tendonitis should have a "painful arc" on abduction of the shoulder and pain on resisted movement of the affected tendon. The completely normal physical examination of the shoulder excludes rotator cuff tendonitis. Although irritation of the acromioclavicular disease can produce pain between the shoulder and the neck, this pain should be brought on with abduction of the shoulder between 90 degrees and 160 degrees. The normal shoulder examination makes acromioclavicular disease less likely. Acromioclavicular disease does not usually cause weakness of the elbow extensor and finger abductors.

References

1. Boyce RH, Wang JC. Evaluation of neck pain, radiculopathy, and myelopathy: imaging, conservative treatment, and surgical indications. *Instr Course Lect.* 2003;52:489–495.
2. Rao R. Neck pain, cervical radiculopathy, and cervical myelopathy. *J Bone Joint Surg Am.* 2002;84-A(10):1872–1881.
3. Ylinen J, Takala EP, Nykanen M, et al. Active neck muscle training in the treatment of chronic neck pain in women. *JAMA.* 2003;289(19):2509–2516.

241. A frail 91-year-old woman with Alzheimer's dementia (recent Mini–Mental State Examination score, 12 of 30) is transferred to the emergency department from her nursing home for evaluation and management of severe agitation. For the past 2 days, she has been irritable, pacing, and threatening to hit other residents. She has also been having more trouble sleeping and has made vague claims that others are trying to harm her. A few hours ago she punched another resident. The patient has a history of heart disease and mild chronic obstructive pulmonary disease, both currently under good control. She also has a history of recurrent urinary tract infections but is on no prophylactic medications. In the emergency department, she was cooperative during triage evaluation, but after being placed in a room, she got out of bed and walked the hall, seeming confused. When redirected back to her room, she became agitated, insisting that she had to go home and would not cooperate with testing.

What is the most appropriate next step in the management of this patient?

(A) Administer lorazepam 1 mg intramuscularly
(B) Administer haloperidol 2 mg intramuscularly
(C) Assign a nurse to spend one-on-one time with her
(D) Administer olanzapine 5 mg sublingually
(E) Restrain the patient to obtain a blood and urine work-up

ANSWER: C

This patient has had an acute onset of behavioral agitation, with a paranoid theme, that has escalated to violence over a few hours. The primary differential diagnoses are agitation related to an underlying medical problem (hence, delirium) and a psychotic disturbance related to Alzheimer's disease. Clarifying this differential requires a more careful mental status examination and a laboratory work-up. However, this cannot be accomplished until the patient has been calmed. Given the time course, full work-up can probably wait, so restraining the patient is too aggressive in this case. If the patient appeared obviously medically ill or in distress and did not cooperate with the necessary evaluation, then restraint might be necessary. However, the emergency department team can try to de-escalate the situation; the best first approach is nonpharmacologic. Since this patient was cooperative on arrival, she may be calmed with careful individual attention and re-orientation. This strategy should be allowed sufficient time to succeed. If it fails, pharmacologic intervention may be needed.

Given the patient's paranoia, the possibility that she is suffering from delirium, and her frailty, an antipsychotic is the preferred first-line agent. Benzodiazepines are inferior to antipsychotics for managing delirium. The choice of antipsychotic agent is important. There are three general options: high-potency typical agents (haloperidol, droperidol, fluphenazine), low-potency typical agents (chlorpromazine, thioridazine), and atypical antipsychotics (olanzapine, risperidone, ziprasidone, quetiapine). Atypical antipsychotic agents have not been adequately assessed for the management of acute agitation in frail elderly patients with dementia; their comparative safety, efficacy, and speed of onset in this setting is unknown. For that reason, they are best used as second- or third-line agents. Low-potency antipsychotics have unacceptable rates of adverse effects (especially excess sedation, hypotension, arrhythmia, falls) in frail elderly persons and should not be used in the emergency setting. There is substantial clinical experience for managing acute aggression and agitation with haloperidol and related high-potency typical agents. In addition to antipsychotic effects, these agents are acute anxiolytics and have motor effects that slow patients down physically. Lower doses are needed in frail elderly persons than in younger persons.

References

1. Lyketsos CG. Diagnosis and management of delirium in the elderly. *J Clin Outcomes Manage.* 1998;5(4):51–62.
2. Rabins PV, Lyketsos CG, Steele CD. *Practical Dementia Care.* New York: Oxford University Press; 1999.
3. Tueth MJ. Dementia: diagnosis and emergency medical complications. *J Emerg Med.* 1995;13(4):519–525.

242. An 86-year-old woman who lives in a nursing home is evaluated because she has several pressure ulcers. She has advanced vascular dementia. Medications include benazepril, aspirin, and a multivitamin. She is able to walk if she uses a front-wheeled walker and has assistance from two other persons. Nurses' notes indicate that she has been getting more combative over the past several months and that her oral intake has been steadily dropping.

On examination, she is able to follow simple two-step commands. She has severe expressive aphasia. Weight is 44.5 kg (98 lb), down from 50.9 kg (112 lb) 3 months ago. She has two stage III pressure ulcers: one, 4 × 6 cm, is located on her buttock; the other, 3 × 3 cm, is over the left mid-scapular region. She has several bruises, ranging in size from 2 × 2 cm to 5 × 7 cm, on the inner aspect of her upper arms, and a large bruise (8 × 12 cm) on her medial right breast and sternum. When asked how this occurred, the attendant explains that the nurse's aide who was working with her yesterday evening had to "fight" to get her ready for a bath.

Laboratory results are normal except for total protein, which is 5.9 g/dL, and albumin, which is 3.3 g/dL.

Which of the following is the next step in caring for this patient?

(A) Discontinue aspirin
(B) Remove the nurse's aide from direct patient care.
(C) Transfer the patient to a new nursing home.
(D) Reassign nurse's aide to a different patient.

ANSWER: B

The most urgent next step is to protect this and other vulnerable older adults from possible abuse. Thus, it is essential to remove the nurse's aide from direct patient care while investigating for possible mistreatment. Although there is not enough information to conclude that mistreatment has occurred, a number of issues raise concern. First, this person has several risk factors that increase her likelihood of being abused: she is demented, she requires a lot of assistance with activities of daily living, and she is combative. The physical findings also are suspicious: bruises on the inner aspects of her upper arms may indicate that she is being grabbed with significant force, and a bruise on the breast is an uncommon finding that demands further investigation. A reasonable suspicion of abuse must be reported to state authorities. The person who is the possible perpetrator should not be allowed to continue interacting with patients during the investigation. Transferring the patient to a new nursing home or reassigning the nursing assistant to a different patient would protect this patient but not other patients.

Daily low-dose aspirin may make some people prone to easy bruising but would not explain the unusual location of her bruises. If the patient bruises easily, there should be bruises in locations such as the dorsal hand or forearm; these areas are frequently bumped for benign reasons and do not raise a suspicion. It is unlikely that a person with her level of function sustained a bruise on the breast and sternum without another person's being involved or at least witnessing the event that led to the bruise. In this case, the explanation that she resisted a bath is not adequate. A person who bruises easily and who is resistant to care may have bruises in multiple locations where she is handled by caregivers. The finding of an isolated bruise on her chest wall is not consistent with the given history.

It is important to work toward reducing the patient's agitation. Older adults who are agitated and combative are more likely to be mistreated in nursing homes and may injure others. Before a medication is started, however, medical and psychosocial factors that may be contributing to her behavior should be addressed. For example, the patient may be in pain because of her wounds, or her combativeness may be a protective response to this particular aide's handling. Also, environmental factors may be contributing to her agitation. Once these issues are thoroughly explored, medication may be considered.

References

1. Joshi S, Flaherty JH. Elder abuse and neglect in long-term care. *Clin Geriatr Med.* 2005;21(2):333–354.

2. MacLean DS. Preventing abuse and neglect in long-term care Part II: clinical and administrative aspects. *Ann Long Term Care.* 2000; 8(1):65–70.

3. Thomas DR. Improving outcome of pressure ulcers with nutritional intervention: a review of the evidence. *Nutrition.* 2001;17(2):121–125.

243. A 70-year-old woman comes to the office because of fever that has persisted for nearly 1 month. She has daily fevers to 38.8°C (102°F) and marked fatigue. She has a history of osteoarthritis, for which she takes occasional acetaminophen. Physical examination is normal except for temperature of 38.5°C (101.3°F). Laboratory studies are normal except for hemoglobin (11 g/dL), alkaline phosphatase (170 U/L), and erythrocyte sedimentation rate (70 mm/h). Urinalysis, blood cultures, purified protein derivative skin testing, and computed tomography of the chest, abdomen, and pelvis are normal.

Which of the following is most likely to provide the diagnosis?

(A) Indium 111 tagged leukocyte scan
(B) Positron emission tomography
(C) Temporal artery biopsy
(D) Bone marrow biopsy
(E) Liver biopsy

ANSWER: C

Fever of unknown origin is most commonly due to infection (particularly endocarditis, tuberculosis, intra-abdominal abscess), malignancy (primarily lymphoma and rarely leukemia), or collagen vascular disorders. In patients aged 65 and older, giant cell arteritis accounts for up to 18% of cases of fever of unknown origin. If infection and malignancy are unlikely given negative cultures and normal results on both purified protein derivative testing and computed tomography, the most appropriate test is temporal artery biopsy. The diagnosis is also suggested by mild anemia, elevated erythrocyte sedimentation rate, and abnormal alkaline phosphatase level, all common in giant cell arteritis. In the absence of other abnormalities in the laboratory and radiologic tests performed already, additional diagnostic testing would not be warranted.

References

1. Levine SM, Hellmann DB. Giant cell arteritis. *Curr Opin Rheumatol.* 2002;14(1):3–10.
2. Liozon E, Boutros-Toni F, Ly K, et al. Silent, or masked, giant cell arteritis is associated with a strong inflammatory response and a benign short term course. *J Rheumatol.* 2003;30(6):1272–1276.
3. Norman D. Fever in the elderly. *Clin Infect Dis.* 2000;31(1):148–151.
4. Tal S, Guller V, Gurevich A, et al. Fever of unknown origin in the elderly. *J Intern Med.* 2002;252(4):295–304.

244. A 79-year-old woman comes to the office for a routine examination. History includes atrial fibrillation, diabetes mellitus, osteoarthritis, class III heart failure, and coronary artery disease. She had a myocardial infarction 9 years ago. Medications include furosemide 40 mg twice daily, acetaminophen 500 mg four times daily, potassium chloride 10 mEq every morning, lisinopril 5 mg every morning, warfarin 2 mg daily, metoprolol 25 mg twice daily, a multivitamin daily, and glipizide 20 mg twice daily. Her blood glucose monitoring record over the past 2 weeks lists glucose concentrations ranging from 195 mg/dL to 225 mg/dL. She reports no signs or symptoms of hypoglycemia.

Laboratory studies:

Sodium	137 mEq/L
Potassium	4.3 mEq/L
Glucose	200 mg/dL
Urea nitrogen	20 mg/dL
Creatinine	1.7 mg/dL
Hemoglobin A_{1C}	8.5%

What is the most immediate need at this time?

(A) Start metformin.
(B) Start insulin.
(C) Start rosiglitazone.
(D) Discontinue metoprolol.

ANSWER: B

This patient has uncontrolled diabetes mellitus and requires additional treatment. Of the available options, insulin is the best choice. Both metformin and rosiglitazone are inappropriate choices because of this patient's comorbidities. Metformin is not recommended because she has kidney insufficiency (as suggested by serum creatinine levels above 1.4 mg/dL and estimated creatinine clearance of 25 mL/min to 28 mL/min) and heart failure requiring pharmacologic treatment. Both of these conditions may increase risk for lactic acidosis, a rare but serious metabolic complication that can occur with metformin accumulation during treatment. Thiazolidinediones such as rosiglitazone are not recommended in patients with New York Heart Association class III or IV cardiac status because they can cause fluid retention that may lead to or exacerbate heart failure.

Metoprolol is indicated in this patient since she has a history of myocardial infarction. β-Adrenergic blockers are underused in clinical practice, especially in older patients with diabetes mellitus, possibly because of concerns that they may interfere with diabetic control by worsening glucose tolerance or that they mask warning signs and symptoms (such as tachycardia and changes to blood pressure and pulse) of acute hypoglycemia. Clinically, the use of selective β-adrenergic blockers has little effect on glucose metabolism. Further, insulin-induced hypoglycemia occurs far less commonly in patients with type 2 than type 1 diabetes, and other manifestations of hypoglycemia, such as dizziness and sweating, may not be significantly affected. The benefit of metoprolol use after myocardial infarction outweighs the theoretic potential for impairment in glucose control.

References

1. Calabrese AT, Coley KC, DaPos SV, et al. Evaluation of prescribing practices: risk of lactic acidosis with metformin therapy. *Arch Intern Med.* 2002;162(4):434–437.
2. Care California Healthcare Foundation/American Geriatrics Society Panel in Improving Care for Elders with Diabetes. Guidelines for improving the care of the older person with diabetes mellitus. *J Am Geriatr Soc.* 2003; 51(5S):265–280.
3. Di Bari M, Marchionni N, Pahor M. Beta-blockers after acute myocardial infarction in elderly patients with diabetes mellitus: time to reassess. *Drugs Aging.* 2003;20(1):13–22.
4. Horlen C, Malone R, Bryant B, et al. Frequency of inappropriate metformin prescriptions. *JAMA.* 2002;287(19):2504–2505.
5. Masoudi FA, Wang Y, Inzucchi SE, et al. Metformin and thiazolidinedione use in Medicare patients with heart failure. *JAMA.* 2003;290(1):81–85.

245. You are consulted about an 82-year-old woman for preoperative assessment before surgical repair of a fractured hip. She has longstanding rheumatoid arthritis treated with methotrexate for 10 years and has multijoint involvement, with significant deformity of her metacarpal-phalangeal joints bilaterally. She has never smoked and has no cardiac or pulmonary symptoms.

On physical examination, blood pressure is 136/76 mm Hg, heart rate is 80 per minute, and respiratory rate is 14 per minute. There is no jugular venous distention, her lungs sound clear, and her cardiac examination is normal. A 12-lead electrocardiogram is normal.

Which of the following should be obtained prior to surgery?

(A) Spirometry
(B) Full pulmonary function testing with diffusion capacity
(C) Cardiopulmonary stress testing
(D) High-resolution computed tomography of the chest
(E) Lateral neck radiograph

ANSWER: E

Because of longstanding rheumatoid arthritis, this patient may have atlanto-axial subluxation (C1 on C2), which would put her at risk for spinal cord trauma during neck extension in standard orotracheal intubation. If atlanto-axial subluxation is present on lateral neck radiograph, the anesthesiologist should perform intubation with the neck in neutral position. Although patients with rheumatoid arthritis may have associated lung disease, including pulmonary fibrosis, bronchiolitis obliterans organizing pneumonia, pleural effusions, and rib cage deformity, this patient has no pulmonary symptoms to warrant a specific evaluation. Spirometry, full pulmonary function testing, cardiopulmonary exercise testing, and high-resolution computed tomography of the chest (to assess for interstitial lung disease) have no role in the evaluation of asymptomatic patients.

Pulmonary toxicity develops in 2% to 8% of patients receiving methotrexate. The majority of patients who develop methotrexate pulmonary toxicity do so within the first year of therapy, although cases have been reported as late as 18 years after the drug was initiated. Methotrexate pulmonary toxicity presents with common respiratory symptoms, depending on the type of pulmonary toxicity (eg, acute methotrexate pneumonitis with fever, chills, malaise, cough, and dyspnea). Evaluation for methotrexate pulmonary toxicity in this patient would not be warranted since she has no pulmonary symptoms.

References

1. Perez T, Remy-Jardin M, Cortet B. Airways involvement in rheumatoid arthritis: clinical, functional, and HRCT findings. *Am J Respir Crit Care Med*. 1998;157(5 Pt 1):1658–1665.
2. Tanoue LT. Pulmonary manifestations of rheumatoid arthritis. *Clin Chest Med*. 1998; 19(4):667–685.
3. White D, Mark E. A 53-year-old woman with arthritis and pulmonary nodules. *N Engl J Med*. 2001;344(13):997–1004.

246. A 72-year-old man is brought to the emergency department from his nursing home because he has a moderate viral upper respiratory infection accompanied by worsening behavior, including agitation, mild paranoia, verbal aggression, confusion, and nonadherence with his medication regimen. He has also become more dependent in activities of daily living. He has mild mental retardation of unknown cause, obesity, chronic obstructive pulmonary disease, diabetes mellitus type 2, mild hypertension, obstructive sleep apnea, and dementia attributed to alcohol abuse. He has a 30 pack-year history of smoking. He has no history of mood, thought, or anxiety disorder. His only behavior-modifying medication is a cholinesterase inhibitor for dementia, the dose of which has been unchanged. He has continuous positive airway pressure treatment at night, but it is difficult to get him to use it or take his medications since his behavior has deteriorated. He snores loudly at night, and the nursing staff reports evidence of apnea. He is excessively sleepy and has diminished alertness.

Physical examination is consistent with upper respiratory infection. He is cooperative about taking his medications while in the emergency department. There is no evidence of other new infection, occult illness, or change in his dementia. Psychiatry consultation finds no sign of a mood, thought, or anxiety disorder and suggests that his behavioral changes may be consistent with changes in his sleep disorder.

Which of the following is the most appropriate immediate management for this patient?

(A) Add a low-dose atypical antipsychotic medication.
(B) Add a mild stimulant medication.
(C) Switch cholinesterase inhibitors.
(D) Discharge the patient and reinstitute continuous positive airway pressure.
(E) Expand scope of diagnostic testing.

ANSWER: D

The onset of this patient's challenging behaviors coincided with his upper airway infection and his refusal to use continuous positive airway pressure. His loud snoring, excessive somnolence, witnessed apnea, and mental status changes indicate inadequately treated obstructive sleep apnea. Resumption of continuous positive airway pressure may be all that is needed to return the patient to his previous behavior level. His airway status and adherence may improve with positional changes, such as having him sleep in a more upright position, or sewing a soft object into the back of his sleepwear to keep him from sleeping on his back. Disturbed sleep can cause significant mental status changes and behavioral disturbances that may mimic psychosis, delirium, or dementia. Sleep disorder may be caused by simple obesity, and certain genetic disorders, such as Down syndrome, are associated with an increased incidence of obstructive sleep apnea. In Down syndrome, weight gain, hypognathia with reduced upper airway, and muscle hypotonia make obstructive sleep apnea more likely.

Adding even a low dose of an antipsychotic may worsen the sleep disorder by further disrupting sleep patterns and lowering the level of alertness. It may increase the potential for serious adverse effects such as tardive dyskinesia and extrapyramidal symptoms.

Adding a stimulant to this patient's regimen may improve alertness, but considering the patient's several health conditions, the risk would seem to outweigh any potential benefit.

Changing the patient's cholinesterase inhibitor is not warranted. The timing of the symptoms does not suggest a change in his dementia. If anything, discontinuing the cholinesterase inhibitor could be considered, since no controlled trials support the use of these agents in dementia secondary to alcohol use.

Further hospitalization and testing seem unnecessary and would only increase health risks. An extended in-patient stay may diminish a person's prehospitalization level of independence.

References:

1. Brylewski J, Wiggs L. Sleep problems and daytime challenging behaviour in a community-based sample of adults with intellectual disability. *J Intellect Disabil Res.* 1999;43(Pt 6):504–512.
2. Davidson PW, Janicki MP, Ladrigan P, et al. Associations between behavior disorders and health status among older adults with intellectual disability. *Aging Ment Health.* 2003;7(6):424–430.
3. Gunning MJ, Espie CA. Psychological treatment of reported sleep disorder in adults with intellectual disability using a multiple baseline design. *J Intellect Disabil Res.* 2003; 47(3):191–202.
4. Heller T, Janicki M, Hammel J, et al. *Promoting Healthy Aging, Family Support, and Age-Friendly Communities for Persons Aging with Developmental Disabilities: Report of the 2001 Invitational Research Symposium on Aging With Developmental Disabilities.* Chicago: The Rehabilitation Research and Training Center on Aging with Developmental Disabilities, Department of Disability and Human Development, University of Illinois at Chicago; 2002.
5. Simpson N. Delirium in adults with intellectual disabilities and DC-LD. *J Intellect Disabil Res.* 2003;47(S1):38–42.

247. The effect of physical activity on bone density is most highly correlated with which of the following?

(A) Frequency of activity
(B) Duration of activity
(C) Intensity of activity
(D) Type of activity
(E) Volume of aerobic activity

ANSWER: D

The health benefits of physical activity are generally proportional to the amount of physical activity. When activity is performed above minimum thresholds for frequency, duration, and intensity, health benefit depends mainly upon the volume (energy expenditure) of aerobic activity. The dose-response relationship between physical activity and disease risk varies by disease in a manner that is incompletely understood. Cardiovascular disease risk decreases with volume of aerobic activity over a wide range of volume. Furthermore, it has been demonstrated that the beneficial effects of physical activity on health are independent of other risk factors. In particular, beneficial effects have been found to be independent of body mass index. Blood pressure shows little dose-response effect, as most of the effect of physical activity on blood pressure occurs at low levels of activity. The effect of activity on bone density is less related to volume of aerobic activity and more related to the type of activity, with resistance training and high-impact activities correlating with benefit.

References

1. Liu-Ambrose TY, Khan KM, Eng JJ, et al. Both resistance and agility training increase cortical bone density in 75- to 85-year-old women with low bone mass: a 6-month randomized controlled trial. *J Clin Densitom*. 2004;7(4):390–398.
2. Tanasescu M, Leitzmann MF, Rimm EB, et al. Exercise type and intensity in relation to coronary heart disease in men. *JAMA*. 2002;288(16);1994–2000.

248. An 82-year-old woman comes to the office because she has a 3-day history of pruritic rash and swelling of both legs. History includes heart failure, hypertension, and coronary artery disease. Medications include aspirin, hydrochlorothiazide, atenolol, candesartan, and atorvastatin.

On physical examination, the patient has flat, nontender purpura involving both legs with 2+ pitting edema. Urinalysis shows 4+ protein and 4+ erythrocytes.

Which of the following is the most likely cause of this patient's symptoms?

(A) Aspirin
(B) Atenolol
(C) Hydrochlorothiazide
(D) Candesartan   Atacand
(E) Atorvastatin

ANSWER: D

This patient has features consistent with a drug eruption and acute nephritic syndrome secondary to candesartan therapy. Angiotensin-II receptor antagonists generally have a side-effect profile similar to that of placebo, but adverse events reported in the literature include angioedema, pancreatitis, hepatotoxicity, and acute renal insufficiency; Henoch-Schönlein purpura has been demonstrated.

Aspirin, atenolol, hydrochlorothiazide, and atorvastatin can cause a drug eruption, but none of these is associated with acute nephritic syndrome.

References

1. Bosch X. Henoch-Schönlein purpura induced by losartan therapy. *Arch Intern Med*. 1998;158(2):191–192.
2. Fervenza FC. Henoch-Schönlein purpura nephritis. *Int J Dermatol*. 2003;42(3):170–177.
3. Morton A, Muir J, Lim D. Rash and acute nephritic syndrome due to candesartan. *BMJ*. 2004;328(7430):25.

249. A 71-year-old man comes to the office for evaluation of dementia. He describes short-term memory loss (repeating questions, forgetting to do things), he gets lost easily, and he has recent difficulty operating the television channel changer or lawn mower. The only other symptoms he describes are mild social withdrawal and occasional crying spells. The changes have progressed gradually over several years, but they have accelerated in the past 6 to 9 months. He has a history of well-controlled hypertension, type 1 diabetes mellitus, hypercholesterolemia, and coronary heart disease. He takes aspirin, metoprolol, insulin, and atorvastatin. He has no psychiatric history.

Physical and neurologic examination is normal, with no signs of gait disorder or focal findings. General mental status examination is normal. His score on the Mini–Mental State Examination is 18 of 30; he missed 6 points on orientation, 3 on recall, 2 on serial sevens, and 1 on intersecting pentagons. Laboratory studies are normal. Magnetic resonance imaging of the brain shows moderate atrophy and moderate white matter change reported as consistent with microvascular disease, but no infarcts or lacunes.

What is the most likely cause of this patient's dementia?

(A) Dementia with Lewy bodies
(B) Major depression
(C) Frontotemporal degeneration
(D) Alzheimer's disease
(E) Vascular dementia

ANSWER: D

This patient has a dementia syndrome (amnesia, apraxia, disorientation) that has progressed over several years and recently accelerated. He has mild psychiatric symptoms and multiple cardio-vascular risk factors, but no history of cerebrovascular events. Magnetic resonance image of the brain shows white matter change with no infarcts. Vascular risk factors and brain vascular disease are now believed to be risk factors for the onset and progression of Alzheimer's disease. Alzheimer's dementia has primarily cortical features (amnesia, apraxia, agnosia, aphasia), a gradual onset and progression, and is associated with a normal neurologic examination. Vascular dementia often has mixed cortical and subcortical features (dysmnesia, dysexecutive function, delay, depletion).

In the presence of occasional mild depressive features, major depression is not likely to cause this degree of cognitive impairment. As the patient has no history of depression, the symptoms began later in life and are therefore most likely attributable to dementia. Frontotemporal degeneration is unlikely because the clinical picture shows little or no personality change or "frontal-executive" symptoms, which typically occur before the onset of memory loss in frontotemporal dementia. The picture is not typical of dementia with Lewy bodies because the cognitive decline does not appear to have short-term fluctuations, and there are no hallucinations, delusions, gait disorder, falls, or parkinsonism. To diagnose vascular dementia, current criteria require, in addition to dementia, evidence of cerebrovascular disease. The patient has cardio-vascular disease and risk factors, but no cerebrovascular history. In addition, the neurologic examination is normal. Brain imaging reveals white matter change, but no infarcts. White matter change of this sort is common in aging persons; its clinical significance is unclear in the absence of focal neurologic findings or gait disorder. Thus, while this patient likely has atherosclerotic disease of brain blood vessels, the atherosclerosis does not appear to have led to infarcts or loss of tissue consistent with what is seen in vascular dementia.

References

1. Groves WC, Brandt J, Steinberg M, et al. Vascular dementia and Alzheimer's disease: is there a difference? a comparison of symptoms by disease duration. *J Neuropsychiatry Clin Neurosci.* 2000;12(3):305–315.
2. Iadecola C, Gorelick PB. Converging pathogenic mechanisms in vascular and neurodegenerative dementia. *Stroke.* 2003; 34(2):335–337.
3. Rabins PV, Lyketsos CG, Steele CD. *Practical Dementia Care.* New York: Oxford University Press; 1999.

250. An 84-year-old woman comes to the office accompanied by her daughter for evaluation of progressive weight loss. The patient thinks she has good nutrient intake. She denies problems sleeping, depressive symptoms, change in bowel habits, or other active medical problems. She has had no serious illness or surgery in the past 5 years. She takes a daily multivitamin but is on no other regular medicines. She has lived alone since her husband's death 7 years ago. The daughter states that her mother is less active socially than before and spends most of her time reading, knitting, or watching television. The daughter is convinced that her mother has cancer; her father also started losing weight before metastatic cancer was diagnosed. A mammogram done 6 months ago and a screening colonoscopy done 2 years ago were normal.

The patient weighs 54.5 kg (120 lbs; body mass index 22 [kg/m^2]), 12% less than the prior year. The remainder of the physical examination is normal. Mini–Mental State Examination score is 28 of 30, and Yesavage Geriatric Depression Scale (short form) score is 2 (not depressed).

Apraxia : The inability to execute a voluntary motor movement despite being able to demonstrate normal muscle function

Agnosia : The inability to recognize & identify objects

Stool guaiac, urinalysis, complete blood cell count, electrolytes, and liver, renal, and thyroid function tests are normal, as is chest radiography. Electrocardiography reveals normal sinus rhythm.

Which of the following is now indicated?

(A) Computed tomographic scan of the abdomen
(B) Upper and lower endoscopy
(C) Upper gastrointestinal study with small bowel follow-through
(D) No further diagnostic testing

ANSWER: D

When older patients have involuntary weight loss, the potential causes are often readily identifiable by history and physical examination alone. When this is not the case, a more thorough diagnostic evaluation is warranted. Data suggest that the probable cause is usually identified by a focused evaluation that begins with the same basic panel of tests as this patient obtained. Additional tests are warranted only if abnormalities are identified with initial testing. If focused evaluation is unrevealing, watchful waiting is more appropriate than extensive undirected testing. In the case presented, the initial evaluation did not identify any abnormalities, so efforts to address her known risk factors for weight loss, such as social isolation and low level of physical activity, would probably provide more benefit to her than additional diagnostic testing.

References

1. Bouras EP, Lange SM, Scolapio JS. Rational approach to patients with unintentional weight loss. *Mayo Clin Proc.* 2001;76(9):923–929.
2. Hernandez JL, Riancho JA, Matorras P, et al. Clinical evaluation for cancer in patients with involuntary weight loss without specific symptoms. *Am J Med.* 2003;114(8):631–637.
3. Lankisch P, Gerzmann M, Gerzmann JF, et al. Unintentional weight loss: diagnosis and prognosis: the first prospective follow-up study from a secondary referral centre. *J Intern Med.* 2001;249(1):41–46.
4. Wallace JI. Malnutrition and enteral/parenteral alimentation. In: Hazzard WR, Blass JP, Halter JB, et al., eds. *Principles of Geriatric Medicine and Gerontology.* 5th ed. New York: The McGraw-Hill Companies, Inc; 2003:1179–1192.

251. An 82-year-old woman is brought to the emergency department because she fell in the snow and was unable to get up. It is not clear how long she had lain on the snow before a neighbor found her. Her medications are nortriptyline, which was recently initiated for treatment of depression, a multivitamin, docusate, and occasional acetaminophen. She is admitted because her pulse is 46 per minute and temperature is 35.5°C (96°F). Shortly after admission she became agitated and was successfully treated with haloperidol, but subsequently she has become progressively obtunded and is now unresponsive.

On physical examination, she is comatose, cyanotic, and hypoventilating. Her face and eyelids are puffy, and her skin is dry and yellowish. Neurologic examination demonstrates myoclonic jerking in multiple muscles and generalized hyporeflexia. Tapping on a muscle with a reflex hammer produces a transient swelling that resolves spontaneously.

Which of the following is most likely to improve this patient's condition?

(A) Lactulose
(B) Phenytoin
(C) Potassium
(D) Pyridostigmine
(E) Thyroxine

ANSWER: E

This patient is displaying features of myxedema coma, which responds to treatment with thyroxine. Hypothyroid encephalopathy can develop in persons with known hypothyroidism, in persons with acute autoimmune thyroiditis, or in persons, like this patient, with previously unrecognized hypothyroidism in whom stress triggers acute decompensation. Examples of such triggers include bacterial infection, trauma, cold exposure, anesthesia, and medications such as nortriptyline, barbiturates, and phenothiazines. Myxedema coma is characterized by progressive obtundation, often with multifocal myoclonus and even seizures. These nonspecific features can be seen in many metabolic encephalopathies. In myxedema coma, however, muscles can display a myotonic-like transient swelling when tapped, and reflexes are typically reduced. More generalized features of hypothyroidism may also be evident in affected patients, such as dry, rough skin with yellow discoloration, puffy face and eyelids, and loss of the outer eyebrows. Patients in myxedema coma are often hypothermic and cyanotic, and display both bradycardia and hypoventilation. Myxedema coma should always be considered in the differential diagnosis of coma of undetermined cause, especially in older persons during winter.

Persons with hepatic encephalopathy or adrenal insufficiency may display features of metabolic encephalopathy, but the skin changes, puffy eyelids, hypothermia, bradycardia, hyporeflexia, and myoedema upon muscle tapping suggest hypothyroidism in this patient. Lactulose improves hepatic encephalopathy but has no effect on hypothyroid encephalopathy. Phenytoin may be appropriate for patients who have recurrent seizures as a component of a metabolic encephalopathy, but its use is not necessary for multifocal myoclonus. Electrolyte disturbances are not a direct component of myxedema coma, although adrenal insufficiency (Addison's disease) may coexist with myxedema coma and is often accompanied by the triad of hyponatremia, hyperglycemia, and hyperkalemia. Pyridostigmine is effective treatment for myasthenia gravis, which produces muscle weakness, but not altered consciousness.

References

1. Ringel MD. Management of hypothyroidism and hyperthyroidism in the intensive care unit. *Crit Care Clin.* 2001;17(1):59–74.
2. Wall CR. Myxedema coma: diagnosis and treatment. *Am Fam Physician.* 2000;62(11):2485–2490.
3. Wijdicks EFM. *Neurologic Complications of Critical Illness.* Oxford: Oxford University Press; 2002:166–167.

252. A 68-year-old woman who recently moved to an assisted-living facility is referred by her nurse for evaluation of excessive emotionality and inappropriate sexually seductive behavior toward men. In the office, she is wearing considerable make up and jewelry, a provocative V-neck shirt, and a mini-skirt. She states that the nurses in the assisted-living facility are "insensitive and aloof, unable to reverberate with the strong emotional discharge surrounding my wonderful peers," and that they are "jealous of my extensive popularity. I have always had great success with men, though they all turned out to be jerks in the end." Her daughter, who accompanies her, rolls her eyes during much of the interview, interjecting that her mother has always been unstable and angry, that she switches moods easily, and that she is now actually much better as she has not threatened suicide in the past few months. Mental status examination reveals normal rate and rhythm of speech, normal motor activity, euthymia, and no perceptual abnormalities. Cognitive examination is normal.

Which of the following is the most likely cause for the patient's behavior?

(A) Frontal lobe dementia
(B) Bipolar disorder, manic type
(C) Schizotypal personality disorder
(D) Borderline personality disorder
(E) Narcissistic personality disorder

ANSWER: D

This patient displays excessive emotionality and attention-seeking behavior, alternating between idealization and devaluation. Her longstanding history of affective instability, intense anger, and suicidal threats fulfills criteria for diagnosis of borderline personality disorder. Patients with borderline personality disorder have a pattern of unstable and intense relationships, impulsivity, identity disturbance, and chronic feelings of emptiness. In contrast, persons with narcissistic personality disorder are typically grandiose and arrogant, have feelings of entitlement, lack empathy, need to be admired, and are often exploitative in their interpersonal relationships.

Frontal lobe dementia is often accompanied by disinhibited behavior but is also associated with neurologic and cognitive symptoms, which this patient does not have. Also, the behavioral symptoms that accompany dementia are a change from the baseline behavior pattern, whereas this patient's behavior is longstanding. Her physical presentation raises the possibility of mania, but mania would be also associated with characteristic mental status changes (agitation, elated mood and affect, pressured speech, distractibility). Persons with schizotypal personality disorder may be bizarre, but they are distant and avoid close relationships.

References

1. Gabbard GO. *Psychodynamic Psychiatry in Clinical Practice.* 3rd ed. Arlington, VA: American Psychiatric Press, Inc.; 2000:411–462.
2. Sadock B, Sadock V. *Kaplan and Sadock's Synopsis of Psychiatry.* 9th ed. Philadelphia, PA: Lippincott Williams and Wilkins; 2003:808–810.
3. Sanislow CA, Morey LC, Grilo CM, et al. Confirmatory factor analysis of DSM-IV criteria for borderline personality disorder: findings from the collaborative longitudinal personality disorders study. *Am J Psychiatry.* 2002;159(2):284–290.

253. An 86-year-old woman comes to the office because she has mid-back pain at rest and with activity that has worsened over the past few months. She has longstanding osteoporosis with previous compression fractures at T10 and L1. She reports no other symptoms. Medications include calcium, vitamin D, and risedronate. After her last compression fracture 2 years ago, she was started on calcitonin, but it was discontinued after 1 month because of continued back pain and the development of rhinitis. Acetaminophen and over-the-counter nonsteroidal anti-inflammatory agents around the clock provided no relief. After her last visit 3 months ago, she began acetaminophen with hydrocodone (750 mg/7.5 mg), 1 tablet every 6 hours. This regimen provided better pain control initially, but she now rates her pain as 7 out of 10 on most days and states that it limits many of her activities, including bathing and dressing.

Physical examination reveals moderate kyphosis and mild tenderness to palpation over her mid-spine and the surrounding paraspinous muscles. Neurologic examination demonstrates intact lower extremity reflexes, strength, and sensation. Radiography of her thoracic and lumbar spine shows severe degenerative disc disease along with the old compression fractures at T10 and L1; no new vertebral fractures or other processes are visualized.

What is the most appropriate management strategy for this patient?

(A) Increase the acetaminophen with hydrocodone to 1 tablet every 4 hours around the clock.
(B) Switch to immediate-release oxycodone.
(C) Evaluate for kyphoplasty.
(D) Refer for physical therapy.
(E) Add cyclobenzaprine.

ANSWER: B

The World Health Organization pain management ladder recommends beginning with nonopioid analgesia for mild pain and advancing to combination (nonopioid-opioid) analgesia and then opioid therapy for control of moderate to severe pain. Acetaminophen and combination medication failed to relieve this patient's pain. The dose ceiling of the nonopioid component of the combined nonopioid-opioid agents limits their use. In this case, the acetaminophen with hydrocodone dose (750 mg/7.5 mg) cannot be increased to 1 tablet every 4 hours, as this would exceed the maximum dose of acetaminophen (4000 mg per day). Given her persistent pain and functional status limitations, opioid analgesia should be started and titrated until she is comfortable.

Kyphoplasty is a minimally invasive procedure typically performed by a spine surgeon. A needle is introduced into the vertebral body, a balloon tamp is placed to reduce the fracture, and polymethylmethacrylate, a cement-like material, is injected to fill the void. The procedure reduces pain from vertebral fractures in patients with subacute osteoporotic fractures that are less than 3 months old. This patient's vertebral fractures are too old, and because of this, she is not a candidate for this procedure.

Physical therapy is often a useful adjunct in the management of pain. Therapy might include modalities such as strengthening and stretching, heat, ultrasound, and evaluation for transcutaneous electrical nerve stimulation. This patient would likely benefit from physical therapy, but given the severity of her current symptoms, it is essential to get her pain under control first.

Patients with back pain from vertebral fractures may also have surrounding muscle spasm. This patient's symptoms suggest a degree of paraspinous muscle spasm. Although a muscle relaxant (eg, cyclobenzaprine) might provide some benefit, her primary symptoms appear to be related to her vertebral fractures, and she needs to have this pain controlled first. In addition, because muscle relaxants have significant adverse effects (drowsiness, dizziness, confusion), if they are used at all, they need to be started at a low dose and titrated as needed.

References

1. AGS Panel on Persistent Pain in Older Persons. The management of persistent pain in older persons. *J Am Geriatr Soc.* 2002; 50(6):S205–S224.
2. Ballantyne JC, Mao J. Opioid therapy for chronic pain. *N Engl J Med.* 2003;439:1943–1953.
3. Phillips FM. Minimally invasive treatments of osteoporotic vertebral compression fractures. *Spine.* 2003;28(15):S45–S53.

254. In a nursing facility, which of the following is the best approach to identify residents at risk for development of pressure ulcers and to monitor existing pressure ulcers?

(A) Develop risk and monitoring scales specific to that facility.
(B) Implement the Braden scale and the Pressure Ulcer Scale for Healing (PUSH).
(C) Implement the Braden and Norton scales.
(D) Implement the PUSH tool and the Pressure Sore Status Tool (PSST).

ANSWER: B

Developing and validating institution-specific scales is not practical when validated scales already exist. Risk assessment using a standardized scale should be performed on all nursing-home residents upon admission, readmission, return from hospitalization, when there is a significant change in condition, and during quarterly assessments. The two most widely used tools to assess risk are the Norton scale and the Braden scale.

The Norton scale comprises five clinical categories (physical condition, mental state, activity, mobility, and incontinence). The Braden scale comprises six clinical categories (sensory perception, moisture, activity, mobility, nutrition, and friction and shear). A score of 16 or lower on the Norton scale or 18 or lower on the Braden scale indicates increased risk for development of pressure ulcers.

The most widely used validated instruments for assessing the healing of pressure ulcers are the time-consuming Pressure Sore Status Tool (PSST) and the briefer Pressure Ulcer Scale for Healing (PUSH). The PSST is made up of 13 wound characteristics, including depth, size, undermining, type of exudates, and edema. The PUSH tool assesses size of ulcer, exudate amount, and tissue type.

References

1. Dimant J. Implementing pressure ulcer prevention and treatment programs: using AMDA clinical practice guidelines. *JAMDA.* 2001;2(6):315–325.
2. Lyder CH. Pressure ulcer prevention and management. *JAMA.* 2003;289(2):223–226.
3. Theaker C. Pressure sore prevention in the critically ill: what you don't know, what you should know and why it's important. *Intensive Crit Care Nurs.* 2003;19(3):163–168.

255. A patient receives a diagnosis of psychosis associated with Alzheimer's disease. Pharmacotherapy with an atypical antipsychotic is initiated.

Which of the following is more likely with an atypical than with a conventional antipsychotic agent?

(A) Greater likelihood of remission of psychotic symptoms
(B) Reduced rate of falls and injury
(C) Reduced incidence of tardive dyskinesia
(D) Lower incidence of somnolence
(E) Absence of QTc prolongation

ANSWER: C

Although conventional and atypical antipsychotic agents are similarly effective for the treatment of psychotic symptoms in elderly persons with dementia, their adverse effects differ. Atypical antipsychotics are the treatment of choice for psychosis in Alzheimer's disease because they have lower rates of extrapyramidal symptoms, especially tardive dyskinesia. Tardive dyskinesia is a syndrome of choreiform movements that may emerge after sustained antipsychotic therapy. It is often disfiguring and, in the elderly person, can affect dentition, swallowing, and respiration. Tardive dyskinesia is much more common in elderly than in younger patients treated with antipsychotics. With conventional antipsychotics (eg, haloperidol), the 1-year incidence of tardive dyskinesia is over 30% in older patients and around 5% in younger patients. With atypical antipsychotics, the 1-year incidence of tardive dyskinesia in older patients decreases to less than 5%.

Both conventional and atypical antipsychotic agents are associated with sedation and, less commonly, falls and injury in older patients with dementia. All antipsychotic agents may prolong the QTc interval, though the clinical impact of this is unclear.

References

1. Dolder CR, Lacro JP, Leckband S, et al. Interventions to improve antipsychotic medication adherence; review of recent literature. *J Clin Psychopharmacol.* 2003;23(4):389–399.
2. Kinderman SS, Dolder CR, Bailey A, et al. Pharamacological treatment of psychosis and agitation in elderly patients with dementia: four decades of experience. *Drugs Aging.* 2002;19(4):257–276.

256. A 67-year-old woman with recently diagnosed metastatic ovarian cancer comes to the office for a follow-up visit. She has new symptoms of nausea and vomiting. Several months ago, the patient underwent debulking surgery and chemotherapy, but there was extensive carcinomatosis on follow-up imaging 3 months later, and her CA-125 level has remained high. At her last appointment, she acknowledged that her cancer will not be cured and stated that she is reluctant to undergo further invasive procedures or to be rehospitalized. Her current nausea and vomiting started 2 days ago. She has been unable to tolerate any oral intake and has not had a bowel movement in 4 days. Her only medications are acetaminophen with codeine as needed and docusate sodium stool softener every morning.

On examination, the patient appears thin and uncomfortable. She is afebrile. Blood pressure is 98/60 mm Hg, and pulse is 105 per minute. Cardiopulmonary examination is unremarkable aside from tachycardia. The abdomen is markedly distended with decreased bowel sounds, tympany on percussion, and diffuse tenderness on palpation. Rectal examination is normal, with no stool in the vault.

In addition to providing the patient with morphine, which of the following is the most appropriate management strategy for this patient?

(A) Diverting colostomy
(B) Nasogastric suctioning
(C) Octreotide *Sandostatin*
(D) Atropine
(E) Ondansetron *Zofran*

ANSWER: C

This patient has classic signs and symptoms of intestinal obstruction. Cancer patients may develop a bowel obstruction for various reasons, including intraluminal obstruction (eg, by tumor mass), direct infiltration of the bowel wall (eg, colon carcinoma), external compression of the lumen, carcinomatosis causing dysmotility (eg, ovarian cancer), and intra-abdominal adhesions (eg, from postoperative changes). Symptoms of obstruction are generally due to the normal physiologic processes of the intestine (peristalsis and secretion of fluid, electrolytes, and enzymes) plus the inflammatory process caused by the obstruction.

Bowel obstruction in patients with advanced cancer can be managed with conservative therapy. This patient does not wish to undergo further procedures or hospitalization, and her request should be honored. Thus, surgery is not an option, and placement of a nasogastric tube, which may be uncomfortable, should be avoided. Opioids such as morphine and antiemetics such as prochlorperazine relieve pain and nausea, respectively. Ondansetron, a selective serotonins 5-HT(3)-type receptor antagonist, will also relieve nausea and vomiting, but other, less expensive antiemetics should be tried first. Antisecretory agents such as antimuscarinic anticholinergic drugs (eg, scopolamine or atropine) and somatostatin analogs (eg, octreotide) are effective in the management of intestinal obstruction. Octreotide has fewer adverse effects than antimuscarinic agents and has been shown to have superior improvement in symptoms. It can be administered subcutaneously or intravenously with minimal adverse effects.

The care plan for this patient with metastatic ovarian cancer has shifted from a focus on cure to comfort. She is an ideal candidate for home hospice and its multidisciplinary approach to terminal illness. Home hospice nurses can manage an octreotide pump, and the Medicare hospice benefit would cover this treatment.

References

1. Doyle D, Hanks G, Cherny N, et al., eds. *Oxford Textbook of Palliative Medicine*. 3rd ed. Oxford: Oxford University Press; 2003.
2. Muir JC, von Gunten CF. Antisecretory agents in gastrointestinal obstruction. *Clin Geriatr Med*. 2000;16(2):327–334.
3. Mystakidou K, Tsilika E, Kalaidopoulou O, et al. Comparison of octreotide administration vs conservative treatment in the management of inoperable bowel obstruction in patients with far advanced cancer: a randomized, double-blind, controlled clinical trial. *Anticancer Res*. 2002; 22(2B): 1187–1192.

257. An 84-year-old woman living in a retirement home has over the past week become increasingly agitated, especially at night. She climbs out of bed, and on at least one occasion she fell, sustaining a bruise on her hip. She has a 2-year history of cognitive decline consistent with Alzheimer's disease. She has type 2 diabetes mellitus treated with glyburide and chronic obstructive pulmonary disease treated with a salmeterol inhaler. Staff at her retirement home report that she has been a poor sleeper since she was admitted 18 months earlier, but she is otherwise cooperative and cheerful. On examination, she appears fearful and complains of criminals coming into her room at night to attack her.

Which of the following is the best initial management strategy?

(A) Use of side rails on her bed at night
(B) Music therapy in the evening
(C) Physical examination and routine laboratory testing
(D) Treatment of hip pain with acetaminophen
(E) Use of bright-light therapy to improve sleep

ANSWER: C

This patient's 1-week history of agitation and psychosis is suggestive of delirium. In older adults with dementia, recent behavioral changes should precipitate review of their medical status and medications to exclude potential causes of an intercurrent delirium. Many common causes can be ruled out with physical examination, routine blood work, urinalysis, chest radiograph if indicated, and review of recent medication changes.

Use of side rails or any type of physical restraint may increase her risk of harm, leading to entrapment or death. Music therapy is a nonpharmacologic intervention that has been studied in randomized controlled trials. If physical examination and other investigations exclude delirium, this type of intervention could be considered for reducing agitation. Treatment of pain with non-narcotic analgesic medication is an important aspect of management and may contribute to a decrease in agitation. For this patient, however, the behavioral change clearly preceded the fall. The use of bright lights has been shown to improve sleep-wake cycle disturbances in some studies but not consistently. It is unlikely to be helpful for this patient who also demonstrates psychotic behaviors.

References

1. Burns A, Byrne J, Ballard C, et al. Sensory stimulation in dementia. *BMJ*. 2002;325(7376):1312–1313.
2. Camp CJ, Cohen-Mansfield J, Capezuti EA. Use of nonpharmacologic interventions among nursing home residents with dementia. *Psychiatric Serv*. 2002;53(11):1397–1401.
3. Herrmann N. Recommendations for the management of behavioral and psychological symptoms of dementia. *Can J Neurol Sci*. 2001;28:Suppl 1:S96–S107.
4. Howard R, Ballard C, O'Brien J, et al. Guidelines for the management of agitation in dementia. *Int J Geriatric Psychiatry*. 2001;16(7):714–717.

258. A 75-year-old woman comes to the office because of unilateral pain and swelling along the medial hindfoot and ankle regions. The symptoms began approximately 1 month ago without any history of trauma. She has noticed a progressive flattening of the arch of the foot as compared with her other foot. The patient is otherwise healthy.

On physical examination, she is afebrile and has normal vital signs. Neurologic and vascular examination of the feet is normal. There is pain on palpation of the foot, with overlying edema just posterior and distal to the medial malleolus. Weight bearing demonstrates a unilateral flatfoot deformity. She has difficulty standing on her toes because of pain and weakness. Radiographs of the affected foot show no fracture or joint dislocation, but there are structural alignment changes consistent with a flatfoot deformity. Radiographs of the other foot are normal.

Which of the following is the most likely diagnosis?

(A) Stress fracture
(B) Plantar fasciitis
(C) Achilles tendinitis
(D) Posterior tibial tendon rupture
(E) Tarsal tunnel syndrome

ANSWER: D

Posterior tibial tendon rupture commonly develops insidiously with overuse and results in swelling and pain along its course in the posteromedial ankle. The untreated tendinitis progresses to gradual shortening of the tendon and rupture. The hallmark presentation is the gradual development of a unilateral flatfoot deformity. When the posterior tibial tendon (the primary supinator of the foot) fails to operate effectively, the medial arch collapses. Rupture most commonly occurs just distal to the medial malleolus, perhaps because of the relative hypovascularity of the region, and may lead to severe disability and chronic pain. Radiographs demonstrate changes consistent with a flatfoot deformity. Magnetic resonance imaging is the gold standard for diagnosis. Pronated feet and ankle equinus deformities predispose the foot to posterior tibial tendon ruptures, as they increase the mechanical demand placed upon the tendon. Rheumatoid arthritis also has been associated with this condition.

Although a calcaneal stress fracture may induce localized pain and swelling, radiographic changes would usually be evident 3 weeks after the traumatizing event. Also, there would be no flatfoot deformity. Plantar fasciitis causes pain on the plantar surface of the heel, which is usually exacerbated by weight bearing after prolonged rest. Although commonly associated with flat

feet, plantar fasciitis would not result in the gradual new development of this deformity. Achilles tendinitis generally results in pain and edema localized to the posterior ankle region directly over the tendon itself. Achilles tendinitis is related to overuse but is not associated with a unilateral flatfoot. Tarsal tunnel syndrome is a compression neuropathy of the posterior tibial nerve that results in pain and numbness radiating to the plantar foot and toes. It does not cause the foot to flatten.

References

1. Anderson RB, Davis WD. Management of the adult flat foot deformity. In: Myerson MS, ed. *Foot and Ankle Disorders.* Philadelphia, PA: WB Saunders; 2000:1017–1038.
2. Meehan RE, Brage M. Adult acquired flat foot deformity: clinical and radiographic examination. *Foot Ankle Clin.* 2003;8(3):431–452.

259. A 75 year-old slight woman comes to the office because of pain on the posterior aspect of her ankle. She has type 2 diabetes mellitus. She has recently begun an exercise program that consists of 3-mile hikes in the hills behind her home three times a week. On physical examination, there is tenderness on palpation of the Achilles tendon at its insertion into the heel and localized edema. Pedal pulses are palpable and there are no neurologic deficits. Maximal ankle joint dorsiflexion with the knee extended is less than 5 degrees and elicits pain. Plantar flexor motion about the ankle is normal. Radiographs are unremarkable.

Which of the following is the most likely diagnosis?

(A) Gout
(B) Plantar fasciitis
(C) Achilles tendinitis
(D) Anterior tibial tendinitis
(E) Tarsal tunnel syndrome

ANSWER: C

Overuse injury of the Achilles tendon is common in patients who participate in regular, prolonged weight-bearing activities. Running or walking on hills causes additional strain. The most common complaint is point tenderness of the posterior aspect of the heel, either at the insertion site of the Achilles tendon or slightly proximal to it. The pain can also be elicited with forced dorsiflexion of the ankle joint. Commonly, patients also have an equinus deformity due to inadequate stretching, which further strains the tendon. Diabetic patients in particular are prone to equinus deformities, as the chronic elevated glucose levels can cause intratendinous collagen glycosylation, which reduces the elasticity of the tendon. With chronic inflammation of the tendon, radiographs show a retrocalcaneal spur at the insertion of the Achilles tendon.

Gout most commonly affects the great toe (podagra), but it also affects the ankle, foot, and knee. However, gout of the ankle would have developed more acutely than in this case, and it would have been associated with warmth, erythema, and pain with plantar flexion, and tenderness on palpation of the ankle.

Plantar fasciitis pain occurs on the plantar surface of the heel. Anterior tibial tendonitis (shin splints) is also an overuse syndrome, but with pain localized to the anterior ankle or leg. Tarsal tunnel syndrome is a compression phenomenon of the posterior tibial nerve as it traverses by the medial malleolus of the ankle. Affected patients generally have burning pain or tingling in the arch and foot.

References

1. Myerson MS, Mandelbaum B. Disorders of the Achilles tendon and the retrocalcaneal region. In: Myerson MS, ed. *Foot and Ankle Disorders*. Philadelphia, PA: WB Saunders; 2000:1367–1397.
2. Paavola M, Kannus P, Jarvinen TA, et al. Achilles tendinopathy. *J Bone Joint Surg Am.* 2002;84-A(11):2062–2076.

260. A 79-year-old woman comes to the office because of pain, swelling, stiffness, and mild erythema of her right forefoot. She is healthy and takes no medications other than vitamins and calcium. The patient recalls an injury 4 months earlier, in which a package of frozen chicken fell on the foot from a top-loading freezer compartment of her refrigerator. She recalls that the foot swelled immediately and became discolored and painful. At the local hospital emergency department, radiographs of her right foot showed no evidence of fracture. She was advised to take anti-inflammatory medications, apply ice to the area, and rest and elevate the foot. Although the discoloration from the original injury subsided, the swelling has persisted and the pain is now excruciating.

On physical examination, there is exquisite pain on palpation of the right forefoot. The skin over the metatarsal area is warm, erythematous, and dry. The toes are cool to touch, with mild cyanosis over the dorsum. Neurologic findings are normal. Pedal pulses are palpable. Repeat radiographs reveal periarticular soft-tissue swelling and patchy osteoporosis involving the metatarsals and metatarsal phalangeal articulations. Serologic tests for antinuclear antibody and rheumatoid factor are negative, and electromyography and nerve conduction velocity studies are normal.

Which of the following is the most likely diagnosis?

(A) Tarsal tunnel syndrome
(B) Raynaud's phenomenon
(C) Rheumatoid arthritis
(D) Reflex sympathetic dystrophy
(E) Stress fracture

ANSWER: D

The most common cause of reflex sympathetic dystrophy is trauma resulting from fractures, dislocations, sprains, amputations, crush injuries, or even minor cuts of the toes or feet. Other causes include surgery, diabetes mellitus, hemiparesis, venipuncture, infections, and neoplasms. The signs and symptoms of reflex sympathetic dystrophy—pain, swelling, stiffness, and skin discoloration—are usually sufficient for diagnosis. Three-phase bone scan demonstrates diffuse uptake in the blood flow, pool, and delayed phases, and can confirm the diagnosis. Radiographs show patchy osteoporosis, which may progress to a ground-glass appearance. Diagnostic criteria are pain and tenderness in the extremity, soft-tissue swelling, decreased motor function, trophic skin changes, vasomotor instability, and patchy osteoporosis.

Tarsal tunnel syndrome is a compression syndrome of the posterior tibial nerve. Percussion of the posterior tibial nerve may produce a positive Tinel's sign that radiates to the top of the forefoot. There usually is decreased sensation. Raynaud's phenomenon is characterized by episodic pallor of the digits with paresthesia, followed by cyanosis, and finally rubor, warmth, and a throbbing sensation (white-blue-red skin changes). With osteoporosis, radiographs show trabecular bone resorption and intracortical tunneling. With stress fractures, radiographs may initially be normal, but the fracture site should be visible 4 to 6 weeks after injury. Rheumatoid arthritis can affect the joints of the foot, with erythema, joint swelling, and pain or passive and active range of motion. However, there would be no cyanosis on examination, and the radiographs would show changes characteristic of rheumatoid arthritis, not osteoporosis.

References
1. Kosin F. Reflex sympathetic dystrophy syndrome. *Primer on Rheumatic Diseases.* 2000;274–275.
2. Vacariu G. Complex regional pain syndrome. *Disabil Rehabil.* 2002;24(8):435–442.

261. Which of the following statements regarding adult day care is true?

(A) The concept of adult day care originated in the United States.
(B) The National Adult Day Services Association (NADSA) regulates adult day care.
(C) The costs of adult day care are paid out of pocket.
(D) Individuals with cognitive impairment are poor candidates for adult day care.

ANSWER: C

Adult day care began in England in the 1950s, when patients were found to recover faster if they were discharged from the hospital early and returned for day treatment. In 1972 in the United States, the National Council on the Aging formed the National Adult Day Services Association (NADSA) to specifically address the issue of adult day care. The purpose of NADSA is to "promote the concept of adult day services as a viable community-based option for disabled older persons within the larger constellation of long-term care services." Regulation of adult day care differs by state. The federal government does not regulate adult day care, nor does it mandate that states do so. NADSA offers standards and guidelines for adult day care as a template for states choosing to regulate the industry.

The cost of adult day care is paid out of pocket by the consumer. Daily fees can range from several dollars to $185, depending on the region of the country and the services utilized. Some programs offer sliding-scale payment options for low-income clients.

Adult day care programs are targeted to older persons with physical impairment or mental confusion who require supervision, social opportunities, or assistance with activities of daily living. The services vary widely from program to program. Typical programs include transportation, social services, meals, nursing care, personal care, counseling, therapeutic activities, and rehabilitation therapy.

References
1. *Connecticut Association of Adult Day Centers Information Handbook.* Provided by the Connecticut Association of Adult Day Centers, 300 Research Parkway, Meriden, CT 06450. Telephone 203-379-4437.
2. Handy J, Bellome J. Adult day service: the next frontier. *Caring.* 1996;15(12):24–26,28,30–33.
3. Tischer G. Ensuring proper interactions between inpatient/residential settings & home health agencies. *Caring.* 2003;22(9):24–26,29.

262. A 75-year-old woman comes to the office for consultation regarding use of estrogen therapy. She has active gastroesophageal disease with heartburn and occasional hot flushes. She had a hysterectomy at age 55 for uterine bleeding. She has a family history of hip fracture and reports that she is "sensitive" to many medications. She took estrogen in the past but discontinued use after 1 month because of breast tenderness. A recent bone mineral density test shows osteopenia at the femoral neck (T score, −1.8). Adequate calcium intake and vitamin D are recommended, but she also wants to restart estrogen therapy.

Which of the following should be recommended?

(A) Conjugated equine estrogen and medroxyprogesterone, 0.625 mg/2.5 mg daily
(B) Conjugated equine estrogen, 0.625 mg daily
(C) Conjugated equine estrogen, 0.3 mg daily
(D) No additional therapy

ANSWER: C

Because the lifetime risk of fracture increases with decreasing bone mineral density, the prevention of progressive bone loss is an important goal. This woman has osteopenia, and prevention of osteoporosis is warranted. The U.S. Food and Drug Administration (FDA) has approved several therapies for the prevention of osteoporosis, including estrogen, risedronate, alendronate, and raloxifene.

A regimen of 0.3 mg conjugated equine estrogen (half the typical replacement dose) prevents bone loss when given with adequate amounts of calcium and vitamin D. Breast tenderness is minimized with the lower dose. A recent trial using 0.25 mg estradiol (one fourth the usual replacement dose) demonstrated beneficial effects on bone turnover and bone mineral density, with breast and endometrial adverse effects equal to those of placebo. The FDA suggests that alternatives be considered if estrogen is needed only to prevent bone loss or osteoporosis. Bisphosphonates (risedronate, alendronate) are effective but have associated gastrointestinal adverse effects that may limit their use in a patient with a history of gastroesophageal reflux disease. Similarly, raloxifene may exacerbate hot flushes.

The Women's Health Initiative found that estrogen therapy reduces the risk of fractures and colorectal carcinoma but increases the risk of breast cancer and cardiac disease.

References

1. Prestwood KM, Kenny AM, Kleppinger A, et al. Ultra low-dose micronized 17β-estradiol on bone density and bone metabolism in older women: a randomized placebo-controlled study. *JAMA.* 2003: 290(8):1042–1048.
2. Recker RR, Davies KM, Dowd RM, et al. The effect of low-dose continuous estrogen and progesterone therapy with calcium and vitamin D on bone in elderly women: a randomized, controlled trial. *Ann Intern Med.* 1999;130(11):897–904.
3. Rossouw JE, Anderson GL, Prentice RL, et al.; Writing Group for the Women's Health Initiative Investigators. Risks and benefits of estrogen plus progestin in healthy postmenopausal women: principal results from the Women's Health Initiative randomized controlled trial. *JAMA.* 2002;288(3):321–333.

263. Which of the following has been demonstrated in randomized controlled studies to be an effect of postmenopausal estrogen replacement?

(A) An increase in bone density
(B) A decrease in high-density lipoproteins
(C) An increased risk for colorectal cancer
(D) Primary and secondary prevention of heart disease

ANSWER: A

Evidence from the Women's Health Initiative shows that estrogen increases the risk of cardiovascular and thrombotic events while decreasing fracture and colorectal carcinoma rates. This is contrary to earlier epidemiologic and observational studies that suggested a 35% to 50% decreased risk of cardiovascular events with estrogen. The results of the earlier studies may be due to estrogen effects on the lipid profile (specifically, an increase in high-density lipoprotein cholesterol), selection bias inherent in observational studies, or survivor benefit— estrogen users tend to be healthier and more health conscious, and they seek more medical care than women not on estrogen. These factors confound interpretation of the results of the observational studies.

In a secondary prevention trial, estrogen did not protect against cardiovascular events. Patients in the estrogen group had a higher mortality in the first 6 months of the study, but lower mortality in years 3, 4, and 5, which suggests that benefits from estrogen may require years to manifest. The study demonstrated improvement in lipid profiles for women receiving estrogen. However, a study assessing angiographic changes in women with coronary disease who had estrogen or placebo therapy found no differences between the groups.

The estrogen-progesterone arm of the primary prevention trial of estrogen therapy (Women's Health Initiative) was discontinued early because of adverse events in the treatment group, including an increase in cardiovascular events. The estrogen-only arm showed similar findings. At present, these larger randomized trials do not show a benefit of estrogen in primary or secondary prevention of heart disease.

References

1. Herrington DM, Reboussin DM, Brosnihan KB, et al. Effects of estrogen replacement on the progression of coronary artery atherosclerosis. *N Engl J Med*. 2000;343(8):522–529.
2. Hulley S, Grady D, Bush T, et al. Randomized trial of estrogen plus progestin for secondary prevention of coronary heart disease in postmenopausal women. *JAMA*. 1998; 280(7):605–613.
3. Rossouw JE, Anderson GL, Prentice RL, et al.; Writing Group for the Women's Health Initiative Investigators. Risks and benefits of estrogen plus progestin in healthy postmenopausal women: principal results from the Women's Health Initiative randomized controlled trial. *JAMA*. 2002;288(3):321–333.
4. Shumaker SA, Legault C, Kuller L, et al. Conjugated equine estrogens and incidence of probable dementia and mild cognitive impairment in postmenopausal women: Women's Health Initiative Memory Study. *JAMA*. 2004;291(24):2947–2958.

INDEX

NOTE: References are to question numbers, preceded by Q.

A

Abdominal CT, Q90, Q134
Abdominal pain
  acute, Q134
  postprandial, Q90
Abdominal strengthening exercises, Q150
Abuse
  mistreatment, Q130, Q242
  neglect, Q66, Q130, Q201
Acamprosate, Q122
Acetaminophen, Q253
  for arthritis pain relief, Q48, Q88
  with codeine, Q50
Achalasia, Q106
Achilles tendinitis, Q259
Acral lentiginous melanoma (ALM), Q30
Activated protein C, Q206
Activities of daily living (ADLs), Q69
Acute Care for the Elderly (ACE) units, Q80
Acute flaccid paralysis, Q4
Acute nephritic syndrome, Q248
Adherence to medications, Q108
Adjustment disorder, Q109
Adrenal masses, Q78
Adult day care, Q55, Q96
  for Alzheimer's disease, Q161, Q216
  costs of, Q261
Adult Protective Services, Q130
Advance directives, Q123
Age
  and nursing-home placement, Q69
  and postoperative risk of respiratory failure, Q75
Age-related changes
  in pulmonary function, Q53
  in sodium levels, Q58
  in stem cells, Q196
  that result in dizziness and sensorineural hearing loss, Q229
Aggressive behavior in dementia, Q215
Aging women, Q145
Agitation
  acute, Q241
  with dementia, Q215, Q241
  in frail elderly, Q241
  management of, Q43, Q44, Q65
  with mild mental retardation, Q64
Agoraphobia, Q181
Albumin, Q75
Alcohol, Q111, Q182
  dependency, Q122
  reducing consumption of, Q143
Alcohol-Related Problems Survey (ARPS), Q221
Alcoholism
  risk of, Q39
  screening for, Q221
  vitamin deficiency in, Q142
ALM. See Acral lentiginous melanoma
Aloe vera, Q155
α-Blockers, Q68

Alprazolam, Q103
Alprostadil, Q135
Alzheimer's disease, Q98, Q249
  behavioral management in, Q102
  delay in progression of, Q137
  effects on caregivers, Q161
  management of, Q55, Q161, Q216
  psychotic disturbance related to, Q241
  See also Dementia, Lewy bodies
Amantadine, Q12, Q52
American Thoracic Society care guidelines for tuberculosis, Q92
Amiodarone, Q82, Q157, Q180
Amlodipine, Q61
Ammonium lactate cream, Q104
Amyotrophic lateral sclerosis, Q4
Androgen levels in women, Q72
Anemia
  evaluation of, Q148
  hypoproliferative, Q148
  management of, Q42
Anergy testing, Q204
Angiodysplasia, Q77
Angiography, splanchnic, Q90
Angiotensin-converting enzyme inhibitors, Q164
  for acute myocardial infarction, Q169, Q224
  for atrial fibrillation, Q180
  for heart failure, Q180, Q203
Angiotensin-receptor blockers, Q169, Q180
Ankle pain, Q258
Anterior choroidal artery occlusion, Q149
Anterior spinal artery occlusion, Q118
Anterior tibial tendinitis, Q259
Antibiotics, Q159. See also specific drugs
  for community-acquired pneumonia, Q73
  for endocarditis prophylaxis, Q94
Antibodies, anti-Yo, Q194
Antidepressants, Q100, Q103
Antiepileptic drugs, Q103
Antihypertensives, Q202
Antioxidants, Q137
Antipsychotic agents
  for agitation, Q241
  atypical, Q255
  low-dose, Q246
Antiretroviral therapy, Q236
Antithrombin III, Q206
Anxiety disorder, generalized, Q24, Q109, Q233
Aortic stenosis, Q164
Aortic valve replacement, Q164
Aortoenteric fistulas, Q77
Appendicitis, Q134
Appetite restoration, Q34
ARPS (Alcohol-Related Problems Survey), Q221
Arterial stiffness, Q160
Arteriovenous malformations, Q77

Arthritis
  osteoarthritis, Q5, Q48
  pain relief in, Q88
  rheumatoid, Q162
Arthroplasty, total joint, Q48
Aspiration pneumonia, Q13
Aspirin, Q82
  adverse effects, Q248
  for atrial fibrillation and heart failure, Q180
  daily low-dose, Q242
  herbal interactions, Q94
Assisted-living facilities, Q133, Q216
Assistive listening devices, Q45
Atenolol, Q88, Q157, Q248
Atherosclerosis, systemic, Q90
Atorvastatin, Q152, Q248
Atrial fibrillation
  new-onset, Q180
  treatment of, Q82
Atrophic vaginitis, Q31
Atropine, Q125, Q256
Audiograms, diagnostic, Q14
Audiology, Q45
AudioScope test, Q193
Auditory brain stem response test, Q175
Auditory hallucinations, Q112
Autism, Q103
Autoimmune thrombocytopenia, Q47
Automatic cuffs, Q160
Autonomic neuropathy, Q176
Avoidant personality disorder, Q6
Awakening, early-morning, Q158

B

B-cell lymphoma, chronic, Q47
Back extensor resistive exercise, Q179
Back pain, Q223
  acute, Q57
  lower back pain, Q8, Q150
  mid-back pain, Q253
Back protection maneuvers, Q150
Bacterial overgrowth, small bowel, Q188
Bacterial vaginosis, Q222
Balloon aortic valvuloplasty, Q164
Baroreceptor sensitivity, decreased, Q160
Behavior problems
  agitated aggressive behavior with dementia, Q215
  nighttime disruptive behaviors, Q62
Behavior support plans, Q103
Behavioral change
  causes of, Q102
  disability resulting in, Q20
Beneficence, Q22
Benign paroxysmal positional vertigo (BPPV), Q46, Q91
Benign prostatic hyperplasia
  erectile dysfunction with, Q176
  mild to moderate, Q197
Benztropine, Q52

Bereavement, Q217

Berg balance test, Q138

β-Blockers
for acute MI, Q169
for atrial fibrillation and heart failure, Q180

Bethanechol, Q239

Bilateral occipital lobe infarction, Q208

Biofeedback
-assisted pelvic muscle training, Q26
for bladder training, Q76

Biopsy
excisional, Q120
fine-needle aspiration biopsy, Q140
incisional, Q30

Bisphosphonates, Q87

Bladder, overactive, Q110, Q119, Q239

Bladder cancer screening, Q136

Bladder contractility, impaired, Q220

Bladder training, Q76

Bleeding
diverticular, Q77
rectal, Q77
risk of, Q155
vaginal, Q172

Blood pressure
drug effects on, Q234
monitoring, Q138, Q160

Blood-pressure control. *See also* Hypertension
life-style interventions for, Q3
for stroke risk reduction, Q59

Bone density, Q247

Bone homeostasis, Q152

Borderline personality disorder, Q6, Q252

Bowel obstruction, Q256

BPPV. *See* Benign paroxysmal positional vertigo

Brachytherapy, Q9

Braden Scale, Q254

Brain imaging
in dementia, Q63
in gait disturbance, Q212
magnetic resonance imaging, Q138, Q212

Breast carcinoma, intraductal, Q146

Breast disease, Paget's, Q146

Breathing-related sleep disorders, Q158

Bright-light therapy, Q2

Buprenorphine, Q184

Bupropion, Q49

Buspirone, Q49, Q215

C

Calcaneal stress fractures, Q258

Calcitonin, Q57

Calcium, Q152

Calcium alginate dressings, Q11

Calcium antagonists, Q169

Calcium carbonate, Q57

Calcium channel blockers, Q202

Calcium citrate, Q57

Calf pain, Q33

Calorie counts, Q15

Calorie restriction, Q105

CAM. *See* Confusion Assessment Method

CAM-ICU. *See* Confusion Assessment Method of the Intensive Care Unit

Cancer
colon, Q32, Q187
intraductal carcinoma the breast, Q146
lung cancer, Q98, Q230
metastatic ovarian cancer, Q256
multiple myeloma, Q25, Q148
oral cancer, Q124, Q128
ovarian cancer, Q194
paraneoplastic cerebellar degeneration, Q194
prostate cancer, Q9, Q50, Q87, Q170

Candesartan, Q248

Candidiasis, vulvar, Q31, Q116

Cardioversion, Q82

Caregiver stress, Q214

Caregiving, Q115
Alzheimer's disease and, Q161
burdens on, Q62
community services related to dementia, Q214
women caregivers, Q145

Cataract surgery, Q209

Cataracts, bilateral, Q64

Causalgia, Q18

Ceftriaxone, Q73

Celecoxib, Q35, Q88, Q162

Cerebellar degeneration, paraneoplastic, Q194

Cervical disk disease, Q240

Cervical spine radiography, Q212

Cervical spondylosis, Q118

Charcot's foot, Q36

Chemotherapy
adjuvant for colon cancer, Q187
for stage IIIB non-small cell lung cancer, Q230

Chest angiography, Q144

Chest pain, Q169

Chest physical therapy, Q159

Cholinesterase inhibitors, Q246

Chronic B-cell lymphoma, Q47

Chronic obstructive pulmonary disease
management of, Q11
postoperative complications, Q159
postoperative risk of respiratory failure, Q75

Chronic pelvic pain syndrome, Q136

Chronic prostatitis, Q136

Chronic renal insufficiency, Q42

Circadian rhythm advances, Q158

Citalopram, Q44, Q198

Clavulanate plus gentamicin, Q73

Clomipramine, Q49

Clonazepam, Q215

Clopidogrel, Q141

Clostridium difficile diarrhea, Q163

Clozapine, Q165

Coagulopathy work-up, Q172

Cochlear implants, Q85

Codeine, Q50

Coenzyme Q$_{10}$, Q52

Cognitive-behavioral therapy for panic disorder, Q233

Cognitive deficits, drug-induced, Q198

Cognitive impairment, mild, Q86

Colitis, nonspecific, Q77

Colon cancer
adjuvant chemotherapy for, Q187
screening for, Q32

Colonoscopy, Q32, Q134

Coma, myxedema, Q251

Communication, family, Q153

Community-acquired pneumonia, Q73

Community services
dementia caregiving, Q214
Program of All-Inclusive Care for the Elderly (PACE), Q96

Compression fractures, vertebral, Q8

Compression stockings, Q234

Computed tomography, Q63
abdominal, Q90, Q134
of pelvis, Q136

Computed tomography angiography, Q144

Confusion, worsening, Q67

Confusion Assessment Method (CAM), Q95

Confusion Assessment Method of the Intensive Care Unit (CAM-ICU), Q92

Conservatorship, Q127

Contact dermatitis, Q104

Continuous positive airway pressure, Q2, Q246

Coronary artery disease
prevention of, Q126
risk factors that modify LDL goals, Q126
risk reduction for, Q235

Cortical blindness, Q208

Corticosteroids
to minimize risks of postoperative pulmonary complications, Q159
for temporal arteritis, Q107

Cortisol, Q72

Costs of adult day care, Q261

Cruzan v. Director, Department of Health of Missouri, Q238

Cyclobenzaprine, Q253

Cyclophosphamide, Q87

Cystoscopy, Q239

Cysts, popliteal, Q33

Cytochrome P-450, Q100

D

D-dimer testing, Q101

Daytime sleepiness, Q35

Decision makers, surrogate, Q123

Decision making, Q22, Q64

Deep-vein thrombosis
diagnosis of, Q101
risk factors for, Q144

Delirium
causes of, Q231
clinical features of, Q95
diagnosis of, Q92
drug-induced, Q67, Q198
with mechanical ventilation, Q93
prevention and treatment of, Q43

Delusions, Q69, Q112

Dementia, Q174
agitation with, Q215, Q241
Alzheimer's, Q249
behavioral changes in, Q102
clinical features of, Q95
community services related to, Q214
end-stage, Q13

evaluation of, Q63, Q249
frontotemporal, Q102
HIV-associated, Q236
with Lewy bodies, Q41, Q44, Q102, Q165
psychosis in, Q165
sleep disturbances with, Q185
vascular, Q93, Q98, Q102, Q249
See also Alzheimer's disease, Lewy bodies
Dementia-related psychosis, Q112
Desmopressin, Q68
Dental treatment preparation, Q94
Dentures, Q128
Dependent personality disorder, Q6
Depression, Q93
with Alzheimer's disease, Q55
major, Q98, Q109, Q147, Q177
prevalence of, in long-term-care facilities, Q51
with psychotic features, Q98
with sleep disturbances, Q111
treatment of, Q34, Q74
Dermatitis
contact, Q104
seborrheic, Q27
Detoxification, opioid, Q184
Detrusor hyperactivity with impaired bladder contractility, Q220
Diabetes mellitus, Q5
oral conditions with, Q128
type 2, Q178
uncontrolled, Q244
Diabetic neuroarthropathy, Q36
Diarrhea, *C. difficile*, Q163
Diazepam, Q24
Dietary modifications, Q126
Dietary sodium restriction, Q29
Digital rectal examination, Q170
Digoxin, Q164, Q225
Digoxin toxicity, Q67, Q225
Dilation and curettage, Q172
Diltiazem, Q180, Q224
Diphenhydramine, Q88
Diphenoxylate, Q125
Discoid lupus erythematosus, Q27
Disulfiram, Q122, Q143
Diuretics, Q29, Q202
Divalproex sodium, Q44
Diverticular disease, Q77
Dix-Hallpike positioning maneuver, Q46
Dizziness
age-related changes that result in, Q229
benign paroxysmal positional vertigo (BPPV), Q46, Q91
migraine-associated vertigo, Q167
Do-not-attempt resuscitation—do-not-intubate orders, Q22
Domestic violence, Q182
Donepezil, Q198
Dressings for pressure ulcers, Q11, Q190
Drinking patterns, Q39, Q143
Driving evaluation, Q38
Drotrecogin alpha (activated protein C), Q206
Drug addiction, Q184
Drug eruptions, Q104, Q248

Drug-induced delirium, Q67, Q198
Drug-induced photosensitivity, phototoxic, Q219
Drug-induced xerostomia, Q168
Dry eye, Q218
Dry skin, Q104
Duplex ultrasonography, Q90
Dyspareunia, Q192, Q222
Dysphagia
diagnosis of, Q106
pharyngeal, Q171
Dyspnea associated with terminal illness, Q10

E

Eczematous rash, Q146
Edema, Q29
Elder abuse, Q242
mistreatment, Q130, Q242
neglect, Q66, Q130, Q201
Electrocardiography, Q166
Electroconvulsive therapy, Q34, Q55
Electronystagmography, Q175
ELISA (enzyme-linked immunosorbent assay), Q101
Emollients, Q104
End-of-life care, Q22
dyspnea associated with terminal illness, Q10
hospice consultations, Q16
racial differences in patient preferences for, Q153
Endocarditis prophylaxis, Q94
Endometrial assessment, Q172
Enoxaparin, Q206
Entacapone, Q52
Environmental modifications for agitation, Q65
Enzyme-linked immunosorbent assay (ELISA), Q101
Epley maneuver, Q46
Equine estrogen, conjugated, Q262
Erectile dysfunction
causes of, Q176
treatment of, Q135
Erythrocytosis, Q228
Erythropoietin, Q42
Escitalopram, Q100
Esophagoscopy, Q106
Estrogen, Q139
Estrogen cream
for mixed incontinence, Q76
for vulvovaginal disorders, Q222
Estrogen replacement, postmenopausal, Q263
Estrogen therapy
conjugated equine estrogen, Q262
oral estrogen, Q192
Etanercept, Q107, Q162
Ethnicity
and antihypertensive effects, Q202
and nursing-home placement, Q69
and preferences for end-of-life treatment, Q153
Euthyroid sick syndrome, Q195

Excisional biopsy, Q120
Executive Interview (EXIT) test, Q19, Q127
Exercise(s), Q126
abdominal strengthening exercises, Q150
back extensor resistive exercise, Q179
pelvic muscle exercise, Q76
progressive resistance training, Q99
shoulder range-of-motion exercises, Q28
Exposure therapy, Q181

F

Failure-to-thrive syndrome, Q200
Falls
assessment for risk of, Q226
with femoral neuropathy, Q186
reduction of risk of, Q138, Q174
unexplained, Q56
Family caregiving, Q62
Family communications, Q153
Fatal neglect, Q66
Fatigue, Q138
Feeding, gastrostomy, Q171
Feeding tube placement, Q191
Femoral neuropathy, Q186
Fentanyl, Q50
Fever of unknown origin, Q243
Fexofenadine, Q205
Finasteride, Q197
Fine-needle aspiration biopsy, Q140
Fistulas, aortoenteric, Q77
Flaccid paralysis, acute, Q4
Fluconazole, Q222
Fluid replacement, Q211
Fluoxetine, Q192, Q205
Fluvoxamine, Q100
Fluxoetine, Q100
Fondaparinux, Q206
Foot problems
Charcot's foot, Q36
rash, Q183
stress fractures, Q71
Fractures
hip fracture, Q121
hip fracture rehabilitation, Q81, Q131
intertrochanteric, Q121
osteoporotic, Q40, Q179
risk reduction, Q152
stress, Q71, Q260
thoracic vertebral, Q223
vertebral compression, Q8
Frail elderly with dementia, Q241
Frontal lobe dementia, Q252
Frontotemporal dementia, Q102
Furosemide, Q68, Q88, Q152

G

Gadolinium contrast, Q63
Gait disturbance, Q212
Gastrostomy, Q129
Gastrostomy feeding, Q171
Generalized anxiety disorder, Q24, Q109
with panic attacks, Q233
Genital prolapse, Q232
Gentamicin, Q73
Giant cell (temporal) arteritis, Q107, Q141
Giardiasis, Q188

Ginkgo biloba
  antiplatelet effects of, Q94
  risk of bleeding with, Q155
Glaucoma, open-angle, Q79
Glipizide, Q178
Glucosamine, Q155
Gout, Q259
Granulomatous disease, Q83
Growth hormone, Q72
Growth hormone deficiency, Q117
Guillain-Barré syndrome, Q4
Guns and suicide risk, Q182

H

Hallucinations, Q41
  auditory, Q112
  management of, Q44
  and nursing-home placement, Q69
Haloperidol, Q165
Hand tremors, Q41
Health care decisions, Q22, Q64
Hearing aid checks, Q45
Hearing aids, Q213
Hearing Handicap Inventory for the
  Elderly—Screening Version (HHIE-S),
  Q45, Q175, Q193
Hearing loss, Q213
  with presbycusis, Q151
  screening for, Q175, Q193
  sensorineural, Q229
Heart disease, Q61
Heart failure
  "diastolic," Q180
  discharge medications for, Q180
  exacerbation of, Q22
  treatment of, Q203
Heparin, Q141
  for acute MI, Q224
  low molecular weight, Q224
  unfractionated, Q206
Hepatic toxicity, Q207
Herbal medications
  antiplatelet effects of, Q94
  risk of bleeding with, Q155
HHIE-S (Hearing Handicap Inventory for
  the Elderly—Screening Version), Q45,
  Q175, Q193
Hip fracture rehabilitation, Q81, Q131
Hip pain, Q257
Hip protectors, Q57, Q174
Hip surgery
  postoperative pulmonary complications,
    Q159
  preoperative assessment, Q245
  preoperative management, Q121
Hispanic women, Q79
HIV-associated dementia, Q236
Home blood-pressure monitoring, Q160
Home-health care, Q216
  hospice, Q13
  out-of-pocket expenses, Q89
  physical therapy, Q89
  respiratory therapy, Q89
Hospice care
  and bereavement, Q217
  consultation for, Q16

  for end-stage dementia with aspiration
    pneumonia, Q13
  for failure-to-thrive syndrome, Q200
Hospitalization
  of incapacitated patients, Q22
  out-of-pocket expenses, Q89
House calls, Q227
Human immunodeficiency virus-associated
  dementia, Q236
Humoral hypercalcemia of malignancy, Q83
Hydrochlorothiazide, Q61, Q88, Q234
  adverse effects of, Q168, Q248
  effects on calcium and bone homeostasis,
    Q152
Hydrocodone, Q253
Hydrocolloid dressings, Q11
Hydroxide stain, Q183
Hydroxychloroquine, Q162
Hyperparathyroidism, primary, Q83
Hyperalimentation, peripheral, Q125
Hypercalcemia, humoral, Q83
Hypermetamorphosis, Q102
Hyperorality, Q102
Hypertension, Q5
  causes of, Q88
  drug-induced, Q234
  and heart disease, Q61
  management of, Q3, Q25, Q210
  with obesity, Q3
  pseudohypertension, Q108
  resistant, Q108
  "white-coat," Q160
Hypochondriasis, Q54, Q109
Hyponatremia
  delirium in, Q231
  euvolemic, Q37
  SSRI-induced, Q231
Hypopituitarism, Q117
Hypoproliferative anemia, Q148
Hypotension
  orthostatic, Q138, Q160
  postprandial, Q160
Hysteroscopy, Q172

I

Ibuprofen
  digoxin interactions, Q67
  effects on blood pressure, Q234
Implants, cochlear, Q85
Incisional biopsy, Q30
Incontinence, urinary. *See* Urinary
  incontinence
Infection
  upper airway, Q246
  West Nile virus, Q4
Influenza prophylaxis, Q12
Inner ear changes, Q229
Insomnia
  associated with depression, Q111
  treatment of, Q35
Insulin, regular, Q178
Insulin-like growth factor (IGF)-1, Q117
Insulin lispro, Q178
Insulin therapy, Q178, Q211, Q244
Insurance
  long-term-care, Q133
  supplemental, Q14

Intertrochanteric fractures, Q121
Intestinal obstruction, Q256
Intraductal carcinoma of breast, Q146
Intraepithelial neoplasia, vulvar, Q31
Intramuscular testosterone, Q114, Q192
Intraocular lens implantation, Q209
Intravenous pyelography, Q136
Intrinsic sphincter deficiency, Q119
Iodine 123 thyroid uptake scan, Q140
Itching, generalized, Q104

J

Jejunostomy, Q125
Joint arthroplasty, total, Q48
Junctional nevus, Q120

K

Kava, Q207
Klüver-Bucy syndrome, Q102
Knee osteoarthritis, Q48
Knee radiography, Q212
Kyphoplasty, Q253

L

Labyrinthitis, Q167
Lactulose, Q251
Lateral neck radiography, preoperative, Q245
Left ventricular dysfunction, Q164
Lenticulostriate artery occlusion, Q149
Lentiginous melanoma, acral, Q30
Lentigo maligna, Q120
Lentigo maligna melanoma, Q120
Levodopa-carbidopa, Q35
Levomethadyl acetate, Q184
Levothyroxine, Q152
Lewy bodies, dementia with, Q41, Q44
  behavioral changes in, Q102
  psychosis in, Q165
  See also Alzheimer's disease, Dementia
Libido, Q72
Lichen sclerosus, Q31, Q116, Q222
Life-style interventions, Q3
Limb movements, periodic, Q35
Lisinopril, Q88, Q234
  for heart disease, Q61
  for hypertension, Q61, Q210
Litigation for negligent care, Q201
Long-term-care facilities
  depression in, Q51
  environmental concerns, Q65
Long-term-care insurance, Q133
Longevity, extended, Q117
Loop diuretics, Q234
Lorazepam, Q2, Q49, Q185, Q198, Q215
Low-air-low mattress, Q7
Low-density lipoprotein (LDL), Q126
Low molecular weight heparin, Q224
Lower back pain, Q8, Q150
Lubricants, water-soluble, Q192
Lumbar spinal stenosis, Q33
Lumbar spine instability, Q150
Lung cancer
  metastatic, Q11
  non-small cell, Q230
  occult, Q98

Lutein, Q155
Lymphoma, chronic B-cell, Q47

M

Macular degeneration, Q20, Q189
Megakaryocytopoiesis, exuberant, Q47
Magnetic resonance imaging, Q63
  abdominal, Q90
  of brain, Q138, Q212
  with gadolinium contrast, Q63
Malabsorption, Q188
Malformations, arteriovenous, Q77
Malignancy. *See also* Cancer
  humoral hypercalcemia of, Q83
Malignant lentigo of elderly people, Q120
Malignant pleural effusion, Q11, Q230
Malignant skin lesions, Q120
Masses, adrenal, Q78
MAST-G (Michigan Alcoholism Screening
    Test—Geriatric Version), Q221
Mattresses, low-air-low, Q7
Mechanical ventilation, Q93
Median neuropathy, Q118
Medicaid, Q84
Medicare, Q5
  compensation for house calls, Q227
  hospice benefits, Q13
  Part A, Q14, Q84
  Part B, Q14, Q84
  Program of All-Inclusive Care for the
    Elderly (PACE), Q96
Medicare Advantage (Medicare Managed
    Care, formerly Medicare Plus Choice, or
    Medicare HMO), Q5
Medications. *See also specific medications*
  adherence to, Q108
  and erectile dysfunction, Q176
  out-of-pocket expenses, Q89
Medigap insurance, Q84
Megestrol acetate, Q191, Q200
Melanoma
  acral lentiginous, Q30
  lentigo maligna, Q120
  in situ, Q120
Melatonin, Q111, Q185
Memory loss, Q86
Meningioma, parasagittal, Q118
Men's health
  benign prostatic hyperplasia, Q197
  osteoporosis, Q139
  suicide risk, Q156, Q182
Mental retardation, Q103
  mild, Q64
Mental status changes, sudden, Q93
Metabolic syndrome, Q3
Metastatic lung cancer, Q11
Metastatic ovarian cancer, Q256
Metformin, Q178, Q244
Methadone, Q184
Methotrexate, Q107, Q162
Methyltestosterone, Q192
Metoprolol, Q61, Q177, Q244
MGUS. *See* Monoclonal gammopathy of
    undetermined significance
Michigan Alcoholism Screening Test—
    Geriatric Version (MAST-G), Q221

Middle cerebral artery occlusion, Q149
Migraine-associated vertigo, Q167
Milk-alkali syndrome, Q83
Mini-Mental State Examination (MMSE),
    Q19, Q127
Mirtazapine, Q35, Q191
  for insomnia, Q110
  for weight loss, Q129
Mistreatment, Q130, Q242
MMSE (Mini-Mental State Examination),
    Q19, Q127
Modafinil, Q35
Monoclonal gammopathy of undetermined
    significance (MGUS), Q25
Morphine, Q10
Moxifloxacin, Q73
Multiple myeloma, Q25, Q148
Mutations associated with extended longevity,
    Q117
Myeloma, multiple, Q25, Q148
Myocardial infarction
  acute, Q169, Q224
  hypertension and heart disease from, Q61
Myxedema coma, Q251

N

Nalmefene, Q122
Naloxone, Q184
Naltrexone, Q143, Q184
Naproxen, Q154
Neglect, Q130
  fatal, Q66
  litigation for negligent care, Q201
Nerve conduction studies, Q212
Neuroarthropathy, diabetic, Q36
Neuropsychologic testing, Q19
Nicotinic stomatitis, Q199
Nighttime awakening, Q65
Nighttime disruptive behaviors, Q62
Nipple rash, unilateral eczematous, Q146
Nitrates, long-acting, Q169
Nocturia, Q68
Nonketotic hyperosmolar syndrome, Q211
Nonsteroidal anti-inflammatory drugs, Q234
Nortriptyline, Q55, Q154, Q177
Nurse's aides, Q242
Nursing care, Q241
Nursing home care, Q216
  assessment for risk of falls in, Q226
  burdens on caregiving that lead to, Q62
  for incapacitated patients, Q22
  out-of-pocket expenses, Q89
  payment for stays, Q84
  risk factors for placement in, Q69
  transitions for caregiver after placement,
    Q115
  weight loss in, Q191
Nutritional recommendations, Q171
Nutritional risk assessment, Q15
Nutritional status
  evaluation of, Q23
  improvement of, Q125
Nystagmus, Q91

O

Obesity
  hypertension with, Q3
  and postoperative risk of respiratory failure,
    Q75
Obsessive-compulsive disorder, Q49
Obsessive-compulsive personality disorder,
    Q237
Obstructive pulmonary disease, chronic
  management of, Q11
  postoperative complications, Q159
  postoperative risk of respiratory failure,
    Q75
Occipital lobe infarction, bilateral, Q208
Occlusive dressings, Q190
Occupational therapy, Q1
Ocular motor abnormalities, Q142
Olanzapine, Q215
Ondansetron, Q122, Q256
Opioids
  addiction to, Q184
  detoxification and maintenance, Q184
  for pain relief in prostate cancer, Q50
Oral cancer, Q124, Q128
Oral conditions with diabetes mellitus, Q128
Oral lesions, Q124
Oral nutritional supplements, Q129, Q171
Orthostatic hypotension, Q138, Q160
Oseltamivir, Q12
Osteoarthritis, Q5
  of knee, Q48
Osteoporosis, Q5
  in men, Q139
  reduction of vertebral fractures, Q179
  risk of fractures, Q40
  treatment of, Q21, Q57, Q81
Outpatient prescription medications, Q89
Ovarian cancer, Q194
  metastatic, Q256
Overactive bladder, Q110, Q119, Q239
Overflow incontinence, Q154
Oxybutynin, Q154, Q197
  anticholinergic effects, Q198
  for mixed incontinence, Q76
  for overactive bladder, Q239
Oxycodone
  abuse, Q184
  for pain relief, Q50, Q253
 P
PACE. *See* Program of All-Inclusive Care for
    the Elderly
Paget's disease of the breast, Q146
Pain
  abdominal, Q90, Q134
  back, Q57, Q223
  calf, Q33
  in cervical disk disease, Q240
  chronic pelvic pain syndrome, Q136
  hip, Q257
  lower back, Q8, Q150
  mid-back, Q253
  plantar fasciitis, Q259
  shoulder, Q28, Q240
Pain relief
  in arthritis, Q48, Q88
  in prostate cancer, Q50
Palpitations, Q157

Panic disorder, Q98, Q109, Q181, Q233
Paralysis, acute flaccid, Q4
Paraneoplastic cerebellar degeneration, Q194
Parasagittal meningioma, Q118
Parathyroid hormone (teriparatide), Q21
Parenteral nutrition, total, Q125
Parkinson's disease, Q52
Paroxetine
    complications of treatment with, Q231
    cytochrome P-450 interactions, Q100
Paroxysmal positional vertigo, benign, Q46, Q91
Pelvic muscle exercise, Q76
Pelvic muscle training, biofeedback-assisted, Q26
Pelvis
    chronic pelvic pain syndrome, Q136
    computed tomography of, Q136
Peptic ulcer disease, Q5
Percutaneous coronary angioplasty, Q164
Periodic leg movements, Q35, Q68, Q158
Peripheral hyperalimentation, Q125
Personality disorders
    borderline, Q252
    dependent, Q6
    obsessive-compulsive, Q237
Pessaries, Q232
Pharyngeal dysphagia, Q171
Phenytoin, Q141, Q251
Phenytoin concentrations, Q205
Phenytoin toxicity, Q205
Pheochromocytoma, Q108
Phlebotomy, therapeutic, Q228
Photosensitivity, drug-induced, Q219
Phototoxic drug-induced photosensitivity, Q219
Physical activity
    effects on bone density, Q247
    long-term effects on CAD risk, Q235
Physical therapy
    chest, Q159
    home, Q89
    for reflex sympathetic dystrophy or
        shoulder-hand syndrome, Q18
    for shoulder problems, Q28
Physician-assisted suicide, Q238
Pityriasis rosea, Q27
Plantar fasciitis, Q258
Plantar fasciitis pain, Q259
Pleural effusion, malignant, Q11, Q230
Pneumonia
    aspiration, Q13
    community-acquired, Q73
Podagra, Q259
Polycythemia, Q114
Polycythemia vera, Q228
Polymeric oral supplements, Q129
Popliteal cyst, ruptured, Q33
Positional vertigo, benign paroxysmal, Q46, Q91
Positioning, Dix-Hallpike, Q46
Positron emission tomography, Q63
Posterior inferior cerebellar artery occlusion, Q149
Posterior lens capsule, opacified, Q209

Posterior tibial tendon rupture, Q258
Posttraumatic stress disorder, Q181
Postural hypotension. See Orthostatic
    hypotension
Postvoid residual urine testing, Q154
Pramipexole, Q35
Prednisone, Q141, Q162
Premature beats, ventricular, Q157
Presbycusis, Q151
Pressure Sore Status Tool (PSST), Q254
Pressure Ulcer Scale for Healing (PUSH), Q254
Pressure ulcers
    litigation for negligent care involving, Q201
    mattresses for care of, Q7
    occlusive dressings for, Q190
    risk assessment for, Q254
    treatment of, Q11
Progesterone, Q72
Program of All-Inclusive Care for the Elderly
    (PACE), Q96
Prompted voiding programs, Q110
Propafenone, Q157
Propoxyphene, Q50
Prostate cancer
    follow-up management of, Q87
    pain relief in, Q50
    screening for, Q170
    therapy for, Q9
Prostate-specific antigen (PSA) levels, Q154
    annual screening, Q170
    measurement of, Q60
Prostatitis, chronic, Q136
Pruritus
    generalized, Q104
    vulvar, Q116
Pseudoachalasia, Q106
Pseudohypertension, Q108
Psoriasis, Q27, Q104
PSST (Pressure Sore Status Tool), Q254
Psychiatric emergency, Q156
Psychiatric evaluation, involuntary, Q156
Psychosis
    dementia-related, Q112
    in dementia with Lewy bodies, Q165
    major depression with psychotic features, Q98
    treatment of, Q165
Psychotherapy, Q64, Q233
Pulmonary disease, chronic obstructive
    management of, Q11
    postoperative complications, Q159
    postoperative risk of respiratory failure, Q75
Pulmonary function changes, age-related, Q53
Purified protein derivative skin test, Q204
PUSH (Pressure Ulcer Scale for Healing), Q254
Pyridostigmine, Q251

Q

Quetiapine, Q165, Q174

R

Racial differences
    in antihypertensive effects, Q202
    in nursing-home placement, Q69
    in preferences for end-of-life treatment, Q153
Radiography, Q212
    of knee, Q212
    lateral neck, preoperative, Q245
Ramipril, Q88
Range-of-motion exercises, shoulder, Q28
Rash
    of nipple, Q146
    phototoxic drug-induced photosensitivity, Q219
    tinea pedis, Q183
Raynaud's phenomenon, Q260
Reading disability, Q79
Rectal bleeding, Q77
Reflex sympathetic dystrophy, Q18, Q260
Refusal of therapy, Q238
Rehabilitation
    hip fracture, Q81, Q131
    stroke, Q1
Renal insufficiency, chronic, Q42
Reporting mistreatment, Q130
Resistance training
    back extensor resistive exercise, Q179
    progressive, Q99
Respiratory failure, Q75
Respiratory therapy, home, Q89
Respite care, Q216
Rest periods, Q174
Restless legs syndrome, Q158
Restraints, Q43, Q174
Reticulocyte count, corrected, Q148
Retinal examination, Q212
Rheumatoid arthritis, Q162
Rhythm disorders, Q157
Right of refusal of therapy, Q238
Rimantadine, Q12
Rinné test, Q175
Risedronate, Q57
Risperidone, Q103
Rivastigmine, Q44
Rosacea, Q27
Rosiglitazone, Q178, Q244
Rotator cuff tears, Q28
Ruptured popliteal cyst, Q33

S

Safety, driver, Q38
Salivary stones, Q128, Q168
Scabies, Q104
Schizoid personality disorder, Q6
Schizophrenia, late-onset, Q112
Screening
    admission, Q204
    for alcohol use disorders, Q221
    annual PSA screen, Q170
    for colon cancer, Q32
    for hearing impairment, Q175
    for hearing loss, Q193
    for prostate cancer, Q170
    for tuberculosis, Q204
Seborrheic dermatitis, Q27

Seizures, Q97
Selective serotonin reuptake inhibitors, Q231
Selegiline, Q52
Self-injurious behavior, Q103
Sensorineural hearing loss
    age-related changes that result in, Q229
    with presbycusis, Q151
Sepsis, Q206
Sertraline
    for depression, Q55, Q74, Q177
    for obsessive-compulsive disorder, Q49
Shoulder-hand syndrome, Q18
Shoulder pain, Q28, Q240
Shoulder range-of-motion exercises, Q28
SIADH (syndrome of inappropriate
    antidiuretic hormone), Q37
Sialoliths, Q128, Q168
Sildenafil, Q135
Skilled nursing facilities, Q1, Q201
Skin, dry, Q104
Sleep disturbances, Q68, Q158
    apnea, Q68, Q158
    associated with major depressive disorder,
        Q111
    breathing-related disorders, Q158
    with dementia, Q185
    disruptive behaviors, Q62
Sleep hygiene, Q2
Sleepiness, daytime, Q35
Small bowel bacterial overgrowth, Q188
Small bowel series, Q134
Smoking cessation
    benefits of, Q113
    indications for, Q199
Social phobia, Q181
Sodium levels, Q58
Sodium restriction, Q29
Somatization disorder, Q54, Q109, Q173
Sotalol, Q157
Spinal instability, lumbar, Q150
Spinal stenosis, lumbar, Q33
Splanchnic angiography, Q90
Spondylosis, cervical, Q118
Squamous cell carcinoma, oral, Q128
Squamous cell hyperplasia, vulvar, Q31
St. John's wort, Q74, Q100
Standard of care, Q201
Statins, Q152, Q177, Q180
Stem cells, Q196
Stimulants, Q246
Stomatitis, Q128, Q199
Strength training
    abdominal exercise, Q150
    progressive resistance training, Q99
Stress
    caregiver, Q214
    posttraumatic stress disorder, Q181
Stress fractures, Q260
    calcaneal, Q258
    in foot, Q71
Stress incontinence
    surgical intervention for, Q119
    treatment of, Q26
Stroke
    pure (isolated) sensory, Q149
    risk reduction of, Q59

seizures after, Q97
    swallowing disorders related to, Q191
Stroke rehabilitation, Q1
Substance abuse, Q182
Suicide, physician-assisted, Q238
Suicide risk, Q156, Q182
Sulfasalazine, Q162
Sundowning, Q93
Supplemental insurance, Q14
Surgery
    cataract, Q209
    discontinuation of supplements before,
        Q155
    hip fracture, Q121, Q245
    hip replacement, Q159
    postoperative pulmonary complications,
        Q159
    postoperative risk of respiratory failure,
        Q75
    for stress incontinence, Q119
    upper abdominal, Q75
Surrogate decision makers, Q123
Swallowing disorders, Q191
Swallowing evaluation, Q125
Syncope
    unexplained, Q166
    vs unexplained falls, Q56
    of unknown cause, Q132
Syndrome of inappropriate antidiuretic
    hormone (SIADH), Q37
Syringomyelia, Q118
Systemic atherosclerosis, Q90
Systemic lupus erythematosus, late-onset,
    Q17

T
Tadalafil, Q135
Tamsulosin, Q68, Q197
Tardive dyskinesia, Q255
Tarsal tunnel syndrome, Q259, Q260
Temazepam, Q111
Temporal arteritis, Q107, Q141
Temporal artery biopsy, Q243
Tendinitis, anterior tibial, Q259
Terazosin, Q239
Teriparatide (parathyroid hormone), Q21
Terminal illness, Q10
Testosterone
    intramuscular, Q114, Q192
    for libido improvement, Q72
    replacement, Q135
Thalamoperforate artery occlusion, Q149
Theophylline, Q159
Thiamine (vitamin B1) deficiency, Q142
Thoracic vertebral fracture, Q223
Thrombocytopenia, autoimmune, Q47
Thrombosis, deep-vein
    diagnosis of, Q101
    risk factors for, Q144
Thyroid hormone, serum, Q195
Thyroid nodules, Q140
Thyroid uptake and scan, Q140
Thyrotropin concentrations, Q195
Thyroxine, Q251
Tibial tendinitis, Q259
Tibial tendon rupture, posterior, Q258

Ticarcillin, Q73
Tilt-table testing, Q70, Q132
Tinea pedis, Q183
Toe-walking, Q71
Tolterodine, Q76, Q205
Total joint arthroplasty, Q48
Total parenteral nutrition, Q125
Toxicity
    digoxin, Q67, Q225
    hepatic, Q207
    phototoxic drug-induced photosensitivity,
        Q219
Training
    pelvic muscle, Q26
    resistance, progressive, Q99
Transrectal ultrasonography, Q136, Q170
Transurethral resection of the prostate, Q239
Trazodone, Q185, Q215
Tremors, hand, Q41
Triamcinolone, intra-articular, Q48
Tuberculosis
    admission screening for, Q204
    current guidelines for treatment of, Q92
Tuning forks, Q193
Tympanometry, Q175

U
Ulcers
    peptic ulcer disease, Q5
    pressure ulcers, Q11, Q190
Ultrasound
    of abdomen, Q134
    duplex, Q90
    transrectal, Q136, Q170
    vaginal, Q172
Upper abdominal surgery, Q75
Upper airway infection, Q246
Upper gastrointestinal lesions, Q77
Urge incontinence, Q110
Urinary incontinence
    mixed, Q76
    overflow, Q154
    stress, Q26, Q119
    urge, Q110
Urine testing, postvoid residual, Q154
Urosepsis, Q80
Uterine prolapse, Q232

V
Vacuum tumescent devices, Q135
Vaginal bleeding, Q172
Vaginal lubrication, Q192
Vaginal ultrasound, Q172
Vaginitis, atrophic, Q31, Q116
Vardenafil, Q135
Vascular dementia, Q93, Q98
    behavioral changes in, Q102
    diagnosis of, Q249
Vascular ectasia, Q77
Venlafaxine, Q177, Q231
Venous thromboembolic disease, Q144
Ventricular premature beats (VPBs), Q157
Vertebral fracture
    compression, Q8
    osteoporotic, Q179
    thoracic, Q223
Vertebrobasilar insufficiency, Q167

Vertebroplasty, Q223

Vertigo
  age-related changes that result in, Q229
  benign paroxysmal positional vertigo, Q46,
    Q91
  migraine-associated, Q167

Vestibular neuronitis, Q167

Vibrating tuning forks, Q193

Video urodynamics, Q136

Violence
  domestic, Q182
  escalation to, Q241

Vision loss, Q209
  bilateral, Q79
  cortical blindness, Q208
  mild mental retardation with, Q64

Vision testing, Q138, Q189

Vitamin B$_1$ (thiamine) deficiency, Q142

Vitamin E, Q137

Vitamin K, Q152

Voiding, prompted, Q110

VPBs. *See* Ventricular premature beats

Vulvar candidiasis, Q31, Q116, Q222

Vulvar disease, Q31

Vulvar intraepithelial neoplasia, Q31

Vulvar pruritus, Q116

Vulvovaginal disorders, Q222

W

Warfarin, Q82, Q152, Q180

Weakness, Q138

Weber test, Q175, Q193

Weight loss
  assessment of, Q129, Q225, Q250
  in failure-to-thrive syndrome, Q200
  intervention for, Q129
  in nursing-home residents, Q191
  postprandial abdominal pain with, Q90
  progressive, Q250
  recent, Q23
  reduction of, Q34

Wernicke's encephalopathy, Q142

West Nile virus infection, Q4

Whisper test, Q193

"White-coat" hypertension, Q160

Women's health
  aging, Q145
  androgen levels, Q72
  dyspareunia, Q192
  osteoporotic fractures, Q40
  ovarian cancer, Q194
  reading disability, Q79
  vulvar candidiasis, Q31, Q116, Q222
  vulvovaginal disorders, Q222
    X

Xerosis, Q104

Xerostomia, Q128, Q168

Y

Yohimbine, Q135

Z

Zaleplon, Q185

Zanamivir, Q12

Zoledronic acid, Q87

Zolpidem, Q2, Q35, Q88, Q111, Q185

THE BOSS

Springsteen

ELIANNE HALBERSBERG

SHARON STARBOOK™ CRESSKILL, N.J. 07626

Acknowledgements

This is an unauthorized biography. Members of Springsteen's entourage kept emphasizing this during our conversations at the Meadowlands on August 11, 1984. Again I remind them, lack of authorization was certainly not due to lack of effort. Constant attempts to reach the necessary sources proved futile. Requested parties were always "not in right now," telephone messages were never returned, numbers were disconnected, registered letters were sent back unclaimed.

Springsteen fans don't need anyone to explain his magic—they live and breathe it. To the thousands whose lives have been touched by this man and his music, those with whom I have spent hours waiting for tickets, exchanging Springsteen stories; those who so willingly shared their feelings about rock and roll's most honest and respected performer, I hope these pages help capture some of that truth.

My deepest thanks to:

Mills and Cheryl Fitzner:
For your encouragement and invaluable friendship throughout the years.

Bruce Lubin:
For recommending me to the publishers and suggesting I write this book.

and, of course, Bruce Springsteen:
For everything. May your "Glory Days" never end.

This is a SHARON STARBOOK™
Copyright © 1984 by Sharon Publications Inc., All rights reserved. No part of this work may be reproduced or transmitted in any form or by any means, electronic or mechanical, including photocopying and recording, or any information storage or retrieval system without permission in writing from the publisher.

Editor: Mary J. Edrei
Cover and Book Design: Rod Gonzalez
Research: Bruce Lubin, Gary Azon, and Paul Castori
Manufactured in the United States of America

Chapter 1 ———————————————————————————— 11
THE EARLY YEARS

Chapter 2 ———————————————————————————— 17
APPEL, HAMMOND AND THE FIRST ALBUM

Chapter 3 ———————————————————————————— 21
THE E STREET BAND SHUFFLE

Chapter 4 ———————————————————————————— 25
NINETEEN SEVENTY-FIVE AND THE ANTHEM

Chapter 5 ———————————————————————————— 33
LAWSUITS, LABOR AND THE ALBUM SHIPS GOLD

Chapter 6 ———————————————————————————— 41
BOOTLEGS, M.U.S.E., BAND PROJECTS AND A TOP TEN HIT

Chapter 7 ———————————————————————————— 53
AN ACOUSTIC MASTERPIECE

Chapter 8 ———————————————————————————— 59
SPRINGSTEEN SPRINGS BACK

Chapter 9 ———————————————————————————— 69
THE E STREET BAND: THE PERFECT COMBINATION

Chapter 10 ——————————————————————————— 79
THE PRINCIPLES: A CAST OF MILLIONS

DISCOGRAPHY

Introduction

Bruce Springsteen, rock's most humble hero, returns in 1984 with *Born In The U.S.A.,* his seventh album in eleven years. Skillfully backed by the E-Street Band (Roy Bittan, Clarence Clemons, Danny Federici, Garry Tallent, Steve Van Zandt, and Max Weinberg), Springsteen's long-awaited followup to 1982's acoustic *Nebraska* carries the tradition of his previous works—honest, intense lyrics; powerful music; rough, passionate vocals.

Born In The U.S.A. marks some firsts for Springteen—both surprising, but perhaps inevitable. With the release of the successful first single, "Dancing In The Dark," Springsteen entered the world of music videos, a field he had explored only once with "Atlantic City," a track from *Nebraska* featuring a black-and-white clip in which he does not appear. "Dancing In The Dark" was also re-mixed as a twelve-inch dance single.

Springsteen's audiences have been predominantly in the 18-to-35 age group, but with his recent playlist success (his last radio hit was "Hungry Heart" from *The River* album) and the rotation of the video, he is acquiring younger listeners. Some critics foresee this as the preliminary step toward the so-called "teen idol trap" insuring commercialization and overexposure. They speculate that this "new wave" of Springsteen fans may become a risk factor—a potential threat to the man and his music—to the phenomenon we have come to know as "The Boss."

Springsteen is foremost a poet; a realist painting graphic scenarios through his music. Over the years he has introduced an ever-increasing audience to an entire spectrum of characters, all linked by a common bond of frustration—a frustration stemming

from their bleak, desolate lives; characters so vivid, desperately seeking justice in an unjust world, surrounded by pain, the anguish of desire, the loneliness of growing up and growing old, finding their escape in ways that often turn against them. Springsteen's protagonist is in each of us, and there lies the reason that so many have praised him. Through his words we realize that we are not alone in our basic needs.

And so, *Born In The U.S.A.* takes up where *Nebraska* left off. In that two-year lapse, Springsteen fans waited, albeit impatiently, for this album. This is the group that has grown with him, matured together since the days of *Greetings From Asbury Park, New Jersey.* But since that time a new entity has emerged—America's youth, those just discovering the world so aptly described in Springsteen's

lyrics: the restlessness, dreams and relationships; the agonies of small-town life and discontents of working-class hardships. That "teen" crowd will be a part of Springsteen's current tour. His new listeners, the product of a society plagued by unemployment, economic strife, insecurity, and frequent hopelessness—themes that make up the songs of Springsteen's album.

In 1975, with the release of *Born To Run*, Springsteen was heralded for resurrecting the essence of a musical genre that many feared had been permanently buried under glitter, disco, and punk. He remains one of the few performers in contemporary music to successfully, and consistently, uphold those traditions, and in doing so, his conviction makes believers of us all.

Honest, intense music—Bruce Springsteen and Clarence Clemons, their timing is impeccable, and they play off each other with a childlike innocence, all their own.

*The guitar was more than just a hobby for
Bruce Springsteen—it was an obsession.*

Chapter 1

THE EARLY YEARS:
"MUSIC SAVED ME"

reehold, New Jersey. A small middle-class factory town fifteen miles inland from the boardwalk and arcades of Asbury Park; a few miles from U.S. Highway 9, the one that would eventually be immortalized in the song of a native son. A town that would probably have remained in the background, unheard of by most, had it not been for the man who would put Freehold, his hometown, on the map.

Bruce Frederick Springsteen was born September 23, 1949, to Adele and Douglas Springsteen. He has two younger sisters, Virginia and Pamela. Their background is Dutch/Italian. Mr. and Mrs. Springsteen married when he got out of the Army. She worked as a secretary; he held several different jobs over the years: in a mill, as a cab driver, a guard at the jail. The Springsteens' spent various times living with Mrs. Springsteen's parents, and Bruce was a student at parochial school for eight years, a period in his life that he hated and still looks back on with bitterness and disdain.

Springsteen has never hidden his negative feelings toward school, having openly recalled "hating" the experience. Ignored by classmates with whom he did not fit in, Springsteen grew up a loner, "always on the outside looking in," he has often said. The pain of a solitary existence (a subject that is explored again and again in his lyrics) made the youngster look for other outlets, other companions. He came to discover the most reliable, consistent friend of the friendless—music—the one thing that was always there; an escape from cruelty and loneliness. "Music saved me," he would later say; indeed, as it has saved many of us.

The true moment of enlightenment for Springsteen came when he was nine years old. Like millions of other families, Sunday nights were reserved for the Ed Sullivan Show; and it was on one of those Sundays, in September 1956, that Bruce Springsteen laid eyes on and heard "The King," Elvis Presley. Elvis—the sexy young man with the Southern drawl, slicked back hair, tight clothes, and that sneer! Elvis—his guitar slung low on his gyrating hips, his rough-and-tumble voice. The daring young rebel was considered too risque for television and they would only show him from the waist up. He frightened parents, made the girls cry and swoon, and gave young men across the country a role model. Young Springsteen was so overwhelmed by Presley that his mother bought him a guitar the next day. But his hands were too small, formal lessons were out of the question (after all, that's not how Elvis did it!), and he put the instrument away for five years. He never put away his dreams. He often recalls that he just couldn't imagine anyone seeing Elvis and not wanting to be Elvis!

In 1963, Springsteen bought his first real guitar for $18 at a pawn shop, and a cousin taught him some fundamental chords. He has since remarked that the first time he stood in front of a mirror with his guitar was also the first time he was actually able to tolerate the reflection that stared back at him. He had found the magic, and in no time it dominated his entire life. The guitar was more than a hobby—it was an obsession. Never one for technical study, Springsteen had an unusual flair to listen and learn. And how he listened: Elvis, Sam Cooke, The Beatles, Fats Domino, Chuck Berry, The Rolling Stones, Eric Burdon and The Animals, Manfred Mann with vocalists Paul Jones, Roy Orbison, Mitch Ryder, Gary "U.S." Bonds, the Motown, and Stax Sounds.

The newfound joy was not shared by his parents. They apparently had other things in mind for their son's future; trying to convince him to change his

career plans, telling him the same thing that all parents tell their offspring: "You need something to fall back on." He knew better. Springsteen has frequently mentioned the tension between his father and himself during those adolescent years. (The father-son conflict would later be confronted in universal terms that all young people could relate to in songs like "Adam Raised A Cain" and "Independence Day.") He has also noted that he never felt that his parents understood exactly what his music meant to him. Springsteen has indicated in various interviews that the two "unpopular" things in his house were him and his guitar, but he was never deterred. Instead, he had discovered his freedom, his dream, and his ambition. There would never be anything more important—music was (and remains) his priority, it was what his life would center around, it was his reason for being.

Springsteen was in and out of local bands for a while, like any other musician. In 1965 he joined The Castiles, a Freehold group managed by "Tex" Vinyard. Their first gig was at a local high school. The Castiles' repertoire consisted of all the current rock hits, a few so-called nostalgia tunes, and, eventually, they wrote and performed some original ma-

The boardwalk, Asbury Park.

terial. They played for civic clubs, in parking lots, trailer parks, drive-in movies during intermission, even at the local prison and at an asylum. They were developing quite a following in the Jersey area, and in 1967 they cut a demo at a New Jersey studio that was never released, even locally. During that same year The Castiles were hired for a month of bookings at the Cafe Wha in New York's Greenwich Village. But as high school ended, so did The Castiles. The members parted ways, to seek out different careers, different interests. However, Bruce Springsteen, having just graduated from Freehold Regional High School, had acquired valuable experience from those years and they served to reaffirm his convictions. Determined to continue his life of music, Springsteen joined Earth, a heavy-metal-style group.

It was about this time that Springsteen discovered the up-and-coming musicians' gathering place—Asbury Park. The summer resort, which has a history dating back to 1870, is a city in Monmouth County, New Jersey, on the Atlantic Ocean, fifty miles south of New York City. Its beach houses, arcades, hotels, and the boardwalk that stretches the entire length of its one-mile beach would later be in-

The Stone Pony, one of Springsteen's regular hangouts.

lyn, the four became Child. That name already being used by another area group, they changed to Steel Mill. This was the first band to really set Springsteen's career into full swing. Through Steel Mill, Springsteen (who at this time was sporting shoulder-length hair) became known outside of New Jersey. Steel Mill's popularity was widespread. Their sound was a mixture of heavy metal, rock, and blues. During this period Springsteen was enrolled at Ocean County Community College, but his days as a college student were short-lived.

In early 1969 the Springsteens relocated to California, but their son chose to stay behind in Freehold. He lived for a while in the family's house, and later with friends. In the summer of that same year, Steel Mill's manager, Tinker West, took the group to California, where they were booked at the Fillmore West and at Esalen, a self-actualization spa. The group received rave reviews from the San Francisco *Examiner*'s Phil Elwood. Reportedly, this trip across the country also gave Springsteen the opportunity to fully learn to drive a car, something too that would become an important aspect of his life and that would play a recurring role in his lyrics.

Although relatively successsful, the California performances broke no major ground for Steel Mill. They returned to New Jersey, and shortly thereafter, bassist Vinny Roslyn was replaced by Miami Steve Van Zandt. By 1971 Steel Mill, despite their popularity, called it quits. Springsteen then formed Dr. Zoom and The Sonic Boom, a multimember assemblage that played a variety of sounds, and whose onstage antics included an ever-present Monopoly board. The group lasted all of three dates. After that came the Bruce Springsteen Band, a ten-piece outfit that featured horns and female singers. Finding the right combination of people took six months. The final product lasted for two shows, but it bonded the relationships of Springsteen, Lopez, Tallent, Federici, Van Zandt, and pianist/guitarist David Sancious, a classically trained musician who would appear on Springsteen's first two albums. The Bruce Springsteen Band was reduced to a five-piece, but did not last in this version, either. The other members were working day jobs; Springsteen refused to let anything else come before his music. The group broke up and Springsteen went the solo route. Somewhere within this period Springsteen allegedly found Clarence "Big Man" Clemons, playing saxophone for an area group led by Norman Seldon.

fluential in Springsteen's writing; his lyrics would bring to life his experiences in Asbury Park, detailing its attractions and "landmarks." It was at The Upstage, an Asbury Park club that Springsteen would meet Miami Steve Van Zandt, Garry Tallent, Danny Federici, and Vini Lopez. They would all play a part in the formation of the E Street Band.

Earth's history is short; Springsteen spent some time with the group, but as he met an increasing number of musicians at The Upstage, his musical direction began to veer from the people with whom he was playing. Having been discovered by Danny Federici and Vini Lopez, the two approached him one night at the club and, with bassist Vinny Ros-

Next page: Springsteen refused to let anything come before his music. Inset: When he first saw Elvis Presley "The King" he was so overwhelmed that his mother bought him a guitar the next day.

chapter 2

APPEL, HAMMOND,
AND THE FIRST ALBUM

In 1971 Springsteen was being managed by Carl "Tinker" West, who met New York songwriters/ producers Mike Appel and Jim Cretecos. West arranged for Springsteen to audition for Appel, and although the latter was impressed with the young singer's talent, the two somehow lost contact. Springsteen decided to move to California, this time for good, but again the West Coast didn't offer what he was looking for and he returned to New Jersey. Springsteen was eventually able to reach Mike Appel again for an audition, and a few days later Springsteen signed a management and publishing contract with Appel and his company, Laurel Canyon. The inexperienced and trusting Springsteen signed the contract one night on the hood of an automobile in a parking lot, innocent of legalities and provisions. Unfortunately, this candid faith would later work to his disadvantage.

In May 1982 Appel, in his reputed aggressive style, was able to schedule a meeting between Springsteen and John Hammond, Vice-President of Talent Acquisition for CBS Records, whose credits included signing Aretha Franklin, Billie Holliday, and Bob Dylan to that label. Springsteen apparently

Greetings From Asbury Park, New Jersey.

performed "It's Hard To Be A Saint In The City," and Hammond was immediately impressed. He booked Springsteen for a show at a New York Club, The Gaslight. CBS Records' then president, Clive Davis, shared Hammond's enthusiasm, and on June 9, 1982, Springsteen was signed to a ten-album contract.

Springsteen had stated his musical experience as eight years with bands and two years as a solo artist. When preparations began for his first album, the company was apparently expecting a solo debut. Springsteen had other plans. He called in his Asbury Park friends and co-workers: Gary Tallent, bass; Clarence Clemons, saxophone; David Sancious, guitar and piano; and Vini Lopez, drums. The album was recorded in three weeks and produced by Appel/Cretecos team. *Greetings From Asbury Park, New Jersey* was released in January 1973. "Blinded By The Light"/"Angel" was the first single. While the album with the postcard cover was not exactly a commercial success, its diverse cast of characters and complex lyrics brought a fresh change of pace to the music scene of the early 1970s. Shortly after the album's release, Springsteen and Band (with the addition of Danny Federici on organ) began a club tour of the New York, Boston, Philadelphia, and Chicago areas. In May 1973 "Spirit In The Night"/"For You" became the second single.

From May 30 through June 15, Springsteen toured with Chicago. The ten dates were decidedly mismatched in billing, with Chicago audiences not primed for Springsteen and vice versa. The tour was Springsteen's last as an opening act. From then on it would be his shows, his equipment, his venues.

In July, Springsteen wrapped up his first series of concerts playing a six-night engagement at New York's Max's Kansas City, co-headlining with reggae giants Bob Marley and The Wailers before a capacity crowd of 200.

Despite the definite rock edge of *Greetings From Asbury Park, New Jersey* Springsteen fell victim to the fate that all artists must face at some point— comparisons and categorization. Springsteen was struck hard, and the label pinned to him was one that he would have trouble ridding himself of: "The New Dylan." He was yet another in a long string of performers to be tagged as such. The comparisons may have been inevitable; after all, Springsteen was signed to CBS Records by John Hammond, the same man who signed Dylan. Springsteen's song-

"The New Dylan"

writing also was deep and personal, which many people felt put him in the same genre as Dylan, and there was also the fact that for two years prior to *Greetings From Asbury Park, New Jersey* Springsteen had been functioning as a solo act. There were also the physical aspects that some people saw— Dylan and Springsteen sharing similar styles of dress (jeans and work shirts), and basic physical traits that were viewed by some as similarities (their hair, beards, and body frames).

Although Springsteen has expressed his admiration for Dylan, and has also been known to perform an intense acoustic rendition of Dylan's "I Want You" (doing a much slower and passionate version than the original), that is the extent of any similarities. Springsteen's roots are deeply planted in the original rock and roll traditions, and once he had assembled his band, those elements came forward in full volume.

The label had been attached to him, though, and it was going to haunt him for the next few years. It was also the first of many barriers that Springsteen would encounter and eventually overcome. They would take time and would cause him more problems as he tried to establish himself and build a solid reputation, but Springsteen's dedication and confidence would see him through.

chapter 3

THE
E STREET BAND AND SHUFFLE

In fall 1973, Springsteen was back in the recording studio, working on his second album with his band: Clemons, Federici, Lopez, Sancious, and Tallent. Offering a reflective look at life on the Jersey shore, *The Wild, The Innocent, and The E Street Shuffle* was released in November 1973. No singles were issued, nor did the album receive extensive airplay, but the reviews were favorable. Springsteen and Band backed the album with shows in small clubs and halls in a few markets, and began to develop their following.

On February 23, 1974, Vini Lopez left the E Street Band. He was replaced by Ernest "Boom" Carter, a friend of David Sancious. Springsteen and the Band's live shows were developing into the fundamentals of today's performances: long, demanding, and out of the league of any other artist. He was spending more time on stage, close to two hours, playing songs from his albums, material not yet released, and rock classics from Elvis, Gary "U.S." Bonds, Chuck Berry, and Manfred Mann. Springsteen's story-telling skills had also been incorporated as part of the show. He has since become known for the tales he recounts to his audiences—

Jon Landau was so moved by the intensity of Springsteen's performance, that he wrote one of the most emotional, inspiring rock reviews ever printed.

adventures in Asbury Park, experiences with various members of the E Street Band, the hardships encountered while growing up in Freehold. Whether factual or fabricated, Springsteen has an unsurpassable ability for making these stories completely believable, and it is probably impossible to find another performer who can match his rapport.

Springsteen's tour was not only gaining length, but was also increasing in popularity. He was overwhelming audiences in every city. Even in areas where he was virtually unknown, word of mouth was drawing crowds and every show ended with standing ovations and everyone shouting for more.

From April 9–11, 1974, Springsteen and Band played a three-night benefit at a bar called Charley's Place in Boston's Harvard Square. In the window of the club was posted a copy of a review of *The Wild, The Innocent, and The E Street Shuffle*, written by Concord resident Jon Landau, who wrote for the Boston-Cambridge weekly *Real Paper*, and was also responsible for *Rolling Stone*'s record-review section. Springsteen happened to be reading Landau's posted column when the writer arrived at Charley's Place. They were introduced and spoke for a while, and the show left Landau very impressed. One month later, on May 9, Springsteen and Band returned to the Harvard Square Theatre. Landau, so

moved by the intensity of Springsteen's performance, wrote one of the most emotional, inspiring reviews ever printed, one that in its entirety has since become a landmark in music journalism. That review contained the now-famous statement in which Landau predicted having seen the future of rock and roll in Bruce Springsteen. CBS Records, seeing the infinite opportunities in that quote, launched an advertising blitz centered around it, and with the combination of Springsteen's amazing concerts and the mass promotion by CBS, sales of the first two albums began to increase. Consequently, pressure and expectations also mounted as time drew closer for recording the next album.

In July 1974, David Sancious left the E Street Band after being offered a recording contract with Epic Records. Sancious, pursing a solo career and playing with a number of jazz-rock bands along the way, was joined shortly after by Ernest Carter. Springsteen was facing cancelled dates, two band vacancies, and a delayed album. He and Mike Appel ran an ad in *The Village Voice* to announce the openings, and auditioned several musicians. In August, drummer Max Weinberg and pianist Roy Bittan became part of the E Street Band. Meanwhile sessions resumed, unsuccessfully, to record a new album and mix a new single.

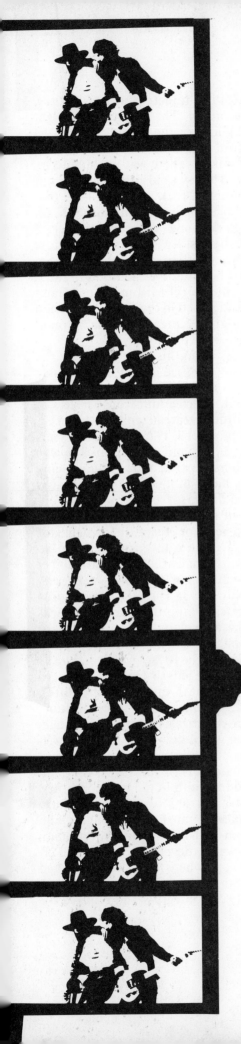

Chapter 4

1975 AND THE ANTHEM

t was November 1974. A year had gone by since the release of *The Wild, The Innocent, and The E Street Shuffle*. Springsteen was nowhere near its followup. Jon Landau had moved to New York, and his friendship with Springsteen was growing. By early 1975, Landau had heard the demo tapes, had attended recording and mixing sessions, and was becoming a regular member of Springsteen's group. Springsteen valued Landau's opinion highly, and in March 1975 Landau accepted Springsteen's offer and became co-producer, working with Mike Appel. In April, under Landau's suggestion, Springsteen and Band relocated their recording sessions from New York City's 914 Studios to the Record Plant, and Jimmy Iovine was hired as engineer. His previous experience included work with Phil Spector and John Lennon. With all the previously scheduled shows completed, all efforts were thrown into the new album. What followed were grueling hours in the studio, beginning at 3:00 in the afternoon and ending at 6:00 the next morning, sometimes running for a consecutive 24 hours. The group had projected a July release date, but by August there was still no album. Springsteen, an un-

Bruce Springsteen, the man and his music, offered honesty and integrity and restored belief that rock and roll was from the heart.

bending perfectionist, rejected take after take, recording after recording. The horns weren't right on one song, the guitar or the saxophone solo on another. The record company waited, the public waited, the band waited. There was pressure to release the product. There was also the ever-present stigma of the "future of rock and roll" label that hung like a mixed blessing over Springsteen's head. Would he live up to everyone's expectations, including his own? Was he just a victim of hype whose name would fade away with so many others? During this time there had been another addition to the E Street lineup. Former Steel Mill member Miami Steve Van Zandt had joined in the recording session to help with horn arrangements and background vocals; Springsteen asked him to stay.

Springsteen was taking his time finishing the product, refusing to sacrifice quality for the mere sake of having a new album out on the racks. He labored over each cut, rejected numerous masters of the album, rerecorded, rearranged, and remixed, until finally, on September 1, 1975, almost two years after the release of his second album, *Born To Run* was out. An emotional portrait of day-to-day living, *Born To Run* was an instant classic in its candid description of the dreams, frustrations, turmoil, and desperation of routine work, lost loves and friendships, of the need for escape, the struggle for survival, the insatiable quest for freedom so deserved. The album entered the charts at Number 84, then shot to Number 8 in its second week, eventually reaching Number 3. The album went gold shortly after its release (approximately six weeks later), then soon became platinum. Along with the release of the album, a single was issued: "Born To Run"/"Meeting Across The River," which despite its four-and-a-half-minute length (among standard three-to-three-and-a-half minute radio hits), reached Number 23 on the charts. "Born To Run" (the single) became America's first major introduction to Springsteen, who was enthusiastically welcomed by previously disenchanted rock fans. Turned off by the trends and fads of the 1970s, they had given up hope and lost faith in the music industry. Suddenly, amidst a barrage of glitter, platform shoes, electronic dance music, strobe lights and discos, a blue-jean-and-T-shirt-clad young man burst onto the airwaves, devoid of any special effects, resurrecting hope where for so long there had been none. Bruce Springsteen, the man and his music, offered honesty and integrity, and restored the

< *Springsteen with Miami Steve Van Zandt. They've been close friends since they were 16. Above: Relaxing with two of his many admirers.*

belief that rock and roll was actually from the heart—that it could still bring salvation to its listeners, who recently had been subjected to mass quantities of product that lacked substance, that lacked the traditions and values that had once been bestowed upon it. Within those four-and-a-half-minutes, Springsteen reaffirmed the convictions that had been dormant under the influence of empty vinyl platters.

From opening riff to final chorus, "Born To Run" offers hope, a chance to escape from broken dreams, an alternative that says things don't have to be this way. Springsteen paints a picture of American lifestyle as seen through the eyes of the working class. This is not the jet-set scene of the wealthy and the upper class. Rather, Springsteen reaches the ideal of an Everyman performer who is as much a part of the audience as the listeners are, someone who understands what it means to be an outsider, to find release in a late night drive after enduring hours under the boss' tyranny, who can relate to human desires, wanting and needing more than what is being offered, and knowing that so much more is deserved. Most important, Springsteen puts those feelings into words, into music, offering an alternate route, an open invitation to travel it with him.

Within the contents of one album, Springsteen examined the pains we think we suffer alone, and made us realize that they are universal. Springsteen also opened new doors for music, bringing back the untarnished look and sound that contemporary music so sorely missed and clearing a path for upcoming groups, making it once again acceptable to play rock and roll for the sake of the music itself, and not for a synthetic image.

Slowly recuperating from the "New Dylan" label, and with the "future of rock and roll" tag less prominent, Springsteen faced yet another obstacle. On October 27, 1975, he was featured as the cover story in both *Time* and *Newsweek* magazines. What might have been considered a great honor by some was also seen as just media hype by others, who insinuated that Springsteen was nothing more than a records-company creation. Although both magazines seemed sincere enough in their attempts to spotlight the career of someone who was being looked upon as a "new sensation," and examine the development of the artist, the publications may have done as much harm as they did good. At the time of the dual cover stories, Springsteen's reputation had become so widespread that every reporter in the country seemed to be taking part in the story.

29

THE BOSS

"Rock's New Sensation" the cover of Time—October 27, 1975.

Everyone wanted an interview. Each magazine devoted several pages to a chronicle of his career, and their own interpretations of his words and music. Springsteen's photo was on the cover of everything from daily newspapers to the leading industry trades, and unfamiliar listeners were caught between believing that the young man from New Jersey was truly this generation's genius, or just another in a series of "next big thing" rock stars who come and go so quickly that it is impossible to keep up with all of them.

Time and *Newsweek* titled their lengthy features "Rock's New Sensation" and "Making Of a Rock Star," respectively, and each went about its own way of narrating the Springsteen story. However, they did cover some common ground: the frustrating school days in Freehold, the "new Dylan" label, and the time spent recording *Born To Run*. The magazines' approaches may have been somewhat different, but both had the same basic goal—to attempt an interpretation and analysis of what some considered the Springsteen mystique—what it was about this young man that seemed to have pushed the record industry into a fit of enthusiasm and was converting listeners by the thousands into enthralled fans. Both publications sought to probe Springsteen's background, to trace the path of his unbelievable success.

Time and *Newsweek* were looking perhaps for answers they thought might exist about this new phenomenon—where he lived, where he was from, what his early years had been like, where he drew his inspiration, what it was about his songs that made them so significant, and why listeners were heralding him as some sort of musical miracle. They interviewed Springsteen, Jon Landau, John Hammond, and various others. They spent time with Springsteen, frequenting the Asbury Park hangouts, looking for those explanations if there really were any.

Granted, both *Time* and *Newsweek* were successful at presenting the Springsteen story, relating his past, offering insight as to the individual behind the songs (not to mention teaching their readers a thing or two about Asbury Park). But again, this was just cause for skeptics to doubt the value of Springsteen, to question the record company's publicity about this ultimate rock star. It was easy for those who were unfamiliar with Springsteen to pass him off as another flash-in-the-pan (as is the oft-chosen description), a marketing attempt to bestow yet another money-making idol on the music industry.

"bears a striking resemblance to Dylan . . ."

Newsweek in particular, by the mere selection of its headline (although certainly with no intention of doing any harm to its subject), added to the incredulity about Springsteen's worth and his ability to stand on his own merits. They alluded to the ever-present comparison, stating that he "bears a striking resemblance to Dylan . . ." and detailing again the "future of rock and roll and its name is Bruce Springsteen" article. Looking back at the 1975 *Newsweek* feature, perhaps the most ironic, and even amusing, moment in the entire spread is a statement from Warner Bros. Records President Joe Smith who at the time said, "He's a hot new artist now, but he's not the new messiah and I question whether he will establish an international mania. He's got a very long way to go before he does what Elton has done, or Rod Stewart or The Rolling Stones or Led Zeppelin."

Indeed!

Johnny Lyons, lead singer of Southside Johnny and the Asbury Jukes, is a much welcomed, frequent guest of Bruce on stage.

chapter 5

LAWSUITS, LABOR, AND THE ALBUM SHIPS GOLD

n November 1975 Springsteen and Band began a brief European tour, playing in London, Stockholm, and Amsterdam. In December they returned to the United States and continued the tour. During a concert at C. W. Post College in Greenvale, Long Island, a recording was made of the group performing "Santa Claus Is Coming To Town," complete with Springsteen asking Clarence Clemons if he had been a good boy all year. The priceless track was released only to a few radio stations, where it received tremendous airplay. The record was not commercially issued until 1981, when it appeared on a children's album, *In Harmony 2*. The "Born To Run" tour came to a close at the Tower Theatre in Philadelphia.

Springsteen began 1976 with the release of a second single, "Tenth Avenue Freeze-Out"/"She's The One." With the start of the new year, things seemed to be on the positive side for Springsteen. The "hype" was proving to be fact, not just publicity. Album sales were skyrocketing, the tour had been a success, Springsteen had gained the respect and adulation of industry and skeptics alike. In the early part of the year various E Street Band members

Springsteen sings of human strife and internal conflict; the universal struggle of trying to live, not just exist.

worked on some outside projects, Jon Landau contributed production guidance to other material, and Springsteen polished new songs for his next album, which was projected for an early summer release following a previously scheduled spring tour. Little did anyone know that Springsteen's past—the naivete of an unsuspecting young man signing a contract in the parking lot of a club—was about to surface in what would be a long, painful experience.

In January and February 1976, as money began to come in from record sales, it became clear that Springsteen's contract with Mike Appel and Laurel Canyon was shortchanging Springsteen, while tipping the royalties scale completely in Appel's favor. Springsteen, who had signed the contracts spontaneously, with never a thought to having them examined by an attorney, began to realize the injustice of the deal. However, he still "liked" Appel, recognized the fact that Appel was one of the first people to believe in him, and simply could not turn his back. He hoped to work out some kind of arrangement with Appel and straighten things out. Supposedly, some sort of agreement was reached, but it was an on-again-off-again thing that was eventually thrown out by Appel. In March, Springsteen and Band set out on their tour, criss-crossing the South, Midwest, and Northeast, with no particularly set route taking them from area to area. The tour continued until May 28, 1976, coming to a close at the U.S. Naval Academy in Annapolis, Maryland.

What followed was a complex, confusing ordeal. In May 1976 Mike Appel allegedly tried to intervene (unsuccessfully) on the gross from six Springsteen performances in an effort to collect the management commission he claimed was owed to him in back pay. On July 27, 1976, the formal lawsuit with Appel began; "Conflict of interest" was the reported charge. Springsteen, claiming that he had not been properly advised of his rights, allegedly filed breach of contract against Appel. According to reports, there were discrepencies in royalty payments. Worst of all, Springsteen had unknowingly relinquished all the publishing rights to his songs to Mike Appel and Laurel Canyon, giving the company complete freedom to do as they pleased with his material. Springsteen reportedly asked for compensation for damages incurred, and sought to dissolve any prior contracts with Appel.

On July 29 Appel countered Springsteen's suit. Appel reportedly claimed "piracy" on the part of Jon Landau, and obtained an injunction preventing

Springsteen goes on stage to greet good friend Robert Gordon.

Few artists, if any, devote so much time and effort to their work.

He has so much respect for his listeners—he refuses to give them anything less than one-hundred percent.

Landau and Springsteen from entering a studio together. Appel reportedly also charged Springsteen with breach of contract.

The next ten months were shadowed by a series of legal battles, during which, of course, Springsteen could not record his next album. Inadvertently, this situation got CBS Records involved in the fiasco.

In the meantime, Springsteen went back on the road from September to November 1976, covering ground from Los Angeles to New York, playing his first engagement at the Spectrum in Philadelphia, and wrapping things up with a six-night sellout at New York City's Palladium Theatre. Despite the fact that Springsteen was touring with no new album to coincide with the shows, the tour was a tremendous success. He did perform some new songs during the course of the tour, several of which eventually appeared on his fourth album.

In March 1977 Springsteen filed another motion in his continuing struggle with Mike Appel. The next two months kept both men in the courtroom, going through the unpleasant sequence of testimony and defense. Finally, on May 28, 1977, it was announced that Springsteen and Appel had reached a final settlement. The details of the agreement were never revealed; instead, reporters were simply told that the two men had "satisfactorily resolved their differences." It was reported, however, that Mike Appel retained his rights to a percentage of royalties from Springsteen's first three albums, and a five-year production deal for Laurel Canyon with CBS Records. Springsteen won back the rights to all of his material, was granted the right to select his own producer, and all of his ties with Mike Appel were legally dissolved. Springsteen could now return to the studio with Jon Landau to record his long-awaited album.

On June 1, 1977, Springsteen and Band entered Atlantic Recording Studios, with Landau producing and Jimmy Iovine as engineer. Not pleased with the sound, they moved the sessions to The Record Plant. As is always the case with Springsteen, the sessions were slow and painstaking. The result was *Darkness On The Edge Of Town.* Like *Born To Run,* there is a recurring theme of escape on the album, but it is handled differently. The characters here have matured; they seek explanation; they are laden with guilt, anger, and frustration. They loathe a situation that they feel powerless to change, but know they must. Cursing the injustices of the hardships they are forced to endure, these protagonists are fighting to rise above their immediate state, to be more than just victims of circumstance. They are searching for answers, demanding due respect. They symbolize anyone who has sacrificed in order to survive; anyone who has ever looked back and wondered "what if," who has suffered humiliation, received no recognition for efforts, who has hungered for a change but is not certain of fitting in. *Darkness On The Edge Of Town* is a deeply personal album that tells the story of human strife and internal conflict; the universal struggle of trying to live, not just to exist.

Springsteen, Landau, and Steve Van Zandt began mixing *Darkness On The Edge Of Town* in early 1978, with assistance from Charles Plotkin. Mixing was complete in early spring. In May, Springsteen and the E Street Band began a seven-month U.S. tour that would continue until January 1, 1979, with only one break from October to November. The tour covered 86 cities and totalled 109 shows.

In June, just a few weeks after the start of the tour, *Darkness On The Edge Of Town* was released and reportedly shipped gold. Marking almost three years since the release of *Born To Run, Darkness On The Edge Of Town* entered the charts at Number 39, climbed to Number 10 of the following week, and eventually reached Number 5. The first single, "Prove It All Night"/"Factory," peaked at Number 33. Within a short period of time the album was certified platinum.

By July 1978 Jon Landau had become Springsteen's manager.

Springsteen—never a weak moment, never an imperfection in his art.

chapter 6

BOOTLETS, M.U.S.E., BAND PROJECTS, AND A TOP-10 HIT

 n July 7, 1978, Springsteen and Band performed at The Roxy in Los Angeles. The show was the first of several summer concerts that would also be simultaneously broadcast on various radio stations. This also meant an open market for bootleggers. Actually, illegitimate Springsteen tapes had been circulating for years, but by 1978 the illicit recordings had become a booming business. They reached their peak with the "Darkness On The Edge Of Town" tour, as Springsteen had by then reached "superstar" proportions. Bootlegging had gotten totally out of control, as new tapes of rehearsals, studio work, and live shows were constantly being released. The problem was multifaceted: by having his material released by outside parties, Springsteen was basically losing power over his copyright, something he had struggled so hard to gain control of two years earlier. Much of the bootlegged tapes contained unreleased material, never meant to be heard outside of the studio, again a violation of copyright. But the tapes were in high demand by Springsteen fans, some of whom felt entitled to gather as much as was available of Springsteen's work (no matter how it had to be obtained) because of the value

With a cheerful smile and exuberant energy, he gives his fans exactly what they want.

they placed on him; others simply because some of Springsteen's most poignant masterpieces are among those he has never released, and bootlegs were the only means of obtaining and appreciating these works on a permanent basis. There was no denying the emotion and drive captured on the in-concert tapes, such as the most popular "Main Point" (1975) and "Winterland" (1978) shows. The demand was so high for the bootlegs that the tapes were being pressed, and some major-market record stores were selling copies directly off the shelf, displaying them next to the CBS-issued Springsteen albums. Fans were handing over $15 to $20 (at least) per copy, and from there more cassettes and copies were made and distributed. The fault did not really lie with the fans who purchased, duplicated, and traded tapes amongst themselves—they were just trying to own anything available that involved their idol. The real blame was on the actual bootleggers —the ones who stole Springsteen's material, then sat back and collected a small fortune at the expense of the performer and his fans.

In August 1978, determined to put a stop to boot-legging, Springsteen was back in court, this time with CBS Records backing him, suing for damages against the bootleggers. Reportedly, five defendants in California were charged with breach of copyright and unauthorized use of Springsteen's name and material. A similar suit was allegedly filed in New

Jersey against a resident of the state. The popularity of Springsteen bootlegs seems to have subsided in recent years; at least they are seldom mentioned openly among Springsteen followers or in trade headlines reporting more tapes discovered. The bootlegs, however, remain available, are still circulating, and since 1978 updated material has probably become part of the bootleg catalogue.

On January 1, 1979, Springsteen and Band drew the "Darkness On The Edge Of Town" tour to a close in Cleveland, Ohio. It would be another two years before they performed a full-length concert. In April, Springsteen was in the studio again, this time at the Power Station in New York City, laying down some tracks for his next album. Unfortunately, a mid-month accident while riding around on his three-wheel motorcycle caused Springsteen to injure his knee, thus tying up the recording process during his recovery. This was but the first in a series of delays that would hold up the album's release. Recording sessions are the same for every Springsteen album: he constantly brings in new material, records, scraps the results and starts over, writes more songs, records, changes the arrangements, scraps the finished project. Springsteen's fanatical obsession with detail will not allow him to release something if there is one tiny flaw, even if it is not noticeable to the listener; or if he is left with the slightest element of doubt about the final take. He

Springsteen is more than just another singer; he's not a star. He's basic—an everyday kind of person.

spends infinite hours rerecording, rearranging, remixing, and, often, ultimately rejecting. Consequently it can take a couple of years before the material meets his satisfaction and he deems it ready to be heard by the public. It is this dedication on the part of the performer that makes him special. Few, if any, artists devote so much time and effort to their work, and, without fail, Springsteen always delivers perfect material. He could easily overlook minute blemishes that no one else would notice and get the product to the people much sooner, but that's just not his style. While this means that the fans have to wait (and wait, and wait) for the next album, no one seems to mind because of the certainty that what will eventually be delivered is Springsteen at his best, with never a weak moment, never an imperfection in his art. It is not just the pride he takes in his work. It is the respect he has for his listeners—to place such value on them that he refuses to give them anything less than one hundred percent.

In 1979 Springsteen revealed what some felt was a surprising side of him—a role many interpreted as that of an activist taking part in a controversial project. During the course of the "Darkness On The Edge Of Town" tour, Springsteen, while in Los Angeles, met Tom Campbell, a veteran of the antinuclear movement. The two had been introduced before at an earlier event and, upon seeing each other again during Springsteen's tour, they rekindled their friendship. The second meeting took place some time after the incident at Three Mile Island when the nuclear reactor came close to a meltdown. Located in Pennsylvania, Three Mile Island had a shocking effect, not only on local residents but on the entire nation, increasing awareness of the possibility of nuclear disaster. Surrounding states were deeply shaken by the incident. The 1978–1980 period was filled with antinuclear rallies, protests, and concerts, and antinuclear coalitions were established in numerous cities. During this time Tom Campbell, Sam Lovejoy, Howard Kohn, and David Fenton joined forces with Jackson Browne, Bonnie Raitt, John Hall, and Graham Nash to form Musicians United For Safe Energy, or M.U.S.E. They planned a large fund-raising/educational/interest-gaining benefit at Madison Square Garden. Campbell approached Springsteen about the possibility of his participation, and Springsteen expressed interest.

The move was a first. Although strains of political/social/economic views are evident in much of his material, Springsteen was, and remains, careful not to commit himself to any such groups; to avoid any alliances; yet he did agree to take part in the M.U.S.E. concerts after being familiarized with the details of the event. However, unlike most of his contemporaries, Springsteen made no statements as to what stand he took on the issue. While Jackson Browne, John Hall, and Graham Nash were avid spokesmen for the event, Springsteen, who was inevitably the draw for attendance, remained silent.

M.U.S.E. week at Madison Square Garden was scheduled for September 19–23. Preliminary rallies were held, and the list of artists appearing during the five-night benefit included the M.U.S.E. founders, and help from The Doobie Brothers, Nicolette Larson, Jesse Colin Young, James Taylor, Carly Simon, David Crosby, Stephen Stills, Chaka Khan, Tom Petty and The Heartbreakers, Ry Cooder, Peter Tosh, Gil Scott-Heron, Willie Nelson, Raydio, Sweet Honey In The Rock, Poco, and more. Springsteen agreed to play hour-long sets on September 22 and 23, and authorized having his performances recorded for use on an upcoming M.U.S.E. concert album, also a benefit project, planned for release later that year. Springsteen also agreed to having his performance filmed for M.U.S.E. concert movie. The M.U.S.E. shows were Springsteen and Band's first in more than nine months and, predictably, those were the nights that were sold out. The Springsteens devotees were there in abundance, making things just a bit tense for those artists with the truly unenviable task of opening for Springsteen. Thousands of voices kept up an incessant chant of "Bruce! Bruce!" from the moment they entered the Garden until the final note of Springsteen's final song.

The outcome of the M.U.S.E. concerts, aside from the obvious proceeds raised, was some of the finest onstage footage ever caught on videotape, with Springsteen and The E Street Band delivering an absolutely scorching performance. Brief though it was, it captured the essence of Springsteen in concert and, according to many of the "No Nukes" movie viewers, made everyone else's performance pale severely in comparison! The film, which was released in summer 1980, featured Springsteen doing "Thunder Road," Gary "U.S." Bond's "Quarter To Three," and a new piece, "The River." The "No Nukes" album, a triple set which was released in time for Christmas 1979, was packaged with a notice that proceeds were going to the M.U.S.E. cause;

it contained Springsteen's "Mitch Ryder Medley" (which has since become known as Springsteen's "Devil With The Blue Dress Medley") and a duet with Jackson Browne on "Stay," the Maurice Williams and The Zodiacs tune.

Between the time Springsteen agreed to the M.U.S.E. benefits and the actual shows, he had almost been hibernating in the studio, putting the finishing touches on his new album with help from Jon Landau and Miami Steve Van Zandt. Soon 1979 had come and gone, and there was still no sign of a new album. Meanwhile the other members of the E Street Band began 1980 by becoming involved with other projects. Roy Bittan lent his skills to such artists as David Bowie, Graham Parker, Jim Steinman, and Ian Hunter. Max Weinberg also worked with Steinman and Hunter, and with Ellen Foley. Clarence Clemons and Garry Tallent experimented with record production and area artists. Clemons played on recordings by other artists. Danny Federici worked with British performer Graham Parker.

There was still no album from Springsteen, who had recorded about 40 songs for the project. In May, Springsteen, Landau, and Van Zandt took the package to Los Angeles, where 20 songs were selected for a double album, to be mixed by Charles Plotkin. With the set complete, Springsteen was ready to reassemble the E Street Band for their first world tour, which would cover the U.S., Canada, Europe, Australia, and Japan. The tour commenced on October 3, 1980, in Ann Arbor, Michigan, where Springsteen's close friend Bob Seeger joined him in an encore of "Thunder Road."

On October 17, 1980, Springsteen's fifth album, *The River*, was released. It entered the charts at Number 4 on November 1, and was Number One the next week. Once again, *The River* encapsulated some of the standard Springsteen images—cars and girls. And again, there was the "escape" theme. But this time, Springsteen took things a step further. Mixing elements of rock, blues, folk, country, rockabilly and ballads, Springsteen composed a series of vignettes, introducing us to characters who are often struggling, trapped by internal conflicts. Despite a selection of upbeat songs, there is a gripping shadow of sadness blanketing *The River*. The peo-

ple Springsteen writes about on this album are caught up in the efforts of survival. They no longer look beyond for new challenges. Instead, they are facing unpleasant realities, plagued with the ghosts of the past.

On November 8, 1980, the first single from *The River*, was released: "Hungry Heart"/"Held Up Without A Gun." The single, a surprisingly melodic, upbeat song (for Springsteen), which featured delightful "pop" backup harmony from Flo and Eddie, was also Springsteen's first Top 10 hit. "Hungry Heart" entered *Billboard*'s Hot 100 and quickly climbed to Number 5.

Springsteen's concerts had escalated to his marathon four-hour shows, which contained only a brief intermission at the halfway point. With the advent of a Top 10 hit, Springsteen was now receiving full-time AM and FM airplay, and more and more new converts were joining the millions of faithful devotees who were spending days in front of ticket

offices to get the best seats, and who were following him across the country. Springsteen concerts had become more than just a night out at the arena. They had become a pilgrimage as people drove, flew, hitchhiked, and bussed across numerous state lines to be a part of "The River" tour again and again.

There was Mark, from Los Angeles, who was traveling from city to city with the tour. He had taken a break from his college classes, determined to see every show Springsteen did. His feeling was "College will be around all year; Springsteen won't."

Joe, from Philadelphia, was traveling the entire East Coast to see Springsteen. Columbia, South Carolina, marked his 150th Springsteen show, and he was proud to announce that he had been in the audience on that famous night on May 9, 1974, at the Harvard Square Theatre to witness the performance that inspired Jon Landau's "future of rock and roll" statement. Joe said he still had a copy of

THE BOSS

that piece, which he felt put into words what everyone in the audience was thinking that night.

Kathy, a native of Washington, D.C., quit her job in time for "The River" tour, withdrew all her savings from the bank, packed a travel bag with some clothes and a few essentials, and took off to follow Springsteen. She waited outside the arena every night after the show for just a glimpse of him, and said she had been lucky enough to actually meet him that way on a few occasions. Her prized possession was her Springsteen tour book/program, which he had autographed for her.

There was also on unidentified young lady who became quite famous in her city, and on her college campus. She was pursuing her degree in a southern capital city where Springsteen did one show, but she was originally from "up north," according to the people who told her story. They could not remember exactly where she was from, but thought it might have been Rhode Island. What they did re-

member was sitting next to her at a concert in the southern city. Prior to the show she was telling everyone around her that she had gone home for the Christmas holidays and learned that Springsteen was playing at Madison Square Garden, all dates sold out. Determined to see him, she bought one ticket from a scalper for $250. She told her friends that during "Sherry Darling," Springsteen pulled a girl up from the audience onto the stage and danced with her. She told everyone that her life would be complete if someday her prayers were answered and she could have that one dance.

During an intermission at the southern concert that Thursday night, it was announced that tickets for Springsteen's upcoming show there would go on sale the following Monday morning. The people near her noted that she told her friends, "I'm going to wait in front of the box office! Please bring me some blankets later!" and ran out of the building. After the concert the people went by the box office to check if she was there. They found her sitting in the below 20° cold, and by that time, more people had begun to set up camp. They would remain there until Monday morning (when the tickets would sell out in a matter of hours).

The same people who saw the girl at the other concert recognized her at the Springsteen concert in February, seated front row center. And when the big moment arrived, and Springsteen tore into "Sherry Darling," he pulled that same hysterical, crying young lady up on the stage to dance. Ten thousand people cheered their way through Springsteen's concert that night, but there was no doubt who was the happiest person in the crowd!

These people are but a select few among the millions who share this love for Springsteen. But all the labels that they have attached to him: "Superstar," "Phenomenon," "Messiah," "Genius," haven't touched the guy from New Jersey. Springsteen remains one of the guys—no ego, no star trip, no jaded, burned-out attitude. Throughout the adulation and the success that leads so many popular figures into a world of excess and indulgence, Springsteen has never changed his ideals or his values. To this day the man still sports jeans and T-shirts, still "hangs out" in Asbury Park clubs, still doesn't smoke, rarely drinks (and if so, in moderation), and refuses to touch drugs.

Springsteen does more than just walk out on stage and go through the motions. He pushes himself, the Band, and the audience far beyond the

usual limits. For a minimum of four hours (he would probably play all night if he could get away with it), he keeps the crowd on their feet. They sing, cheer, dance, and put on almost as much of a show as he does. Springsteen's concerts are an all-or-none situation, and everyone gets in on the act. But there's more. Springsteen insists on a sound check before each performance, and in typical Springsteen fashion this doesn't mean checking things out and running through four or five songs. Sound checks for Springsteen take up to three hours, often throwing in material that is not on the song list (E Street members have reported that this often happens during the concert as well, with Springsteen calling a song that they haven't done in years and catching everyone by surprise). Springsteen is also notorious for checking the sound from all points in the arena, every night, moving from section to section, from the front row to the last seat at the very top of the highest row, to make sure everything is at its best for his audience.

In Februrary 1981 another single was released

from *The River*: "Fade Away"/"Be True." It reached Number 20. On February 13, Springsteen and The E Street Band postponed the European segment of their tour that was scheduled to begin at the end of the month. The reason—Springsteen was suffering from exhaustion. On April 4, the nine-week European excursion got underway in Hamburg, West Germany, and covered 11 countries: Germany, Switzerland, France, Spain, Belgium, Holland, Denmark, Sweden, Norway, England, and Scotland. The European visit closed at the International Arena in Birmingham, England, on June 8.

Springsteen's summer tour of the United States opened on July 2, for six sold-out shows at the 20,000 seat Brendan Byrne Arena in the Meadowlands sports complex in East Rutherford, New Jersey. The arena, an $85 million complex, was said to have been constructed as a multiuse facility structured toward rock and roll—with sound panels and insulation. Located just outside New York City, the Brendan Byrne Arena opened its doors in 1981, and it somehow seemed appropriate that Springsteen

should come home to be the first performer upon its stage. Tickets to the six-night stand were sold by mail order only, and the arena received enough requests for Springsteen to have played 19 sold-out shows.

August took Springsteen and the E Street Band to California for three nights at the Los Angeles Sports Arena. On August 20, during that set of shows, Springsteen played a benefit before a sold-out crowd of 15,000. The procedes went to the 8000-member Vietnam Veterans of America, the largest veteran organization, and to several local Los Angeles veterans' organizations, such as the Los Angeles Mental Health Clinic. Springsteen's benefit sparked interest for additional veterans' benefit concerts by Pat Benatar in Detroit and Charlie Daniels in Saratoga Springs. Springsteen's involvement in the cause reportedly stemmed from his friendship with Ron Kovic, a disabled veteran. Springsteen and Jon Landau looked into various veterans organizations and after conferring with the Vietnam Veterans of America's vice-president,

Michael Harbert, and veteran Bobby Muller, the show was confirmed. The concert raised $100,000 for the organization, and it was reported that a Springsteen poster was also being sold to raise more funds for the veterans.

"The River" tour came to a close on September 14, 1981, at the Riverfront Coliseum in Cincinnati, Ohio. Springsteen and Band had been on the road eleven months. That fall the "No Nukes" concert became available on video cassette, introducing the excitement of those performances to a larger audience, many of whom had never seen the movie because of its limited-market distribution. In November the *In Harmony 2* album was released, containing the live version of "Santa Claus Is Coming To Town."

Getting some well-deserved rest after a lengthy tour.

chapter 7

AN ACOUSTIC MASTERPIECE

 pringsteen closed 1981 and opened 1982 quietly. There was no mention of a new album, nor was his name appearing anywhere in print. Springsteen seemed to have removed himself carefully from the spotlight, and fans assumed he was in a seclusion of sorts, getting some well-deserved rest after the lengthy tour. It also seemed likely that Springsteen was writing songs for his next album.

In March 1982 Springsteen began recording sessions for his next release. Some demos were cut at his home, and later there were band sessions at two studios in New York City: The Power Station and The Hit Factory. Projected dates were reported, rumors were circulating—new album out in spring, tour in summer; album out in summer, tour in fall. Finally fall was officially here but, predictably, there was still no album.

In October 1982 *Nebraska*, Springsteen's sixth album, was released. Dramatically different from any of his other works, *Nebraska* was recorded on Springsteen's own portable four-track cassette recorder, and featured only Springsteen and his guitar. The story goes that Springsteen recorded the songs as a demo, then with the E Street Band, but

Left: A publicity shot by Columbia records. Above: Rock's most humble hero.

was not satisfied with the results. He then rerecorded the songs alone in the studio, but decided the final product lacked the raw feeling of his demos, so he scrapped those tapes as well and went back to the originals. *Nebraska* is a stark look at a bleak America. There is none of the usual "escape" theme, none of the cars and girls motifs, no faith, no hope, no dreams. *Nebraska* paints a very depressing picture of a land and a people who have suffered the wounds of a failed economy, a broken dream. They are victims of crime, unemployment, poverty, deprevation, humiliation. *Nebraska* has been compared to the works of Woody Guthrie; it has been called a recorded version of John Steinbeck's novels. *Nebraska* deals with the plight of the doomed, people

to whom life has dealt a tremendous unfair blow. Their destinies were not blessed with luck. These are America's downtrodden, the weary and destitute. Through them, Springsteen opens our eyes to situations that we often do our best to shut out. He instills compassion in us by making things that much clearer. But Springsteen's words tie the characters of *Nebraska* into one another—through situations, repeated phrases; through the unbreakable bonds of family, of blood; the knowledge that some things, immaterial ones, cannot be taken away, and likewise must be defended. Springsteen's lyrics are simple in structure, but their meaning is complex. He sings in a hushed tone, accompanied only by the haunting strum of his guitar, in the style of the solo folk-

The incredible joy "The Boss" has in performing is really something to behold to audiences worldwide.

influenced album that the record company expected from Springsteen the first time that they brought him into a recording studio.

Releasing an album like *Nebraska* as a follow-up to *The River* was a risk for Springsteen—a risk that the fans might not react the same way, that radio airplay would be out of the question. Where would the disheartening acoustic ballads fit in among synthesized new music and Top 40 hits? (Some stations did pick up on "Atlantic City" and rotated it somewhat as an album cut extra.) Springsteen was ready for the challenge, willing to take the chance, to release an album full of emotions that seemed to have been building up and waiting to be set free, perhaps even confronted. Whatever the case, *Nebraska* surprised even its creator with its success. It entered the charts at Number 29, and rested firmly at Number 4 the next week. It also became one of, if not *the* most critically acclaimed album of 1982, with press and

listeners praising Springsteen's courage and wisdom. A gripping expose of an America that most people would prefer to believe does not and could not exist, *Nebraska* is a masterpiece, a phenomenal work by one of the most ingenious songwriters of our times.

No single was released from *Nebraska* in the U.S., but "Atlantic City"/"The Big Payback" was released in Britain. Stateside, Springsteen had just released his first official video, a dismal black-and-white portrayal of the New Jersey shore to accompany "Atlantic City." Neither Springsteen nor any members of the E Street Band appear in the video. There were rumors of a solo Springsteen tour following the release of *Nebraska*, but they proved to be no more than rumors. Fans wondered just where *Nebraska* material would figure in the next Springsteen tour with the E Street Band, whenever it might be.

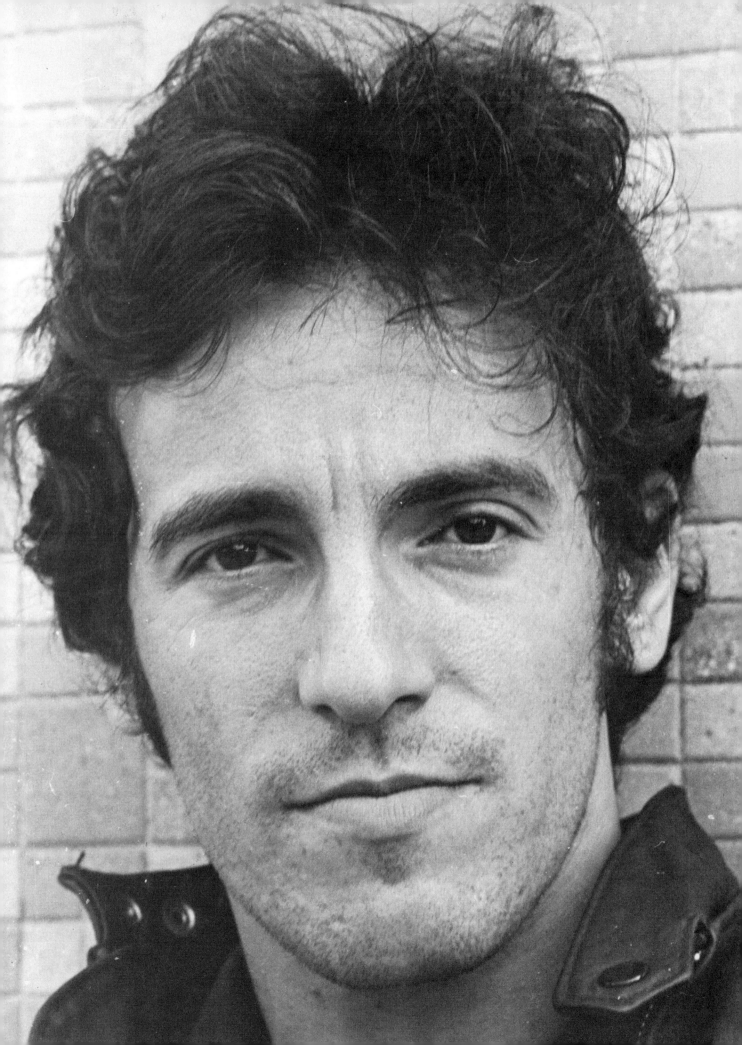

On June 29, 1984 Springsteen's 14-month "Born In The U.S.A." tour opened at the Civic Center in St. Paul, Minnesota.

chapter 8

SPRINGSTEEN SPRINGS BACK

**R**ecording sessions picked up again in winter 1982, but for the first time in almost nine years the E Street Band was undergoing changes. Miami Steve Van Zandt was seriously involved with his own group, Little Steven and The Disciples Of Soul. Assisted by E Streeters Danny Federici, Clarence Clemons, Garry Tallent and Max Weinberg, Van Zandt's group released their first album *Men Without Women* in December 1982. Van Zandt had not broken ties with Springsteen; rather, this was looked upon as an outside project between Springsteen albums. But 1982 became 1983 and there was no album on the way. On October 10, 1983, Clarence Clemons and his band, The Red Bank Rockers, also released their first album, *Rescue!*

The year passed with only rumors and speculation about the next Springsteen album, his first with the E Street Band in almost four years. By spring it was rumored that the album was complete and final mixing was being done. But in April 1984 Springsteen fans were dealt a sudden shock—Steve Van Zandt had made official his decision to leave the E Street Band and pursue a solo career. The news was devastating. Van Zandt had been an integral part of

Above and Right: Bruce Springsteen—Byrne Arena—August 1984.

Springsteen's career since those days in Asbury Park. Onstage he was Springsteen's story-telling sidekick, his "acting partner" for the in-concert antics and routines. On album, he was the man behind the guitar parts. In the studio, he was part of the production, arranging, and mixing. It was hard to imagine the E Street Band without Van Zandt. There were questions raised about motives and behind-the-scenes reasons for his departure. The only answer that ever came from within the Springsteen camp was that Van Zandt reportedly felt the time had come to concentrate fully on his own group. Fans wondered if there was more to the story than what was being revealed. They wondered if he would ever return. Most of all, they wondered who would take over for him.

On May 4 the much-anticipated new single from Bruce Springsteen and the E Street Band was released: "Dancing In The Dark"/"Pink Cadillac." Fans had been wondering what Springsteen's new material would be like, and just how much he had changed over the past three years, considering the drastic transitions that the record business had undergone. The popularity of music videos had been single-handedly credited with bringing a battered industry back to its feet after a several-year slump that left record sales at an all-time low and saw major acts cancelling blocks of tour dates. The "new music" invasion had launched an entire spectrum of debut acts onto the charts, making electronic sounds and pulsating rhythms highly fashionable. Heavy metal saw a resurgence and the leather-and-spikes look became common as daily wardrobe. Dance mixes grew into such a wonder toy that even the most unexpected artists were delving into the world of 12-inch singles, a style so individual that it even earned its own hits chart in the pages of *Billboard*, alongside the Hot 100, Top Rock, Pop, Rhythm and Blues, Country-Western, and Adult Contemporary. Where would Springsteen fit in among all this?

"Dancing In The Dark" is an unexpectedly up-beat song, for Springsteen. It has all the makings of a chart hit—uplifting tempo, sing-along harmonies, a catchy chorus, lots of backbeat. Those contemporary ingredients are just surface characteristics. Lyrically, it is still one-hundred percent Springsteen—the frustrated persona looking for something different, dissatisfied with himself, in need of a change of action. Springsteen has again captured the agitation and futility that so many of us feel; our inner

conflicts, the lack of confidence, the urge to make something happen, combined with the uncertainty of exactly what it is we are looking for.

No one was surprised when "Dancing In The Dark" vaulted to the top of the charts. It was, in fact, Springsteen's highest charting single to date, surpassing "Hungry Heart." It made the national Top 10 within four weeks of its release, shot to Number 4 in its fifth week, and peaked at Number 2.

Springsteen took the song two steps further. He entered the newfound circle of dance singles, issuing a 12-inch remix of "Dancing In The Dark," which at first made many fans wonder if he was selling out this time, going the commercial route as it is fre-

quently put. The 12-inch version was a shock at first listen, and was met by mixed reactions from many Springsteen fans, but it didn't take long to appreciate the worth of this new extended version, which again moved quickly to the top. The dance mix of "Dancing In The Dark" has also expanded Springsteen's airplay, making him a crossover artist for the first time in his career.

"Dancing In The Dark" was also Springsteen's screen debut, as he made his first official appearance in a video (excluding in-concert clips and quick shots in other artists' works). Directed by Brian DePalma, the video features Springsteen and the E Street Band in concert, although the shots of the

band members are very brief, with most of the footage concentrating on Springsteen. The video was filmed on June 28 at the Civic Center in St. Paul, Minnesota, before a house full of lucky fans recruited just for the event. Rather than go through the scenario plot-minimovie that most artists opt for in videos, Springsteen went straight to the heart of his song—"live" tape, which was certainly the most effective way of portraying any of his works. Despite the fact that the "show" was under the supervision of a director, as opposed to just a spontaneous clip of a concert ("Rosalita," "No Nukes"), "Dancing In The Dark" still managed to portray the excitement of Springsteen and the E Street Band

in action.

It has been reported that the "Dancing In The Dark" video project originally began as a concept video, under the direction of Jeff Stein, whose credits include The Cars and Billy Idol. Midway through production, Springsteen changed his mind about the project, which did not surprise anyone. Movie director Brian DePalma ("Carrie," "Dressed To Kill," "Scarface," etc.) was brought in to take over the video, which Springsteen decided would be the in-concert version.

On May 15, 1984, Springsteen recruited the newest addition to the E Street Band—guitarist/friend Nils Lofgren, whose musical background includes

Left: Clarence Clemons "The Big Man" and Springsteen. Clemons is easily 50 percent of Springsteen's story-telling act. Above: In 1969, on a trip cross-country to California, Bruce learned to drive a car.

nine solo albums and both studio and road work with Neil Young. Lofgren's boyish charm, musical and physical dexterity, and on-stage antics made him the ideal choice.

CBS Records launched an avalanche of promotional materials in advance of the release of the Springsteen single and the new album *Born In The U.S.A.* Record stores received advanced glossy fliers notifying them of the upcoming campaign. They advance-promo'd the album by calling it "The newest rock 'n' roll classic from America's classic rock 'n' roll legend. . . ." They listed Springsteen's lyrical, musical, and technical growth" and said the soon-to-be-released album was the one "to thrill his millions of fans—and a natural to win over legions of new ones." CBS took things a step further on the flier, calling Springsteen ". . . *the* artist who depicts American rock 'n' roll to music fans, critics, and musicians all over the world!" and described *Born In The U.S.A.* as a "fantastic album filled with great rock 'n' roll, and intense ballads with a feeling only Bruce Springsteen can create." To the untrained or unassuming eye/ear, this crusade could have been mistaken for hype, an encore performance of the "future of rock and roll" fanfare of CBS in the 1970s. Of course, by now, everyone knows better and no one has any doubts about Springsteen. So, when CBS began their full solicitation for the album—by mid-May record stores were boasting tremendous album cover blowups, photos, wall-

Despite his immense popularity, he has never sold out to the glamorous life. He is still the guy from Freehold, New Jersey.

length teletype-style announcements of what was coming soon; plus MTV was also running ads— everyone had faith in the product. CBS's pre-album praise and excitement was common knowledge for Springsteen fans. There was really no need to try to convince anyone about the quality of what we were going to hear. We all knew it would be perfect! The only problem was trying to keep the heightened tension under control while waiting for the release date to finally arrive!

On June 4, admist the expected fanfare and commotion, *Born In The U.S.A.* was released. Radio station request lines were flooded, airplay rotation couldn't keep up with the calls. Record stores could hardly keep up with demand. *Born In The U.S.A.* entered at Number 9 on the Top Album charts, which was the highest entry position of any album in the past two years. Within three weeks *Born In The U.S.A.* had reached Number One, and was nearing platinum status. Meanwhile, *Born In The U.S.A.* also entered at Number 2 on the British Charts.

During the last week of July/first week of August, the album's second single, "Cover Me"/"Jersey Girl" was released, and was listed as one of the nation's hottest adds, listing a total of 132 markets. "Cover Me" entered the charts at Number 52, climbed to Number 40, and had reached Number 29 after only three weeks on the charts, no doubt on its way to the Top 10.

On June 25, 1984, there was yet another change in the Springsteen entourage. Patti Scialfa was added to the E Street Band as a backup vocalist, after Springsteen heard her sing in an Asbury Park bar. She joined the group only three rehearsals prior to the tour.

On June 29, 1984, Springsteen's 14-month "Born In The U.S.A." tour opened at the Civic Center in St.

Paul. The tour, his first in three years, is currently in full swing, and the group is at its best. Springsteen, sporting a new look (the result of running, weight-training, and a change in eating habits —reportedly he is now including vegetables in his diet and has broken his tradition of morning, noon, and night meals of Pepsi's and cheeseburgers), is back on his nightly four-hour-plus marathons, covering material from all seven albums, including some very intense moments from *Nebraska*.

Springsteen's tour is again taking him into Europe, Japan, and Australia, and, as always, Springsteen and the E Street Band are breaking sales records wherever they are scheduled to play.

The Springsteen legend is growing as the tour progresses. Truly music's most important element, Springsteen is anything but a product of the entertainment world. He remains the people's performer, "one of us" to his fans, who each believe that they know him in their own way. Despite his immense popularity, he has never sold out to the glamorous life. He is still the guy from Freehold; the casual, unassuming, somewhat shy individual whose heart and soul belong to his music above anything else. He maintains a mutual respect for the people who work with him and the millions who love him. Devoid of "rock star" vices and attitudes, Springsteen is a rarity—a drug-free, alcohol-free, nonsmoker who makes his living in an admirable way, surrounded by a medium ridden by the "sex, drugs, rock and roll" cliche. Springsteen has retained his feelings for the working-class audience about whom he writes. The pleasures and freedoms of adolescence—the Asbury Park clubs, jam sessions in shoreside bars, the boardwalk, long drives—remain his pleasure today. He has not given in to trends or fallen victim to fame. Springsteen has, above all, upheld his beliefs, his understanding of what it means to be young, to be outcast, to want what is justly due but so unjustly taken away. Most important, he has remained honest with himself and with us. And that honesty, that trust, is what makes millions of people follow him across the country; makes them worship his every word. Springsteen does not sing *to* us, he sings *with* us, celebrates with us, laughs with us, and even cries with us. How lucky we are to have such a spokesman—one who shares our feelings, brings back the enchantment we sometime forget still exists, ignites within us that spark of adventure, that quest for something new, and who takes us with him on that never-ending ride!

*Clarence Clemons,
Bruce Springsteen
and Nils Lofgren.*

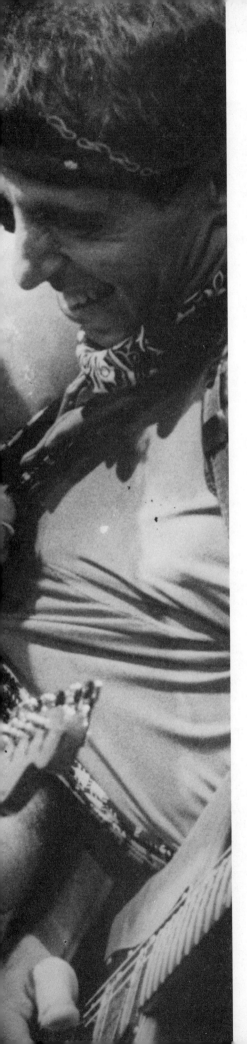

chapter 9

THE E STREET BAND: A PERFECT COMBINATION

There have been a number of personnel changes in the E Street Band since Springsteen first assembled them in 1972. The lineup that appeared with him in 1974 has been intact since that time, and while their names and photos appear on every album and they are periodically mentioned in magazine and newspaper articles, they still seem to keep in the background to some extent. Springsteen's band is more than just a group of musicians thickening the sound. They are highly talented individuals whose skills and personalities merge completely with Springsteen and with each other.

ROY BITTAN

Affectionately known as "Professor," Springsteen's piano player is also adept with synthesizers, organ, and accordian. Bittan hails from Rockaway Beach, New York. He joined the E Street band on August 23, 1974, replacing David Sancious, who was offered his own recording contract by Epic Records. Bittan's first band was called The Noblemen, and it was reported that he was the only member of the E Street Band (other than Springsteen) with actual recording experience. Bittan had also

Clarence Clemons, "The Big Man."

toured with the production of *Jesus Christ, Superstar,* and had played with the Pittsburgh Symphony. Since joining the E Street Band, Bittan's outside projects have included recording and/or touring with such artists as Dire Straits, Air Supply, Stevie Nicks (Bittan was her keyboardist on last year's "Wild Heart" tour), Meatloaf (playing on his debut album, *Bat Out Of Hell,* in 1978), Bonnie Tyler, David Bowie (on the albums *Station To Station,* and *Scary Monsters*—playing on and helping arrange the latter), Jimmi Mack, Graham Parker, Ellen Foley, Garland Jeffreys, and Ian Hunter.

CLARENCE CLEMONS

Nicknamed "The Big Man," Clemon's background includes some time as a teacher in a reform school and as a linebacker for a minor league team. Clemon's football future seemed quite optimistic, with tryouts for the Dallas Cowboys and the Cleveland Browns, until an unfortunate injury sustained in an automobile accident changed his plans for athletics. Since joining the E Street Band, Clemons (who has been with Springsteen since *Greetings From Asbury Park, New Jersey*) has been given credit for returning the saxophone to its rightful predominant role in contemporary music. Clemons, whose first band was The Vibratones, reportedly began playing the saxophone when he was still a child. The story of how he and Springsteen met seems to vary per concert, depending on which version

Springsteen decides to tell. Some outside reports have it that they were introduced by a mutual friend on the boardwalk in Asbury Park. Others say Springsteen heard Clemons playing at an Asbury club and they met directly. No matter what the story, Clemons is easily fifty percent of Springsteen's story-telling act, dramatizing the in-concert tales together, with a spoken and musical chemistry that must be seen to be appreciated. Their timing is impeccable, and they play off each other with an almost childlike innocence—prancing, facing off, chasing each other around the stage.

On June 11, 1981, Clemons and the E Street Band celebrated the grand opening of his club, "Big Man's West," in Red Bank, New Jersey. On October 10, 1983, Clemons and his band, The Red Bank Rockers, released their first album, *Rescue!* The album contains eight songs, and includes contributions from Desmond Child, Ellie Greenwich, Clemons, and Springsteen (who wrote and co-produced "Savin' Me"). Along with quite a list of background vocalists and musicians (including Springsteen), The Red Bank Rockers consisted of Clemons—saxophone, percussion, and background vocals; John "J. T." Bowen—lead vocals; David Landau—guitar; Ralph Schuckett—keyboards; John Siegler—bass; and Wells Kelly—drums. The single from *Rescue*, entitled "Woman's Got The Power," was accompanied by a video featuring Springsteen as a car wash attendant. Recently it was noted that Clemons made a cameo appearance in country-western star Ricky Scagg's video "Honey (Open Up The Door)."

Clemon's enthusiasm and warmth extend beyond the stage. After shows, in the early morning, in hotel lobbies, restaurants, shops, or parking lots, Clemons is always ready to sign autographs, pose for photos, and answer spontaneous questions from fans and reporters. The hearty smile never fades, and everyone is treated like an old friend. Clemons is grateful to his audiences, and is quick to point out their importance. "It's really us and them," he says, noting the roaring adulation of the concert crowds. "We give and they give, and that's really what makes it happen; the way we build off of each other." It's obvious the power that Springsteen has over his audiences; the control he could have over crowds of 20,000, at times reminiscent in their response to that of masses in the hands of a political leader. Clemons admits that it can be almost frightening, but says the positive aspects of what Springsteen and

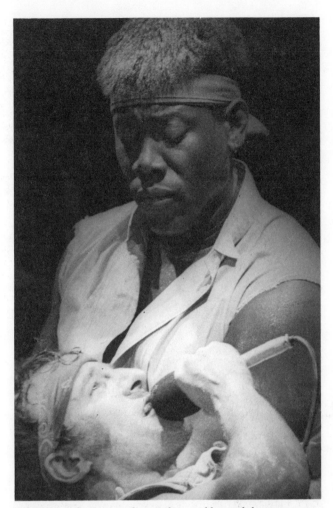

Clemons' enthusiasm and warmth extend beyond the stage.

the E Street Band are doing hopefully have some effect. "It's a clean, wholesome show—no negative aspects—it's all pure, and," he adds, "if we can touch just one more person each time and bring those wholesome ideas forward, then that's an accomplishment." When asked about the decision to release a dance-mix of "Dancing In The Dark," Clemons explained that the initial idea came from CBS Records. "Remixes have become the things to do," Clemons notes. "I wouldn't call it 'commercial' on our part, though. It's more like adapting to the times, which is necessary for any artist." He adds that the latest single, "Cover Me," is also being remixed for a possible 12-inch release. Clemons also mentioned that The Red Bank Rockers have been working on other projects as of late, but hope to have a new album out around the first of the year.

DANNY FEDERICI

This Flemington, New Jersey, native is a longtime musical associate of Springsteen's. Federici plays organ, piano, accordion, and glockenspiel, and lists The Legends (a high school group) and Bill Chinnock as past credits. Federici was playing in a band with Vini Lopez when they discovered Springsteen. They added Vinny Roslyn on bass and became Child, which became Steel Mill. Federici has worked almost constantly with Springsteen since 1968, with Steel Mill and later with the ill-fated ten-piece Bruce Springsteen Band, making him one of the longest-lasting musical associations Springsteen has had. Projects outside of the E Street Band for Federici, in the studio and/or on the road; include Joan Armatrading and Graham Parker And The Rumour (Federici played the organ on their 1980 album, *The Up Escalator*).

NILS LOFGREN

The agile guitarist grew up in Chicago, then later lived in Maryland and Washington, D.C., where, as a teenager, he played with a succession of bands until finally forming Grin with drummer/vocalist Bob Berberich and bassist/vocalist Bob Gordon, and, eventually, Lofgren's brother Tom. Lofgren, proficient on piano, accordion, and guitar (having been influenced greatly by artists such as Jimi Hendrix and The Rolling Stones), was building a reputation and, in 1971, his skills caught the attention of Neil Young and Danny Whitten's Crazy Horse, who recruited Lofgren for some session work on their debut album. *Crazy Horse* underwent a number of

personal problems and, upon their parting of ways, Neil Young, determined not to let Lofgren's talent slip away, applied the guitarist's skills to his classic album *After The Goldrush*, bringing Lofgren national recognition. He was 17. Lofgren went back to Grin, and a subsequent recording contract with Columbia resulted. They cut a self-titled debut in 1971, followed by *1 + 1* in 1972. Grin endured the opening-act slot for quite some time but never achieved major status. In 1972 they released *All Out*; its success was minimal. By 1973 Neil Young was assembling musicians for another tour and Lofgren readily accepted the offer, which took him across the U.S. and Britain. After the tour Lofgren returned to Washington, put Grin back together, and they signed with A&M Records. *Gone Crazy* was released in 1973 but sales were low, and by June 1974 the band had broken up. In 1975 Lofgren released his first solo album, *Nils Lofgren*, for A&M. The album, which also featured Wornell Jones on bass and Aynsley Dunbar on drums, was critically acclaimed, and Lofgren, accompanied by his brother Tom, began touring and building up a following of his own. He was 24 when *Cry Tough*, his 1976 release, made the U.S. and British charts. Since then Lofgren has released seven more albums. The latest, *Wonderland*, had him back on the road, displaying his performance skills. In addition to music, Lofgren is also an accomplished gymnast; his concerts' final moments are notorious for his backflip from a minitrampoline. (This bit of acrobatics is adding an extra touch to the final moments of Springsteen's concerts as well!) In may 1984 Lofgren became an official E Street Band member, filling in after the departure of Steven Van Zandt. Lofgren and Springsteen knew each other well, and Lofgren quickly adapted to the E Street entourage, playing and performing with as much flexibility and ease as the original members.

PATTI SCIALFA

The stunning lady with the powerful voice is from Deal, New Jersey. Claiming her voice as her instrument, Scialfa lists The Rolling Stones, Motown, David Bowie, Bob Dylan, Joni Mitchell, and her own grandfather as her influences. The blues/rock/country inspirations she mentions come through on stage. At first a surprising element (many Springsteen fans were a little baffled by the news of a female backup singer, although in 1974 Suki Lahav also toured with Springsteen, contributing some vo-

cals and playing violin), Scialfa has had no problems fitting in or delighting audiences. Her stage presence adds a distinct touch of charm and sweetness to the show (she also carries this wonderful attitude with her offstage, as she is inevitably being recognized and swarmed by fans), and her duets with Springsteen on "Out In The Street" add a whole new dimension to the song. Scialfa came to the E Street Band via experience with David Sancious (Springsteen's original piano player), David Johansen (formerly of The New York Dolls), and Southside Johnny And The Asbury Jukes. The story has it that Springsteen heard Scialfa singing in an Asbury Park bar, was completely taken by her voice, and recruited her on June 25—barely enough time to prepare for opening night on June 29!

GARRY TALLENT

The former Neptune High School student allegedly met Springsteen in a New Jersey shore bar. After listening to Springsteen's sets, Tallent reportedly approached Springsteen and convinced him to give a listen. Tallent, an avid rockabilly fan, wound up in Springsteen's short-lived band Dr. Zoom and The Sonic Boom, making the bass player another of Springsteen's original musical collaborators. Tallent has reportedly helped out Ian Hunter and has done some production work for other artists. However, to date, his touring experience is exclusive to Springsteen, with whom he has worked since January 1971.

STEVE VAN ZANDT

Springsteen's guitarist has also been a close friend since the two were 16-years-old. Van Zandt was the bass player for Steel Mill during the late 1960s and was also second guitarist for the Bruce Springsteen

Top Left: Bruce Springsteen and Miami Steve. Top Right: Nils Lofgren. Above: Max Weinberg and Nils Lofgren.

Clarence Clemons, Bruce Springsteen and Nils Lofgren. Springsteen tours are a ritual—a truly incredible experience.

Band during the summer of 1971. Van Zandt, another regular on the Asbury Park music circuit, reappeared in 1975 and made his first album performance with Springsteen on *Born To Run*, doing background vocals and horn arrangements. At that point Van Zandt was officially recruited to be a member of the E Street Band. His outside projects centered mostly around another Asbury Park group, Southside Johnny And The Asbury Jukes, fronted by close friend Johnny Lyon. In 1976 Van Zandt produced the Jukes' debut album *I Don't Want To Go Home*, for which he wrote the title track. Van Zandt did a lot of production for The Asbury Jukes, arranging, writing, and playing guitar on some of their later albums. By the time of Springsteen's 1978 release, *Darkness On The Edge Of Town*, Van Zandt was sharing production credits with Springsteen and Jon Landau. In December 1982, the period between *The River* and *Born In The U.S.A.*, Van Zandt released an album entitled *Men Without Women* by his own group, Little Steven And The Disciples Of Soul. With Van Zandt writing, arranging, producing, singing, and playing guitar, the years with Springsteen were an obvious influence on the new group's sound, making them a must for any Springsteen fan. Van Zandt and his band did some shows, but there was never any doubt about his priorities with the E Street Band; Van Zandt was back in the studio for recording and production sessions for *Born In The U.S.A.* In 1983, Little Steven And The Disciples Of Soul released their second album *Voice Of America*. In April 1984, shortly before the release of "Dancin' In The Dark", word was confirmed that Van Zandt was leaving the E Street Band to concentrate on his own group. Little Steven And The Disciples Of Soul went back on the road, wrapping up a tour on August 17 in San Francisco, then returned to New York to prepare for a European tour. An invitation from Springsteen must have been irresistable, because on August 20 Van Zandt joined Springsteen and the E Street Band during the last of 10 sold-out shows at the Brendan Byrne Arena in East Rutherford, New Jersey. Van Zandt jammed with the group on "Two Hearts," and with 20,000 fans screaming for more, Van Zandt stayed aboard for one of Springsteen's classic rock and roll medleys.

Clemons and Springsteen performing in London, June 1981.

On stage with the E Street Band, Van Zandt was like the stooge for Springsteen's routines. Together they would stalk across the stage, Van Zandt playing the silent role to Springsteen's dramatic stories. Their moves never slipped a beat in the timing of the song or the story, and they related their far-fetched adventures so convincingly that a packed arena sat quietly, hanging on the suspense of every word, swept up in the plot. The news of Van Zandt's departure was disheartening to the fans, many of whom are still skeptical as to why such an integral part of the band would leave so unexpectedly, prior to the tour. Whatever the ultimate reason, Van Zandt's decision was sad news to everyone, and it is believed that Springsteen's touching farewell song "Bobbie Jean" is *Born In The U.S.A.*'s goodbye to Steve Van Zandt.

MAX WEINBERG

Born in South Orange, New Jersey, Weinberg came to the E Street Band via audition. The story goes that Weinberg, who had been in and out of bands since the age of 13, was studying his craft in New York when he responded to Springsteen and Mike Appel's ad in *The Village Voice* looking for a drummer. Supposedly, thirty musicians were auditioned and Weinberg was the final choice, becoming an E Street Band member on August 23, 1974, in time for the recording of the *Born To Run* album (with the exception of the title track which had been

previously recorded with Ernest "Boom" Carter on drums). Other than the E Street Band, Weinberg's recording and/or touring experience includes work with Meatloaf on the *Bat Out Of Hell* album, Ian Hunter, Bonnie Tyler, Ellen Foley, and Garland Jeffreys.

Weinberg also recently explored a new field—he authored a book entitled *The Big Beat*, which spotlights many of his influences, and what is often rock's most overlooked talents—drummers. Weinberg interviewed some of the leading figures in Rock's rhythm, and the book also aroused the interest of NBC's syndicated "Source" Network. The result was a two-hour radio special hosted and produced by Weinberg and based on his book. Reportedly Weinberg insisted that the radio program follow the format of *The Big Beat*, and the show's music included cuts from Elvis Presley, James Brown, Little Richard, Aretha Franklin, The Rascals, Led Zeppelin, The Beatles, and many others. The program also featured interviews with 14 of the industry's prime drummers, among them Ringo Starr, and D. J. Fontana, who played with Elvis Presley, and it also had an exclusive interview with Dave Clark that was said to have been his first radio interview in almost 20 years.

CHARLES PLOTKIN

While not a member of the E Street Band in the formal sense, Charles Plotkin deserves some mention because of his extensive work as Springsteen's producer, having worked with the artist since 1978, on *Darkness On The Edge Of Town* and all of Springsteen's albums since. The functions of a producer vary—some also function as engineers. Plotkin is not one of those, nor does he ever write, sing, or play on any of the material he works with. Some artists choose to assume all of their production responsibilities with no outside help from anyone, feeling that they know their music better than someone who is not a part of the act. Others, like Springsteen, are open to a third party's opinion of their ideas; open to suggestions for arrangements, various administrative aspects, and general supervision of the project and its outcome. Plotkin has performed in those capacities with Springsteen for six years, and the results have never been anything less than monumental.

Plotkin's experience in production is diverse, and his list of credits is long. Among them are: Bob Dylan, Bette Midler, Orleans and Tommy Tutone.

The need to see him again and again remains inexplicable.

No two of his performances are ever alike. Springsteen has enough material to give his audiences something new every time.

THE PRINCIPLES:
A CAST OF MILLIONS

hen the name Bruce Springsteen comes up in conversation, the first question is usually "Have you ever seen him in concert?", followed by "How many times?" Springsteen isn't just a performer that you see once a year when his tour passes through your area. Springsteen tours are a ritual, an experience. It's as though the three-year span between tours is merely empty time for planning the next excursion for fans. They collect shows like points in a contest —the idea is to see as many shows as possible, regardless of distance or expense. It's easy to get caught up in this challenge because of the emotional tie between performer and audience. For someone who really loves Springsteen—not just a casual listener, but someone whose whole life practically revolves around the man (and there are many)—the need to see him again and again remains inexplicable. There is just something—a feeling, a bond, a satisfaction about his concerts that no one and nothing else can equal.

There are his performances. No two are ever alike. Springsteen has enough material to give something new each time, whether he's performing some of his unreleased masterpieces such as "The Promise" or

"Roulette," pulling an unexpected cut from an early album, like "Sandy" or "For You," or perhaps one of his songs made famous by another artist, for instance "Fire," "The Fever," or "Because The Night." There are the older tunes, the ones that influenced Springsteen and the E Street Band during their adolescent years, the ones by the artists they most admire—Manfred Mann's "Pretty Flamingo," Gary "U.S." Bond's "Quarter To Three," and so many more; enough to keep up the variety and make each show individual. There is Springsteen himself. Onstage for at least four hours a night, his energy level never subsides by even one degree. The constant drive, the effect-free, unadulterated music—just pure rock and roll the way it was meant to be and, thanks to Springsteen, the way it is again—leaves the audience physically exhausted but emotionally gratified for days after the concert. Springsteen's shows are guaranteed to be everything and more. There's never a chance that he'll come out in an "altered" state and stumble through a show, never a possibility that his state of mind will be anything less than positive. The man simply never has a bad night. Springsteen and Band don't perform *for* the audience, they perform *with* them. When Springsteen tells one of his stories, he's telling it to 20,000 of his closest friends. When he extends the microphone to the audience, the entire crowd sings. Even the strictest security guards have been known to clap their hands and join in on the chorus! And when Springsteen makes that nightly leap into the audience, he's not surrounded by 10 muscle-bound bodyguards. Springsteen gives his fans the ultimate test of trust every night with that jump, and they always pass with a perfect score. Try to picture any other "major" act having enough faith in his fans, enough confidence in them to actually join them in the midst of the arena with no fear of being grabbed or mobbed. Springsteen has this assurance, and the mutual respect between him and his fans make it possible for him to get this close, knowing that he is one of them and that they will treat him as such.

Most of all, there are the people, and no tribute to Springsteen would be complete without devoting a chapter to them. Every show brings them in from all points of the U.S. and Canada, and part of the fun and adventure of traveling to Springsteen concerts is meeting so many new people and sharing the unity that ties Springsteen fans together, the understanding they have about each other; being able to discuss Springsteen with others who feel the same way. The themes of his lyrics: loneliness, frustration, anguish, the search for change, the freedom of basic pleasures, are all common grounds that Springsteen's fans can relate to, and that is the bond running through the tremendous crowds that attend his performances; the strength that makes each show so powerful. Twenty-thousand hands are raised with his, 20,000 voices sing with him, and when the houselights are turned up, as is the custom during his final encore, the flood of moving figures reaching up into the farthest corners of the hall creates an electricity that no other performer can claim. During those moments Springsteen, who sees this same response at every show, somehow always looks as if he is experiencing it for the first time—his joy and gratitude are so sincere and unrestrained.

No other artist receives such love and devotion from his fans and, while every city where Springsteen plays sells out and greets him with mass hysteria, there's nothing to compare with what happens when New Jersey's boy comes home! Appropriately the first act ever to play at the Brendan Byrne Arena, Meadowlands Sports Complex in East Rutherford, New Jersey, in 1981, Springsteen sold out six nights there; but what he did at the Meadowlands in 1984 went beyond anyone's expectations.

At a capacity of 20,000, selling out just one night at the Meadowlands is an accomplishment in itself. This year Springsteen sold out 10 nights—and did so in 28 hours. Tickets for the shows, dated August 5-6, 8-9, 11-12, 16-17, and 19-20, were sold in two separate periods that totaled 28 hours. The tickets were sold only through selected Ticketron outlets by phone, and through Teletron and Meadowlands' Charge-A-Seat, with a limit of six tickets per person per call. Desperate fans, however, were buying tickets for as many shows as possible, hoping to see Springsteen all 10 nights. The sales record Springsteen set was previously unheard of in the first hour alone. Beginning at 8:00 a.m. on Tuesday, June 19, through Teletron and 30 selected Ticketron outlets in metro New York, New Jersey, and Connecticut, 16,000 tickets were sold. That's an average of 266 tickets per minute; double the rate of any other Ticketron/ Teletron sales. Through Teletron alone, 29,000 tickets were sold the first day—this broke the agency's records for sales during the entire week before. On that day the New Jersey telephone company was facing 120,000 calls per hour all day, and the tremendous increase in number was attributed to Springsteen. (One fan later reported that the

Every show brings Springsteen's fans from all points of the U.S. and Canada. No other performer receives such love and devotion.

81

charge lines had been so congested that the number had to be changed because no one could get through!)

On the second day of sales (during the 28-hour period), Teletron sold 21,000 tickets. In addition, Ticketron sold 113,000 over the two-day period, and 39,000 were sold by the Meadowlands' Charge-A-Seat outlet.

By using the Ticketron/Teletron/Charge-A-Seat method, Meadowlands' officials felt they would assure fans of getting the best seats first, and would minimize the problems of scalping. Unfortunately this was far from being the case. Scalping is, after all, big business and easy money; most often for people who are not even fans of the performer and have no intention of seeing the show themselves. These people are just looking for "quick bucks" and they are seldom disappointed. Because of the demand for tickets at the Meadowlands, many fans were unable to get through the telephone lines at all and were left empty-handed. Some said they would have preferred braving a week or more of camping out in front of the box office to be assured of hard tickets than to have called and called and received nothing. Springsteen, who is vehemently opposed to ticket-scalping and has expressed his outrage publicly on numerous occasions, had an ironic situation on his hands, probably unknown to him. The very people he has tried so hard to expose and exclude were having a field day in the Meadowlands parking lots. Desperate fans were counting out up to $350 for a pair of Springsteen tickets into the hands of unscrupulous, insensitive thieves who think nothing of taking advantage of Springsteen devotees, and capitalize on the name of the performer furthest removed from any such type of filthy business. Actual cost of Springsteen tickets was $16.00, plus a service charge of about $2.00, rounding out the total to some $18.00 apiece.

There is something so special about seeing Springsteen at the Meadowlands—something that makes his performances there stand out from other places. Put simply, the people at home feel a closeness to him that no other area can match, because he is theirs. Springsteen never abandoned New Jersey for a more glamorous life, and his fans appreciate him for this. He still lives in Jersey (his home is now in Rumson), still frequents Asbury Park (ask any Jersey fan—most will tell you they have seen Springsteen at an Asbury club or they know someone who has!). He still relates to what they are all going

through, what it's like to grow up there, and he talks about it on stage. Springsteen and New Jersey are part of each other, and that's a treasure no other state can claim.

Springsteen's Meadowlands concerts in August 1984, brought in people from all areas, across state lines, and many were seeing him for the first time. There are also younger fans discovering him; but no matter their age, they all share the same opinion about what draws them to Springsteen: his words. Springsteen fans are eager to talk about their devotion to him, and their words are worth relating because they speak for all of us and say more than anyone else's attempted analysis.

Robin is from Jersey City and has been listening to Springsteen for nine years. The Meadowlands show was her 15th Springsteen concert, and she planned trips to Connecticut and Pennsylvania to see him again. "It's everything about him," she says, "His attitude, his approach, his lyrics—especially his lyrics."

Sue is from Wallington and discovered Springsteen when *Born To Run* was released. She tried to get tickets for all 10 nights at the Meadowlands, but could only get them for three shows. She has seen Springsteen "countless times," and says, "It's the way he says things" that makes him exceptional.

Richie and Richie share more than their first names. They are best friends, both from Secaucus, and both were seeing Springsteen for the first time. They are both fifteen-years-old, and have been Springsteen fans for several years. They represent the "new" group in the audience, the younger crowd. But, says one, "You're never too old or too young to listen to Springsteen, because his songs are the kind that everyone can relate to." Springsteen is more than just another singer, says the other; "He's not a 'star'—he's basic, an everyday kind of person." The fact that Springsteen hails from their home state is significant, because "Everybody always knocks New Jersey on television and in other ways, so it's good to have someone representing Jersey in a good way, especially someone like Springsteen."

Jackie and Dore are from Philadelphia, and they are among those who follow Springsteen from city to city. They've been listening to his music for eight years, and camped out in front of a North New Jersey Ticketron office for two and a half days to get tickets to all 10 Meadowlands shows. New Jersey marked their 13th show on the "Born In The U.S.A." tour. Dore followed Springsteen on the "Darkness

On The Edge Of Town" and "The River" tours, and the Philadelphia shows in September 1984 would mark the 100th time she had seen Springsteen in concert. She says, "It's his energy. No other performer gives 100 percent all the time. He does." Jackie adds, "I can't put it into words, what he does to me. I've never felt the way I do when he's on that stage!"

Kim is from Morris Plains. She saw Springsteen once on "The River" tour and had tickets for three nights at the Meadowlands. "I've been listening to him since I was in the seventh grade," she says, "when my sister bought *Born To Run*. His lyrics mean so much to me. I listen to him every day. The way he says things, the way he puts his feelings into words and the way he sings—it seems like he feels the way I do. He's not 'Hollywood' or anything like that, he's still a guy from Jersey."

David drove an hour and a half from his Connecticut home to see Springsteen. Although he has been a fan since the release of *Greetings From Asbury Park, New Jersey*, the Meadowlands was his first Springsteen concert. "He makes me feel good," is his explanation, "like there's no difference between me and him. Through his singing and his words, I feel like he's letting me know he cares."

Ray and Chris made an eight-hour drive to the Meadowlands from their home in Columbus, Ohio. They had seen Springsteen the month before in Cincinnati and Cleveland, and saw three shows on "The River" tour. In Jersey, they paid $45 apiece to get in the Meadowlands. Their seats were in the fifth row, but they waited for a while outside after show time to make their purchase, on the assumption that, as the evening progressed, the scalpers would drop their prices in their hurry to unload extra tickets. Ray recalls, "We heard a live radio broadcast of Springsteen in August 1978 and we've been hooked ever since. The way he expresses himself on stage— no one else has that kind of feeling or emotion."

Dave and Rooney had a seven-hour drive from Pittsburgh to the Meadowlands. They discovered Springsteen in 1978 when they were high school freshmen. The Meadowlands show was their fifth Springsteen concert. Rooney explains, "Springsteen puts on the greatest show there is. I relate to him, because everthing he sings about is like my own life."

Tom is from New York and says that both he and his brother have been Springsteen fans since the early days. Tom explains, "My brother and his wife were vacationing in Europe for the summer. When I

Above: Shaking hands of fans who adore him. Above: Hauling photographer Lynn Goldsmith away after she disobeyed his rule of taking no pictures, at the M.U.S.E. Concert, September 1979.

Clemons and Springsteen: *"We give and they give and that's what really makes it happen,"* says Clemons. *"We build off each other."*

found out Springsteen was doing 10 shows at the Meadowlands, I said to myself, 'I've got to have tickets for every one of his shows.' Well, I must have been the first person on that phone when they went on sale, because I managed to buy a pair for every night! Then I called my brother over in Europe to tell him my good news and you know what? Next thing I know, he says he's coming back home! Leaves his wife waiting for him in Europe and he catches the next flight back to New York so he can go see Springsteen 10 times with me!"

Siobhan and Kerry are from New York and were seeing Springsteen for the first time at the Meadowlands. Siobhan says Springsteen is different from most of his contemporaries because "His lyrics mean something. He doesn't just put words together because they sound good or to sell records. He really has something to say."

Laura and Brett flew in from Los Angeles for one night at the Meadowlands. They made close to a five-hour flight and said that the trip was something they had jokingly discussed doing. They became serious about the idea when some friends in New Jersey told them they had tickets. Brett had seen Springsteen on five previous occasions, Laura on three. Their interest in Springsteen came about some time after they had heard him for the first time. Laura recalls, "I got the *Darkness On The Edge Of Town* album and I liked it a lot, but I got into him seriously with *The River*. I was a big Jackson Browne fan, and I went to see *No Nukes* at the

movies, which both he and Springsteen were in. Up until that point I thought it was all hype. 'Born To Run' was a really good song, but I was like, 'So what, another rocker.' Then I saw him in *No Nukes* and I just couldn't believe it. I was immediately converted."

Brett remembers, "I bought *Born To Run* because I wanted to know what all the excitement was about, but at the time it didn't really affect me. Then I heard a live radio broadcast from The Roxy during the 'Darkness On The Edge Of Town' tour—it was so unlike anything I had ever heard. I could tell just by listening—he came across so different, so honest and so real. In a way, you feel like you know him personally through his music."

Tom is from North Jersey, and the Meadowlands was his fifth Springsteen arena show. He first started listening to Springsteen when *Born To Run* was released, then bought *Greetings From Asbury Park, New Jersey* and *The Wild, The Innocent, and the E Street Shuffle*. Since then he has bought all of Springsteen's albums the same day that they went on sale. While Tom is as devoted a fan as Springsteen could hope for, he is also exceptionally realistic in his perception of Springsteen's career. "Don't get me wrong," he says, "it's great to see how popular he has become, because he is so good and he's worked so hard for this, but sometimes his overwhelming popularity becomes a bit disheartening. It's like, some of his best material is on his first two albums, but he's at a point now where he just can't include all those songs, so something has to be left out and that's really sad, because the further he goes, the less older songs he'll do, and to me, those are like the essence. You listen to him and follow him for all these years and you tell yourself he's still the same, but in your heart you know that's impossible because everyone changes. For instance, my favorite way to see Springsteen is in small clubs, and I wish I could experience that again, but I know it can never happen."

Tom's point is valid. The more Springsteen's popularity increases, the more people each want a few minutes of his time and, unfortunately, he has less and less of it to give to a constantly growing number of demands from fans and media. Not that he doesn't try. His reputation is widespread as the one performer who won't ignore or abuse his fans. He signs autographs when he can, stops to talk, and has often mentioned the thrill of seeing all those people waiting for him at the back door of the arena after the show. His fans have enough faith in him to believe that he will never change when it comes to facing them.

Every Springsteen fan has a fantasy of actually getting to know their idol, perhaps to meet him and have the chance to talk to him, and to get a better understanding of the man whose words mean so much. Likewise, each one wants to think of himself or herself as the Number One Springsteen fan. There is, however, one person who has earned this title. Her name is Obie, and she has supported Springsteen's career for about 17 years. She was one of the first to recognize the talent and potential Springsteen had long before his first album, and she has remained loyal ever since. Springsteen is grateful. Obie's name appears on album and tour program credits, and two front row seats are reserved for her at any show she attends.

Obie would never take advantage of her friendship with Springsteen as a means of publicity; but over the years she has become well known among Springsteen fans, most of whom have never seen nor met her, but have heard about her somehow. When spotted at concerts, it's common to find fans gathering around her, not necessarily to ask questions about Springsteen but just for the chance to meet this special person, the ultimate Springsteen fan and his close friend, who somehow finds the time and patience for everyone.

Springsteen fans each have a favorite story, one they witnessed, read, or heard from someone else, a

Springsteen gives his all, one-hundred percent.

special incident involving Springsteen—something he said or did that stands out and merits being told again and again. The following is just that—an unforgettable moment, the details of which are as clear in 1984 as they were three years ago when they were observed; an account that best captures the qualities in Springsteen that makes him so unique and so exceptional in the eyes of his fans.

It was mid-February 1981 and Springsteen was nearing the end of the southern segment of "The River" tour. After a show in a capital city, his only

Top: Springsteen waved enthusiastically and the cheers grew louder for "The Boss." Above: Springsteen and Nils Lofgren. Lofgren quickly adapted to the E Street entourage, playing and performing with as much flexibility and ease as the original members.

performance in that state, a crowd of some 200 had gathered at the back door of the Coliseum. Security forced them to leave, saying that the closest they could remain was on a corner across the street from where the tour bus was parked. The crowd relocated, but after an hour or so of waiting in the rain in temperatures below twenty degrees (and steadily dropping) the group thinned out until only fifty people were left, soaked and freezing, but not about to give up catching a glimpse of Springsteen as he exited the Coliseum and got on the bus. After what seemed an eternity, the "big moment" arrived. As Springsteen emerged, the crowd cheered and applauded. Springsteen waved enthusiastically and the cheers got louder; he climbed up on the bus and it pulled away. But instead of driving up the street toward town, the bus U-turned, crossed the street and parked at the curb where everyone stood, silenced by disbelief. Springsteen stepped out into the rain and thanked everyone for waiting. Suddenly the group came to life. Everyone wanted photos and autographs. One of Springsteen's security people stressed, "One at a time." Springsteen promised, "Don't worry, I'm not going anywhere until I talk to everybody." One fan gathered up his nerve and commented, "Hey Bruce, you're gonna catch a cold in this rain!" "It's okay," Springsteen smiled, "if you guys can do this for me, I can do it for you."

One young lady had broken everyone's heart. A New Jersey native, she was attending college in the south and was sobbing pitifully as she gazed at her idol. Finding herself face to face with Springsteen, she handed him a small stuffed animal. "His name is Bruce," she choked through her tears, "and I've had him all of my life. I named him after you." Springsteen seemed genuinely taken by this flood of emotion. "You named him after me?" he repeated gently, "Thank you, that's really nice." "I want you to have him." she sniffled, "because he's the only thing I have to give you. I'm from New Jersey and your songs remind me of home." By now Springsteen was completely involved. "You really want me to have him?" She nodded. Springsteen accepted the gift, took her hand, and smiled. "Thank you so much," he said, "I know how much he means to you, and I really appreciate it." He placed the little animal on the dashboard of the bus. "I'm going to put him right here until I'm finished, okay?" She nodded again, still sobbing as she stepped aside.

Springsteen continued his hospitality in the rain for at least another 45 minutes.

DISCOGRAPHY AND EXTRAS

GREETINGS FROM ASBURY PARK, NEW JERSEY

"Blinded By The Light"
"Growin' Up"
"Mary Queen Of Arkansas"
"Does This Bus Stop At 82nd Street?"
"Lost In The Flood"
"The Angel"
"For You"
"Spirit In The Night"
"It's Hard To Be A Saint In The City"

Released: January 1973
Singles: "Blinded By The Light"/"Angel,"
           January 1973
           "Spirit In The Night"/"For You,"
           May 1973

Musicians
Bruce Springsteen: Vocals, electric and acoustic
  guitars, congas, harmonica, some bass and
  piano
Clarence Clemons: Saxophone, background vocals
Vini Lopez: Drums, background vocals
David Sancious: Piano, organ
Garry Tallent: Bass

Guest Musicians:
Richard Davis: Upright bass
Harold Wheeler: Piano

THE WILD, THE INNOCENT, AND THE E STREET SHUFFLE

"The E Street Shuffle"
"4th Of July, Asbury Park (Sandy)"
"Kitty's Back"
"Wild Billy's Circus Story"
"Incident On 57th Street"
"Rosalita (Come Out Tonight)"
"New York City Serenade"

Released: November 1973
Singles: None

Musicians

Bruce Springsteen: All guitars, harmonica, mandolin, recorder, and lead vocals
Clarence Clemons: Saxophone, background vocals
Danny Federici: Accordion, piano, organ, background vocals
Vini Lopez: Drums, background vocals
David Sancious: Piano, organ, electric piano, clarinet, soprano sax, background vocals
Garry Tallent: Bass, tuba, background vocals

Guest Musicians

Richard Blackwell: Congas and percussion
Albany "Al" Tellone: Baritone sax on "E Street Shuffle"

This is Springsteen's only album issued without a lyric sheet.

BORN TO RUN

"Thunder Road"
"Tenth Avenue Freeze-Out"
"Night"
"Backstreets"
"Born To Run"
"She's The One"
"Meeting Across The River"
"Jungleland"

Released: September 1, 1975
Singles: "Born To Run"/"Meeting Across The River," September 1, 1975
"Tenth Avenue Freeze-Out"/"She's The One," January 24, 1976

Musicians

Bruce Springsteen: Vocals, guitar, harmonica
Roy Bittan: Piano, glockenspiel, harpsichord, organ
Clarence Clemons: Saxophone
Danny Federici: Organ
Garry Tallent: Bass
Max Weinberg: Drums
David Sancious: Keyboards on "Born To Run"
Ernest "Boom" Carter: Drums on "Born To Run"

Guest Musicians:

Steve Van Zandt: Background vocals, horn arrangements on "Tenth Avenue Freeze-Out"
Randy Brecker: Trumpet, flugelhorn
Michael Brecker: Tenor saxophone
David Sanborn: Baritone saxophone
Wayne Andre: Horns
Richard Davis: Bass
Suki Lahav: Violin
Charles Calello: String arrangements

This was the last album produced by Mike Appel, and the first by Jon Landau. Steve Van Zandt became a permanent member of the E Street Band at the time of these recording sessions.

DARKNESS ON THE EDGE OF TOWN

"Badlands"
"Adam Raised A Cain"
"Something In The Night"
"Candy's Room"
"Racing In The Street"
"The Promised Land"
"Factory"
"Streets Of Fire"
"Prove It All Night"
"Darkness On The Edge Of Town"

Released: June 1978
Singles: "Prove It All Night"/"Factory,"
            June 1978

Musicians:
Bruce Springsteen: Vocals, lead guitar, harmonica
Roy Bittan: Piano
Clarence Clemons: Saxophone
Danny Federici: Organ
Garry Tallent: Bass
Steve Van Zandt: Guitar
Max Weinberg: Drums

THE RIVER

"The Ties That Bind"
"Sherry Darling"
"Jackson Cage"
"Two Hearts"
"Independence Day"
"Hungry Heart"
"Out In The Street"
"Crush On You"
"You Can Look (But You Better Not Touch)"
"I Wanna Marry You"
"The River"

"Point Blank"
"Cadillac Ranch"
"I'm A Rocker"
"Fade Away"
"Stolen Car"
"Ramrod"
"The Price You Pay"
"Drive All Night"
"Wreck On The Highway"

Released: October 17, 1980
Singles: "Hungry Heart"/"Held Up Without A
            Gun," November 8, 1980. This became
            Springsteen's first Top 10 single.
            "Fade Away"/"Be True," February 1981

Musicians
Bruce Springsteen: Vocals, electric 6- and 12-string
    guitars, harmonica, some piano
Roy Bittan: Piano, organ, background vocals
Clarence Clemons: Saxophone, percussion, back-
    ground vocals
Danny Federici: Organ
Garry Tallent: Bass
Steve Van Zandt: Acoustic and electric guitars,
    some lead guitar, harmony vocals, background
    vocals
Max Weinberg: Drums

Guest Musicians
Mark Volman and Howard Kaylan (Flo and Eddie):
    Background vocals on "Hungry Heart"

Springsteen and the E Street Band spent 15
months in the studio completing this album.

NEBRASKA

"Nebraska"
"Atlantic City"
"Mansion On The Hill"
"Johnny 99"
"Highway Patrolman"
"State Trooper"
"Used Cars"
"Open All Night"
"My Father's House"
"Reason To Believe"
"The Big Payback"

Released: October 1982
Singles: None in the U.S.; however, "Atlantic
            City"/"The Big Payback" was issued
            in Britain.
Musicians
Bruce Springsteen: Vocals, guitar

The album was recorded on Springsteen's four-
track, portable home cassette recorder.

BORN IN THE U.S.A.

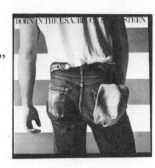

"Born In The U.S.A."
"Cover Me"
"Darlington County"
"Working On The Highway"
"Downbound Train"
"I'm On Fire"
"No Surrender"
"Bobby Jean"
"I'm Going Down"
"Glory Days"
"Dancing In The Dark"
"My Hometown"

Released: June 4, 1984
Singles: "Dancing In The Dark"/"Pink Cadillac,"
              May 4, 1984
           "Cover Me"/"Jersey Girl," August 1984
           "Dancing In The Dark" also released as
              a 12-inch dance single remixed by
              Arthur Baker.

Musicians

Bruce Springsteen: Vocals, guitar
Roy Bittan: Synthesizer, piano, background vocals
Clarence Clemons: Saxophone, percussion, background vocals
Danny Federici: Organ, glockenspiel, piano
Garry Tallent: Bass, background vocals
Steve Van Zandt: Acoustic guitar, mandolin, harmony vocals
Max Weinberg: Drums

Guest Musicians:

La Bamba: Background vocals on "Cover Me" and "No Surrender"
Ruth Jackson: Background vocals on "My Hometown"

Springsteen and the E Street Band spent close to two years recording and mixing this album. Springsteen reportedly scrapped the project three times during the recording process.

The song "Darlington County" has also become a topic of interest for Springsteen fans in South Carolina, who are convinced that Springsteen named the song after their area. Darlington is, in fact, a Carolina county, site of the Southern 500 stock car race. Darlington officials have wondered why Springsteen selected their county as the subject of a song, but CBS Records publicists told reporters in North and South Carolina that it was merely "a racing song without being a racing song" and that the title was likely to attempt to "conjure up the image of racing." Regardless, Springsteen's South Carolina fans are delighted that he knows about their county, and will certainly make their pleasures known when Springsteen and Band bring their current tour to the South.

SPRINGSTEEN EXTRAS

Springsteen's material is mostly exclusive to his own albums; however, a few of his songs (performed by Springsteen and the E Street Band) have appeared on other recordings, some of them listed below.

No Nukes—the album—was released around Christmas 1980, with proceeds going toward the M.U.S.E. (Musicians United for Safe Energy) antinuclear cause. On this triple-album set, Springsteen is featured doing the Mitch Ryder medly ("Devil With The Blue Dress," etc.) and in a duet with Jackson Browne on "Stay," the Maurice Williams and The Zodiacs tune.

In Harmony 2—released in November, 1981, this anthology of children's music by rock stars contains an in-concert performance of Springsteen and the E Street Band doing "Santa Claus Is Coming To Town." This track, which was issued as a 12-inch promotional single, was recorded on December 12, 1975, at C. W. Post College, Greenvale, Long Island.

"Risky Business"—Summer 1983—the soundtrack of this movie features a brief segment of "Hungry Heart."

"Baby It's You"—Summer 1983—another motion picture soundtrack—this one includes "It's Hard To Be A Saint In The City," "She's The One," "Adam Raised A Cain," and "The E Street Shuffle."

"Prove It All Night"—1978—a live recording was issued to a selection of radio stations.

BRUCE SPRINGSTEEN AS REQUESTED AROUND THE WORLD

"Sherry Darling"
"The River"
"Cadillac Ranch"
"Hungry Heart"
"Out In The Street"
"Born To Run"
"Badlands"
"Prove It All Night"
"Rosalita (Come Out Tonight)"

Issued in 1981 as a demonstration album for radio stations only, this album coincided with "The River" tour, even listing the entire world-tour itinerary on the back cover, and reportedly contains the most-often-requested Springsteen songs during that period, as charted and surveyed around the world.

VIDEOS

"Rosalita"—this clip was filmed July 8, 1978 at the Phoenix, Arizona, Coliseum. Six years later it is still being shown on a number of music video and entertainment programs.

No Nukes—The M.U.S.E. concert documentary film was released in summer 1980. Springsteen and the E Street Band are featured doing "Thunder Road," Gary "U.S." Bond's "Quarter To Three" and introducing a new song, "The River."

"Atlantic City"—1982—a grim black-and-white video portraying life on the Jersey shore. Neither Springsteen nor any member of the E Street Band appear in this clip.

"Woman's Got The Power"—October 1983—this video accompanied the first single from *Rescue*, the debut album by Clarence Clemons and The Red Bank Rockers. Springsteen makes his "acting debut" portraying a car wash attendant.

"Dancing In The Dark"—July 1984—Springsteen's first official video, directed by Brian DePalma, captures Springsteen and The E Street Band "in concert" before a crowd in St. Paul, Minnesota.

CONTRIBUTIONS

Springsteen and the E Street Band have contributed to other artists' work. Some examples:

Springsteen has appeared on tracks by The Dictators and Lou Reed, and performed background vocals on "Endless Night" with Graham Parker and The Rumour on their 1980 album *The Up Escalator*.

Most members of the E Street Band have also been involved in studio and tour projects with other artists.

SPRINGSTEEN MATERIAL BY OTHER ARTISTS

Springsteen's works have been covered by a number of other performers. In addition, he has also written songs specifically for other artists, and has done some extensive work with other acts.

SOUTHSIDE JOHNNY AND THE ASBURY JUKES

Southside Johnny Lyon, Springsteen, and Steve Van Zandt's friendship goes back to the early days at The Upstage in Asbury Park. In June 1976 the Asbury Jukes released their debut album, *I Don't Want To Go Home*. Steve Van Zandt, who produced the album, also wrote the title track. The album included "The Fever" and "You Mean So Much To Me," both songs by Springsteen, who also wrote the album's liner notes.

In May 1977 the second Asbury Jukes album, *This Time It's For Real*, was released. Again produced by Steve Van Zandt, the album contains three Van Zandt/Springsteen compositions: "Little Girl So Fine," "Love On The Wrong Side Of Town," and "When You Dance."

The third Jukes' album, *Hearts Of Stone*, also produced by Van Zandt, was released November 4, 1978. It contains two Springsteen songs: the title track and "Talk To Me," plus a Springsteen/Van Zandt/Lyon tune, "Trapped Again."

Springsteen also recruited former Asbury Jukes singer Patti Scialfa as his backup singer for the "Born In The U.S.A." tour.

GARY "U.S." BONDS

Springsteen had been performing Gary "U.S." Bond's songs for years, having cited him as an in-spiration numerous times. In 1981 Springsteen had the chance to play an important part in Bond's comeback album *Dedication*, released on April 15. Produced by Steve Van Zandt, the album also features the entire E Street Band. The album contains three Springsteen songs: "Dedication," "Your Love" and "This Little Girl," which was released as a single; plus a Bonds/Springsteen duet on a new version of the old Cajun tune "Jole Blon."

In June 1982 Bonds' *On The Line* album was released. The album was produced by Steve Van Zandt, and the E Street Band again took part in the music. Seven Springsteen songs are included on the album: "Hold On (To What You Got)," "Club Soul City," "Love's On The Line," "Rendezvous," "Angelyne," "All I Need," and "Out Of Work," which was also released as a single and reached Number 21 on the Hot 100 Charts.

COVERS PREVIOUSLY RECORDED BY SPRINGSTEEN

"For You"—from *Greetings From Asbury Park, New Jersey*—covered by Greg Kihn.

"Spirit In The Night"—from *Greetings From Asbury Park, New Jersey*—released as a single by Manfred Mann's Earth Band on April 3, 1976, and reached Number 97 on the charts. It reentered the charts on April 30, 1977 and climbed into the Top 40.

"Blinded By The Light—from *Greetings From Asbury Park, New Jersey* was covered by Manfred Mann's Earth Band and entered the Hot 100 on November 20, 1976. It went to Number 1 and marked the first time anyone made it to the top of the charts with one of Springsteen's songs.

"4th Of July, Asbury Park (Sandy)"— from *The Wild, The Innocent, and The E Street Shuffle*—covered in the mid-1970s by The Hollies.

COVERS NOT RECORDED BY SPRINGSTEEN (NOT A COMPLETE LIST)

"Because The Night"—the story has it that while Jimmy Iovine was working on the *Darkness On The Edge Of Town* album for Springsteen, he was also producing Patti Smith's album in a studio next door. Iovine brought her the song, she reworked some of the lyrics, and released it in April 1978. It became a Top 20 hit. Springsteen still performs the original version in concert, but has never recorded it. It appears on numerous bootlegs, however.

"The Fever"—this song appears on the debut album by Southside Johnny and The Asbury Jukes. It was also recorded by several other artists, including the Pointer Sisters in 1978. Springsteen has allegedly recorded the song himself, but never released it. This one also appears on several bootlegs, including the notorious Winterland, California, live tapes, December 15, 1978.

"Fire"—was released in 1978 by Robert Gordon on his album with Link Wray, *Fresh Fish Special*. The Pointer Sisters also released it that same year on their *Energy* album, and took it to Number 2 on the Hot 100.

This is another popular in-concert song for Springsteen, featuring some of the best on-stage interplay and duets between him and Clarence Clemons. "Fire" has become an audience favorite, and consequently is available on numerous bootlegs.

"Rendezvous"—Springsteen began performing this in concert about 1976. In 1979 the song was released on Greg Kihn's album *With The Naked Eye*.

"Protection"—the song was written by Springsteen for Donna Summer's self-titled album released in August 1982. Springsteen played the guitar solo on the song.

BOOTLEGS

Bruce Springsteen has probably been the victim of bootleggers more than any other artist in recording history, or certainly the artist whose problems with bootlegs have been most publicized. Studio outtakes dating back to the days of Steel Mill remain in circulation, and almost all of Springsteen's die-hard fans seem to own at least one piece of illicit material. Bootleggers have made a fortune from Springsteen, in ways comparable to ticket scalpers —by charging outrageous prices and making successful sales to eager fans. Springsteen has gone out of his way to try to alleviate these problems, albeit unsuccessfully, even going so far as lawsuits. The bootleg situation has been rectified somewhat—at least the illegal tapes are no longer sold by reputable record chains as part of their Springsteen catalogue. As long as the entertainment industry exists, however, bootleggers (and scalpers) will continue their "get rich quick" methods, knowing they will always find a buyer.

Ever since Springsteen took bootleggers to court in California and New Jersey, the word "bootleg" seems to have become taboo among Springsteen fans, who are more reluctant now to discuss their collections of tapes and albums. The thrill of owning these recordings, obviously, was because it is the one means of obtaining any form of "live" album by Springsteen and the E Street Band, or of completing a collection of his material. Furthermore, most of the tapes (especially the studio outtakes) contain exceptional material that never made its way even into the concerts, much less the albums. The early tapes also contain different versions of the album tracks, with different tempos and sometimes radically changed lyrics and an occasional instrumental version. Springsteen fans are intrigued with these preliminary recordings that often trace the development of a song from chord progressions to final take. Some of the tracks contained on the live and studio tapes have become vintage Springsteen to many fans, who can discuss these classics with as much knowledge and expertise as when they talk about each new release.

A surprising number of people, the majority of them in major-market cities where bootleg albums were sold, have access to the tapes, and it is not difficult for a newcomer to hear some of this rare material. Anyone who has spent several days camping out for tickets with thousands of other Springsteen fans has probably had the chance to listen to a wide variety of tapes, since campers all tend to bring their own music, and take advantage of the vigil to exchange information and opinions about Springsteen. By the time the bootlegs have reached this group, though, the tapes are in what sounds like their hundredth pressing—a recording of a recording of a recording, and so forth. Vocals are barely audible, the music is muffled, the cassettes filled with static, and the tapes obviously have no monetary value to a bootlegger. None of the flaws are important to the listeners, who cherish even the faintest sound that they know is Springsteen.

Therefore, the tapes deserve mention only because they are common subject matter among the fans. It is important to note, however, that the people who obtained the tapes (as opposed to those who actually made the tapes) are in no way trying to infringe upon or violate Springsteen's material by owning them. They simply treasure them as rare souvenirs.

BOOTLEG VIDEOS

Actual footage of Springsteen and the E Street Band in concert is rare—virtually unheard of. Not much is ever mentioned about bootleg videos, but there probably are a few available. Word has spread about one such tape, simply known as the "Cleveland Show." The tape quality is said to be dreadful, having been duplicated so many times, and allegedly contains mostly material from the *Darkness On The Edge Of Town* album, a few songs from *Born To Run*, and some selected cuts from *Greetings From Asbury Park, New Jersey*, and *The Wild, The Innocent, and the E Street Shuffle*. There are also, supposedly, some Springsteen extras, such as instrumentals, and a "new" song—"Sherry Darling." The video also is said to feature Springsteen doing some of his own favorites from the artists that influenced him. There have been guesses that the show was taped either on August 9, 1978, at The Agora (the same night as the live radio broadcast), or when Springsteen returned to the Richfield Coliseum in Cleveland in December 1978/January 1979. The real mystery is how the show was successfully taped and distributed.

ALTERNATES

Many of Springsteen's studio outtake bootlegs contain several versions of one song, with Springsteen playing solo, with the E Street Band doing different introductions or instrumental breaks, or playing the song on a completely different beat. Some of the bootlegs (in concert as well as in the studio) contain songs that appear on Springsteen albums, but with different verses, other names given to the personas. Most interesting are recordings of songs that contain familiar lines or entire verses that later became the foundation for a completely different song. These "alternates" are being mentioned as a point of interest in considering the complicated process of writing and developing the songs, and as a statement of fact regarding illegal tapes and the versions of songs that were heard in concert during early Springsteen tours.

B-SIDES

Springsteen's early singles contained B-sides also on the respective albums:

Greetings From Asbury Park, New Jersey
"Blinded By The Light"/"Angel"
"Spirit In The Night"/"For You"

Born To Run
"Born To Run"/"Meeting Across The River"
"Tenth Avenue Freeze-Out"/"She's The One"

Darkness On The Edge Of Town
"Prove It All Night"/"Factory"

With the release of *The River*, Springsteen's singles were issued with previously unreleased B-sides,

making the singles collectors' items in a sense as follows:

The River
"Hungry Heart"/"Held Up Without A Gun"
"Fade Away"/"Be True"

Nebraska
"Atlantic City"/"The Big Paycheck"—this release was issued only in Britain.

Born In the U.S.A.
"Dancing In The Dark"/"Pink Cadillac"
"Cover Me"/Jersey Girl"—this Tom Waits composition is also being featured by Springsteen and the E Street Band as part of their song list on the "Born In The U.S.A." tour.

OTHER STARBOOKS FROM
SHARON

REACH OUT *The Diana Ross story* (ISBN #0-89531-036-8)	Leonard Pitts, Jr.	**$5.95**
PAPA JOE'S BOYS *The Jacksons story* (ISBN #0-89531-037-6)	Leonard Pitts, Jr.	**$5.95**
HOLLYWOOD HUNKS (ISBN #0-89531-034-1)	Jacquelyn Nicholson	**$5.95**
MUSICMANIA (ISBN #0-89531-036-4)	Robyn Flans	**$5.95**
MR WONDERFUL *The Stevie Wonder Story* (ISBN #0-89531-078-3)	Leonard Pitts, Jr.	**$5.95**
BOB HOPE (ISBN #0-89531-077-5)	Leonard Pitts, Jr.	**$5.95**
JUDY & :LIZA (ISBN #0-89531-079-1)	Michael S. Barson	**$5.95**
THE GLAMOUR GIRLS OF HOLLYWOOD (ISBN #0-89531-076-6)	Leonard Pitts, Jr.	**$5.95**
THE MAGIC OF MICHAEL JACKSON (ISBN #0-451-82089-4)		**$4.95**
THOSE INCREDIBLE JACKSON BOYS (ISBN #0-89531-086-4)		**$2.95**
INSIDE DURAN DURAN (ISBN #0-451-82096-7)		**$4.95**
THE VAN HALEN SCRAPBOOK (ISBN #0-451-82102-7)		**$4.95**
THE BOY *The Outrageous Boy George* (ISBN #0-451-82101-7)		**$4.95**
BREAKDANCING (ISBN #0-451-82095-9)	Curtis Marlow	**$5.95**
OVER FORTY AND FABULOUS (ISBN #0-451-82103-3)	Arthur Stern	**$6.95**
THE YEAR OF THE PRINCE (ISBN #0-451-82108-4)		**$4.95**
THE BOSS BRUCE SPRINGSTEEN (ISBN #0-451-82109-2)	Elianne Halbersberg	**$5.95**

For purchase of any of the above titles, send above price, plus $1.00 postage and handling to: Sharon's Sales Dept. 105 Union Ave., Cresskill, N.J. 07626.